A
DECADE
OF
HOPE

Also by Dennis Smith

A
DECADE
OF
HOPE

Stories
of Grief and Endurance
from 9/11 Families
and Friends

Dennis Smith

WITH DEIRDRE SMITH

VIKING

VIKING

Published by the Penguin Group
Penguin Group (USA) Inc., 375 Hudson Street,
New York, New York 10014, U.S.A.
Penguin Group (Canada), 90 Eglinton Avenue East, Suite 700, Toronto,
Ontario, Canada M4P 2Y3 (a division of Pearson Penguin Canada Inc.)
Penguin Books Ltd, 80 Strand, London WC2R 0RL, England
Penguin Ireland, 25 St. Stephen's Green, Dublin 2, Ireland
(a division of Penguin Books Ltd)
Penguin Books Australia Ltd, 250 Camberwell Road, Camberwell,
Victoria 3124, Australia (a division of Pearson Australia Group Pty Ltd)
Penguin Books India Pvt Ltd, 11 Community Centre,
Panchsheel Park, New Delhi–110 017, India
Penguin Group (NZ), 67 Apollo Drive, Rosedale, Auckland 0632,
New Zealand (a division of Pearson New Zealand Ltd)
Penguin Books (South Africa) (Pty) Ltd, 24 Sturdee Avenue,
Rosebank, Johannesburg 2196, South Africa

Penguin Books Ltd, Registered Offices: 80 Strand, London WC2R 0RL, England

First published in 2011 by Viking Penguin, a member of Penguin Group (USA) Inc.

1 3 5 7 9 10 8 6 4 2

Copyright © Dennis Smith, 2011
All rights reserved

Page 365 constitutes an extension of this copyright page.

Library of Congress Cataloging-in-Publication Data

Smith, Dennis, 1940-
A decade of hope : stories of grief and endurance from 9/11 families and friends /
Dennis Smith with Deirdre Smith.
p.   cm.
ISBN 978-0-670-02293-9
1. September 11 Terrorist Attacks, 2001—Personal narratives.   2. September 11 Terrorist
Attacks, 2001—Social aspects.   3. Grief—United States.   I. Smith, Déirdre.   II. Title.
HV6432.7.S635   2011
974.7'10440922—dc23   2011023325

Printed in the United States of America
Set in Warnock Pro
Designed by Francesca Belanger

For the families of the 2,974 lost on 9/11,
those men and women and children who endured the suffering
of that time and who have found whatever it took to integrate
that day into each following day of the last decade

And for Lee Ielpi, Rescue Co. 2, FDNY (ret.),
whose words and actions are invariably inspiring

. . . we will not fear, though the earth should change, and though the mountains slip into the heart of the sea; though its waters roar and foam, though the mountains quake at its swelling pride. Listen. . . . the God of Jacob is our stronghold. Listen.

—Psalm 46:1-3, 7

I am leaving you with a gift—peace of mind and heart. And the peace I give is a gift the world cannot give. So don't be troubled or afraid.

—John 14:27

Contents

Acknowledgments

I want to thank and acknowledge the goodwill and the inspiring strength of the twenty-five interviewees within these pages who allowed themselves to speak so freely about their lives and loss. It would be an understatement to say that it was difficult for them to again call upon those memories of the worst times in their lives.

The president of Viking, Clare Ferraro, has been generous in supporting the efforts of the 9/11 community, and her friendship is much appreciated. Rick Kot is the most reliable editor a writer could possibly have, and I deeply thank him for everything he has contributed to making this a more meaningful book and me a more thoughtful scribe. I appreciate editorial assistant Kyle Davis for his relentless attention. I would like to convey a big thanks to the team of Viking professionsals, from the book designer, Francesca Belanger; jacket designer, Eric White; to all of those who shepherd a book from the initial proposal through the editorial process; and to those whose sales and marketing efforts bring it finally to the public. My agent, Al Zuckerman, has represented giants in the publishing industry, but he, as Vasari said about Raphael, always found time for the common man. Thanks, Al. FDNY commissioner Sal Cassano and NYPD lieutenant Gene Whyte offered good advice and help that are manifested in the pages of this book. Teresa Grogan-Lustberg has again offered consequential direction, this time in suggesting I ask Valary Oleinik to transcribe the recordings of what became more than thirteen hundred pages of manuscript. Thank you, Valary, for enduring the difficulty of listening to these many heartfelt and very moving interviews. Jennifer Adams and her staff at Tribute, the 9/11 families memorial center on Liberty Street, helped to recommend the right balance of interviews among the many thousands of possibilities. I will always appreciate their support. I thank my children Brendan, Dennis,

Sean, and Aislinn for keeping me in the front of their collective mind. And, finally, I thank my daughter Deirdre, whose intelligence and writing skill helped me mold these interviews into a coherent whole called *A Decade of Hope*.

—Dennis Smith, New York City, May 13, 2011

Introduction

Never before in American history had our peace and well-being been so suddenly, fully, and unalterably changed as they were on the morning of September 11, 2001. On that Tuesday morning all Americans suffered, and many around the world suffered with us. The suffering grew more intense as the days turned into weeks and the weeks into months, as the powerful images of search and recovery, funerals, and honors were presented to us. Now, as those months have grown into the accumulated years of a decade, most of us are still very much haunted by the horror of that day, and we continue to feel the pain within that memory.

But for thousands of Americans—the spouses, children, parents, siblings, and loved ones of the 2,974 men, women, and children killed in the World Trade Center, in Shanksville, Pennsylvania, and in the Pentagon—memory can be a cruel master.

How have they gotten through this time, these people who directly experienced the loss of someone vitally loved? How have they dealt with such a public and historically important loss, a loss that they were reminded of each day in newspapers and magazines and on television? How have they faced the absence of a family member at every milestone celebration—birthdays, graduations, engagements, marriages?

How have they rebuilt their lives? How have they found the inner resilience to transcend the grief of their loss—and the pain of wondering what might have been for the individuals lost that day? I wondered if the suffering of 9/11 became an obstacle for every thought that was meant to be hopeful, every plan to build for tomorrow. Was every thought framed within the shadows of terrible loss? Was peace possible for these families, or was there a continuing maelstrom of sadness?

I have spent a life working in the emergency services, from a time of great social unrest in the South Bronx to that field of absolute destruction at the World Trade Center on 9/11. I arrived at Ground Zero immediately following the fall of the North Tower, and I stayed for fifty-six days. I attended dozens of funerals through those early months of September, October, and November of 2001, so along with the thousands who lined up outside those churches and temples I came to share as much as was possible the depth of family grief.

What I sought to discover in the interviews in this book is how these individuals found the courage and the hopefulness to move forward in their lives, to ensure the containment of their families, to grieve and to honor, and to understand the consequence of this very visible tragedy on their future. And, for many, to see how they were able to transform their grief into productive ends.

Faith, compassion, and charity are required to attain the greatest of virtues—hope. We need to believe that the world of tomorrow will be a good world, populated by moral and well-meaning people. It is why we have eulogies—to celebrate the good of a life, for we rely on the memory of that good to serve us in molding a life of decency as we step into our future.

It is easy to say that we must believe in the goodness of our future, and that our collective future can be better than our past. But it is not easy to live with the memory of loss even when building a better tomorrow. At the heart of it all, it takes moral character and goodness to go on.

A
DECADE
OF
HOPE

Dan Nigro

Dan Nigro was the chief of operations when he drove with Chief of Department Peter Ganci over the Brooklyn Bridge from the Fire Department's Brooklyn headquarters. "This is going to be the worst day of our lives," Chief Nigro uttered as they watched the smoke rising from the North Tower. Not long after, Chief Ganci asked him to walk the perimeter of the buildings to do an additional evaluation. The South Building came down when he reached the Church Street side of the complex, and he ran for his life. He never saw Chief Ganci again.

Before the collapse I was on Church Street. I was heading to the lobby of the South Tower, which was a shortcut back to the command post on West Street. If you went through the South Tower, then through the Marriott Hotel, you could stay fully in the interior as you walked. All I saw on Church Street were pieces of the building and pieces of the plane. I thought that the South Tower would be a safer route back.

But then a guy came out of the crowd. If this had happened in a movie you would think it was an integral part of the film, because he literally stopped me. I wanted to say "I'm really in a hurry," but this guy was shouting, "My wife is in the North Tower!" I knew the guy, and knew that his wife had had a baby three months before. These things triggered in me the sense that I couldn't run away from him, and so I told him, "Nobody's cell phone works. She's fine, I'm sure. . . . Don't worry, don't worry." I didn't really believe it, not with what I saw all around me. But no sooner did we turn around and begin to walk fifty feet toward the South Tower than the building came down.

When the South Tower fell, we ran to a big, substantial place, a Starbucks, figuring it would be easy to get into. I grabbed the door handle; it was locked. That was the second time that I felt I was destined to get hit with the building. Once again we were outside, and I thought we were too close to the falling tower to find safety. But we were on Dey Street, midway between the North and South towers, and because of the way that the buildings were laid out, I guess we were far enough inside the doorway to feel that we would be safe. My aide that day was Adam, who is my nephew. He had on only a short-sleeved FDNY shirt and no helmet, typical of the way our aides work. He did not expect to be put into a firefighting position. So we got into a corner, and I got on top of him, and we waited to see what would happen. The sound was a huge, screeching roar. The only thing that landed on us was that thick dust and light debris. There was enough of it, though, to make me feel very worried: *When is it ever going to stop?* I asked myself, and *When will we be able to breathe again?*

The black cloud just enveloped us, and the dust got everywhere—in the nose, the ears, the eyes, every crevice. And then it suddenly stopped. After that extremely loud noise came those unbelievable minutes of quiet—a forbidding silence. We picked ourselves up, and I couldn't see more than twenty feet. I could see a car parked at the curb, ten or fifteen feet from us, that was half crushed by something. In a moment of dark irony, I was happy that it had hit the car and not us. I didn't see anyone in our area who needed help. I don't know what our mental state was at the time, but I would say that we were extremely confused.

You could say that this guy who stopped me in concern about his wife was a random thing. He came out of the crowd and prevented me from being either in the building or directly under the building, which is where we would have been. People who believe that things are for a purpose would say that there was some other reason for it. Some would say this is how random our life is.

I do remember clearly that I wanted to get back to the command post. The most direct route there would have been to turn right and try to go through the plaza there that separated the towers, but all that was there now was a mountain of collapse. It dawned on me to go down Broadway and then turn and head over to West Street. A couple of building mainte-nance guys pulled us into a building—I guess we looked like ghosts—and we were able to wash some of the stuff out of our eyes and ears in their washroom.

So we continued downtown to try to head west. But suddenly there was that terrible sound again. We weren't really in a position to see the building coming down, but this huge cloud came and covered us again. Later I saw in some of the pictures how the cloud mostly blew to the south and east, and followed us to where we were.

When the North Tower fell, it was, at least for us, not as bad as the first time. But it was still frightening to everyone, as it added to the sense of calamity. We waited a short time for the cloud to disperse again, and could see the Fire Department communications van to the south of us. We ran down to it, thinking they had to know what was going on. We saw Dr. [David] Prezant [FDNY chief medical officer; see page 28] standing there with a few firefighters. I said, "What's going on? You can't tell from the radio who's in charge. Where is the command post? Who's running this operation?" I was really surprised when the guy said that Chief [Thomas] Haring, a deputy chief in the Bronx, was in charge of the command post, which was now on Broadway just south of City Hall.

I was stunned. Had everyone been killed? Where was Chief Ganci? Commissioner [William] Feehan? Chief [Donald] Burns? The command post, originally west of the buildings was now east, not even on the same side of the buildings. So all of us walked back: Dr. [Kerry] Kelly [FDNY chief of health services], Dr. Prezant, myself, my aide, and a few firefighters who I think were assigned to Engine 10 and Ladder 10.

We got up to the post where Chief Haring was and learned that it was just an operations post, for there were so many fires burning and people hurt, and that the real command post was still at West Street. So we left the doctors there, because they were dealing with some injured people. They had set up a triage center in a drugstore, I think.

Someone I knew from Ladder 111, Vince Conway, was there, and said to me, "Pete is missing." I think that's the first news I got about Chief Ganci. I saw that this then placed me in charge, and I continued to make my way to the command post. On West Street, a few blocks north of the Trade Center, we formed somewhat of a command post setup. Chief [Frank] Cruthers and some of the other staff chiefs were there. They confirmed that Chief Ganci and Commissioner Feehan had been together and were now missing. As we learned later, almost everyone, with the exception of Jay Jonas and those miracle guys in the stairway of the North Tower, was missing, gone, never to be seen alive again. Which was the case with Pete Ganci and Bill Feehan and Donald Burns and all of them. I was the highest-ranking person now operating.

Thinking about it now, part of what was in my head was disbelief: *How could this have happened?* The first thought that entered my mind when the building was coming down was disbelief that I was going to be killed by the collapse of the World Trade Center. It just didn't make any sense to me. Afterward, knowing that both of the towers were gone, I came to accept that it had happened, though it wasn't really registering in the reality part of my head. It was hard, maybe impossible, to put everything together. Days later I read a lot of the official department interviews, and many people had the events out of sync. They might have remembered they were in a certain location, but we know that they couldn't have been at that place at that time. The day happened in such a once-in-a-lifetime fashion.

We have always fought fires in a certain way: You've seen this happen before; you've seen that happen before. We usually know what to expect. Small things sometimes do occur at a fire or an emergency that are unexpected, but for everyone in the Fire Department, this was completely off the page. So taking charge at that point, I tried to fall back on things that I knew, like sectoring the disaster area, for instance. There was so much going on that I realized that I had to assign my ranking people in charge of each area so we would have some semblance of being organized. The area that came to be called Ground Zero was sectioned into quarters, each led by a single chief. It was organized in our typical fashion: Captains, battalion chiefs, deputy chiefs, and other people worked together as trained companies, as teams, even if they had never met one another [before]. They hooked up with one another, and in some way, maybe common cause, followed the directions of the higher-ranking people, and it worked. Even the chief who was in that North Tower stairwell tried to continue to be a chief. Under the worst possible circumstances, we did form an organization that worked.

We learned that morning about the Pentagon and about another plane that went down. There were many rumors that this was certainly bigger than just two planes. The first few times that warplanes flew overhead, hearing that sound of jet planes again certainly shook everybody up on the ground. For days I think people believed that we were going to be attacked again. Everyone was on edge.

I sensed that our loss was almost incomprehensible. When we got back to the command post the information was incomplete. People weren't really transmitting on the radio. I wasn't hearing enough to know the full extent. Of course I knew we lost hundreds but had no idea how many. Did we lose everybody who was earlier seen? Almost everybody? Did we lose a thousand people? The numbers were just numbing, beyond what you could say, think, or anticipate.

High-rise buildings on fire have never fallen down. How did this happen? History shows there had been localized collapses in high-rises, and I think some of us expected that. But even the worst fires, at the end of the day there was still a building standing. This was the first time. In fact, as we found subsequently, even in controlled demolitions, no building had ever collapsed into itself as the Twin Towers did.

Back at the command post I could actually see that some people, like Chief [Peter] Hayden and Chief [Joseph] Pfeifer, whom I knew had been in the building, were now safe, and that was a pocket of good news among the bad. People from the West Street command post had gone into the basement of the Financial Center and had come back out. Some of them had realized what was going on. But we were having a hard time and were only learning what had happened as we interacted at the command post and walked around the scene. But throughout that day I still had no idea how many people were missing, except that it was an incredibly high number. None of us knew.

We were all familiar with the fact that people can survive in pockets after collapses for days and days and, in a few rare cases, as long as thirteen days. We did think there would be more people alive, injured, especially since there were many underground levels. As it turned out, there were very, very few.

I thought that the people whose transmissions on the radio came through from that North Tower stairwell were confused, and that they were actually in a different building. I didn't believe anyone could be alive in that pile of rubble—not there, in that position. If they had said we were on Promenade B or one of those levels downstairs, it would have sounded more rational but for thirteen of them to survive in that stairwell, it's still a miracle.

As we made our way around the building again and started to do our searches, however, it was becoming quickly apparent that there weren't going to be survivors here. We called it a rescue operation for a few weeks, but after the first few days it was getting harder to believe that. We never lost consideration for the hope within families, however. Some of them wanted to believe that, like in earthquakes, we'd pull someone out ten days

later, so we certainly acted as though we were going to pull people out, and
we worked as hard and as fast as we could to find people to pull out. But it
was becoming more and more apparent that it just wasn't going to happen.
And it didn't.

We were assured through our mutual aid agreements that various fire
departments would assist us in covering many other parts of the city. They
came in from all over Long Island and Westchester County and staffed
some of our firehouses that day and that night. At the scene we had adequate people. At major fires, Pete Ganci used to say, "We have 210 engines,
so keep sending me engines until I tell you to stop." We had an enormous
resource of fire companies here in New York that was unavailable to anyone
else in the country. So despite our terrible losses, we still had a huge number of people to do this task downtown. While I never felt that we didn't
have adequate staffing there, it was difficult to stabilize the situation, because the whole perimeter was on fire, and so much damage had been done
to the water mains: 90 West Street, a huge building, was on fire on the south
side; on the north we had 7 World Trade Center completely in flames. Either
of these would have been the fire of the year for us, but we were also trying
to stabilize many, many smaller fires.

We had no chance of committing enough people to put out the fires
burning uncontrollably at 7 World Trade Center, so we decided that we
would stop operating there because of the danger of the collapse of that
building. We pulled everyone to a safe distance, which proved to be a good
move, because all forty-seven stories of the building came down around
five o'clock. The fact that everyone was out of the way, and no one else was
hurt, was a small consolation at the end of the day.

We knew that 7 World Trade Center had a large diesel-fuel tank. It had
been a controversy to allow diesel fuel in that building, which was meant
to be used for the city's Office of Emergency Management and to power
emergency generators for the stock-trading operations that went on in that
building. So we knew that there was fuel in there to add to the problem,
and once that building came down we could recommit everyone to what
we were doing.

At some point late that afternoon the fire commissioner, Tom Von
Essen, came back to the scene, and he said, "You're now the chief of department." Officially I was promoted on Sunday morning, and following that
we had a big promotion ceremony to replace all the officers we had lost. So

there were promotions in every rank that day. It was held outside of head-quarters on Sunday morning.

The fires continued to burn for months in that pile, intensely. I'm not sure when and at what point they were declared under control. We would get daily aerial infrared photos from the [federal] government showing where fires were still burning under the pile, so we could see what was getting better and what was changing.

At times I thought it was beyond our capabilities as a fire department to rebuild ourselves and accomplish our work at the Trade Center. Who does something like this? How could we? Maybe we needed the army to come in. But we have a lot of talent in the Fire Department, and a lot of people put together a system that worked. And we did it rather rapidly and on the run. Technically, it was a Fire Department–managed operation, but a lot of agencies were involved. We did use the federal resources, and logistical-support people who were used to running massive forest fires helped. FEMA [Federal Emergency Management Agency] teams came in from all over the country. The design and construction bureau, the city department that supervises construction, had a big role also, as did the Police Department, and the Port Authority, which owned and ran the property. But the Fire Department maintained control of the situation through-out. Some people didn't want to believe that we were in charge—some, I think, were quite offended by that—but it was a Fire Department operation until June of 2002, when it was handed over to the Port Authority.

Certainly one of the lessons of this entire experience was my own inadequa-cies. You do the best you can, but if you think you're up to the task of something like 9/11 and the aftermath, you're fooling yourself. You think you can brush aside the pain of the death of these people by gallows humor, or by saying, We're firefighters, we're gonna be tough. And that doesn't work. I was not up to the task of everything that challenged us. There were times when I was terrible at home. We all had frustration, and whom do you take your frustration out on? Usually the people closest to you, because, in your mind, they don't understand what you're doing. They don't appreci-ate what's going on, so you shout at them and get angry with them. Look-ing back, there were certainly incidents like that that I'm not proud of.

Maybe it took me some time to realize the proper sequence of the events of importance to prioritize what we were doing. Supporting the firefighters who survived and were still around needed to be attended to. We were all worried about the next attack, as we weren't all convinced that this particular operation was over. Maybe something else was coming? Other buildings? The Empire State Building? Transportation hubs? We thought about these things every day, at least until the end of 2001. And the families of those who died . . . Everyone had different needs. Everyone had different expectations of what we would or could do for them. What we *should* do for them. Mayor [Rudy] Giuliani, I thought, was great with us, with the families. I think eventually we did a good job with them.

Thankfully there were so many people within the department who were talented, and who made up for my own inadequacies, because I couldn't be at the WTC site every minute of every day. I couldn't be at every one of the 343 funerals. I couldn't be at every interagency meeting that was held. There was a limit to what I could physically do, mentally do. Members of our department helped out, with funerals, especially. People did a great job making me look like I did a good job, I think. I owe a lot to them. The further it gets from those days, the more I realize that if I hadn't had a lot of people to lean on in this department, I would have been completely shot day one. I would just have had to walk away from it. Crawl up, roll up into a ball, and be totally useless, because it was an overwhelming task for anyone to do without that caliber of help. But I had it.

I never got used to the funerals; I don't think anyone did. There were 343—it was one, and then one more, and one more. It wasn't just a big number: These were individuals with families, relatives, friends. Invariably these firefighters were the nicest people in their neighborhoods. They were the coaches of the Little League teams. They worked at soup kitchens. They were good and solid individuals. They took care of their families. You heard this every day for months. You saw the kids who lost their fathers, mothers who lost their sons, and I always tried to feel that I was a sponge that would absorb everyone's grief. I was never good at watching sad movies; I'd always be the one crying. So I'd go to these funerals, and I'd come out and feel weak just witnessing this profound grief. What happened to so many families was overwhelming. At times I'd speak, and the effort of writing a speech and delivering it in some presentable manner made it possible for me to get through that particular day. I'd have to put on a strong face.

The firefighters did a good job with that too. They didn't break down at the funerals, and they were strong for the families. People were assigned to each family to take care of them. The bagpipe band figured a way to cover every funeral, to give that special Fire Department dignity that is so meaningful to the family. We didn't think it possible, but they did it. We have a Ceremonial Unit, which got very good at making every funeral move forward like clockwork. I was pretty sad that we had to get good at managing funerals, but as a department we did, though it took its toll on everybody.

I can think of only one or two funerals of members who were not buried from a church. I can't believe that all of these people were churchgoing folk, but I think everyone's spirituality grew during this period. Maybe the highlight for me was when I went to Rome in November. The Italian government asked me to send a few firefighters, including a group of family members of those who had died, and they asked me to come as well. At first I said, "I can't go. There's too much here." They said it was only for two days, and that the group was going to have an audience with the pope at the Vatican. To see the pope seemed to be time well spent for me and for the department and, certainly, going to St. Peter's for a mass dedicated to the FDNY members lost on 9/11 conducted by the pope was historic. I was almost speechless when it came time to go up and say something to him. It was overwhelming, and I felt very uplifted by it for months after that.

The terrorism of 9/11 was a worldwide event and reached that extraordinary level where we had the pope praying for us. Not only for the people who had died and for their families, but for all the people who were continuing the work down in Ground Zero, and those protecting everyone else in the city. I'd never been across the Atlantic before, and I came back with an outlook that was certainly stronger from that visit, stronger from just being near Pope John Paul II, who will soon be a saint. I did feel just being in his presence that he had an aura.

To this day I ask myself what I could have done differently. I was the chief of operations, a big responsibility. What would have resulted in less of a loss of life? Did I do my job adequately? Or would somebody else have done a better job? Chief Ganci was in charge, but I also had a lot of high-ranking experience. I was the second in command and had as much responsibility in that incident as anyone. And I still wish there was something I could have done differently.

There have been times when people asked me, "How could you send my husband into the building like that? How could you do that?" And that's a good question. I understand someone's asking that, and it hurts to hear it. But I also understand it hurts me less than it does her. It's not an off-base question—not everyone patted us on the back to say, Don't feel bad, I don't blame you. People were angry with the department for what happened. Some people, not many. Most families were unbelievably gracious in dealing with their loss, and not getting on us, but it was a day-to-day struggle just trying to find some sort of balance. Even the firefighters wanted to know, What are you going to do different next time? I mean, if we get called to the Empire State Building now, what are you going to do differently? You're in charge. How are you going to keep us safe? And the wives would ask, How are you going to keep my husband safe? Do you know?

And I didn't know. I could not give them a guarantee to keep our people safe. No one could, and you can't guarantee it today. But we've had a decade to look back and change our policies. Maybe we can keep a higher percentage of the members safe, but we cannot say unequivocally that this will not happen again. We all know this is firefighting, and there is much stress involved with that. And danger.

That's why I'm a believer in the randomness of things rather than the purposefulness of them. It wasn't that the good or the kind were spared above others, or that one life was more valuable than another. I was spared, and some other person's life was taken. I'm sure many of those lives were more valuable than mine, and their families may have needed them more than mine needed me. I don't know. Certainly many, many of them were better people than I, as I learned at the funerals, hearing the eulogies.

St. Paul says that you see through a cloudy glass, and someday you'll see it clear. Someday there will be a clearness to this, and then all of us might go, Aha, that was it. But no, this is not understandable. I've tried to tell myself that maybe I should be out there doing more good in the world, because there was a reason that I was saved, and the reason was that I was going to do something great with my life. I've had ten years, and I've done okay during that time, but I certainly haven't made an impact on the world in the past decade, unless there's something coming up that I don't know of.

My father is a retired firefighter and has always given me good advice— an old firefighter's advice. Some months after 9/11 he told me to go to every firehouse that had lost people. There were about ninety such firehouses, so each night I'd go out and stop at a few on the way home. I would talk to the members, and say, "I'm sorry about your loss." Sometimes it was a short visit, and everybody was like, Okay, fine, nice to see you, Chief. In other places it was very spirited—a lot of anger, a lot of fear—and I spent hours getting roughed up in the kitchen. But I took the blows, as they say, and I think it was very good advice from my father. It showed them that I was out there listening to the guys, thinking about them, caring about what they said, caring about what they felt. I might not be able to change everything that they wanted me to, but I listened.

My retirement was a sudden thing, really. In September of 2002 I did not get a tenured appointment from City Hall, so I put my retirement papers in. It shouldn't have been, but I just let it be; I was now going to be without a job within thirty days, so I decided to visit every battalion, got every fire company together. So again at night I would stop at a few battalions, and companies would come over with the rigs, and I spoke to each one of them, thanking them for what they had done, which made me look good. I got a lot of honors, including the [Cavalier] of the Republic of Italy, and the [National Order of the] Legion of Honor, Chevalier of France. I might be one of the few people in this country to have been awarded both of those, and the only reason that I was was because of the firefighters in New York City.

It was a good way to go out, and the last day on the job I went back to Ladder 123. I had always had a lot of respect for that company, and although I never worked there, I had a son-in-law there, and a nephew. I took the irons [an ax and a Halligan tool] that night, and I was on the back step [a term for being on the fire truck]. It was my last tour of duty in the FDNY.

I was still a firefighter, even after all those thirty-three years, having risen through the ranks: lieutenant, captain, battalion chief, deputy chief, assistant chief, chief of operations, chief of department. I don't know if I was still on full duty, or even legal, but I was going out the way I came in. I found that what I missed when I got promoted through the ranks is what I liked about the job in the first place: the actual firefighting with people I trusted. So it was kind of like going full circle for me, and I left the job in a pair of jeans, a pair of work boots, and a T-shirt. Fortunately, there were no memorable fires that night, and I thank the people of Brooklyn for that. I was an older version of the guy who came on the job in 1969, and rode the back steps of many different fire trucks. It was a lot of fun with the firefighters in the kitchen, and so it was a nice way, a good way, to end my career.

It did not come the way I wanted it at the time, as I had planned to stay in the job practically until they threw me out. But again, things don't always happen the way you think they are going to happen, so you make the best of how it goes. It was quite a year, and I have trouble remembering other parts of my life in the Fire Department because of that last year. I was once asked in an interview if, other than the World Trade Center, I could name some other fires I had been at that were memorable. And I couldn't. Because once those buildings collapsed, it was like the hard drive in my mind took up all the memory, and there was no room for other recorded events. Sometimes they come back to me now, but at the time I couldn't even think of things that hadn't occurred in that twelve-month period, from September 11, 2001, to September 9, 2002, when I retired.

If you were a survivor of Pearl Harbor, I think that would always be the defining event of your life, no matter what else happened to you. Certainly because I am a survivor of September 11, and was chief during that time, my life subsequent to that has become centered around 9/11. That's all I think about. But it had such an impact on my life that I think I'm a better person now. I'm more apt to think about people's feelings. I've become more in touch with the importance of everything that I do every day, and how nice it is to have these days. To have a life, even the parts of it that aren't so much fun, is still something to experience. If I get delayed at an airport—the kind of minor inconvenience that used to drive me crazy—it doesn't seem to matter anymore. Such things have much less impact now, because all of us who were there were impacted by something so big that all else seems pretty small in comparison. Some people, unfortunately, have never gotten over it enough to function. Some, maybe many, lost the way they used to be, the way they enjoyed their life, because it hurt them so badly. They weren't able to get to the point where they could compartmentalize that hurt, and live with it. Not everyone can simply say, You know, it's time to move on. That's unrealistic—you don't move on to a place where this is no longer a part of you. It's always a part of you. I'm lucky enough to have been able to have a life after 9/11 that's been wonderful. It doesn't mean that I don't have pain, but I can still see beauty, and enjoy each day.

I think some of us knew that the World Trade Center was built outside of the building code in New York. I can't speak for people there that day who were knowledgeable about the details. I knew about it because it was Port Authority, and the authority is exempt from local building codes. I don't know if any of our department leadership was on the job when it was being built, but maybe we were just at the beginning of our careers. Were any of us aware that those trusses might have rendered the building less strong than others that we'd been in? Probably not. We were probably not as aware of the skeletal structure as we should have been. And that speaks to some of the inadequacies I felt afterward. Here I was, in a very high position in the department, and I didn't know this. We all should have known more, maybe. But I can only speak for myself. I have always considered myself to be knowledgeable, but I wasn't as knowledgeable as I thought I was.

I've seen one of the chief structural engineers of the Trade Center [Leslie Robertson] on TV since, and he doesn't feel that way, but I'll let him deal with whatever demons are in his head. And I'm sure they're there, each and every day. I have enough of them in my own head to deal with. Here we had the biggest buildings in New York, and I don't remember ever seeing a fire-load analysis of those structures. We probably were just creatures of experience. In the New York City Fire Department most everything we do is based on our experiences. Overseas a lot of the chiefs have to have degrees in engineering to reach the highest levels in their departments. In New York we've always had a guy who has been to five thousand fires leading us. It did work, for the most part, but it didn't work very well that day.

So we have the firefighting issues, the construction issues, and the issues of the attackers. I'm always shocked by how casual people remain in this country about the whole issue of Islam, that they are willing to believe that these nineteen people who hijacked the planes were an aberration, that everyone else in the Muslim world is just peace and love. There's no way we have to be nice, that we have to be kind, that we must consider it could be our fault that this happened. Because we're not nice to others around the world, it's *our* fault? I'm not willing to buy that; I think it's crap. I think people who want us to believe in the "it's a few radicals" idea have some nerve. They want to sacrifice another few thousand people, another 343 firefighters, with this stupidity.

We're a country built on individual rights; I hear this all the time. How far do we extend that? How far? Should we stop searching people going onto planes? Why do we have to ask politely when we want to question these criminals about their behavior? Let's not worry about our society, some politicians seem to be saying, but let's worry about them. Let's not worry about the people they are going to kill. Let's worry about the well-being of the killers. And it's going to happen again. The firefighters still think about it every day. Their families think about it. My two daughters think about it, with their firefighter husbands, that firefighters are out there and could be sacrificed again.

We should, must, remain vigilant against people who want to harm us. I don't know how we can solve their problems. I don't know what they want. What is it that they want? What is it that sent these people out to kill us? What is their goal? If the goal is the destruction of our culture, then the only answer for us can be to defend ourselves and our families to whatever extent we have to.

I think our intelligence community was persistent, for instance, in staying after bin Laden, and that persistence paid off. I was in no way gleeful when I received word of his death, but considering the life he chose, the life of a mass-murdering criminal, he certainly got what he deserved.

I don't think the forces that brought us to 9/11 have disappeared or dissipated. We might have pushed some Taliban out of Afghanistan, but they're still there, a force in that world that sees whatever we're doing over here as evil. I'm offended when people think that anyone who took a stance against building a mosque near Ground Zero is a racist or a Muslim hater. Look at it this way: Muslims killed many of my friends, killed family members of some of the people who said I don't like the idea of a mosque down by Ground Zero, and so I am sensitive to the subject. We have to be sensitive to those 9/11 families who think this. We owe it to them. They're not saying that they believe there shouldn't be Muslims in America or that Muslims don't have a right to exist. The idea of building a mosque has now grown to that of building a great Muslim cultural center, and it is just too close to a place that's considered sacred to many people. Why would one think these family members should get over it?

No one is saying that every Muslim in the world is to blame for 9/11, but it is undeniable that a battle exists between some segment of people who believe in the Muslim faith and what we would call the West. I think everyone can agree to that. It's not just a few guys, and once we get rid of those guys who are locked up somewhere in a cave, it will all end. I don't think anyone believes that. The world continues to be very dangerous, and I am afraid that the next attack could be even more heinous than 9/11.

I'm talking about a nuclear or radiological event that will affect many thousands of people for many years. I don't have a security clearance, so I don't know what intelligence we're gathering around the world, but just the knowledge that there are people out there who are willing to put a bomb in their shoe or their underwear—that disturbs me. People danced in the streets after 9/11, and I know there would be people who would dance in the streets if a nuclear device were to be detonated in Times Square.

Can they be successful? I'm not so afraid of it that I'm living out in a cabin in Montana. My family and everyone else I know lives here in New York. We are still the biggest target. We are not running away from it, but certainly we know that it's possible. In one way we in New York are very fortunate, because we have good leadership in our Police and Fire departments. We all benefit from that. For now, anyway.

Ray Kelly

Ray Kelly is the only official to hold the office of police commissioner of the city of New York under two mayors—David Dinkins and Michael Bloomberg— separated by eight years. He is a man who was molded by the caring and the personal motivations found within a close-knit Irish Catholic family. He is perhaps the most educated police commissioner who has ever served a major police department (a group that includes President Theodore Roosevelt). A former U.S. Marine, he brings to his leadership style the values of integrity, strength, and courage that were taught in his training and refined on the battlefields of Vietnam. He is known as a creator of innovative and important programs and policies designed to keep the public protected from the social hazards of crime and safe in the midst of New York City's greatest challenge to the security of the homeland.

I was the youngest of five—three brothers and one sister—and my parents were loving, hardworking people. I always remember my mother working—she had a part-time job as a checker at Macy's. My father was basically a milkman for a significant period of time, until there was a change in the law, brought about by [Mayor Fiorello] LaGuardia. LaGuardia was not a hero in our household. To the best of my knowledge, the milk regulations were changed so that you could now buy it in supermarkets, and so the price was lowered. As a result, the route deliverers basically went out of business. My father then worked on the docks, and then in the Brooklyn Navy Yard. When the war was over, he was out of work. I remember him shaping up in the *New York Times*, and then he got a great job as a clerk in the Treasury Department in the IRS. In his fifties he would go to work wearing a suit and tie, something I had never seen previously.

When I was born we lived at Ninety-first Street and Columbus Avenue, in a five-story tenement that has since been torn down. I went to St. Gregory's School, which is still on Ninetieth between Amsterdam and Columbus, and when the neighborhood became bad we moved to Queens, where I attended eighth grade at St. Theresa's in Sunnyside. I then went to St. Ann's Academy in Manhattan, which was moved to Queens and, though it had existed for over one hundred years, its name was changed to Archbishop Molloy. It's still a good school today.

In college I majored in economics, within the School of Business at Manhattan College. In those days you had to have 144 credits to graduate, and so I took many diverse courses—Spanish and history, accounting, psychology—and found them to be interesting and insightful. But it was the School of Business, so statistics and those sorts of courses were in the core of the curriculum. And I also had a big dose of theology.

I was also working in Macy's part time. My mother had gotten me a job as a stock boy, but I saw an advertisement looking for college students to do part-time work in a path to become a police officer. Adam Walinsky in the Lindsay administration helped create the police cadet program, which was the first effort on the part of municipal police agencies to bring college graduates into police departments. I had no relatives in the police department, but this advertisement seemed to be a window into this mysterious organization—and I didn't particularly want to continue as a stock boy. I was in the first class of police cadets, and we were looked at somewhat strangely by the uniformed members of the department, because we were all so young. We went to work in a variety of administrative units. I worked in the lost property section, and then in the communication division, where I would man the switchboard. And I worked alongside other college students doing that. And that's how I took the test to be a police officer. You had to take the test, and pass it, to remain in the cadet program.

About a month after I graduated with a commission as a second lieutenant, I went on active duty in the marines. I had three older brothers, all of them in the Corps, so I sort of felt compelled to go into the marines as well. They would bring home Marine Corps paraphernalia and that sort of thing when I was young, so I was fascinated by it. While family environment was very important to me, and obviously, Catholic school provided a sound educational foundation, I think it's fair to say that my experiences in the marines have also been important. Marine Corps values mean a lot to me, because those core values—honesty, determination, fairness, and courage—stay with you your whole life. You don't realize it, and don't consciously think about it every day, but they really do impact on how you approach life, approach problems, deal with people.

When I left the Marine Corps in late 1966–early 1967 I came back to the NYPD training school. Now I had just come from Vietnam, so chaotic situations were not unusual for me, but we were taken to the range, fired fifty rounds of ammunition, given blue uniforms and guns, and within three days put right out on the street on patrol with a more experienced uniformed officer. This was a highly unusual occurrence, and we would never do it today. I went to Brooklyn, where there were disturbances in East New York and Bedford-Stuyvesant—garbage cans being thrown off the roof and that sort of thing. So we were in the thick of it before we really had any training.

The sixties were very tumultuous. Most people today don't remember, or they aren't old enough to remember, that there was a lot of street disorder. The sixties and early seventies were fraught with civil unrest.

I started going to St. John's law school at night, got promoted to sergeant, [and] began working in East Harlem, where I worked a lot of midnight tours on patrol. It was a very busy time, and a violent time. When we look at crime statistics today, they pale in comparison to those days. The job was a lot more dangerous back then, and a lot more uncertain in terms of what we might encounter. In 1971 or '72, twelve police officers were killed. It was definitely dangerous work, but it was exciting too, and I loved it.

At the same time, we had police corruption, which was exposed by the Knapp Commission. Its findings were a major surprise to the average police officer—and might come as a surprise to many people today—as they were not aware of corruption in specialized units, like narcotics. The idea that police would be taking money from drug dealers was something that was considered by members of the department to be total anathema. It was a very hostile environment.

I became first deputy police commissioner under Commissioner Lee P. Brown in February of 1990. Because he was the president of the IACP [International Association of Chiefs of Police], he often had to speak at events in other parts of the country, so as acting commissioner, I gained much experience.

At that period of time we weren't prepared for the development of organized terrorism. Should we have been? Hindsight is twenty-twenty, but the answer is yes. To the extent that there was some hum or buzz about terrorism, it was thought to be a federal problem, and the federal government was addressing that. We were not aware on a municipal level, where we were taking care of the traditional things that police agencies are supposed to. In those days we had a significant amount of crime, and obviously our focus was on suppressing it.

On February 26, 1993, we had the first World Trade Center attack. I remember going there and seeing the magnitude of the event. Of course, what happened on September 11 dwarfs what took place then, but at the time it was a major, major incident. We were involved in rescue and recovery efforts, and then we had specialized units like the bomb squad assist in the investigation. But the assumption was that the federal government would be actively engaged, and we did not see ourselves in those days as having a kind of equal partnership with the FBI. It should have been a wake-up call for the city, and it also should have been a call for us to look behind the federal curtain and see what was going on. When you look back you see that relatively little was going on.

To a certain extent, one of the problems that emerged as a result of the first World Trade Center attack is that it supposedly was solved very quickly, and the individuals were seen as being somewhat inept. A detective in our auto crime division found the differential of the truck that was used and brought it to our police lab. It had a hidden VIN [vehicle identification number], which was traced very quickly to a rental facility in New Jersey. A few days after the attack the bombers came back to get their deposit, claiming that the truck had been stolen. The bombing took place on a Friday, and the following Thursday the arrests were made. When you think about it, the fact that they came back for their deposit wasn't all that illogical, if they were taking the position that they didn't know what happened to the truck, since it had been stolen, but instead they were painted as buffoons. As a result of that I think the attention of the investigative agencies was lowered, or shifted. And as far as the public was concerned, these people were in jail.

But not too long afterward there was another plot in which Jim Fox, who ran the New York office of the FBI, learned from an informant of plans to blow up 26 Federal Plaza, the UN, the Holland Tunnel, and other familiar sights throughout New York City. Suspects were arrested and were again considered to be some sort of buffoons, because they were so sloppy. So while there was a sense that there was a threat out there, it wasn't well organized. Sheikh Rahman was discovered to be in the middle of it, and was ultimately taken into custody, and that was that. Life went on. I left city government then at the end of ninety-three, early ninety-four, and the police department didn't particularly focus on the issue of terrorism.

At that point I went to NYU [New York University] for a short time on the teaching faculty, and then joined a consulting company, for which I went to Haiti for six months to take charge of the international responders. So I was out of municipal police business and doing work for the federal government, now in a totally different sphere. I, too, certainly wasn't focused at all on the terrorist threat.

I do remember, though, sitting in the lobby of the World Trade Center on February 26 with an engineer who had been trapped in the elevator, and who had just cut himself out to safety. He said that they could never take those buildings down. The bomb crater went from the B1 to the B5 level, but they were supported by huge beams. There was some consideration that their plan may have been to take this tower down, perhaps even with the aim of one building falling into the other. But the engineer's insistence that they could never take the building down struck me.

In 1996 I was working for a litigation support company when Bob Rubin, who was then the secretary of the treasury, called and asked for some advice, and then asked if I would be interested in going to the federal government as undersecretary of the Department of the Treasury in enforcement. At that time about 40 percent of all federal law enforcement was in the Treasury Department, including the Secret Service, the ATF [the Bureau of Alcohol, Tobacco, Firearms, and Explosives], and U.S. Customs, and was responsible for all federal law enforcement training, with the exceptions of the FBI and the DEA [Drug Enforcement Agency]. So he asked me to go and become undersecretary for treasury, and I did, in 1996. I was sworn in and had U.S. Customs reporting to me. The customs commissioner left, and I interviewed a lot of people and made some recommendations to Secretary Rubin, who was not happy with them. Finally, I said, what about me for that job? To demote oneself is a fairly un-Washington thing to do, but in 1998 I became the customs commissioner and remained in that position until the end of the Clinton administration. Then, in early 2001, I went to Bear Stearns as head of global security.

So, on September 11, 2001, I was physically in the Bear Stearns building at 345 Park Avenue when the first plane struck. Initially it was said to be a small plane, but then, fifteen minutes later, the second plane hit, and of course it was obviously an intentional act involving terrorism of some sort. We were in the process of building the new Bear Stearns headquarters a block and a half away, and I was told there was panic there. I went to the building and tried to calm people down.

My wife, Veronica, was out of the country, but I was concerned about my son Gregory, who was a reporter for New York 1. I didn't know where he was, and I couldn't contact him. Nor could I contact my other son, James, who was downtown as well. I was also concerned about my home, and I knew, by all indications, that I couldn't get back there, because I lived literally one block away from the World Trade Center, in Battery Park. I didn't know what the vulnerability of my apartment building was. There was a fair amount of—I wouldn't say chaos, but people were very uncertain and didn't know what to do. Some wanted to go home; others wanted to stay. There were problems with transportation. The most memorable thing that day was to witness the first building fall, because you could see part of the South Tower from our building. I thought back to that conversation I had had in the lobby of that very tower on February 26, 1993, about its never coming down. But the building went down. Like so many other people, I was just dumbstruck.

Ultimately the feeling that kicked in was a desire to help in some way, to bring my experience to bear on the issue of arresting and bringing into custody whoever had done this—and preventing something like it from ever happening again. It was a common belief for the next months that another attack was imminent: Something else was going to happen; it was just a matter of time.

The magnitude of the event so far exceeded anything that we had ever experienced. I had been around and had known police officers who were killed in the line of duty, but when I saw the breadth and scope of the impact of losing twenty-three police officers in one hour—that was horrific. Most of the twenty-three police officers killed that day were from the ESU [Emergency Service Unit], which I had served with. I knew Sergeant Michael Curtin, who was also in the Marine Corps Reserve, and who was killed that day.

And then the impact on the Fire Department, losing of 343 men—that was very hard to believe, to internalize. If it had happened in the Police

Department it would have been, percentagewise, the equivalent of twelve hundred officers. Initially the estimates of the overall death toll were much higher than three thousand; some people were predicting as many as ten thousand. The true number was just unknown, and it took days to sort that out.

I was asked by Secretary of Transportation Norman Minetta to come to Washington to join a committee that had been formed to get planes back in the air, as all commercial flying schedules in the Northeast had been greatly impacted by the events. I met with people at the FAA [Federal Aviation Administration] and was involved for a few days, eager to help. There were other conferences, and it was interesting to both the power of the airline industry and the federal regulatory agencies.

Shortly after the attack, in October, I was asked and agreed to endorse Michael Bloomberg for mayor, who was seen as a tremendous long shot after September 11. The day after he was elected he called me. I had my own thoughts about what the city should do in the wake of this attack, but I was not really preparing to come back to the job of New York City police commissioner.

When I took the position my primary thought was that business had to be done differently in terms of protecting our city. Here we had had two major attacks, both at the same site. New York had to do more as an entity to protect itself. We could not rely solely on the federal government. You can offer all sorts of rationales, but the federal government had failed.

The NYPD is an organization of fifty thousand people. That is formidable in size, and we needed to configure the agency in such a way that it would be an integral and important player in protecting the city from a terrorist event. So I started thinking about it, and put up a long sheet of butcher-block paper on which I wrote out the changes in the structure of the department, which is what we have today.

I knew the counterterrorism bureau had to be moved up in importance in the department—there were only seventeen investigators on the terrorism task force at the time of September 11. I knew we needed to have a strong relationship with the FBI. I knew that our intelligence division had to be more formed, and we needed people outside of policing to be a part of it. The police department, not unlike the fire department, is tradition bound, and the question was, Who could I bring in from the outside to head the counterterrorism bureau? Who would be accepted? I decided that, given my background, I wanted a former Marine Corps general to come in and head it. I also knew we needed a medical and scientific component with the ability to assess the threat from chemical, biological, and radiological weapons and to learn how to protect ourselves—that meant a doctor and medical staff. In our intelligence division I wanted to get someone from outside the agency with relevant credentials. And I wanted to build up our language skills, so I looked to have someone come in from the CIA. I wanted to bring in people from federal agencies who were involved in fighting terrorism. All of these guiding principles were written out on the butcher-block paper.

I reached out to Frank Libutti, a lieutenant general who had just retired from the Marine Corps and had tremendous credentials. And he came onboard in January of 2002. I reached out to David Cohen, whom I knew from his time as the CIA head of station in New York. We drafted several retired FBI agents. We were able to hone our own internal language skills while at the same time broadening our recruitment to obtain people with sensitive language capabilities that we thought we needed for our own internal intelligence investigations.

This is a "can do" organization, and by January of 2002 we had our counterterrorism headquarters set up in Brooklyn. You have to consider that people in the first months of any life-changing event are usually trying to find the light switches, so this was quite a remarkable achievement. And we continued to bring in people from other parts of the department.

We thought about going to other countries. When I was customs commissioner we had legats [legal attachés] overseas. One of our concerns was that there might be investigations going forward that involved New York, investigations that we knew nothing about. And I knew a cop-to-cop relationship could work in other countries, as there's a sort of recognition in the international law enforcement community that cooperation works pretty well. I took the experience of having customs legats and tailored it to our needs. The concept was to have what we call trip wires, or listening posts, people in other parts of the world who could give us any sort of heads-up, any information that would better protect New York.

The first location where we put this in place was Tel Aviv, Israel, where we had Detective First Grade Mordecai Dzikansky. We knew that the Israelis would be very supportive of this concept. We sought to identify someone in the NYPD who had strong roots in Israel, and even may have gone to school there. Mordecai—Morty—had gone to Hebrew University for a couple of years, and was now a detective. He was received extremely well. At that time there were lots of suicide bombings in Israel, so we thought we could learn something about what we call *tradecraft* going on, because we believed that it was going to come here.

To get Morty to the site of a bombing within thirty or forty-five minutes, he was given an office with the national police, and he was soon sending back detailed information that we would never have been able to get anywhere else—there's no vehicle for that sort of data to come to municipal police agencies.

In March of 2004, bombings took place as trains were coming into the station in Madrid, Spain, but the bombs themselves had been assembled in pickup vans in the vicinity of outlying stations. Obviously we've been very sensitive to such incidents because of our own train system. We sent Morty to Madrid, as well as a team from our transit bureau that had been involved in helping the MTA design their cars. We found out very quickly from Morty—the Spaniards had good camera surveillance—that some vans had been used to put the bombs together. One of the bombs, which they were using cell phones to activate, had not been detonated, so we had really detailed information on the device. We saw that the bags themselves that carried the bombs were pretty big and weighed about twenty-two pounds. So we got that information out quickly to the patrol force working around our subway stations, and we felt our patrols started to increase the comfort level of the riding public.

On July 7, 2005, bombs went off in London at eight o'clock in the morning. Our guy in London was actually on the subway going to work when it happened, and when he got to headquarters he was able to give us real-time information. We didn't know if this was part of a worldwide event or if it was isolated in London, so we buttressed our uniformed patrols. I called a meeting that day and said that I wanted to have knapsacks and bags checked in the subways but to make sure it passed muster as far as Supreme Court decisions regarding stops and searches went. We put that in place within a couple of hours and are still doing it today. Obviously some of this we do for effect. We want to advertise the effort, and at least get people thinking about the fact that we are aware.

In January of 2011 we sent a top guy, a former member of the Israeli defense force, to Moscow, and he told us some unsettling things. This was just after the Domodedovo Airport bombing, in which 35 people were killed and 168 people were injured, and he looked at the security they had in place there and said it was very lax: Guards who were supposed to be checking the machines were on cell phones; the machines were going off, and people were just allowed to go through. Our guy tested the system with keys in his pockets, and they simply let him go. Mumbai is another example of where we got granular information because of the trip-wire protocol.

We have the right people in place because of our department's size. We have Arabic speakers in Dubai. We've got NYC police officers who were born in Spain, in Madrid. We have people who were born in Israel. We've got Canadian-raised officers in Montreal.

We are still trying to get our arms around the radicalization process. I think you see Peter King [see page 82] taking this issue on, and he'll be doing a lot more of that. In 2007 we published a report by Mitch Silber and Arvia Bhatt, who are part of our intel house. We sent them all over the world. They went to Australia and to the Netherlands and tried to get some understanding of the phenomenon of what they call unremarkable people deciding to kill innocent people in their own country. Their report talks about the four stages of radicalization, and it really is seen as the template for our law enforcement and intelligence community. We're working on the second version of that now to refine it.

We know a fair amount about the radicalization process, where people start, how their ideas change, and when they decide to commit jihad. We are learning more and more about it, but it's no easy task, because we have also seen people who have just radicalized themselves. There are others who have been radicalized by a "sanctioner." If you look at the case of eighteen young men in Toronto, their sanctioner was in essence a custodian in a mosque. Do we see it as a problem in the United States? Yes. But we don't know what we don't know.

When you search for the indicators to identify someone who is going to decide to kill other people, they don't jump out at you. Whom do we watch? What are the tipping points where people will decide to inflict violence? They're not easy to see. We have thousands of people who come here on a student visa. It is probably a good thing overall for this country to have student exchange, but how do you vet them? There are thirty thousand students from Saudi Arabia going to school in Western countries, most of them here.

It is very, very hard to predict where we will be in the future, and no really thoughtful people have come out with anything definitive. A lot is based on economics. People want jobs, but there are no jobs at the end of jihad. If they change their government, that doesn't translate into jobs. So what does that mean? It means more frustration, more uncertainty. Is that an opportunity for the Muslim Brotherhood and other groups like that to come in and take over? Perhaps. We don't know.

One thing we have not seen in all the Middle East turmoil is American flags and Israeli flags being burned. So if you had to pick out one reason for upheavals in the Middle East and in Africa, it is that people want to advance economically. But there's no real structure in place to do this. The only country with the resources to make a difference in other Arab countries is Saudi Arabia, and they haven't really shown the propensity to do that sort of thing so far. Nobody knows the direction these countries will take. Look at Iran in 1979. They got rid of the shah, supposedly for all the right purposes, but the effort was subverted and was captured by radical Islamists. Could that happen today? Yes, it could happen. What do we do about it? It's going to take generations to change this jihadist thinking. My sense is, they are looking for the goods they see everywhere, but these are poor countries, and they are not able to change overnight. If a high-tech economy comes to them, it's going to be well down the road.

Let's assume democracy breaks out. It's a pretty messy process. The reality is that having somebody like Mubarak sit on the top of the Middle East and provide stability was a good thing for us. It's nice to espouse the virtues of democracy, but there are a lot of countries that aren't ready. George Will asked recently, "Would you want to see democracy in Pakistan?" If there's some semblance of democracy that breaks out in certain countries, it doesn't necessarily bode well for us at all. Why? Because the strongman model has worked reasonably well for stability in the Middle East. It's worked reasonably well for the United States. It's worked reasonably well for Israel. Getting away from that is just uncharted water; nobody knows what the result could be. And could these democratic efforts be subverted and negatively change the direction of a country? Absolutely. If it's going to change inevitably, what do we do? We can't necessarily change the tide of history.

I'm not saying everything depends on our military strength, but it's kind of the big guy you need standing behind you. Talk softly and carry a big stick. Our military is the big stick that we've depended on in the past. I think the world might sense the reluctance on our part to use justified, legitimate force, based on the reaction of the American people. The polls show that a majority want us out of Afghanistan, and there's no discernible benefit so far with what's happened in Iraq. Yes, there's some form of democracy, but who knows what that all means down the road? Do we have the will? It may have been undermined by what turned out to be the longest war in our history.

David Prezant

Dr. David Prezant is the chief medical officer of the New York City Fire Department. After the first plane went into the North Tower, he headed for the World Trade Center from his hospital in the Bronx. He soon helped set up a triage station on West and Liberty streets, less than a half block away from the South Tower, the first tower to fall. When it did fall, the building came down in eight seconds. He only remembers seeing people running before he was blown off his feet and thrown through the air.

I was born, according to my parents, at Bronx-Lebanon Hospital, which is on the Grand Concourse. And I lived in that area around the Grand Concourse for the first six years of my life, roughly. We then moved closer to Montefiore Medical Center on Mosholu Parkway, and I started school at PS 80. I had always hoped to go to Bronx Science, but when I was going into fifth grade we moved to Yonkers. There I finished grade school, and then went to Lincoln High School, a normal high school with no science specialization. From there my parents told me that I could go to the college of my choice, but they had only a limited amount of money. I didn't want to burden myself with loans, so I had to think about whether I wanted to go to a state school or a private school. I got into all of the state schools in New York, but I also got into Columbia, which is where I decided to go.

To be closer to campus, I moved to my grandmother's apartment on the Upper West Side. And it was a great experience because (a) I didn't really have a commute, only a five-minute subway ride, and (b) I was able to have the full college experience, with everything right there. Also, I got very close with my grandmother, which was just a very big benefit. Most of us don't live in an extended-family world anymore, and I'm glad I got the chance to do so, because my grandmother was a great person.

I didn't always know that I was going to become a physician. I knew that I was going to do something in science but was not quite certain what.

I majored in biochemistry, and originally I thought I was going to become a PhD scientist in biochemistry or organic chemistry—what a mistake that would have been. But I was convinced that chemistry was my calling. I was incredibly wrong.

Many people think parents want you to become a physician, and I can tell you with 100 percent honesty that in the beginning that was not the interest of my parents at all. They did not care what I chose to do, but based on their own life experiences, they did feel that happiness required a certain amount of security—not money, but security, the ability to control your own destiny and make your own decisions. My dad had always wanted to do certain things but was impoverished growing up, and he did not want the same thing to happen to me. He felt that if I went into chemistry that I would become an automaton, and pharmaceutical companies would just use me and spit me out. And he was probably right. Only a few very brilliant people can really control their own destiny in that industry. And so after a while he lobbied very hard, in a way I found distasteful at times, for me to go to medical school. I hated what he said at the time, but as usual with parents, he was absolutely correct.

So I went to the Albert Einstein College of Medicine in the Bronx. It's a great medical school, but I was completely uninterested for the first two years, at best an average student. However, when I got onto the wards and started seeing patients, I realized how great this field could be, and how you could change things for both individuals and, through teaching and research, for large numbers of people as well. I realized that I wanted to specialize in internal medicine, and did my internship and residency at Harlem Hospital, because I wanted a place where I could learn a lot, and where I really could make a difference. I wanted to be in an impoverished area, where interns and residents were used as physicians, something that is not too commonly practiced in this day and age. At that time, although we had supervision, we were really doing it all ourselves. I was there for three years, and then I went back to Einstein–Montefiore Medical Center to do a pulmonary fellowship to become a pulmonary critical care specialist.

While at Montefiore, the main teaching hospital for Einstein, I ended up meeting two physicians who worked for the Fire Department. One was Dr. Fell, who was a chest surgeon, and the other one was Dr. Rosenbloom, who was a cardiologist. I was not part of their sphere, being a pulmonary doctor, but we'd interact, and we seemed to get along well. By the time I finished my fellowship I was married to a woman who already had two children, so I had substantial financial responsibilities. But I did not want to go into private practice; I wanted to continue doing research and teaching and taking care of patients in a way that did not involve worrying about how much time I spent with them, or billing, and all of those things. I graduated in 1986, a pulmonary physician, and was offered by Einstein the standard rate for an academic pulmonary physician, which is fifty thousand dollars. That is not a lot of money today, and was not even a lot of money in 1986, especially if you have a wife and two children. So I was thinking about what other side jobs I could take, and I remembered that I knew these two Fire Department physicians. Wouldn't that be interesting? The Fire Department must need a lung specialist, with all that smoke inhalation. So my FDNY doctor friends called up Dr. Cyril Jones, who ran the [FDNY's] Bureau of Health Services at that time, and it seemed like [he had] the perfect job for me. I could see all of their pulmonary patients in one day. I could choose a weekend day, so it wouldn't interfere with my work at Montefiore. It would supplement my income and allow me to provide some important service back to the city. And finally, it would enable me to help people in such a noble position as firefighting, where they get smoke inhalation, asthma, and other maladies in order to save lives.

And so that is how I got the job with the FDNY. It was a phenomenal way to give something back to this great city.

In the midnineties, Dr. Jones retired, and the Fire Department began looking for a more state-of-the-art facility, one that would be more actively monitoring and treating—things that I had been doing on my own but that most of the Bureau of Health Services was not doing. Dr. Kerry Kelly then became the chief medical officer, in 1994, and I became the deputy chief medical officer. Today . . . Dr. Kelly is chief medical officer of the Bureau of Health Services. I'm chief medical officer for EMS [Emergency Medical Services] and special adviser to the [fire] commissioner on all health matters. Both Dr. Kelly and I are codirectors of the World Trade Center Medical Monitoring and Treatment Program.

Dr. Kelly's specialty was family practice, and we formed a great partnership. She lives and breathes the Fire Department. Her grandfather was a fire chief, her father was a lieutenant, and she has many cousins on the job. I think of her almost as a Mother Teresa for the Fire Department. She really wants the best medical care for the firefighters, and she's allowed me great latitude in my work. Sometimes a leader is really only interested in leading, but Dr. Kelly is interested in taking people along and allowing them to become the best they can be.

I have a lot of interests, and she has encouraged all of them. Together we developed a medical group practice in an occupational health setting so that we could offer our firefighters state-of-the-art medical care. As a doctor in a large organization, you can easily be labeled the company doctor, and the only way to avoid that label is to constantly practice state-of-the-art medicine. We do not make duty-status decisions in favor of the patient or the department, but medical decisions, and then the duty-status decisions just follow.

I got interested in protective equipment to reduce burns, because the major injury among firefighters was various degrees of burns. We did fascinating studies with bunker gear [outer protective clothing], showing that it reduced burns. These studies got me to know [both] management and [the labor unions] better and develop credibility with them. We did medical studies, and the union leaders, who were very savvy about safety, realized that if you practiced the best medicine it would benefit everyone in the long run.

It was not a question whether I would respond to the World Trade Center on 9/11—it was just a fact. I'm a lung specialist, but when Dr. Kelly and I took over the leadership of the Bureau of Health Services, one of the responsibilities that was unique to the chief medical officer and the deputy chief medical officer was trying to help out when firefighters and EMS workers who worked for the FDNY were perilously injured. So since the midnineties I have been responding to any life-threatening emergency for firefighters. I could go to all the major-alarm fires, because I'm a leader and I have a command presence, but that's not my interest. I love firefighters, and my mom always told me that my two favorite places to visit as a kid were the Bronx Zoo and the local firehouse. I don't like to just stand around fires, but I do go whenever there is a life-threatening injury or the significant potential for life-threatening injuries, or whenever I think I might be of help in a mass disaster. My job gives me that freedom and responsibility. The toughest moments, but the best ones, for Dr. Kelly and me have always been when a firefighter is fatally or near fatally injured, because we are really able to help that family and that person. Anybody who has seen us do that realizes the immense benefit that we bring to them, to that situation.

Before 9/11 there was a fire chief who had a very serious smoke inhalation event, and he went into respiratory distress. He was intubated at the scene and was taken to a small hospital. I arrived shortly afterward, and the medical care was excellent, but it rapidly became evident to me that their ability to provide the same high-level medical care throughout his hospital admission, especially at nighttime, was not going to be what this patient needed. And therefore I went into the waiting room, and I introduced myself for the first time to his wife. It's a situation in which I had not been that patient's physician, I'd never met the family, and I was now asking that his wife trust me and my advice that, despite the potential for additional new life-threatening consequences, we should take this patient and move him to a different hospital. As I was trying to explain to her why she should trust someone she had never met, she interrupted me and said, "You can stop talking now, I know who you are, and we're going to do whatever you say." To this day, that is the greatest moment of my life, because it just sums up everything. It sums up the sense of a career in which you're trying to do nothing but help people. Luckily God was watching over me then, and the chief had a great outcome, and is now living a completely normal life.

Our life or our job is made more joyful or sweet because it's not without risks. You can only achieve positive things if you are true to your basic vision and philosophy. But that is not without risks. It was a risky thing to do to take that patient out of a protective environment; he was intubated and in critical condition. If he passed away in that environment, it would have had no consequence to me or the Fire Department, except that we would have lost a soul. If he passed away during transport, it would have had damning consequences to me and to the department's Bureau of Health Services, because he would have passed away under our responsibility. These are very tough experiences to live through, but you become stronger because of them. And they just magnify your life.

On the morning of 9/11 I was doing what I do, and Dr. Kelly and everyone else were doing exactly as always—which was to be aware of the department's health needs. We immediately saw this is a huge event, with the potential for mass casualties that we might be able to triage or treat. It would be incredibly likely that there would be near fatal or fatal firefighter or EMT [emergency medical technician] events that we would interact with, as liaison or whatever. I cannot tell you that I looked at the towers and said, Oh,

343 firefighters and nearly 3,000 people were going to die that day. In fact, it didn't occur to me at all, and interestingly, it didn't occur to me that this was a terrorist event. I only thought, when the first plane hit, that it was an accident, but I knew it's where I belonged, and so I got in the car. On the way my wife called me, saying she had seen on TV that a second plane had hit. You knew then that something crazy was going on here.

Dr. Kelly responded from Staten Island; I responded from the Bronx. She got there a little earlier than I did, but both of us arrived after the second plane had hit and before the first tower collapsed. I parked a few blocks north of the command center, which was on West Street. I went down to the command center and reported there, as I'm supposed to. I saw Chief [Peter] Ganci and spoke to him but did not see Dan Nigro [see page 1] until later on.

In 1993, when the first bombing at the Trade Center occurred, I was not in a position where I could respond. Dr. Jones was then head, and I was really a one-day-a-week lung specialist. I had heard, whether it was correct or not, that there was a doctor who was already in the towers—not a Fire Department doctor, but a regular doctor who had helped a pregnant woman and had set up a little treatment area on one of the floors. I always felt that's what I would have liked to have done in similar circumstances. You were there to help people, not to watch. So now I kept bothering Chief Ganci, whom I knew: "What can I do?" I realized that he had his job to do, and I couldn't really bother him too much, because he couldn't concentrate. To give me something to do, and possibly get me out of his way, he said, "Why don't you go over to West Street and the South Tower, on the corner, and just stay there, and when victims come out you can triage them and decide what they need? We'll send one or two ambulances to meet you."

As I was walking the few blocks there, I saw what I originally thought was debris and then realized was people jumping off of the towers. When I got there I was met by several EMS—I think two—ambulances, maybe three, and by an EMS chief. He looked around, saw where we were, and said, within minutes of my arriving, "This is not the place where we need to be. There's stuff falling. We should not be on the sidewalk here. We should walk into the middle of West Street." Obviously there was no traffic—it had all been cordoned off—so we set up our triage evaluation area there. I, along with the few EMTs and paramedics who were there, followed the EMS chief.

That single decision saved our lives, because within a minute of our turning around and walking toward the Hudson River, somebody realized that the South Tower was collapsing, or that stuff was falling. I was looking away from the tower, and when all of a sudden people in front of me started running toward the water, I said to myself, *What are these cowards running for? What's going on here? We're going to start the triage center, so why are they running?* But you get this sort of herd mentality, and so I started running too, toward the water. It was surreal—I'd never been in war, I'd never been attacked, I'd never experienced a tsunami or hurricane or earthquake or a volcano eruption. So this was a first for me. You hear about experiences in which your life flashes by you in an instant. It is so true. As I was running across West Street I was going over in my head several things, again and again. Number one, I was saying to myself—and I can remember it like it was yesterday—was though I had not seen the tower collapse, I hadn't heard anything either. I have no auditory memory of this at all. I remember the sheer silence afterward, but I don't remember whether the collapse was loud or silent. All I have is people in front of me, and alongside of me, running, and stuff falling all over me and, literally, beams to the left of me and to the right of me. And I said to myself, over and over again, *I have shown up here, and I'm going to get killed, and I have helped no one. This isn't fair.* In the short period of time getting across West Street, I must—at least in my memory—have said that to myself a million times. The other thing I said to myself was that my wife knows I'm here, but she is not going to be able to survive without me. My wife had some medical problems, and I just felt that I was now dying, I had helped no one, and I was hurting my wife in ways that no one could imagine. And this just seemed unfair. And then, before I knew it, I didn't actively jump, but I was blown what felt like halfway across West Street. I became engulfed in debris that was falling and falling and falling, and I thought it was never going to stop.

And then I remembered—this is how stupid you can be, or how stupid I was, because I never try to play firefighter, but I do listen to patients—one guy who came to me maybe twenty years before, and he had a knife on his belt. Firefighters don't come in uniform when they see you unless they are injured on the job. He was not uniformed, but I was wondering why he had such a large knife on his belt. And he told me that a firefighter always needs a knife, because if you got caught in a building collapse, what you needed to do is to get down on all fours, cut a hole in the carpet, pull up the carpet, stick your head under the carpet, and suck out whatever air you could until somebody came and found you. I have no idea whether this is true or not, but I remembered it as I was being engulfed with all this stuff. A firefighter would know how humorous this is. I had no knife, and below me appeared to be asphalt, so I wasn't going to be cutting a hole in anything to get air. But this story came back to me, and I said to myself, *I need to create an air pocket so I can survive. Somebody will find me. The Fire Department will rescue me. They don't know where the hell I am, but they rescue everybody else, so they're going to rescue me.* I was 100 percent convinced of this. I'm telling this because I find it unimaginable that a person could have these thoughts during this event. I am amazed at how these thoughts occur.

So—stuff was falling, I had no idea where I am, and I was wearing everything that I preached a first responder should not wear in a disaster: a sports jacket, a tie, pants, and regular shoes, along with a stethoscope. I had no hard hat—no hat at all—no gloves, no respirator, no SCBA [self-contained breathing apparatus], nothing. I was doing exactly what you should never do in a disaster, which is to take an asset and convert it into a liability. My training made me an asset, but now, caught in this disaster, I was a liability.

I had no idea where I was except that I was somewhere on West Street. I could barely breathe with so much dust, and I couldn't see anything at all. I knew there was stuff above me that I couldn't seem to get out from under, because it just kept coming down, and I ended up lying prone, face-down on a hard surface, which I later found out was actually the asphalt on West Street. But at that time I didn't know. And I got it into my head that no matter how hard it was going to be, I was going to get on all fours. I was going to lift myself up. Obviously I could not stand up to run away, but that's what I would have loved to have done. I was caught in all of this debris, but I was going to get on all fours, because then there would be an air hole underneath me that I could live off of until somebody came and rescued me. Now, the stupidity of this notion did not occur to me at the time.

I was now suffering greater injury, with more stuff getting at my head, because I was not protecting it, and this air pocket that I tried to create just got filled in with dust and debris. But I survived. Everything stopped suddenly, and I was able to crawl out from between crevasses. It seemed that Sheetrock or plywood or beams of some sort must have fallen in a way that created a sort of roof for me. In addition, I was lucky enough to have been blown, or almost catapulted, to the end of West Street, directly under where the pedestrian bridge meets the ground, so there was a sort of natural crevasse that also must have protected me. When you hear on the radio that they had spent, like, $12 million to build a narrow pedestrian bridge over a highway, and you say to yourself, *How could that possibly have cost $12 million?*, I now look at it as money well spent. Build those things as strong as you can. Again, I didn't figure this out in advance; I didn't purposefully aim to be shielded by the bridge. I just ran across the street and got blown under the bridge. I was just lucky.

Let me fast-forward to about 11:00 P.M. that night, after having survived and then having worked the entire day there. Around 11:00 at night I was finally able to call my wife. I said, "I'm okay," and she said, "Thank goodness." She said the towers collapsed, there are no more towers, and I kept telling her about my day, and we kept going back and forth until I interrupted her and asked, "Wait a minute, honey, what did you just say? The towers are gone? What are you talking about?" Because to that moment, I thought that the only things that had fallen were from where the planes had hit. I did not know that the entire tower had collapsed. I wasn't watching TV, so I didn't have any visual images of this. I was very busy thereafter and was looking in the opposite way from the towers. This was a complete revelation to me. And I ask myself how someone could have been down there the whole day and not realized that the whole towers had collapsed. I realized that tower 7 had collapsed, because they asked me to move our triage area, and we had been on Broadway, right in the shadow of tower 7. I don't remember the North Tower collapsing. It might have collapsed while I was still under all of the debris.

Getting back to that morning: When I got out from under the debris I was all alone, but I saw one or two firefighters and fire marshals on the street with me. We started walking away from the dust cloud toward the Staten Island Ferry. I got all the way to the ferry, and that's where I met Dr. Kelly for the first time, and Chief Nigro, as well. Dr. Kelly told me how she had been rescued on two occasions by two different firefighters: one pushed her through a revolving door and another under an overhang, away from the onslaught, which shielded her from the dust clouds. I still did not realize there were collapses, thinking it to be debris from the airplane destruction. She'd actually treated one of our firefighters, who had been severely injured, and helped evacuate him to an ambulance. So she had been able to actually accomplish something.

The three of us walked a little east and up Broadway. When we got close to Vesey Street, Chief Nigro went off on his own to command the event, and Dr. Kelly and I decided to set up our triage center there. So with the help of several firefighters, we broke into one of the buildings on Broadway, where there was a Duane Reade, so that we could get supplies from its pharmacy. We had the firefighters break down two separate entrances, so we would have an ingress and an egress for the wounded. We had anticipated that we would have many injuries, and the two of us would do the best that we could.

Police officers must have known that we were there and directed people to us. We wound up being a magnet for many other health-care professionals who wanted to help, including a surgeon friend of mine whom I didn't know was down there, along with Dr. Ira Feirstein, the psychiatrist from the Fire Department. We built a minitriage area where we could treat the wounded, give them psychological counseling, do eyewashes, albuterol treatments for people who had irritant injuries, and we actually even had a little surgical center in case somebody needed emergency treatment before we could get him to a hospital. We had no major injuries but were treating a lot of eye and nose irritation, giving them nebulizer treatments with albuterol, and a lot of walking wounded as well.

And then, late in the afternoon, a chief came in and said we were in the shadow of tower 7, which could collapse right on top of us, and we had to move our triage area. I was a little upset about this, because we had really organized it very nicely, but we moved to Pace University, across the street from city hall, which turned out to be a better place for us, with a lot more room. When tower 7 fell the dust from the collapse came all the way up the stairs of Pace University, so we just missed the very periphery of that dust cloud. We stayed in our new location, again treating the same types of problems: no life-threatening injuries, just wounded people, eye irritation, and pulmonary irritation. I was helping a lot of people.

I didn't know until the next day that Chief Ganci was gone. I was too busy. I had no idea that 343 firefighters had died. I had no idea how many deaths there were. I had no idea that Father [Mychal] Judge [chaplain of the New York City Fire Department], with whom I was very friendly, had died. I had immense respect for him—immense. And I loved him. When I had been involved previously with some protective equipment research, he was really very helpful to me.

I knew there must have been deaths in the collapse, but my feeling was very strong that my role was to work at and command the triage center. My expertise was not in packaging patients but rather in treating them. "Packaging" is not a negative term but an EMS term for immobilizing people and making [them] ready for transport. There were many people who were doing that, and I needed to be taking care of those people who walked or stumbled out and needed assistance. There were a lot of patients, and we were helping a lot of people, so I felt fulfilled. It was the right decision.

We remained at Pace until about 9:00 P.M. One interesting event occurred then that shows we are all human and can all make serious mistakes. As we were leaving, exhausted, a young woman Rollerbladed up to the Pace center in hospital scrub and said, "I'm here to help."

I realized how much people wanted to help, and I presumed she was a nurse or physician. And she could have been helpful, but I had to disappoint her. I know it sounds strange to say "disappoint," because it's a good thing to not have patients, but I knew I was going to disappoint her. And so I said, "I'm sorry, but there are no patients anymore, and we're closing up our shop, but you might want to go to a local emergency room to see if you can be of any help."

She replied, "No, you don't get it. I'm a veterinarian."

Now she could see in my face complete surprise and a little disgust. I told her, in what I guess was a chauvinistic way, "Give me a break. We've been attacked; there have been hundreds of deaths." I didn't know then that there were actually thousands. This was not the time for a veterinarian to be here to rescue the parakeets and the kittens. We're not going to risk lives to save some parakeets and some kittens.

She now no longer presented the nice personality that she had had a moment before. Her facial expression changed, and she put me in my place, as she should have, and retorted something like, "Listen, buddy, I am a veterinarian, and one of the official veterinarians for rescue dogs in any New York City disaster. You either direct me to where the rescue dogs are or under federal regulation I am closing this site for all rescue dog activities."

And so there I was, now completely realizing that due to my own stupidity I could have stopped rescue activities. Luckily she had the strength
of will to get assertive, and I then directed her to where I thought the rescue dogs were. So that was a good thing. And yes, she was probably more
of an asset at that time than I was.

After leaving Pace we went to visit one or two local hospitals: Downtown Beekman [near Pace University], and then another hospital right over
the Brooklyn Bridge. We then went to headquarters [FDNY headquarters
in Brooklyn], because we thought we might be needed throughout the
night, though it turned out we were not. We slept at headquarters that night,
and the next day we started figuring out what to do in terms of building
for the future.

After 9/11 Dr. Kelly and I went to Fire Commissioner Von Essen, who
was a very prohealth and prosafety fire commissioner, and in my opinion
did more for health and safety than anyone serving before him [Thomas
Von Essen was also a former president of the Uniformed Firefighters' Association, the union that represents the firefighters.]. We told him this had
been a unique exposure, the only time we had been attacked on our own
soil. Forget about the political aspects: From a medical perspective, this
had been a unique exposure.

The cloud that day was very thick and did not fully dissipate: 9/11 dust
is a very heterogeneous mixture. What we at the ground level were exposed
to is called sedimentary dust. By definition it consists of the largest, heavi-
est particles, the particles that fell closest to Ground Zero. As you go farther
out, if you draw concentric circles, the dust that people on the street level
are exposed to is by definition smaller, so many think that the greatest exposure to bad stuff is right at the epicenter of the event. Actually, in terms
of inhalation exposure, that's not always true, because we are able to breathe
in the smaller particles deeper than we can breathe in larger particles. And
sometimes you get more cardiopulmonary and toxic exposures distant
from the epicenter, because that dust is coated with all the chemicals of
combustion and pyrolysis that have been occurring.

What was different about the World Trade Center is that, against common teaching, the people at the epicenter inhaled deeply a ton of stuff.
Common teaching holds that those large particles at the epicenter would
just have caused sinus and upper airway irritation. Because the density was
so high, however, we actually inhaled large particles into our lower airways,

so the World Trade Center is actually the opposite of a typical disaster, and you got greater inhalation injury at the epicenter.

Right around Ground Zero you could not see your hand, but as you walked toward the Staten Island Ferry it became gray. What struck me was the sheer grayness of it. I love old movies, and Ground Zero on 9/11 really did look like the movies that were made about the cold war and the A bomb, the H bomb. There was no color. Everything was black and white. It was very, very cloudy, very dusty, nobody around, and very quiet. Total quiet. It could have been in an old end-of-the-world movie.

I realized that there would be pulmonary consequences that same day, which is why we set up the triage center. But I thought they were going to be the standard smoke-inhalation injury, which is a few days of coughing up stuff and, in certain rare cases, a few months of problems. It was only the next day that my thoughts settled and, after processing what different firefighters had been saying—that the fire smelled different and tasted different—and the fact that there had been much more coughing going on than at a typical fire, that I realized that this could have really catastrophic impacts on people's health.

From a health perspective, we needed to investigate the health consequences of 9/11. We would not be stopped by people saying that if we found problems we were going to open up Pandora's box. The example that we gave Commissioner Von Essen was the historic telephone company fire on Thirteenth Street and Second Avenue in the 1970s. Every firefighter who was there had large PCB [polychlorinated biphenyl] exposure, and all over the world firefighters believe that those who worked at that fire died of cancer. We don't know whether that's true or not. We did not provide medical services; we did not study it. We did not prevent people from thinking that 100 percent of those firefighters died from cancer. If we had been there, do you really think we would have found 100 percent dying of cancer? Even if we found conclusively 90 percent dying of cancer, it would have been better than believing it wrongly. . . . Von Essen agreed instantly. And we then began to fight a battle, which continues today, with the federal government to get the funding necessary to do this right—from a medical perspective and from a science perspective.

FEMA had money for rebuilding New York after the terrorist attack. I think they had $20 billion in emergency funding, and we successfully received a grant of $4.8 million for the first two years. That allowed us to demonstrate to the federal government what I've always believed, which is that you cannot provide a short-term or a long-term medical monitoring or treatment program after a disaster if you're not able to partner with credible local people. And then we had to convince people that our program was state of the art.

We started our 9/11 program before any other 9/11 program in New York City, a year before Mount Sinai started theirs. We have consistently provided top-notch, state-of-the-art medical care and monitoring, and we have provided services that no one else can match, because our dollars go further. We don't have indirect overhead costs that many institutions have for federal funding, and we don't have to advertise to find people. We don't have to search them out, since we know every one of our firefighters and EMS workers. We maintain the retirees in the group, and we keep in touch with them so that we don't have longitudinal dropout, which screws up any long-term medical monitoring and treatment program. It is bad for science and creates barriers for providing medical care to those most in need. The sick people are lost to follow-up, and there is the false impression that everyone is well. The primary goal was clinical service. But again, just like the unions and management know, just like I know, and now just like our patients know: If you're not able to show credibly that there's a need for a program, just asking for it is not enough. This program exists here, and at Mount Sinai for non-FDNY workers, because our scientific studies are credible.

We wanted a sustainable medical program. And so we do clinical service, and we study that service, because in studying it we get to be better by learning what's working and what's not, keeping the program at its freshest level for our firefighters. For example, we did some blood and urine heavy-metal studies right from the beginning, with the first three hundred people, and then, to a lesser extent, with the first ten thousand people we saw. Those studies, showing that heavy metals like lead and mercury were not elevated, indirectly kept the World Trade Center site open when people wanted to close it due to a [misplaced] concern about high mercury levels [and the potential of ongoing exposure to it]. We were able not only to keep the site open but to redirect our dollars into much more useful things, like pulmonary function tests and CAT scans, mental health therapy, things that the group really needed rather than chelation therapy for mercury. So this is a fundamental value of our World Trade Center Medical Monitoring and Treatment Program.

We then made certain decisions that were very helpful. The key decision that we made was advocating right from that day for a monitoring and treatment program. We were capable of doing monitoring, but not in a large-scale concept. We advocated for getting funding so we could do more than what we normally do, like all the heavy-metal tests. We advocated that we would control it—that it would not be outsourced to anyone—because we felt it was a matter of our credibility, and [it was] our responsibility to do it right. And we felt that it would be more sustainable if it was done internally. We also had pre-9/11 data to compare it to, so we would have the objective ability to keep this sustainable. With Von Essen's help we already had built an infrastructure that could be expanded to do this.

Another key decision was in trying to bring in specific, focused resources that would help us. We identified certain things that we were lacking, that we needed. The first thing was to increase radically the counseling involved. We already had a good program in place, which probably provided the best alcohol treatment program in the world and phenomenal counseling services for the one to three firefighter service–connected deaths that we averaged per year. But it was not large enough to handle the activities we needed now.

Remember, we have 12,000 firefighters and 3,000 EMTs and paramedics in our Fire Department, and several thousand civilians: 343 firefighters and 2 paramedics died that day, so we would need to provide counseling services for all 15,000 in the FDNY, and also specific counseling services for the families of the 343 people who died. In the Fire Department, in many of those families, there were additional active or retired firefighters, which compound the impact of a disaster like this. We had learned, even before this, that when a firefighter dies in the line of duty you make a serious mistake if you provide counseling only to his firehouse. Because that firefighter is actually associated with several firehouses—one that he is currently assigned to, one that he served in previously perhaps, one where he was a probationary, and all of those firehouses where he had been detailed to during certain tours. So three to five firehouses may need to be counseled, and if you leave one out of the loop, they feel that they are not getting adequate services. Multiply that by 343, and you've got a massive problem.

So we partnered with the International Association of Fire Fighters [the national parent union of the city's Uniformed Firefighters Association] and other local city institutions to bring in counselors. That was another key decision, and a very important and good one, working with Vinnie Bollen and Rich Duffy in the IAFF. We also advocated strongly with the federal government to provide funds for us to get these services. It was a huge battle, because they wanted to take control of the whole thing. We had the CDC [Centers for Disease Control] come in and draw the blood and urine samples on the first three hundred firefighters we saw, when medical monitoring began on October 1, 2001. The reason we had the CDC get involved was because they have capabilities that no one else has. On a single tube of blood or urine they can process about three hundred chemical analyses for PCBs, dioxins, heavy metals, and various other chemicals of combustion and pyrolysis. The CDC in Atlanta is also considered to be the finest laboratory in terms of quality control.

Here—and this is so cool—was our first sense of how everyone in America wanted to help the 9/11 effort. Our plan was to draw the blood ourselves and then put it on ice and send it to them. Once the CDC agreed to do this for us, however, they sent in their own team to draw the blood. Three guys showed up at the FDNY Bureau of Health Services on the second floor of the MetroTech building in Brooklyn and said, We'll draw the blood for you, package it, and send it off every night. We started talking to them and found out that they were one of the teams that goes to Africa when there's an Ebola crisis. They said they loved being able to help, and it was great for them being able to draw blood when they weren't in a level-A HazMat suit. These guys were real professionals, so it was a great partnership.

A decision was also made to provide a variety of different medications in the initial treatment of patients. However, we decided not to experiment on firefighters and EMS members by providing them with drugs or treatments that had not been FDA approved. We have historically made the decision not to participate in drug trials. There were a lot of people who wanted to offer something that might or might not have been beneficial but was not part of the standard of care, and therefore we did not use their services. Specifically, this would be various nutritional therapies, vitamins, the chelation people down here with the Scientologists. I'm not saying that any of these methods are bad; I'm just saying that they were unstudied and unapproved by the FDA or NIH [National Institutes of Health] or any other sanctioned scientific body. This was a contentious issue for quite some time, but we held fast to this rule.

We realized it was not the Scientologists' philosophy to provide their alternative therapy (sauna etc.) alongside standard medical treatment (respiratory medications etc.). Despite what these alternative therapists said, most patients told us they were having them stop all of their standard medications cold turkey. In out minds it then became an experiment, and we could not really participate in that. The same is true of the people who wanted to talk to us about nutritional therapy or other treatment. None of these things in and of themselves is bad, but in a disaster situation you cannot have a million different paths to wellness. You can have a few, but you can't have a million. There's just too much to do. Everything we do takes effort. Everything takes time. Everything matters. Nothing can exist without impacting on another service, because the effort is so intense. And so we made the decision to concentrate on standard therapies.

One of the things that we at the Bureau of Health Services didn't actively involve ourselves with was the site-safety issues. The Fire Department did an amazing job with on-site safety. If you ignore for the moment long-term illnesses and the psychological consequences of 9/11, only one person was hurt [in the rescue and recovery operations], with a broken leg, and that's it. That's pretty amazing for such a noisy, dirty, and difficult steel- and cement-strewn area. An immense amount of safety training and appropriate decisions were mandated by Chief Dan Nigro and the FDNY in charge of site control.

What I think we neglected, though, was to take a more active role in respiratory and psychological safety than we did. And I'll tell you why this occurred first—not as an excuse but as a learning experience. Both Dr. Kelly and myself are not operations people. We take pride in the fact that we don't run around in uniforms, we don't command the site, we don't act as fire chiefs. Firefighters would have very little respect for us if we did that.

But respiratory and mental health safety protection for the workers at Ground Zero should have also been issues we weighed in on.

However, we're not industrial hygienists or environmental specialists, and initially we didn't understand the nature of the exposure. We knew the number-one objective at the time was rescue, and after the rescue effort was no longer realistic, the goal changed to recovery, to find the victims' remains. Respiratory protection, mental health protection were, and should have been, secondary. If we were there playing Mommy and Daddy, we would have accomplished nothing. So in the first two weeks we were suffering our own trauma. We were planning and advocating for a monitoring and treatment program, and we knew that if we missed that boat, we would never be able to get back on it.

As physicians, if there is, God forbid, a next time, we will advocate strenuously for a more measured [on-site] approach to respiratory protection and for psychological protection specifically. If there's any question, there should be full respiratory protection. That would mean at a very minimum an N95 medical respirator [disposable mask especially efficient for filtering particulate contaminants] rather than a surgical mask, more likely a T100 respirator, the half-face respirators that were given out there two weeks later. And, in a very untenable situation, SCBA, which are masks with air tanks worn on the back. We will advocate not only for the appropriate respirators, but for creating a program in which the masks are worn or the firefighters are ordered to leave the scene. Mandatory is what was missing.

From a mental health perspective, if there is a next time, I think we also have to do a better job at reducing the number of days that any given individual participates [in rescue and recovery efforts]. And that is a very difficult thing to do, because everyone wants to help. And everyone has a family member or a loved one or just a victim that he feels he has to find.

Operationally, it's probably a better management approach to detail workers for a week or a month at a time, but I don't know whether thirty days is too much or two days is too much. There is a lot of variability from one individual to the next, but we have got to truncate exposure in some way. It's a huge Fire Department, and I thought our studies would be able to provide us with magic threshold numbers, but it hasn't happened to date. My instinct and opinion is that we have to rotate people out of these questionable environments on a very frequent basis. And we need shorter periods, to decrease the amount of stress that has to be absorbed.

The Fire Department did nothing wrong. We had never experienced anything like this before. Operational issues correctly took precedence, so don't take into account just one end of my thinking and not the other end. I realize that these are complex issues. I realize why we don't give every firefighter a T100 respirator as part of their standard outfit, because it is inadequate for operating in a fire—a firefighter using it would die of carbon monoxide intoxication. The right mask for a disaster like 9/11 is the wrong mask for everyday firefighting exposures.

I have never spent much time thinking about how much should people be paid for a disability or how much should people's families be paid for the loss of their loved one. What I do know is that, no matter what the decision you make is, you're going to be wrong to someone. Do you make your decision solely on the medical consequences? I explain to firefighters who are going through the disability pension system, which I'm actively involved in, that disability is not based on illness or injury. Every firefighter thinks it is, but that's not the case: It's based on the functional impact of an illness or injury. It's based on whether it is severe enough to prevent you from being a full-duty firefighter. For civilian disabilities a much greater threshold of incapacity is needed to prevent you from doing just regular work—if everything is working correctly, you have to have a very severe injury or illness. One could, if you were the judge, base the decision solely on how that injury or illness impacts you in terms of your function and subsequent life. Or, if you're dead, how it impacts your family.

If you're looking to compensate people based on the loss of the soul, everyone is equal. If you're looking to compensate people on the basis that normal insurance policies do, the rich dead person gets more than the poor dead person. We find that dissatisfying. Likewise, do you put a value judgment on adding dollars because you are a first responder versus a happenstance survivor? In terms of the medical consequence there is no difference. Someone who develops severe asthma who was a first responder and who can't work is no different than a happenstance survivor who develops severe asthma and also can't work. Yet everyone else was running out of that building when the first responders were running in, and there should be a value judgment to that—in terms of how we value human beings' decisions, their lives, and the need to value them—[for] the next time [when] people in emergency response make the same decisions. So, if I were the judge, there would be an extra value for that. Many times there isn't, and the decision is based purely on: How much did you make and how bad is your injury?

Luckily I was able to recover, for the most part, and I felt that I had answered the questions that I asked when I was caught in the collapse, which were,

Why am I down here? Why am I dying when I helped no one? There is an answer to that question: I was down there because I was supposed to be. But from a big-picture plan, I was down there to experience this so that I would have firsthand knowledge of what my own patients and others were experiencing, and so that I could see what was beneficial to me and what might be beneficial to them. After all, it was all about taking care of the patients and taking care of the program. Working with someone like Dr. Kelly is very important, for she is an anchor to taking care of the individual. I know the importance of this program for each person who is hurt.

It's not just about our ability to provide the answers to questions but more about being able to provide the health lifeline to people who need it. This program exists because of the great work it does, the support it has from labor, management, and every patient, the moral imperative, and the scientific findings. But it exists only if politics allows it to, and that requires a huge effort. For me the program is an entity, almost like a human being, and it's synergistic—patients need the program and the program needs the patients. If all you're doing is taking care of the program, you're not taking care of the patients. If all you're doing is taking care of the patients, the program is not going to survive. Dr. Kelly is really the compass for maintaining the balance needed to do both.

I can be with every patient on a schedule, and I think the firefighters really appreciate the fact that when they enter my office—and I'm certain that's true of all of our World Trade Center treating doctors—they are in isolation. Time stops; their need is what's important. I see patients on Sunday, and during the week I am focused on the program. I don't set up my day so patients can come during the week, because I want to maintain my focus on the program. I have to compartmentalize.

There's a third component, which is the analytic process. Early on, in terms of the political aspect of getting funding, we focused on just the Fire Department program, but then we developed cooperative relationships throughout the city, with HHC [the New York City Health and Hospitals Corporation] at Bellevue Hospital, what they call the World Trade Center Environmental Health Center, and the Mount Sinai Consortium, which is not just Mount Sinai but several other hospitals throughout the metropolitan area. Mayor [Michael] Bloomberg has really taken this on as one of the top five funding initiatives for the city, in terms of federal dollars. He has provided city dollars as well. And we've had to now integrate ourselves into the overall city effort. It is different but has great strengths associated with it. It makes certain that people have the necessary tests, that the bills are paid, that there are enough satellites in different areas of the metropolitan area to serve their needs, that programmatic issues are addressed, that there's a CAT scan program, that there are assessments for the needs for specific types of mental health programs, and that priorities are studied—because there isn't an infinite amount of money or time. You have to prioritize people and programming. And then we have to take all of this information and prioritize what we're going to be able to analyze, because we've talked a lot about how the results will drive not only this program but every other program. Now we're considered the cream of the overall program, because we've had all the prior 9/11 data that we've been able to integrate to objectify the problems.

We were the first to publish in the *New England Journal of Medicine* that a World Trade Center cough exists, and that it's a syndrome. We were the first to publish a seven-year 9/11 follow-up study, again in the *New England Journal of Medicine*, showing the effect on pulmonary function. We were the first to show sarcoidosis, a scarring of the lungs and a chronic inflammatory process, that luckily for most people does not usually cause debilitating lung function. But for a few it can, and for a few it can even be life threatening. It's not easy to get articles published in the *New England Journal of Medicine* and the various medical journals that we have published the results of our studies in, but they realized we were not here just to legitimize the program but also to provide credibility, and to use this data to plan for the future, which are all very noble aspects. So it's only by showing these things that you can translate a program from the right and charitable thing to do to the necessary thing to do. It's the necessary things we do that, in a right world, are sustainable. We are also here to do something that only the Fire Department realized was necessary, and we're successful on the analytic side, because when firefighters come in to be seen they ask two questions. They asked these questions before 9/11 and at every bad fire they fight.

The first question is: How am I doing? They're human beings. They want to know how they are doing. The second question is: How are my buddies doing? How is everybody else doing? Your average civilian 9/11 patients exist in isolation. They're human, and they care about all of society, I'm certain, but when they see their doctor they ask, How am I doing? That is not true for the firefighters. They want a serious answer about their cowork-ers. They do not want the wholesale illness of the telephone fire repeated. So when they come in and, after you answer how they are doing, they ask, How are my buddies doing? They realize you can't spend five hours with them discussing it, but they want a serious answer. And that is what has made our analytic program a requirement, and what has made it success-ful, because we realized that the monitoring and treatment program and the analytic program were not separate programs but the same program. We had that vision not on day one, not on day two, but on day minus-one, pre-9/11, a vision shared by everyone at FDNY. All firefighters had the same questions, and they meant them, which is why six years into the program we published a book that we sent out to every firefighter to say, Listen, we care, and here is a book for you. And we're going to update that book. That is why this program succeeds.

My goal for myself is to be a physician until the day I die. I mentioned how my dad had seriously advised me to work in a profession where you could control your destiny. And I realize the importance of that now. My destiny, if I can control it, and as long as my brain is functional, is that I want to work until the day I die. There's nothing better, there's no greater purpose on earth, than being able to help people. Firefighters help people by run-ning into a building, I help people by seeing patients. I'm not alone in that. We all help people in different ways. This is just my way.

We have served our patients, our firefighters, in a 9/11 medical program that has sustainability at the highest levels. Mayor [Rudy] Giuliani and Mayor Bloomberg had exactly the same commitment as ours. Commissioner Von Essen, Commissioner [Nicholas] Scoppetta, and now Commissioner [Sal] Cassano have all had exactly the same commitment as ours. But what counts the most is the patient, and the patient is only going to get these services if the program survives.

This kind of partnership and cooperation is unheard of in a postdis-aster, postcataclysmic event. Our retention rate for medical monitoring is over 90 percent. If you look at the Department of Defense medical pro-grams, or the people involved in the early efforts to build the A bomb, at Hiroshima and Nagasaki, at Three Mile Island, or at any environmental or occupational catastrophe, you will find there is no medical program that has participation above 50 percent, and most of them are happy with 30 percent participation. But we have over 90 percent participation. That is unheard of. That is an amazing, amazing thing.

People often ask me, How do you balance a very active professional life, in which you need to continually be at the top of your game, with a family life, where you have children and a wife or husband who need your time? My answer is that each got a little less time than it deserved, and unfortunately the family got the shorter end of that stick. So my wife spent most of the time with the kids, while I spent quality time either in the evenings or sometimes on a Saturday. But they have grown from great kids to great adults, so no regrets there, except when I look back and see so many photographs that I'm not in. But I was there for every problem. I'm a problem solver to begin with, and both my kids and my wife had come to understand that the family is a team, and each member of the team should do what they do best. And since problem solving is what I do best, they came to use me for that. And it gives me purpose still.

Consideration of family is not just a decision that physicians make. Many busy career people have the same challenge to a lesser or greater consequence, depending on the type of career they have. What I think is very important for a physician is to accumulate life experiences that make you more than a scientist. Patients don't come to you for your scientific knowledge—they expect that, but that's not what they need. They need some level of humanity. You can't have that—or at least most of us can't have that—if we don't live a life of happiness, but also one of sorrow. Those are the things that allow you to connect with patients on a human level, and the fascinating thing about the Fire Department is, it allows the firefighter to connect with you.

To me the Fire Department represents small-town U.S.A. If you ever wanted to be a small-town physician in an urban environment, hook up with a fire department, because it is, in itself, a small town. It's an extended family.

My wife died last year, under tragic circumstances. I had to call the Fire Department to find her body, because the local police and fire departments, in the area of New Jersey where this happened, did not seem to be taking the necessary steps. She drowned, and nobody was around when it happened. There was a boat dock, and it was a very windy, cold night. My wife was wearing a bulky coat, and we believe that she slipped on the dock and fell. She was distraught, very upset, and we think it was just a bad culmination of events. I needed help, so I spoke to some of the chiefs in the FDNY, and they volunteered to assist me. They in turn got various levels of commissioners to agree to help, and to ultimately find my wife's body. Rescue 1 and Marine 1 received the appropriate approvals and searched the waters of New Jersey until they found her.

And so the whole Fire Department knows about my life and, since then, I've had patients connect with me in ways that had never happened before. I've now lived yet another set of experiences, and I can connect with them better. But that's truly underestimating the issue, for what happened is that those firefighters who suffered similar issues and losses after 9/11 now feel more comfortable in sharing their problems with me. It is a great responsibility, but it is such an amazing gift to be allowed into people's lives. I am so much the better, both as a human being and as a physician, for having had these experiences. I wish my wife was still alive—I wish every day that she was still alive. But everything that happens to you, I truly feel, happens for a reason. It's up to us to accommodate or integrate our experiences. We don't know the reasons they happen. That plan is far above us. But it is up to us to try to find a way to take bad things and make them good.

This is what I've been doing, for the weeks, months, and years since 9/11, and will continue to do.

Jay Jonas

When the North Tower fell at 10:28 A.M. on September 11, it brought the total number of men and women killed at the World Trade Center to 2,749. In the midst of this carnage a miraculous and inexplicable event took place: Somehow, when the collapse of this mass of 4.4 million square feet of floor space ended, it left a small open space buttressed by fallen concrete and steel. In this space were twelve firefighters, a Port Authority police officer, and a woman named Josephine Harris. Some minutes before the collapse, Captain Jay Jonas and the men of Ladder 6 had come across Josephine as they hurried to exit the tower, knowing that it was about to fall. She was in great distress, taking only one step at a time as she descended, and she pleaded with them, "Help me." At that moment Captain Jonas and his men determined to take this woman with them, recognizing that she could cost them their lives.

When the collapse started, I was on the fourth floor, looking for a chair for the woman we were rescuing, Josephine Harris. She had a serious case of flat feet and could not walk normally. She is a big woman, and taking the stairs was even more difficult for her. It was an agonizing and slow progress, one step at a time. The South Tower had already collapsed; I could not imagine how many people were already dead. It was just a matter of seconds or minutes before this one would begin to fall. We needed a chair to carry her so that we could run out of the building with her.

I didn't realize it at the time, but the guys I had working for me that day really didn't understand what kind of danger we were in. We had met Captain Billy Burke [see page 182] from Engine 21 when we were still going up the stairs, and when we felt some shaking in the building, he said, "You go check the north windows and I'll go check the south windows." We did that, and then we had a conversation. I thought he was going tell me that a piece fell off the roof, maybe causing a partial collapse in our building. But he said, with kind of a straight face, "The South Tower just collapsed."

I said to my men, "It's time for us to get out of here." They looked at me a little funny, for we'd just climbed twenty-seven floors with a hundred pounds of gear on our backs, and now I'm telling them to do an about-face and go down the stairs. But they knew, they understood. They said, "Okay, Cap," and wanted to start jettisoning some of their equipment, but I told them, "No, keep your equipment with you. Keep your tools with you. You never know; we may need them on the way down."

I'm sure that whatever leadership traits I developed came from observing some of the lieutenants and captains and chiefs that I worked for or with. One thing they all had in common is that the most effective leaders were the ones who remained calm under the highest stress. The more stressful a given situation got, I would consciously slow my speech down and speak softly. That's what I was doing on that day. Billy Butler was in front of me with Josephine's arm over his shoulders, and I would kind of talk to him in a conversational tone, and slowly ask, "Billy, can you move a little faster?"

All of my men—Tommy [Falco], Billy [Butler], Sal Bagastino—came up to me afterward and said, "How were you able to keep it together the way you did? Knowing what you knew, and you didn't cause us any anxiety?" I told them that while I may have been calm on the outside, I was screaming on the inside. When people ask what the scariest part of the experience was, they expect me to say when the building was collapsing. That wasn't it. The scary time was the period between the South Tower's collapsing and the start of the North Tower's collapsing, because it involved the anticipation that something bad was about to happen.

It was like watching a horror movie, when spooky music is playing in the background. Oh, the spooky music was playing in our minds. It was there; it was palpable. We got to the tenth floor, the ninth, the eighth, and I was thinking to myself, *Well, wow, we might make it. We may get out of here.* But, obviously, that didn't happen.

My first instinct, as soon as I heard the *boom boom boom* of the upper floors beginning to hit one another, was to get back to the stairway, to be with my men. And once I got in the stairway, things got very bad. We were being violently thrown around, debris was pelting us on every part of our bodies, and the collapse created very strong wind currents in the stairway. It was like being in an earthquake and a hurricane at the same time.

While I was being thrown around I said to myself, *Well, this is it, I can't believe this is how I'm going to die, but this is it.*

It seemed like an endless amount of time, those floors coming down, closer and closer. Somebody asked me the day after the collapse, "How long did it take for the building to come down?" I said, "I don't know, maybe a couple of minutes." And then I timed it using the news footage they ran so often in the early days: It took only thirteen seconds for the 1,368 feet of that building—110 floors and 360 feet of antenna—to fall.

Once everything stopped—the collapse stopped, the shaking stopped, the wind current stopped, the debris stopped attacking us—it was suddenly dark and still. I was coughing and spitting, trying to get all kinds of debris out of my mouth, my ears, my nose. I then wondered: *Who's still here? Who's still alive?* And once I was able to catch my breath, that's when I called out and gave a quick roll of the names of my men, and Josephine, hoping with each name that they were still alive.

Thank God, they all answered. The next thing I thought: *There has got to be a clue here, for there's got to be a way out.* I responded to a Mayday call from Mike Warchola, the lieutenant in Ladder 5 who was trapped and crushed. He ended up dying that day. But as I came back down after trying to get to him I found a service elevator shaft and [remembered] we all had the lifesaving ropes we carry. I thought, *Hey, we could rappel down this elevator shaft and maybe find the PATH train station and walk to Hoboken, New Jersey.*

I thought it was a brilliant plan. But Tommy Falco, one of my guys, simply said, "Hey, pal, what if we can't get out of the shaft? It's not like we can run back up the stairs and get back here."

Yeah, I thought, *we'll save that for a more desperate time.* So we kept looking for a clue. Initially we tried to continue down the stairs. We felt that maybe we could work our way out, dig or climb, but we didn't go down more than half a flight when word came up from Lieutenant Jimmy McGlynn of Engine 39, who was below us with two of his firefighters trying to save Chief Prunty, who was pinned by concrete and dying a couple of floors— what there were of floors—beneath us. So there was no way out below us, we were told. We kept talking to people on the radio, hoping they would find us. I knew something eventually would happen, but what I did not know was how immense the collapse area was, and that we were the needle in the haystack.

When I finally did make it out to the ambulance I saw Chief Pete Hayden standing on top of a fire truck, directing all the operations. That was inspiring to me. After that, almost elated, I was sitting in an ambulance, getting treated, when a guy came up to me and said, "Hey, that was great, that was unbelievable, that was the most dramatic thing I ever heard on the radio. I've never heard anything like it. Congratulations. You got out." I thanked him, and he said, "By the way, did you see Engine 4 today?"

I thought for a second about what an odd question it was, and said, "No. No, I didn't see Engine 4 today."

And he said, "Oh, my son was working there today."

It hit me like a ton of bricks: *Oh, my God, how many guys do I know who have sons here today?* They were here now, looking for their kids. I hadn't been out ten minutes and I got confronted with this. Then all the names started coming in. Guys were looking for their fathers, and fathers were looking for their sons, and it was just the emotional thread that came with this. And—it's still so raw.

You can read the list of men who died that day: Pete Ganci [the Fire Department's chief of department] was a great guy, a guy who accomplished so much in his life, and was a great leader. Why did he die and not me? I really don't know. People ask if I have survivor's guilt, and I say, Well, yeah, sometimes I do. Especially when I meet widows of firemen who died that day, and I can see it in their eyes, how their whole lives have been affected, as if it had been a trigger event, like a series of dominoes falling down. And how much their lives have changed, how different everything turned out for them. How hard it was, and is, for them. My own wife, Judy, assumed that I was dead, and had been trying to figure out how she was going to tell my kids, until she got word that I was alive. So I could appreciate what a bellwether event it was for these people.

To this day I continue to have little revelations of 9/11. I'll watch video of the building coming down, or I'll see photographs of it, and I'll look at it, and I think I will be able to explain it all. But I can't really tell you.

I can't explain why I'm still here.

People who come to interview me tell me that God was with me that day, and it's really a miracle. I cringe a little when they say that. Are they saying that God was with *me* that day, and that God was not with the other guys? I believe that couldn't be further from the truth. So I've gone through periods where I wonder why we lived and other people didn't. I just know it's not that I'm a better person than anybody else. I knew half of those firefighters who perished in the World Trade Center personally, and they were great men.

So sometimes I wonder: *Why am I deserving of this gift?*

Sometimes my survivor's guilt is tempered by the fact that my job was to go into those buildings and try to save someone, and we did that. And not only did we do that, but I got the chance to bring all my people home that day. All the guys who were working for me were in the same spot that all the guys who died were in, and we just happened to be in that one little pocket, and we all lived.

Now you can make the argument that if we had decided not to stop and save Josephine Harris, we would have died. That's true: We would have died. And stopping to save her was against the grain, as we were definitely going through that fight-or-flight syndrome, and we had decided on flight. We were getting out of the building. And we saw her there, and again, one of my guys, Tommy Falco, says, "Hey, Captain, what do you want to do with her?" I looked at her, and I had a desire to rescue her. But I had opposing desires: I had a desire to save my life and get out of that building. This wasn't like a typical fire, where you are trudging your way through high heat and fire licking over your head and the acrid, killing smoke that firefighters always believe they will get through. Because we all could see, in our mind's eye, what was about to happen, which probably made it a little scarier. But my instincts, which grew from the culture of having been a fireman for twenty-two years at the time, told me to put ourselves into harm's way to save someone, and we did that. We wanted to stop and save her. I don't think I could have left Josephine behind. And, you know, you can say we were given the ultimate payback.

Whenever I go to work, I always have in the back of my mind the possibility that today could be a day like Pete Hayden had. [Pete Hayden was the first arriving deputy chief at the World Trade Center on 9/11.] There's a man I respect more than anyone will ever know, because of his ability and competence on that day of all days, September 11. In the Fire Department we read, we study, we prepare, and we train, but that was so out of the realm of what anyone was used to. At one point when we were trapped in the rubble, we experienced an explosion. It shook the staircase we were in, and Josephine Harris got a little upset. We calmed her down, and Tommy Falco looked at me and said, "Hey, Cap, what do we do now?" And I just looked at him and said, "I don't know. I'm making this up as we go along."

I just had to inject a little humor into the situation, but it's true: There wasn't a manual for this, a book or a course that we could have studied. We just had to rely on our past experience and things that we trained for. And focus—just focus on what our situation was and how we could make it better, and possibly get out of there. I feared that the next attack may be worse, and I just hoped that my experience and my knowledge were going to be able to keep up with it.

I took the terrorism course at the West Point Military Academy. We looked at terrorist events, the history of them, but not so much from a strategic or tactical standpoint. In our training we tried to anticipate different scenarios and evaluate how we would deal with them. It was scary, because we had to try to think along with the terrorists, try to think of what they could do and how we would handle it.

The Fire Department has made some substantial changes. We lost a tremendous number of people—about seventy—who were off duty, who weren't part of the responding units but just showed up. We don't want that to happen again, so guidelines have been set down that instruct firefighters not to respond directly to the scene anymore: They must report to their firehouses and wait for instructions. I think we're a lot better prepared than we were, but I don't know if we can ever reach a good enough state of readiness unless we were in an active state of war—like when the London Fire Brigade was getting hit all the time in World War II.

I made an effort to go to the funerals of the guys I knew. There was never a shortage of funerals to attend. I remember one Saturday there were eleven, and when I looked at the list I realized I knew seven of these guys personally. Which ones will I go to? It was hard, especially in the early days, when I wasn't sure how my presence was going to be perceived.

I experienced reactions that ran all across the spectrum. Some family members were so happy to see me—you know, thank God somebody got out. And I've had the opposite reaction from people I'm sure were going through different phases of the bereavement process. There were two widows who were actively angry at me, and I just couldn't see why. One was a close friend of mine and Judy's, and I asked a family member who had retired from the Fire Department, "What's going on?" He knew where I was coming from. He said, "Well, she's going through a lot right now." And I said, "Well, a lot of people are going through a lot right now." So some of the post-9/11-era process was pretty painful.

It's still hard, and it's left a scar on me. As a battalion chief I worked in a firehouse in Greenwich Village that lost eleven people. I'd be upstairs in my office, and there'd be an announcement over the intercom that a lost firefighter's family members were visiting. They'd have cake and coffee in the kitchen. I would let everybody go down, and I would go down later—just kind of sneak in to see what kind of reception I would get. I would wait and determine if they were happy to see me, or they didn't care, or if they were angry. But generally my experiences with them were great, and I always understood why family members wanted to interact with the firefighters.

Judy knew many of the people who were killed too. She does physical therapy, and many firefighters who were injured on the job over the years went to her office for treatment. We would compare notes—hey, you know this guy, you know that guy—and she took the losses very hard. She would try to protect me from certain things, but as time went on and the list of the dead grew, we started becoming numb.

We became concerned about our kids and how they were dealing with what was happening. A couple of days after September 11, I came down to the kitchen and I was just sitting in the rocker having a cup of coffee when my eight-year-old son, John, came running in to give me a hug, and then went running back into the living room. I looked at Judy and said, "That was nice, but where did it come from?" She said, "Well, I think he just figured it out." He had just figured out that I was inside when the building came down. And when I finally went back to work, he would ask me, "Did they catch bin Laden yet? Did they catch him?" His perception was that [bin Laden] was coming to get me. My youngest daughter, Jane, said, "You're not gonna go inside those buildings again, are you, Daddy?" And I said, "No, those buildings are gone. I can't go in them anymore." It's hard to figure out the way they think, you know? My oldest daughter, Jennifer, was a freshman in high school at the time. We had a parade of people coming into the house to see how I was doing, and she would stay on the perimeter the entire time. She wasn't part of the conversation, but she was listening, just trying to make sure everything was okay, that I was okay.

Right after September 11, I was on medical leave, and my son was play-ing a baseball game not too far from our house. My muscles were still shaking, and I could just close my eyes and reexperience the collapse. But I went to his game, and it had a very calming effect. I try not to miss anything that our kids do, to the point that I'm almost obsessive about it. My oldest daughter is a dancer: We would go to every performance that she had. My son is playing college baseball now, but at the time he was in Little League, and I made every game. I would work out all kinds of work exchanges, what we call mutuals. I would use comp time. Since that time I may have missed maybe three games.

So there is a new sense of joy in immersing ourselves into what our children are doing, and really appreciating it. I'm very, very proud of my children. All three of them have achieved so much in a short period of time. They are very loving and sensitive, and they are humble. But every once in a while, I'll be sitting watching a concert, or go to firehouse picnics and things like that, and hear guys talking about their kids, and remember that there were a lot of my friends who had kids. Those kids don't have fathers anymore. And they don't have that aspect of a father's or a parent's love in their lives anymore. So one benefit that my own kids have is the presence of their father.

Religion and God play a big part in my family. A lot of our education comes from the mass media, and they choose not to highlight religious ideals. The best is not brought out. I don't know that much about the Islamic religion. They believe that you are a believer or a nonbeliever, and you would think that they would want to preach peace and tolerance. But there's not a whole lot of tolerance in that statement: You're either with us or against us. I was raised a Christian, and you're taught to love your fellow man. In my mind that's what religion is all about: to give you a sanctuary from the everyday and learn what God's message is and try to apply that to your daily life, to make your life and the lives of the rest of your family better, and to make your friends' lives better.

You know, if you put people in the same room and they talk to one another, they will get along. They may have different opinions about things, but it seems like when communication breaks down is when things start to deteriorate. For these people to have developed such a hatred for us, dancing in the streets after September 11, we must wonder: What are we doing to make them so mad?

We didn't do anything; they attacked us. I've heard people talk about the situation in Afghanistan and Iraq, saying, "Well, if we didn't do that, maybe the World Trade Center wouldn't have happened," and I say, "Excuse me, the World Trade Center happened before." It was in 1993, only a few years earlier. People have to start developing a tolerance for other nations. There seems to be a tremendous loss of respect for other countries and their laws and their way of life in America and Europe. That's the big thing: We have to fight this tremendous loss of respect for other people.

I was recently talking to a train conductor I know, and, noting that the anniversary was coming up, he asked, "How do you feel about it now, nearly a decade later?"

I answered, "Well, some days it feels like it was twenty years ago, like it was such a long time ago. Some days it feels like it's September 12, 2001. Some days it feels like I am still right there."

I was never as proud to be a fireman as I was that day, a day that was shrouded with so much grief and bereavement, with 343 firemen lost that day. By attaching the number 343 to them it is like saying that they are heroes because they died. But it was easy to die that day. What made them heroes was what they were doing before the building came down, and people lose sight of that. They lose sight that they were witness to the most heroic actions any of us have ever seen. Most people watched the events of September 11 through the lens of a camera, but I saw it from the inside of the building. I saw what was happening inside: Courage under fire. People like Mike Warchola, Faustino Apostol, Patty Brown, Billy Burke, Terry Hatten, Orio Palmer. The hairs on the back of my neck just stand up as I remember their faces.

And the list goes on, all courage and heroism. Listen to the radio recordings of Orio Palmer calling for a "hand line": "We've got numerous involvements of fire up here. We could use a couple of hand lines." He was going to fight acres and acres of fire on all those floors with a couple of two-and-a-half-inch hoses. But I was thinking the same thing: *We can do this, we gotta give it a shot. We can do this.* We were going to attempt the impossible—damn the impossible. There were people up there that needed our help. That is the Fire Department, a selfless profession: You put other people's lives ahead of your own, and, boy, was that principle on display that day.

A few years ago a group of retired firemen in Florida asked me for Josephine Harris's phone number, because they wanted her to come down and give a speech on the anniversary of September 11. I called her to warn her, "You're going to receive a phone call from these guys; they're okay," because she's a private person. The guy who reached her called me back and said, "Well, she'll go if you go." And so I went down, and three thousand people had gathered in a Baptist church—it was a huge place with a very active retired organization. I opened my speech by saying, "Well . . . you know, there was a lot of heroism and courage on display that day, and I'm not sure if you could see it through the lens of the TV camera, but you could feel it. The altruism that was there was remarkable. But a lot of the heroism that you saw on display that day was because those guys were of a generation that had been broken into the job some fifteen, twenty, thirty years ago, and received all the lessons, the esprit de corps, and the organizational culture of the department. And if that earlier generation hadn't taught us those lessons, what you saw on September 11 would have been a lot worse."

This is why retirement celebrations in the Fire Department are such a big thing and are so well attended. Each of us realizes that this man really contributed. He made our careers better. He taught us a lot. Guys don't forget that. They respect it.

Ada Rosario Dolch

Ada Rosario Dolch was the principal of a high school just two blocks from the World Trade Center. On 9/11 she safely evacuated her six hundred students. In memory of her sister Wendy Wakeford, who died that day, Ada helped build a school in Afghanistan that opened in 2005. She currently works with school leaders, and lectures on emergency preparedness and on how to respond and recover from disasters.

We were five girls and one brother, all within seven years of each other, so my mother and father were very busy for a lot of the time. I was the oldest. Then there was my sister Miriam, my brother, Ed, and then three more girls—Rachel, Wendy, and Clara, in that order. I remember five Easter Sunday dresses my mother bought us when we were kids. They were very fluffy and had these big green and pink ribbons and bushy sleeves, like organza. Before church we dressed up my little brother in one of those dresses, either Wendy's or Rachel's. And I can see my sisters now trying to tackle him, and then finally getting this dress on him. He was the only boy in the house, and so we took advantage of that.

I think that's my first recollection of Wendy, and she was having fun. I also remember how we used to tease her. Wendy had this ridiculously thick hair that was extremely straight, so we used to say that there must have been some Chinese in her.

As the oldest I played surrogate mom very often. My mother would leave me with the children so she could run an errand, so she could run to the doctor or dentist. Wendy was six years away from me, but when you're younger that's an eternity apart. The two youngest, Clara and Wendy, were eleven months apart, but spiritually and emotionally they were twins. And losing Wendy brought a severe and intense pain that Clara suffers to this day. She suffers this pain, and simply can't address the issue of 9/11. She still cannot believe that we have been through this and that she has lost someone as close as Wendy. It's been painful for us to watch Clara not able to begin the journey toward recovery. We all hope and pray her time to heal will come sooner rather than later.

We lived on the Lower East Side for a long time, and then moved to Brooklyn. I got married very young—at just nineteen—when the youngest one of us was twelve and Wendy was thirteen. So I had to leave these self-blossoming teenagers behind. I didn't spend a lot of time with them at home then, but they would love to come to my house. We were brought up in a family that was very religious, and my parents were very, very strict Pentecostal Protestants. The girls had very few outings without both parents, and so being able to go to my house was a big thing, something they could do on their own. I lived out in Bay Ridge, a whole other part of the world, out there on Shore Road, where there was a park and the waterside. I remember Wendy, and all of my siblings, always struggling with wanting to be faithful to the upbringing our parents had given us but at the same time trying to spread their own wings and accept God as they wanted to in their hearts—without the limitations that were often put on us under the classification of "this is religion and this is God." And I think they saw me spread my wings through my marriage and realized that there were other things in life. They were beginning to open their eyes to other things, and that was a very interesting experience for me. I was able to show them that God was not just about rules and regulations and thees and thous and don'ts and dos but really One who wanted to know and touch your heart. I'm very happy to have had that experience, to have been able to provide a different angle to the issue of loving God, or worshipping God.

Both my parents came from Puerto Rico when they were young. My mother was fourteen, and my father was sixteen. Two years later they were married on the Lower East Side. My parents both came here looking for the seascape of gold, like just about everyone who comes to America. And, of course, if you're from Puerto Rico you're part of America, and life is going to be easier if you're poor. You're really going to make it big in these great streets of New York. My parents, though, found their life and their streets of gold in factories. So my mother supported our education, because she knew there had to be more than just a sewing machine. She often said, "I don't ever want you to have to find yourself in front of a sewing machine to make a living."

We grew up in a truly complete bilingual environment, because at school everything was in the English language, but we went to a Spanish-speaking church and read the Bible in Spanish. My parents did not speak English very well, but they truly encouraged our English. They were big on: "Let's speak the English." "We don't want you to get confused," I remember my mother saying.

We all went to vocational high school, and so all of us acquired good business skills. But my siblings wondered how I, being the oldest, would get away from a very difficult situation at home, and the strictness of my father holding the reins. I guess they felt that my salvation would come through marriage and college. I went on to Baruch College. And, thank God, thirty-six years later, I'm still a very happily married woman. Wendy went to work, and about three years later she realized that she wanted to get ahead in life, to have better employment opportunities. And so she decided to go to college and got accepted at [the State University of New York at] New Paltz. She was proud of that, our big, tough Wendy—very independent; she knew what she wanted. My husband and I actually drove her up to college, and as we were saying good-bye she wrapped her arms around my husband and said, "Don't let me go." She was twenty-one then, and we realized, *Oh, my God, this is a kid.* She did very well at New Paltz. She also met a lovely young man, got married, finished college, and went to work. Her marriage didn't work out, but it was part of her life, and it wasn't a terrible thing.

She started working at the World Trade Center for a bond house, Cantor Fitzgerald. In 1993, when the center was first bombed, we couldn't find Wendy. We were all in front of the television looking for her but didn't see her coming out. And then it turned out that that morning Wendy had woken up and said, *I'm not going to go to work today, I'm going to go shopping.* And she spent the whole day in a mall and had no clue as to what had happened. Everyone from her office had been evacuated, and luckily everyone was just fine. But so often, after the bombing in 1993, we would hear Wendy say, "I need to get out of here. I don't like this place. I don't like this energy." She was hoping to one day go back to school for her master's degree.

After her divorce, Wendy lived with me for some time, until she found a place of her own in New Jersey, which was very close to our sister Clara. And then she met a young man, a police officer, and about a year later, in

May of 2001, moved in with him. We went to her house for a Memorial Day weekend barbecue. We had met him already a couple of times, but now we could see that they were creating a home for themselves.

One of the things that we always did at the end of September or beginning of October was to go apple picking. Wendy lived in Freehold, and we planned to go to an orchard near her home. But my mom and I wanted to see her before then, and so we decided to meet on her fortieth birthday—August 6, 2001—at the World Trade Center. At this point I was working close by as principal at the Leadership and Public Service High School.

Because she worked for brokers on the 103rd and 104th floors of the tower, she sometimes couldn't get out for lunch, as she was stuck to her table on the trading floor. I told her, "Mom and I, we'll just be right in the mezzanine of your building." We met her there with our presents and cupcakes. We talked and laughed and, because we all have such busy lives in New York, after a few minutes she went back to work, Mom left, and I went back to my school, and life went on. Then came 9/11.

That day was a special election day, for the primaries. It was also the first time that our school building was being used as a voting site, because the area was becoming more of a family community and not just the canyons of nothing but Wall Street office buildings. In fact, some of those office buildings were now being turned into residential apartments, and so there was a need to have a new voting district. The Leadership and Public Service High School was a collaborative effort with Syracuse University, and because some of the members of the advisory board knew Michael Bloomberg, who was on the ballot running for mayor, we were hoping that he would show up at our building to vote. Everything was spiffed up that day, and we were so excited about people voting at a school with the name Leadership and Public Service, as we were really living out our mission. It was another great push for us to continue our public service work.

I got to school by 6:00 A.M. that morning, which was probably one of the most beautiful, most spectacular clear mornings ever. We have an extremely large lobby, and I saw the voting booths spread all over the place. I didn't want my rambunctious teenagers bumping into people who were coming in to vote, so I instructed my custodian to set up two long cafeteria tables to create a dividing line—the voting on one side, and the kids coming in on the other. People began coming in at a quarter to eight, and when I saw that things were running smoothly, I ran upstairs to check on what was going on in the office.

My secretary was actually preparing placards with the names of every teacher for the fire drill we were planning for the next day. When we went outside for the drill, each teacher was to hold up his or her placard so that the children could always find them easily. We had an effective plan for our school, which was enormous—a fourteen-story school building is not very usual. Also, because it was integrated into an office building, the fire codes were very different than they would be for just a schoolhouse.

I sat at my desk to do some paperwork. At 8:30, when classes started, I said to my secretary, "I'm going to run downstairs, just to see who the last stragglers are." I also wanted to check on what was happening with the election. In addition, the battery on my watch had stopped working, so I was going to run into the World Trade Center to get a new battery at Watch World. Since we're such a big school, we had walkie-talkies, so I took my walkie-talkie, which I would never leave without, and my keys, and left. And I never went back upstairs on that day.

At the polls I saw a gentleman who was reading his newspaper, indifferent to what was going on. There was a woman with a little dog, some elderly people, and the policeman who was assigned to the building for the election. As I was speaking with my school safety agents the lights in the lobby went out. *Oh, no*, I thought, *we're having a blackout—probably an electrical mess because of the voting booths.* I believe that when the airplane entered our area it caused a power surge, because there was no [other] reason for those lights to go out. I believe it was because God was watching out for us, and it put me into alert mode. When you're a school principal you're responsible for everybody in the building.

Seconds later the lights went back on. And almost immediately, the first boom resonated. The sound was so intense that you actually shook. I looked over at the police officer in the building, but he was out of there in a flash, and to this day I don't know what happened to that young man. People started screaming and scrambling. I stayed in the lobby and looked up at One Liberty Plaza, and because it's all glass I could see the reflection of the North Tower in it. Garbage started to fly, and I'm wondering, *What the hell is that? What am I watching?* People started spewing into my building for safety, screaming, "An airplane hit! An airplane hit!" They asked for a phone, but I told them we only had an intercom. I wasn't really telling the truth, but I didn't want everyone on the phone. I got on my walkie-talkie and told the assistant principal, who was upstairs, to go and take a look out the window and tell me what had just happened. More and more people were rushing into our lobby, and with all the turmoil going on, and screaming, a few of my kids started coming in. I remember specifically one young man, David, who looked as if he'd seen a ghost. He said, "The World Trade Center was hit." And I said, "Hit with what?" He replied, "An airplane hit the building." I thought to myself, *An airplane*, and pictured a Piper. I pictured a helicopter. A young lady then came in and said, "Ms. Dolch, a big airplane hit."

"Big airplane? What are you talking about, big airplane?" And then I asked her to describe it. She was crying, and had a look of terror on her face, so I sat her down on a big granite bench, and she told me that the North Tower had been hit by a big airplane. And I remember I instantly thought to myself, *Oh, my God, my sister Wendy is there.* And then I said to God, *Please, you have to take care of Wendy, because I have to take care of the kids.*

If I ever write a book, it will be called *The Miracles of 9/11*. Because Wendy was then plucked from my brain; I never thought about my dear sister again, until later on that day. I think I recognized that if I thought about her, I would have been confused. I would have been in an emotional state, and that emotional state would have taken over. I would never have been able to continue to do what I knew I had to do that day, for those kids and that staff and that building were my responsibility Those were truly miraculous moments for me.

There was a lot of scurrying, screaming, people crying, many in hysteria. People wanted to run upstairs for personal items left behind, and I would say no, like a wicked witch of the West. A security officer from the American Stock Exchange came to help. Others were coming in, people I didn't know, and I was afraid. In schools we don't let strangers in our buildings, and it was nerve-racking. Parents were starting to show up, wanting to see their kids, and I told them, "Sorry, you're not going anywhere." I shut down the elevators and told them the elevators didn't work. I had two girls in wheelchairs, I had one girl who had just returned from heart surgery in August, and I had one girl who was 95 percent blind—all she could see was some fog of color. Each had a paraprofessional assigned to her, and I told my assistant principal, "Get them down." A while back we had discussed cherry pickers, and we knew the fire department's trucks couldn't reach the fourteenth floor. While the elevators were still working, we brought the four girls down on them, and told them, except for the blind girl, to leave the building and the area.

I would say God was really directing, because I don't know how the hell I was doing it. My assistant principal said, "Ada, it's not good, what we're seeing from the windows. A lot of things are falling. It's not a good sight, Ada."

I'm always amazed at what happened in those early minutes. I remember asking my assistant principal about the kids in the cafeteria. He said one teacher became like a pillar of salt: She couldn't move away from looking out the window. The kids tried closing the shades before her, and she had to be pulled away. One English teacher told the kids, "Right now all I want you to do is write. Write down what you are seeing and feeling. Write down what just happened, what you experienced." A real teacher, trying to capture those moments. She continued to work, and the students continued writing, but then at 9:03 the second tower was hit.

I was in the lobby, about two hundred yards from the South Tower of the World Trade Center. The plane hit right on our side of the building, and it's such a tall, tall building that the noise was overpowering.

During the previous seventeen minutes my sister in Texas had phoned, and my secretary called for me over the intercom. I refused to get on the telephone with anyone, and my superintendent and the Department of Ed offices were not happy with that. I knew in my head that they had no clue as to what I was going through. I knew if I got on the phone they would distract me, and I couldn't be distracted. I had to stay focused. I created a command center in that lobby. I had to observe people, to communicate, to put this person here, get the teachers, gather the kids. So when the second tower was hit, we had things in place, but then everything shook.

The whole building shook. My secretary was at the window, the equivalent of just a narrow street's distance from the tower, and had a totally unobstructed view of it. She said, "Ada, I could see the windows come in and go out. That's what the boom caused."

We evacuated immediately. We had heard talk—through our walkie-talkies, through police—that it had been a terrorist attack of some sort. My preplanned evacuation site was Stuyvesant High School, but Stuyvesant was all the way on the other side of the Twin Towers. My alternative was Trinity Church, but it was too close. Where could we go? I decided on Battery Park, which would be safe—no buildings. I instructed my assistant principal to get on the loudspeaker and tell everyone that we were going to evacuate. We were going to have an orderly fire drill. No one was to leave their floor until the assistant principal went to the floor and said it was time to go. We did not want all six hundred faculty members and students getting crushed in the halls or stairs. We remained orderly, starting with the fourteenth floor. We had two stairwells, but by the time we got to the fourth floor I had them combine to go down one. I wanted them to come out on the side of Trinity Church, because the other exit was closer to the Trade Center.

I remember I wanted total control. I stood up on one of the polling tables in the lobby, in a dress and high heels, and said, "Listen to me. This is my school building, and I am in control." I don't know if I was crying. I said, "Everyone must leave the building now. We are evacuating. No one can stay in this building. So everyone leave now."

By now my deans of discipline had their bullhorns in the street. My secretary told me that my superintendent wanted to speak with me. I said no phone calls; I will not talk to anybody. My secretary had spoken to another one of my sisters and told her we were fine. It wasn't looking good, but everyone was safe.

I stood at the exit as the kids and everyone were coming down, and I thanked each one of them. "Hold on to someone's hand," I told them. "Don't be alone. Stay close to your teacher. Just walk swiftly, fast as you can, to Battery Park. I'll meet you there."

They're all crying and nervous, "Ms. Dolch, Ms. Dolch!" "There's not anything to be afraid of," I told them. "We're going to be okay. Look, you're here, we're talking, this is me, right? We're talking. We're fine." I said, "You can say your prayers. You're good. Keep going. Go. I'll see you later." And we all walked out. I asked my custodian, "Are you sure there's no one in the building? The kitchen staff?" He assured me that everything was checked twice. I said to the custodian, "I wish I could command you to leave as well, but I know I can't do that." He is the captain of the ship. He stayed behind. I said, "God bless you. God be with you." I left, and as I was going toward Battery Park, I turned around for the first time and looked up. I couldn't believe what I was seeing, these two towers totally on fire.

Even then, I never thought of my sister Wendy. Never. I hadn't spoken about her. Nothing. We kept walking.

On that day we had walkie-talkies everywhere. As we entered Battery Park, the traffic was out of control. People would stop us because of the walkie-talkies, thinking we were public officials, and we told them, "We don't have much information, but we're all going that way." I was directing traffic, making everyone go toward Battery Park.

As soon as we got across the first street going south, the first tower collapsed, the one nearest us, the south one. I heard snaps, crackles, and pops. Snapping, snapping. I looked back and saw this tsunami wave of blackness coming toward us. It was the first time I remember thinking, *I'm going to die now. Phew.* And then I saw that all the kids were running. It's the end of the world. And I remember saying, "Oh, my God in heaven, the kids. . . . Where are the kids going?"

I now started getting pushed and shoved by people. It was a beautiful day, and I was wearing this dress and high heels. You know, I don't wear dresses anymore. I haven't worn a dress since that day. I wear pants now, and I've given up high heels. I remember saying to myself, "My God, forgive me if I have sinned. I'm coming home."

This is my faith. This is who I am. There was a bench at the edge of Battery Park with a fence behind it. I jumped up on the bench and, in my high heels, jumped right over the fence and landed by a tree. There was a bunch of women there, all on the ground. They were wailing, crying out to God, "God have mercy on us," and I just got down on my knees and I joined them. I thought it was a good group.

This black wave now hit us. It jolted us forward. I felt like my neck was getting cut. It felt like my head had been hit by something, but it was just the force that was coming behind that cloud. The air forced from the falling building and whatever was in that air was just really, really striking us. Everything went dark, so black you couldn't see. And then it got in your throat. I couldn't swallow, and what I was swallowing felt like it was cutting my throat. And I remember thinking, *Oh, my God, what's going on here?* And as quickly as it got black, it got gray, then it got a little lighter, and all of a sudden we could see light coming through the ashes. Ash was falling, and we were all stunned. *Oh, we're alive!* The miracle of September 11 happened—I'm still here to talk about it.

There was a man standing next to us saying, "You have to sit, you have to sit, you have to get it out of your throat." And some of the men were actually lifting parts of their clothing off and cutting them into material and putting them in a water fountain that was there. One of them was saying, "You have to wet it, wipe your mouth, and clean it up." I've gone back to look for that fountain, and it's not there. Maybe they've moved it? It could be. I want to believe it was God with an angel looking out for us. It was just a miraculous day for me.

The students were gone. I don't know where they were; they disappeared. I remember sitting, trying to clear out my throat. And then I started walking, and I saw a bunch of kids, and then another bunch of kids. Boats were going to Staten Island, and people were jumping on them. I got on my walkie-talkie: "Where are you? Can you hear me?"

"There are a bunch of kids here," someone said. "We're safe," someone else said. There were a bunch of kids in the Park Restaurant, and just as we began to enter there, the second tower came down. The restaurant people had tried to shut down, as they didn't want anybody coming in, but people broke through the doors. And just as the second tower came down, it got black again. But this time we were shielded a little bit because we were inside the restaurant. The kids—even the rambunctious, real tough boys, the macho men—were down to nothing, full of fear. And one of the things that I always remember: One little girl looked at me, and she said, "Ms. Dolch, you need lipstick."

You need lipstick. It reminded me that she was happy to see me, because she wanted me to be exactly as she always remembered me. But I didn't look so good. The restaurant did have a phone. If you had a landline the phones worked; if you had a cell phone, nothing worked. I said to the restaurant employees, "Listen to me, you've heard every story in the world, but I am a principal of a high school, my kids are all over the place, I just want to make one call to the Department of Education. I want to tell them we evacuated. I'm going to tell them I don't know where the kids are—that's the first thing they ask you—but I can guarantee you one thing, they all left the building, and I guarantee you that they are all safe, because I'm here to tell the story."

Through the walkie-talkies and the bullhorns we were able to gather a lot of kids. It was about eleven o'clock now, and I didn't think anything else was going to happen. We saw the airplanes, the American jets. *We're safe now. The planes are here. We're going to be okay.* Of course, every time a plane came by we ducked. You know, that happened for about three years. I couldn't hear an airplane after that day that my whole body didn't shake.

We knew by then that it was terrorism. Our school safety agents work under the umbrella of the police department, so they were getting direct information. We learned about Pennsylvania and Washington. There were a hundred rumors: California was hit, the White House.

Things began to calm a little. I found my girls in wheelchairs. My little girl who is blind was okay. No one was injured significantly. A teacher broke her toe, and one young man had a severe asthma attack. Everybody else, fine. There were no trains, no buses, and we realized we had to depend on the power of the leg and start going somewhere. I suggested we break up by borough. No one could go north, where the towers were. Everyone had to find another way to get around. I said, "You know what? I live in Brooklyn. Who's going to Brooklyn?" I moved them to one side. "All right, who's going to Queens?" It was decided that my group could cross the Brooklyn Bridge, and so we started to head there.

Then came another miraculous happening for me on that day. A little girl tapped me and said, "Ms. Dolch, I'm really scared." And I answered, "Yeah, we're all a little scared. I'm sorry, I don't know your name: Who are you?" She said, "I'm Charlene Hasan, and I'm one of your new students." But here's the amazing thing about Charlene: She's wearing a Muslim head covering. I had never had a student in my school who wore a head covering. I didn't even know this little girl. It was the fifth day of school, and I always prided myself that I knew all the names of the kids. I even knew their parents' names. But I didn't know my little girl. I said to her, "You don't have anything to worry about. You're going to Brooklyn. I'm going to Brooklyn. Here's what you're going to do. You're going to put your arm in mine, and we're going to walk together. And you're going to protect me, and I'm going to protect you. And we're okay."

That was my little angel who guided my heart. She guided my heart from ever being angry at Muslim people. I can't be angry at Muslim people. I'm angry at some bastards who did some horrendous things, but I could never be angry at Muslim people. We are all God's people. This child guided my heart. I see her often now, and her family. I've visited her home several times to break bread together. She is my angel, and she knows that.

So, with my angel at my side, our group arrived at the Brooklyn Bridge, but we couldn't get across, because it was now being used as a secure way for police, fire, and EMS from Brooklyn. So we had to walk a little farther and go to the Manhattan Bridge. In the middle of the bridge Charlene again said, "Oh, Ms. Dolch, I'm so afraid."

And I kept saying, "Charlene, don't you have faith in God? Look at what you're wearing. Does this mean that you believe in God? And if you believe in God, this is when your faith kicks in. You have to believe we're going to be okay. We're crossing the bridge; I mean, we could sing a song."

We finally made it to the other side of the bridge. Lots of people were there, all in total shock. And then, all of a sudden, I realized for the first time that I had to use the bathroom, and thought of 110 Livingston Street, the Board of Education [now the Department of Education]. The other thing that was on my mind was that my feet hurt from the heels I was still wearing. Heading toward the Board of Ed, I remember Charlene saying, "Ms. Dolch, Atlantic Avenue is right here. I'm going to go to my family." I said, "Are you sure? You going to be okay? You're going to be safe. You can stay with me." She said, "No, no, I'm going to be okay." And I said good-bye to her, and told her I'd see her in school.

My secretary, Lisa, and I reached 110 Livingston Street and, for the first time, I totally lost it—I suppose because I finally felt a little safe. I walked up the steps, but the guard wouldn't let me in. I said to him, "You just don't understand who we are. We've just come out of Ground Zero. You will let me in or you're going to have a crazy lady on your hands!" I might have said I'm going to pee on the floor, or something like that. I was crass. Finally, I was able to call somebody on the inside. I told them my name and my school, and sure enough, they let us in.

Harold Levy was our chancellor then. They brought me into a room where they had been having some kind of a meeting, because there was food out, nice sandwiches. I told them I can't believe where I am right now, and I completely lost it again. Chancellor Levy gave me a box of tissues, because now I was bawling. And I kept thinking back to what must have gone through his head that day: a million point two children in his care, his responsibility, and having no clue where they were. Were they safe? Did they get home? How about children who need medical attention, kids who need medication?

Then I just wanted to hear my husband's voice. We contacted his school, and they were able to get him. It was funny talking to my husband, the calm after the tragedy. Lisa and I waited at the Department of Ed until my husband finally picked us up. I opened the door and got in the car and just said, "What a day, oh, what a day." The things we did not say. I told him I was not telling the story; I couldn't relive it right now. There was no [other] talking.

We took Lisa home, and I just fell to the floor when I got into my house. I'd really lost it uncontrollably and was having a shock moment. Suddenly, still on the floor, I began to ask, "Where's Wendy? Has anybody seen Wendy?"

I have a daughter who was studying in London that semester. She could not reach me in Brooklyn or my sisters in New Jersey, but she called my sister in Texas, who then contacted one of my sisters in New Jersey. There was no other way to communicate. We've since learned about how to communicate and how families should create plans for emergencies. Lessons learned after September 11.

At 5:30 I got a phone call from the secretary of Curtis High School in Staten Island, who told me that more than half of my kids were there, and that they were creating a manifest for me. After that day I learned to keep a list of the names, addresses, and phone numbers of the teachers and students at home, because it was of no value at school. "Are they okay?" I asked. "Are they behaving?" They were contacting every parent, having them call to talk to someone, because the students would be there all night. No one was leaving Staten Island and coming to Manhattan or Brooklyn that day.

Then I got another call, for there was another group of students in New Jersey, because some of the boats skipped Staten Island, went a little farther, and took them to New Jersey. They were all over the place. There were kids all over, staying in school gyms, city halls, government buildings. Every food place was giving them more food than they knew what to do with—Chinese food, Italian food, pizza, McDonald's. I couldn't believe what I was hearing. You know, we're amazing people, Americans—amazing, beautiful people. We get a little cocky sometimes, and we let little stupid things get in our way, but when it's time for us to really pick up our boots and make it happen, we are just amazing people. The giving that went on . . . truly amazing.

That week I never reported to work. I couldn't even think, except for *Where's Wendy? Had anybody heard from Wendy? Did anybody . . . who's going to the hospitals? Who's checking the hospitals? Maybe go to the hos-*

*pitals in New Jersey. Go to the hospitals in Lower Manhattan. . . . Go to ev-
ery hospital. Please, somebody find Wendy. She's probably shopping. She
went shopping. She's stuck in a mall. That's what happened in 1993. Go find
Wendy. Somebody look for Wendy. Where else is Wendy?*

That night, about midnight, a pastor from my church called the house
and said, "I'm standing in front of your school building, your building is
standing straight. Nothing, not a broken window." How did that happen?
Miracles of 9/11. Sometimes I still believe the entire time is like an out-of-
body experience. Except the thing that, of course, is so real to me is: There's
no Wendy anymore. We don't have my sister. Until days later, when we
realized that there was no hope, we were like everybody else, putting up pictures: If anybody has seen this person, please notify us.

Indeed, it wasn't long before we started hearing from the Cantor Fitzgerald people: 658 of its 960 New York employees were lost in the attack. The
news media were saying, "If you were looking for someone who worked for
Cantor Fitzgerald, report to the Pierre Hotel, where a center had been set
up for the company," so we went there several times. They asked us to
identify whom Wendy worked with, what floor she worked on, and her
boss's name. And to look for pictures. Then we went to give DNA, at the
West Side pier that they had set up for receiving samples.

I went back into my school building to collect the belongings of all the
teachers, with my husband and one other person. We filled up garbage bags
with their pocketbooks. Everything was covered in ash, for the windows
had not been completely shut. The *New York Times* from that day was on
my desk, which I actually have at home. Teachers' coffee cups were on desks,
and whatever coffee was there had started to rot away the bottoms of the
cups, and so the coffee had spilled. It was strange, very strange.

Also, I had to get into the vault. My assistant principal had said to me,
you have to go to the vault and get the school's checkbook, so we can at
least write checks for things that we might need. As I stood in front of the
vault I was suddenly sort of paralyzed. Normally I didn't even have to think
about the numbers: My fingers just knew how to spin back and forth, and
it was open. But now I stood in front of the vault and I cried my eyes out.
I could not remember the combination to save my life. I didn't have it written down; I didn't have to—it was ingrained. I had to leave then. Afterward,
I contacted my assistant principal, who told me the combination so I could
go back and open it up.

That's when I first began to understand. I didn't have a name for it then, but I began to understand, *Uh oh, something is wrong*—I wasn't right. I couldn't remember the names of the kids, and I had always known all their names. So that's how I began to realize that I was not normal anymore. What the hell was all of this? It was a lot of pain, a lot of heartache, a lot of anger, frustration, going back to a new school building. My kids were beaten up. The basketball team got beaten up. People just weren't nice. We forgot nice. It just wasn't good at all.

I immediately started to be proactive and got involved in a support group of school leaders and schoolteachers in the Lower Manhattan area. Some bonds were made, and Linda Lantieri, who had worked at the Department of Education for a long time, started something called the Project Renewal. It was really just a meeting, to come together, using some of the philosophy of Parker Palmer, who was a Quaker. We would gather in a circle, and whatever was in your heart came out in silence. It was silence, but we interacted, hugged. And being held gently in someone else's arms during that silence . . . that was really tremendous. It led me to my own spiritual and emotional recovery. We did it weekly, and then it was once a month. And I'm still connected somewhat.

My family . . . we've never sat down and had a powwow. We never sat down and had a conversation about Wendy, to grieve together, cry together. Just never happened. Everybody kind of dealt with it on his or her own. But we were in constant communication with one another. My father performed enough funerals as a minister that I guess he had developed this really hard shell. My sister Clara, the one closest to Wendy, still feels a sense of despair. She has not allowed faith to bubble up in her soul. She's angry—very angry at Muslim people, at anyone who may look like an Arabic person. But everybody heals in a different way. I just like to hold her gently. You know, faith does play a role in giving you some sense that there's a future, and there's life. We'll see Wendy again. Faith is a beautiful thing, and faith really will sustain you. If you have that, this life really doesn't end. There's a pause right now, but there's more to this.

We had a memorial service for Wendy in November. The day after Christmas we got a phone call: They had found remains of Wendy. We all cried, and I could not believe it. They identified her two molars through dental records I had given them. God has a great sense of humor, but it was no joke that they had found her molars. Because Wendy was always smiling.

She always had a big, toothy, mouth-full-of-teeth smile. Her mouth was always open. She was always laughing. That was Wendy. You will never see a picture of Wendy that she doesn't have a big fat smile on her face. *Son of gun*, I thought, *first thing they would find would be her teeth.* You know she's smiling down on us. . . .

A few months later they called us again. They had found a part of her leg, and then, a week or so later, one more call: They found a part of her shoulder. I was very upset and said, "Please do not call us again." I spoke to the family and told them, whoever wanted to take these calls, I would send them on, but I couldn't take them anymore. I can't have my life disrupted this way. Wendy is not a puzzle to be put together. Every time you get these calls it was like someone sticking knives in you. Your emotions just become bitter, it just hurts so much. I said, We know she's gone. So we felt . . . just please don't call us again. And they didn't.

We did not bury her. We have her ashes, and she sits in a box in my sister Clara's house. At first we put her in a mausoleum, because we knew that there could be more remains, and of course we hoped for a lot. We realized that if we buried her it would be a lot more expensive to go back and try to bring . . . And I got a little exasperated again, and said, "Why don't we bring"—oh the dark, sarcastic, bitter sense of humor—"a file cabinet, you know, then we'll know exactly where she is. File it." Then, after the first time we went to the mausoleum, we said, "We're not doing this anymore. This is ridiculous. There's no joy, no nothing coming here." So we took what there was of Wendy and we put the box in Clara's house in New Jersey. Back with her twin. They were two of a kind, and Wendy was as much a best friend to Clara as she was a sister.

I didn't hit rock bottom for about two years, after everything. You don't know what that bottom looks or feels like until you've hit, because when you're the principal of a school there's no time for sitting back and pondering. You don't have time to walk down the street and cry. You've got to get your act together. You've got to graduate the kids. Yes, the world came to me and touched me with sympathy, all of that, but about two years later I just . . . I was angry, I was upset. I was realizing the trauma. I could hear an airplane taking off miles away. People would say, "You can hear that?" Every time a truck went by I just jumped right off my feet. Loud sounds. I was quick, I was sharp. And I knew I wasn't well.

So I started taking a little medication. It was great; it's a beautiful thing to feel relaxed, untroubled. But I knew that medication wasn't going to work for me in the long run. That way of coping doesn't resonate with me. I went to faith: *God, if you're real, and you're a God that heals, and I believe that you are a healer, then you have to heal me, because I can't do this thing. I'm a wife. I'm a mother. I have to make sure that I'm okay.*

And again I turned to the Project Renewal—the resilience work, the work of renewal, renewal of spirit, working through it and participating. Opening yourself up, allowing others into your life in the Parker Palmer method, [according to] everything he wrote. I learned to read his little book, *Let Your Life Speak.* I learned to embrace the seasons of life; that's what his little book is about, the winter of your life and what happens in the winter of your life. Just like winter: When everything is rock solid there are a lot of beautiful things happening underneath the ground that have to break through. Eventually they do. The little crocus makes it through that hard ground, doesn't it? So I knew that I had to strengthen my spirit to get it past the winter and arrive at the spring of my life. I went to healing masses. I went to prayer circles. I opened myself up. I learned about acupuncture for stress. I learned about Reiki. I just became so open to the power of people and healing. Every time I tell the story of that day and of Wendy, it's very healing. Every time I tell the story I honor Wendy.

Not long after the attacks some amazing and wonderful people out in California found me on the Internet. They were all brokers for Prudential Real Estate, and they wanted to volunteer, so they were invited to come and do support work at St. Paul's church downtown. Seventeen of them came to New York for a week, taking their vacation time. This is part of the great outpouring of American love after 9/11. They wanted to meet me for breakfast, and because we were back in our school building by February 1 of 2002, we met at my building. They had just worked an entire night, from midnight to eight in the morning, helping with water and food for the recovery workers. They were tired and exhausted, in their sweatpants and T-shirts, but they came to my school for a beautiful New York City breakfast of bagels and lox. Immediately . . . there was such a bond of joy and love.

Once they were back home, Kathy and Steve Ollerton, my new California friends, continued to be in touch with me and our school. We started an exchange of phone calls, e-mails, and letters between our New York City kids and kids out in California, as a way for them to share their stories, relate their 9/11 experiences. And we actually brought them together: The California kids came to New York City. We called it East Meets West.

For the first anniversary of September 11, Kathy and Steve came back to New York City and went to Ground Zero alongside the rest of my family. The following day we went to the 9/11 family room at One Liberty Plaza, on the twentieth floor, which has a complete view of Ground Zero. They asked me, "What's the legacy for Wendy?" And I said, "I'm an educator; there's only one thing I know, and that's education. And if we don't teach, how will we ever learn? So we have to do something about schooling to memorialize Wendy." And then I thought about it and said, "I'm going to build a school in Afghanistan. What a kick in the head to Osama bin Laden." That's my big sentence, my contribution.

The Ollertons left New York, but back in California they threw their energy into the project, sponsoring things like golf outings and car-washing events to raise funds. Kathy Ollerton was a woman of substance, and she had acquired a lot of these little offices for independent insurance brokers. One of these brokers happened to be a young man from Afghanistan whose family had lost his brother in a very similar fashion to how we lost Wendy. When the Russians came into Afghanistan, to their town, they walked into every house and grabbed whoever was there and took them. Only men— they didn't touch the women. They took his brother, and they never saw his brother again. And so Ibrahim Mojadiddi became the conduit for us to build our school.

Ibrahim's father was a big landowner in Afghanistan, and was well liked. They had nothing but their property, as everything had been destroyed there. The Taliban had taken over, and that was so destructive. Ibrahim wanted to help, so he said, "My family will donate the land." That was in 2004, and that was when the ball really got rolling. The whole project was funded for less than forty thousand dollars.

On July the Fourth of the following year, I traveled to Afghanistan, where we dedicated the school. We met with the minister of education. At the dedication we had the governor of the town, the mayor, and the imams. There were over two hundred people inside this building. The girls sang and chanted, and we gave the boys soccer balls. There is a beautiful sign there where Wendy's name is written in Farsi, and we dedicated a little garden to Wendy. It is just the sweetest thing. It was difficult to grow anything in the middle of this barren, hard land, but they grew flowers. We were treated as if we were royalty. They found grass and bark, and they threw it at us as if kings and queens had arrived. We broke bread with them. We were treated as beautifully as I've ever been treated in my life. Each time we walked in they would say, "God bless America."

I also met the boys and girls. There are over two hundred students in the school, with boys attending in the morning and girls in the afternoon. The boys had previously had to travel over three miles by foot to go to school; the girls simply did not go at all. So this little town now has its own school with Wendy's help. We don't share exactly where it is; we have agreed not to mention the name of the city. The Taliban has become a real stronghold close to this community, and we try to keep it safe.

On my last day there two men had a party in their own home. Of course we were all seated on the floor on beautiful carpets. I only ate rice—I was so afraid of getting sick. These gentlemen came from means and had a cook, and the presentation was just exquisite. When we finished they took out some instruments and started banging away, and the headdress they gave me to wear came off, and we were swaying, and it became just like a revival. There were twelve of us around the floor, but only two women—Kathy Ollerton and myself. Women and men never mix together, but we were mixed for this special occasion. One of the men asked through an interpreter, Would I like to play the drum? I played it as if I knew what I was doing, and said "Oh, this is just like being in church!"

Where we were was just like being in heaven—it was my ultimate healing balm. I had to know in my spirit that I wasn't faking when I said I was not angry toward a whole people. I had to confirm that, and I did. Unfortunately there are some real crazies who have done terrible things, but there are many Christians who have done crazy things too. So while I'm not happy with those insane people, I've met some amazing, beautiful people who I treasure in my heart. And I pray for their safety and their well-being.

I can look at any aspect of nature, whether it's in a photograph or whether it's looking at a tree when I'm in a park, and I appreciate that it's alive. I think about the creator of that tree, and I think there's got to be something bigger and much greater than all that we see in our world. Some people will always say, "Why did God allow evil?" And I say, "Because there's also evil out there. Inevitable evil exists among us." God didn't say there would be no evil: There's a battle and a war going on. So I think to walk on the side of good, to walk on the side of believing that there's a greater good, and that I want a part in that. The good can exist through me, and hopefully through you, too, the same way that the bad has been exposed through other human beings. The good is shown through us. So we each have to shine the light. Light is so critical to me, because if you're in a room, all you do is flick on the light, and there's no longer darkness, and there's no longer that eerie feeling. Well, I want to be that light. I personally have to find a way to play the role that will speak of the good and never give homage to the negative, the evil, and the bad that's in this world.

For me the fundamental question is, How do you allow yourself to open yourself up in life? There's a little faith-based book that many of us read, *The Prayer of Jabez*. Jabez was really an insignificant person in the Old Testament, not even a prophet. But he said a very simple little prayer: "Lord extend my territory. While that's happening, stay close to me." I paraphrase it to say, "Stay close to me, Lord, so no harm will fall upon me." It became a critical book in my life, because that is all I want to say: God, give me an opportunity to touch someone else's life. Give me the opportunity to be in the presence of someone else. Give me an opportunity to touch someone who might be hurting. It's pretty much the prayer of St. Francis of Assisi: Make me an instrument. I don't want to do anything else. I really believe that my calling in life has become, because of Wendy, to be a servant, and however I need to serve, that's what I want to do. I've been an educator my entire life and I cannot think of a greater calling to give me a greater extension of my territory. And, post-9/11, God has really extended my territory.

But look at what has happened ten years later. I traveled around the country speaking about preparedness, and also, I did a very big public speech about faith. Yes, faith and church and school have to be separate. But you can't take away from what is in my heart, who I am. I'm an educator; I love God. God has been my strength. It's not about standing in the front of my school building proselytizing, but rather about showing who you are, where your strength comes from. I would say to kids in my school, I don't care if you believe in this pencil. If this pencil makes you happy, then go with it. But be sure to go with *something*. You cannot, should not, believe you are in this life as an entity of no value, with no connection to a greater being. Let's honor what we believe, And that's my spin on life for the rest of the time I have on this earth. I honor Wendy. And I honor God. That's what I mean when I say, "God, make me an instrument."

Peter King

Peter King (Republican-NY) is the chairman of the Homeland Security Committee of the United States House of Representatives. He has been a congressman since 1993, serving as the U.S. representative for New York's Third Congressional District. He is the son of a New York City police lieutenant.

I was born in 1944 in Manhattan and grew up in Sunnyside, Queens, on Forty-fourth Street between Skillman and Forty-third. Both of my parents were Irish Catholic, and two of my four grandparents were born in Ireland. One was born here but raised in Ireland, and my mother's father was actually Welsh and Episcopalian, but converted to Catholicism.

My father was a city cop. He was promoted to lieutenant and was the director of physical training at the police academy. I knew he had a job at the academy, but no one ever told me until recently that after he retired they put his picture on the wall down there.

We lived just two doors down from the Celtic Cafe, a block and a half from Lynch's Funeral Home, a block and a half from Sunnyside Gardens, where they had the Golden Gloves fights, and a half block from Robert Halls, which was the highest level of clothes that anyone in the neighborhood bought. We had the usual stereotypes for that time. The bar owner was Irish, the delicatessen guy was German, the candy store guy, Jewish. I went to St. Teresa's Grammar School. The nuns had a tough job with over seventy kids in the classroom, and we went to school in shifts of four hours a day.

I always thought it was a really safe neighborhood, but looking back at it now, the brother of the guy who sat in front of me at school went to the electric chair, along with a guy whose father owned a bicycle store. They had killed a guy when a stickup went bad. The neighborhood also had a lot of guys who were locked up, but with all that, it wasn't dangerous. Unless you bothered somebody else, nobody bothered you, and I don't ever remember anyone getting jumped.

We lived almost twelve years in Sunnyside, and then moved to St. Albans on Long Island. I went to Brooklyn Prep High School and looking back on it, I found it tougher than college or law school. Jesuits are totally unforgiving when it comes to your studies. I then went to St. Francis College in Brooklyn. I worked full time during my last two years there, to help pay the bills, while also going to college full time. I saved some money and ended up going to law school at Notre Dame. I graduated in 1969, and right out of law school went into the Sixty-ninth Regiment, U.S. Army. I did almost six months on active duty and four and a half years on reserve duty. A lot of cops and firemen were in the unit.

When I returned, I practiced law in Manhattan for a while. Then I went out to Nassau County, which was not as expensive as the city. I developed a small law firm, got into politics, was elected councilman, and then county comptroller in 1981. In 1992 I was elected to Congress, and I've been there ever since.

I began being absorbed by security matters in our country with the first bombing of the World Trade Center in 1993. Even then, I didn't pay as much attention to it as I should have. Both parties have a retreat at the beginning of each congressional session, and it was while I was at the Republican retreat in Princeton, New Jersey, in 1993 that they announced that a bomb had gone off in the World Trade Center. One of the congressmen in a flat joke attempt said, Any time New Yorkers get killed, that's a good sign. It didn't create a sense of urgency in America or in Congress.

In the early seventies the Croatian freedom fighters set off a bomb occasionally or the Puerto Rican nationals would be involved in a serious shooting or a bombing. These were very tragic events, and usually a few people were killed, but they didn't have consequences beyond. Looking back at the Trade Center bombing now, my initial reaction was that this was a similar incident. I came back to Washington a day or two later, and it wasn't even that big of a thing in the newspaper. My recollection is that Bill Clinton never came to New York to visit the site, and I don't think [Mayor David] Dinkins came back from wherever he was. Ray Kelly basically took over the operation. It just did not register how significant that bombing was, and many concluded it was just some crazy Muslim extremist who was mad at the world. And New York had experienced that before, dating back to the J.P. Morgan Wall Street bombing in 1920.

From February of 1993 through September of 2001, I wasn't on the intelligence committee, so I didn't know of any secret briefings that might have been given, but I never heard the '93 bombing discussed by anyone. It was just out of sight, out of mind.

The evening of September 11, 2001, was supposed to be the annual White House barbecue, which the president hosts for the members of Congress and their families. Both my kids were finally just getting out of school, and my daughter was married, so, rather than paying a bunch of rent every month I had bought a condominium across from the Watergate. My wife, Rosemary, had planned to fly down the night before, but her flight was canceled because of massive thunderstorms, so she was taking the 8:30 A.M. Delta shuttle out of LaGuardia. My chief of staff picked me up that morning right around 8:30 A.M., and as we were driving to the office my daughter called me on my cell phone. Her husband worked about three blocks north of the World Trade Center, and his office looked out at the towers. She told me, before it had been reported on the news or anything else, that he could see out the window that a plane had crashed into the World Trade Center, and she said it was a giant plane. Now my concern was—and it may have been very self-centered, but again, I wasn't even thinking of a terrorist attack—of nothing other than the fact that my wife was on an 8:30 flight that would have been coming up the Hudson at the same time. Right away I was afraid it was my wife's plane, so I called my office, and they called Delta, and all Delta would say was that there had been an accident but couldn't tell us anything else, wouldn't confirm anything. My assistant dropped me off at the Cannon [House] Office Building, where everyone was walking down the hallway, laughing and drinking their coffee, cops were very relaxed, and there was no sense of tension at all. I went into my office, where the TV was on, and just as I walked in I saw the plane hitting the World Trade Center and said, "Oh, they have it on tape." I didn't realize then that it was the second plane hitting. I was still concerned about my wife, and then I turned on my television and learned that the second tower had been hit. *Of course*, I said to myself at that moment, *this is a terrorist attack*.

I still couldn't get in touch with my wife. After the second plane hit my son-in-law had taken off from his building, but he didn't have a cell phone. And then my son, who worked in the Commerce Department, called, but after a false report that a bomb had gone off at the State Department— though then they said it was at the Commerce Department—all the phones went dead there for about fifteen minutes. So I had no indication where my wife, my son, or my son-in-law were. At about 9:21 A.M. my wife called and said, "I don't know what's going on, I don't know how I'm going to get to the White House tonight. They say there are no flights going out today." She had no idea what had happened; they had stopped the planes on the runway, and the pilot announced that all flights had been canceled. I said to her, "Do you know what's happened?" and she said no. I said, "We are at war." It was the first time I heard myself say that. And then they announced it on the plane, and I heard people screaming all around her. I sent someone from my staff to pick up my wife, and then my son called, and my son-in-law called from a cab on the Fifty-ninth Street Bridge. Within a half hour we knew everyone in my family was safe, and as far as I was concerned the whole world was safe for that solitary, brief moment.

Then the Pentagon was hit, and so I ordered everyone to leave. My chief of staff was renting a house near the White House, so I suggested we operate there until we could find out what was going on. As I was going out the door Channel 12, a cable station on Long Island, called and asked to do a one-minute interview. Cops were ordering everybody out, and as I was standing there describing the evacuation, the TV announcer suddenly said, "I can't believe it." I turned around, and over my shoulder on the television I saw the [first] tower was coming down. It was so hard to comprehend. People talking in New York had a split screen of me speaking and the tower collapsing, and I had no idea what would be next.

Where we were going was normally about a fifteen-minute ride, but it actually took nearly two hours to get there. At 10:28 we heard that a plane had gone down in Pennsylvania. I said to myself, *This is too bad, yet with everything else going on—it's just another tragic plane crash.* It never dawned on me that it was part of a bigger situation, or that the plane was aiming for the Capitol. If the plane had hit its target, I would've been less than two blocks away. None of us really associated where we were with what happened, except perhaps the president, and the highway we were stalled on was a highway of American political decision makers. We probably had most of the Congress, Senate, and senior Washington officials locked up in total gridlock.

We got to the chief of staff's house, where my son had planned to meet us. He decided to grab some food first, so that delayed him, and I began to wonder where he was. There was another report that a bomb had gone off at the State Department, which is only about two miles from where I live.

But there was no bomb. From the chief of staff's house we could see convoys of National Guard troops going to the White House. That was sort of a scary thing—combat troops going through Washington and literally racing to the White House. Seeing our troops on the streets was the first thing that really gave me the sense of being in a war zone.

I did not think about the president at that time. I was talking to family and reporters back in New York. The reporters were calling me trying to find out what I knew, and I was asking them what they knew. Around 1:00 P.M. we heard that there was to be a briefing given by the Capitol police in their headquarters next to the Monocle Restaurant. We had no official communication; all of official Washington was shut down, and we were having a briefing in the basement of a small headquarters building next to a restaurant. There was no plan in place to contact members of Congress if Washington or the country was attacked. All of us were on our own that day. There was no central way of communicating with everybody. There were no BlackBerrys. There was no place to call, and it just became a matter of word of mouth.

There's so much that's obvious now, but at the time I was just concerned with suicide bombers. A congressman from Connecticut, Rob Simmons, who is a former CIA guy, said we really had to worry about chemical and biological attacks, which he figured would be the next thing. If this were really synchronized, there would be some chemical bomb going off somewhere or some biological attack, which would really cause the nation to panic.

Inside Capitol police headquarters the police gave us a briefing, and about half of Congress was there. We could see smoke up in the air from the Pentagon. The briefers were asking everyone to stay away from the Capitol, as they didn't know what was going to happen next, and they didn't want to overextend the police. I remember some congressmen insisting they had to go back to the Capitol, so that the country could see them. I know it looked good later on, when they all sang "God Bless America" on the Capitol steps, but I thought at the time that such demands were really irresponsible. First of all, the country was not necessarily looking to us for protection, and secondly, we shouldn't be making the cops' job tougher.

I was really disappointed with all the shouting going on at that briefing. Denny Hastert, the then speaker, and Minority Leader Dick Gephardt had been evacuated somewhere—to this day, I don't know where—and were addressing us on loudspeakers, and people were yelling at them, "No one is going to keep us from the Capitol."

That evening I went to dinner at the Dubliner—trying to eat, talk, get collected somehow. A congressman at the briefing had said, "We have to kill these guys. We have to go to war right away." Another congressman, sitting with me at the Dubliner, said, "Oh, how about all the people *we* kill?"

I should have known that the unity that everyone said was there really wasn't as much there as we thought it was. That night we had another briefing, but half didn't come back for that. We heard Bush's speech on television, and I did a few radio interviews. Then I heard about the people, how many people at Cantor Fitzgerald had been killed, so many hundreds—that was the first that I had learned of it. I took a sleeping pill that night to get to sleep.

The next day, again realizing that this was war, I was trying to go back and think about how would we have done at Pearl Harbor. We got a briefing on the House floor that afternoon by [John] McLaughlin, the number two guy at the CIA. [Attorney General John] Ashcroft was there. I saw FBI director [Robert] Mueller there; he'd just been released from the hospital, back from prostate cancer [surgery] the week before. The head of FEMA [the Federal Emergency Management Agency] was there, and I thought that on the whole it was basically a good briefing. But then again some congressman accused them of covering up, of not giving us all the facts. Then all the yelling really started—it was just so wrong. Another congressman was talking about this terrible disaster, and the members around him were screaming, making partisan points, and I finally just walked out. When you go into these briefings you have to leave your cell phone outside, so I picked mine up and got a voice mail that Jimmy Boyle's son had died. Jimmy Boyle is a former president of the New York City firefighters' union. That was really tough. I called Jimmy, and he said, "My son Michael was killed." Michael Boyle was the first person who died whom I really knew well, so that made me feel even more disgusted with all the screaming going on in Congress. Then I heard about Father Mychal Judge, the Fire Department chaplain, whom I also knew. It was all feeling very real.

On Thursday we went down to the White House for a briefing, and that was interesting. They had gathered all the members of Congress from close to the regions that had been attacked: downstate New York, northern New Jersey, and Virginia. Bush came in, and we all applauded. Outside the room we could see troops with camouflage and the sort of heavy-duty weapons that you never thought you'd see at the White House. The first thing the president announced was that the vice president of the United States had been evacuated, and then he told us that they thought there could be more attacks. He'd been in contact with [Russian president Vladimir] Putin, and with [Pervez] Musharraf from Pakistan, and announced that NATO had gone to DefCon 5, or whatever the top level of alert is. Then he told us that he had agreed to give New York $20 billion. [New York senator Chuck] Schumer said, "Mr. President, I am so startled. I was all set to give long speeches about why we needed the $20 billion. I don't know what to say." Then Bush said, "The only reason I gave it to you was to keep you quiet, Chuck. I didn't want to hear your speeches."

That was good, because everybody laughed, even if it wasn't really that funny. There was so much tension in the room that we truly needed some lightness, so people chose to laugh. And then there was some pontificating. [Republican senator] John Warner from Virginia said, "I sat here when your father was the president during the first Gulf War, and you have my support." It became more about themselves again. Hillary was good; she said, "I'm backing the White House," for the first time, and "I'll support you in any way."

Bush had said in the meeting, please, he didn't want anything to be known about Cheney's being evacuated and asked that nothing be shared outside of the meeting—which was actually a designation of making the meeting classified, so that Congress did not broadcast what we were doing in our government. When I returned to my office I got a call from a reporter I knew at CNN, who asked, "Can you tell us what went on?" And I said, "No, I really can't, this is serious stuff." As I was talking they were announcing Cheney's evacuation on television. Within twenty minutes of a meeting where the president basically swore us to secrecy because we were at war, someone at the meeting had leaked to the press what was considered classified information.

President Bush announced that he was going to New York the next day, and that night I got a call from the White House saying I would be going up with the delegation. On Friday morning, after watching Bush's speech on television from the National Cathedral, we took off from Andrews Air Force Base on an Air Force jet. We landed at LaGuardia and took buses in from there. The streets were strangely empty, especially as we got into the city. People were walking around, but it was an apprehensive walk, a walk of pending doom. We parked about a quarter of a mile north of Ground Zero, and I saw all that white stuff from the buildings, mud on the streets, demolished fire trucks and chief's cars. People were cheering along the way as police, fire, and official cars passed. I saw the Sixty-ninth Regiment guys on duty, and I thought, *Wow*. That hit me: There at the corner of Vesey and West streets were armed troops.

Cardinal [Edward] Egan and Mayors Dinkins and Ed Koch were there. I saw some cops I knew, who told me how bad it was. On television, the reporters were talking about finding survivors. But I spoke to cops, who said that's all bullshit; no one's alive. There were still rumors about hundreds being rescued, and these cops said that there was no chance that anyone was alive. The president arrived and we heard this massive cheering, apparently when Bush got on top of a battered fire truck with Bob Beckwith, a retired NYC firefighter. I spoke to the president briefly, and to Mayor [Rudy] Giuliani. It was a memorable and patriotic time.

The congressional delegation was flying back to Washington, because we had a vote that night—a resolution to take action in Afghanistan. But the next morning was Pete Ganci's funeral, the chief of the FDNY, who [had] lived about a mile or so from me, so I stayed in New York for the funeral. The Secret Service let me off at my car at LaGuardia Airport after being at Ground Zero. The airport was empty; all you saw were Port Authority cops at fifty-foot intervals. As I was driving home on the Grand Central Parkway, I heard many F16s overhead. It was so eerie and unusual for America.

At Pete Ganci's funeral there was a tremendous turnout. The cops dropped off Mayor Rudy Giuliani about a block away from the church. He had just come from Father Judge's funeral in the city, and the funeral of Chief Ray Downey, the famous catastrophe expert. They asked me to go greet him and bring him back to the front of the church. I'd known Rudy for decades, and we didn't always get along, but we had worked things out over a breakfast one day. And I was glad we had resolved any differences.

I could see that Rudy hadn't fully realized the impact he was having on the nation. He had no idea of all the press on television. He was living in the zone, or almost as if he had tunnel vision. As we were walking toward the church, people were applauding and cheering, which seemed to genuinely surprise him.

Later that afternoon I worked up the nerve to go over to Jimmy Boyle's house to pay my respects for Michael. And Jimmy made it easy. I walked in the door, and it was all graciousness—not, *Here's another politician coming in*, and that kind of thing. Jimmy's role was to keep everybody contained, but he did so in as lighthearted a frame as possible. He was speaking to everybody, introducing everyone. It was almost like the classic Irish wake that you read about.

I talked to Jimmy and he had told me he had seen the first plane hit that day and then thought about the first World Trade Center bombing. He remembered that the terrorists had taken refuge in a camera store on Broadway. So Jimmy thought how crazy it would be—and he was going to make a citizen's arrest—if they were there again, hiding out. On 9/11 he actually walked across the Brooklyn Bridge and headed to that camera store, but just as he got to Broadway, the South Tower came down.

About a month later I went back to Ground Zero with some of the 9/11 families. I saw all the destruction again, partial buildings, fallen and bent steel, and that unforgettable smell in the air. I didn't even realize that the buildings had pancaked. I just couldn't imagine . . . where did it all go? Think about the combined two hundred stories of these two buildings, and suddenly there's nothing there, just bits and pieces. How could this ever be put back together? It was like [pictures of] places you see in Germany after World War II or Hiroshima in Japan.

They didn't create the Homeland Security Committee until after 9/11, so it officially began in the next congressional session, in January of 2003. Though it's called a select committee, it is not a permanent one. None of the old-timers wanted it; none of the institutional people wanted it. Why? Because if you create a new committee it takes power from other committees. I was way down on [Speaker of the House] Denny Hastert's list, and not even in the top half when they set it up. What Hastert thought to do to win over the recalcitrant was to put the chairmen of all the powerful committees on the Homeland Security Committee. He said, "That way they'll work with the select committee." Instead, all they did was sabotage it and spend the next two years not showing up for votes, and going out of their way to weaken every bill. It became, at best, like a debating society for two years.

At the end of 2004, though, Hastert became far more serious about it.

He made it a permanent committee; cut its size in half, with twenty-eight or twenty-nine members instead of fifty or sixty, and threw everybody off who was a chairman of any other committee, seeing them as obstructionists. I became chairman of the Emergency Preparedness Subcommittee. I figured that was the one best in tune with New York, to be more aware of the needs of the firefighters and cops, to make sure the preparedness money was coming in, and to ensure that training would be available. And then President Bush appointed the then chairman of the Homeland Security Committee, Chris Cox of California, to be head of the SEC [Securities and Exchange Commission]. So there's an opening, and I decided to run for chairman, even though I was fifth down on the Republican side.

In September of 2005 I was elected chairman of the committee. Republicans lost control in '06, and so I was the ranking member from '07 until January of 2011; then it became a Republican Congress again in 2010 and I was reelected as chairman. During my first term as chairman, which lasted only fourteen months, we did pass the port security bill, and a chemical plant security bill, and restructured FEMA. Also, I was very involved in the Dubai Ports legislation, and I stopped that deal. The Dubai Ports company was going to be given contracts to run major ports in the U.S., and I was concerned about lines for al Qaeda.

At the time of September 11, 2001, I was on the International Relations Committee and the Financial Services Committee. I was very involved in the Irish peace process, and also in Bosnia on the side of the Muslims. I thought that our government had not been doing enough to protect the Muslim community in Bosnia and Kosovo from persecution. Financial Services is always important because of New York's financial industry, and International Relations is where I gained so much insight into our security problems, which is also the reason I supported McCain in 2000.

As of now I'm still on the Financial Services Committee, and the Intelligence Committee, too, where I've been since June of 2009, but that could change, because it is strictly appointed by the speaker. I'm the only member of Congress who's on both the Homeland Security and the Intelligence committees. The Intelligence Committee gives me a clear view from outside; Homeland Security is more inside out. The two together really complement each other, and you see how really dangerous the world is. How at any given time we have to worry about something coming from al Qaeda.

We have to worry about things we think we know about, and even more than that, we have to worry about what we don't know about yet.

I did not see a real attack coming before 9/11, but I did feel it was a dangerous world. After the Iron Curtain came down the general opinion in America was that foreign policy was no longer important, and the United States was safe. But I just saw continuing problems, so I put a lot of work into International Relations. But again, not as far as al Qaeda.

If you go back to the 2000 election, the closest election in our history, I don't think there was a word said about terrorism. We did obviously miss the 1993 statement at the World Trade Center. When you do look at the bombings of the African embassies, when you look at the bombing of the USS *Cole*, and even before that the Khobar Towers in Saudi Arabia and the marine barracks in Lebanon, there definitely was a planned Islamic movement, and we didn't take it seriously enough.

One thing I see with these plots is that they seem to be in motion: people traveling to Pakistan, people going to tribal areas, a lot of contact and transmissions back and forth from suspicious individuals, and you almost never get clear and focused intelligence saying that, for instance, on October 11 we're going to attack a specific building or target. It's always just bits and pieces all over the place. It's been fascinating to watch some of these plots coming to fruition and then have the plotters arrested at the last minute. What's unsettling is when you follow one of these and suddenly everyone involved disappears off the face of the earth. That could mean that the plan has been called back, or there was no plan and we were wrong in the first place. Or that this is now an operation, and we don't know where the people are, and that's terrifying. Also, I think it requires a real change in mind-set for the police and FBI to realize that maybe 999 out of 1,000 plots, or so-called plots, that they follow end up going nowhere. Cops are used to solving a case and locking the perpetrator up, but most of these terrorist investigations end up going nowhere. You have to follow everyone all the way through, and that's so hard. It's going to be a real challenge for leadership to keep everyone focused, because the one you don't follow is the one that's going to happen.

Since 9/11 the big fear has been being attacked from overseas. We've done a good job of stopping that, and we're much stronger now than we were then. Al Qaeda is adapting too, and now they are using people living in this country as well as those living in France and, especially, in England.

They are finding people living in these countries legally who have no known involvement with terrorism and are under the radar screen. In 2009 we had Najibullah Zazi, the guy who had traveled to Afghanistan to be trained as an explosive bomber. Zazi was born in Afghanistan, but he was living here legally—raised in Queens, went to high school in Queens, had a hot dog stand or something downtown, no criminal record at all. And yet he came within days of a massive deadly attack on the subway system. Faisal Shahzad, the guy who brought a car bomb to Times Square in May of 2010, had actually become a U.S. citizen. He traveled back and forth to Pakistan a lot. He was actually questioned, but he gave all the right answers, and there was no reason to be suspicious of him at all.

At the time of the 9/11 attacks I cannot say that I knew the Muslim community very well, yet I probably had a closer relationship with it than almost anyone else in Congress. I was very involved with Bosnia and felt that Muslims were being oppressed there. I sided with them, and it hurt me politically that I supported Clinton on that issue. I thought that Pakistan had a better argument than India about Kashmir. I had spoken at the Islamic Center of Long Island a number of times. The president of that mosque has a daughter who interned at my office wearing full Muslim headgear. I got a human rights award from the mosque. I went to Muslim weddings, and I went to their homes, so I thought I knew them.

After 9/11 I was one of the people who said publicly that we couldn't do to the Muslims what we had done to the Japanese after Pearl Harbor. These are good people; they are proud Americans. But some time around Columbus Day, about a month after September 11, quotes started appearing in *Newsday* from the interfaith director, the president, and the vice president at one of the biggest mosques, and probably the richest one, on Long Island. These guys were doctors—and they were saying there was no evidence of Muslims being involved: It was the CIA, the FBI, the Jews.

The fact that top people within the Muslim community were claiming this was when it first hit me that there must be a total disconnect between the rest of our country and the leaders of our Muslim community—a group living among us who are not assimilated. They were saying the Jews blew up the World Trade Center—really educated people were saying this, people I considered friends. I just could not believe it. And *Newsday* never criticized these quotes, nor did any of our religious leaders. The media would run stories saying we can't have any oppression against Muslims, and I realized then that it was a big issue to even ask any questions. If someone had made the statement that the overwhelming majority—95 percent of Muslims—were great people, but that some in their leadership do not cooperate with our law enforcement officials, he would be branded as being a bigot for even raising the matter.

I started talking to law enforcement, and found again and again, whatever the Koran says or doesn't say, the fact is that too many people in the Muslim community have separated themselves from the rest of the country. There was a Pew poll of American Muslims a few years ago, one of the most respected polls in the country, that found that 65 percent of men between the ages of eighteen and twenty-nine said they were Muslims first; only 25 percent said they were Americans first. Sixty-five percent is a big number when you also consider the fact that 15 percent of Muslim men between eighteen and twenty-nine said they could support suicide bombing. I mean, let's just say there are three million Muslims in America, and 25 percent of them are between eighteen and twenty-nine; that's 750,000 people, and 15 percent of them could support suicide bombing? That's over 100,000 men who said they could support suicide bombing.

There is a knee-jerk reaction to defend Muslim leadership, but the fact is that you can go to almost any city in this country, any precinct in New York and Long Island, and cops will tell you that they get no cooperation whatsoever—that they, the police, are the enemy. There's a major investigation I'm aware of in which families went to the FBI and said their kids were being recruited to be suicide bombers, and when the bureau began an investigation into this, the imams denounced it in one of the mosques. And so no one in that mosque was allowed to cooperate with the FBI.

It is frightening to think that if 15 percent of young Muslim men in our country support suicide bombings, what would that percentage be in Saudi Arabia, Yemen, Jordan, Egypt, Libya, and other countries? We are talking about well into the millions worldwide, and despite what is said, these are not necessarily poor people, or people living in the mountains. The attacks in England, for example, are coming from second- and third-generation Pakistani kids who live middle-income, middle-class lives, with fairly secular, nonsectarian upbringings. In our own country, many in the extremist groups have the same sort of backgrounds. We saw what nineteen hijackers accomplished—to think that there could be millions out there willing to do that.

If you can't identify your enemy, you're not going to defeat your enemy. You have to know who your enemy is, and it's Islamic terrorism. That's why, as chairman of the Homeland Security Committee, I had my first hearing in March of 2011 on the radicalization of Islam, demonstrating that al Qaeda and its affiliates were recruiting Muslim Americans, and local Muslim leaders are facilitating or ignoring that reality. Despite the mindless and hypocritical attacks the mainstream media made against me, I have since acquired so much support from real people.

If I had to make an ethnic generalization about the Muslim community, I would say it was characterized by very low crime, very good family structure, and very solid education. I have met with Muslim leaders, and it's very frustrating. These are doctors, pharmacists, teachers, all extremely educated and very polite, and they would tell me: You know, I'm a doctor, how do you think it makes me feel when people look at me like I might be a murderer? And I ask back: Why, then, won't you ever denounce what these imams are saying on Long Island? They say that these imams don't speak for them. I say, Wait a minute. If Catholic priests got up and said to kill all the Jews, I hope some Catholic leader would stand up and say, This is wrong. When I ask why nobody in the Muslim community stands up, they say, That is not our tradition. So we go in circles.

When my book *Vale of Tears* came out in 2004, I was on a few radio shows and was attacked for being anti-Muslim because I said that I thought that 80 to 85 percent of the mosques in this country were controlled by extremists on the Wahabi side. But in 2000 the State Department [had] held a seminar, a forum on religious extremism, at which a Muslim leader, Sheik Khabani, stated that 80 percent of the mosques had been taken over by extremists. What Muslims say in defense of this is that when extremists come in and take over, the rest of the congregation doesn't really care, because the imam doesn't have the sort of power over them that a priest would have in a Catholic parish, for example. Whether it's 85 percent or 70 percent or 60 percent, that there are that many mosques in America dedicated to Islamic fundamentalism is a frightening proposition.

Also, because many of the Muslims in America are African American, we face the situation of a double political correctness: religious correctness and racial correctness. Many African American prisoners are recruited and converted in prison to radical Islam. There are mosques in the New York and Long Island areas that actually recruit their security personnel from the black Muslims coming out of prison. And the imams who go in there to the prisons—what are they preaching? It's a real issue, and a growing one.

This is an issue for our culture, and for our survival, but it also says something about our national will. If we're not willing to stand up and be willing to seek the truth about this, then we're just kidding ourselves. We must become aware nationally of the issues involved.

Scientists are now working on trying to genetically modify various diseases so we won't have antidotes for them. Say that two people—suicide bombers, in effect—are willing to get smallpox. Fly them over here on planes, have them ride on subways, walk through shopping centers. Smallpox has just a three-day incubation period, so picture the calm devastation they could cause. There is no silver bullet to stop any of this, no wall we can put up.

That's why I said several years ago that the *New York Times* should have been indicted for espionage when they revealed our counterterrorism wiretapping programs on page one, and that we were going after terrorists bank accounts—which is totally legal. If the media used as much effort to criticize and attack al Qaeda and radicalized Islam as they do the CIA or the NSA for intercepting phone calls coming from overseas, we'd be a lot safer.

I'm not optimistic about the debate changing, and I'm not optimistic about the overall mood shifting the way it should. What I am confident of is the people—not at the top level but at the very next level down—are doing a good job despite the lack of support. Here in New York you've got the police and fire departments in the city, and on Long Island, working together, and they are doing a tremendous job. There are major cities in this country that spend almost nothing on counterterrorism. New York, Nassau, and Suffolk are doing a phenomenal job.

It's undeniable that the American people responded against holding the 9/11 trials in New York, they responded against building the Ground Zero mosque, they responded against Obama apologizing to the Muslim nations, so there does exist a concern for national security. The gut instincts of the American people are very good, and we have to translate that to more of a political agenda.

The killing of Osama bin Laden brings a fitting end to a tragic and searing chapter in our history. America has brought final and complete justice to this diabolical terrorist who brought death to so many of our friends and neighbors on September 11, 2001. I truly hope that the family members of those who were murdered on 9/11 will now have some measure of solace and relief.

Ultimately, the American people want to do the right thing, and I'm hoping that the Homeland Security Committee can generate facts that will get people talking. We need to get Americans talking about more issues that have the potential to raise the level of education, the potential to raise an intelligent debate. It's hard to frame that debate, and so far, galvanizing debate into a coherent force hasn't been done. We made a commitment after World War II that all the parties would be opposed to and would fight Soviet totalitarianism and Soviet expansion. The only debates we had over the next forty years involved the question of how we accomplish it—should we be more aggressive, less aggressive, make this overture, or that? We have not had that real commitment on Islamic terrorism. So while I'm optimistic for the long haul, the problem today is that the enemy is so deadly that in the short haul we could suffer real losses.

Lee Ielpi

Lee Ielpi is a retired New York City firefighter and one of the most decorated in New York City history. His son Brendan (see page 115) is also a member of the FDNY. His older son, Jonathan, was a firefighter in Squad 288, which was housed with New York's special HazMat 1 company. Jonathan was lost on the morning of 9/11 along with eighteen other firefighters from the Squad 288 and HazMat 1 firehouse.

I come from a regular American background. I was born in Flushing Hospital and have lived my entire life in Great Neck, on Long Island. My dad came here from Italy as a teenager; my mom's folks came from Italy. They met where they were brought up, in Greenwich Village, married, and had a very simple American life—raising a family, doing the best they could. I owe everything to my mom and dad, who had good family values.

My dad had to work two jobs, and it was very difficult times. My mom had to work just about every Saturday or Sunday. In good weather my dad would put my mother, my grandmother, my sister, and me in the car, and we would go fishing someplace far upstate. My dad knew as much about fishing as the man in the moon, but he wanted to take us out to the country. Dad loved to fish, while my mother would sit there.

From these trips I learned the love of the outdoors, and then I joined the Boy Scouts. Dad then got involved, became the scoutmaster. Our family motto was that we would go on an overnight camping trip every month of the year. *Every month of the year.* And we did.

When I graduated from Great Neck South High I knew enough to get a good job. I got married to my high school sweetheart, worked with my dad and then with my uncle for a while in his big shower door company. But my love was the Fire Department.

Great Neck has an all-volunteer fire department. A very loud siren would blast to let the volunteers know that they had a call. I grew up just four blocks from the firehouse, and I'd hear the whistle and see these big red fire trucks come zipping by. I knew it was a volunteer thing and wondered how I could be one of those firemen. I wanted to race around in the big red fire truck too, have fun, and go through the red lights. And so when I turned eighteen, I joined the volunteers.

I realized right off the bat that it was exciting work, but that it was also helping people. And I love to help people. I think it's fabulous to be able, whether you're a doctor or even somebody who has the ability to sell goods to folks, to do good. Going to a fire and rescuing somebody, or simply saving their belongings—what more could you ask for?

My next thought, of course, was FDNY—to be a fireman in New York City. I listened to my scanner radio, and I could not believe how many fires they went to. Yes, that is what I wanted.

My career changed a little then, because I was drafted during the Vietnam War—actually, for the second time. They tried but did not draft me at eighteen, because I had braces on my teeth. They didn't want to take me then but told me to let them know when the braces came off. It was the first time I had been turned down for anything. The braces came off in May 1968, and in June I got the letter saying, Greetings, we want you. I had been married for almost three years by then, and I was drafted into the United States Army, did my boot camp, and went off to Vietnam.

I did what they tell you never to do in the military—volunteer for anything. They were looking for a few people to go into a reconnaissance unit, which I knew was a small unit that was a pretty tough and front-lines group, so I raised my hand. People who want to do something are always better to be around than people who do things reluctantly. I went to recon, Twenty-eighth Infantry, First Division, and spent a year in Vietnam. My unit was twenty-four guys, and we'd go out in the jungle for a week or two at a time, on whatever mission they told us. Of the twenty-four guys I worked with that year in my unit, twelve were killed, and many were wounded.

Just two days before I had been drafted, I took the test for the New York City Fire Department and passed with flying colors. The FDNY immediately put me on a military list. I was not being paid by the department, but I was building time. After my year in Vietnam I spent six months in the States finishing up my service time. I came out in June of 1970, and in September I was sworn in to the New York City Fire Department.

There is no better way to go through life, and it all just worked out so well. All the guys who in those firehouses were so totally involved in their work, it was great. We went to fire after fire like no one had ever seen before. It was a tough time in the city, but for a firefighter, what better place to be than a firehouse that has fire?

I eventually had four children, and because my wife, Ann, loved to go camping, we brought the babies up doing so. Anne Marie, my oldest, is a schoolteacher, and is married with two children. She still loves the outdoors and goes camping every single summer. Then Jonathan came along, my older son, and Brendan was next. We took Brendan camping at two months old. And then Melissa came along, who is the baby in the family. And everybody's married now.

Jonathan and I went hunting many, many times together. I can remember the first deer that he shot. He thought it was a doe, because it was doe season. It had just become dark as we hung her up, to let the deer hang there overnight, and Jonathan was so happy as we got into our sleeping bags. The next day I was looking at it, and Jonathan was still very proud of his deer. I said, "Jon, nice doe, but there's only one thing wrong." Jon says, "What's that?" I said, "Jon, your doe has a penis and testicles." It was what they call a button buck—its horns never came through, but you can feel little buttons on its head. Everybody cracked up, and it was a good experience for him too.

With time I rose up the ranks in the volunteers and became the chief of the department. My children had never known anything but the Fire Department. When I first became assistant chief, they were just young kids, and I would drive Ann and them around in a chief's car—fire-engine red, gold printing on the doors, lights, siren. My radio would go off for a call, as we had an alarm, and because I couldn't tell the kids to get out of the car and stand on the sidewalk, I would say, "Hold on," and we would be off to the fires, all siren and flashing lights. This was their entire life, all four of them.

I retired from the FDNY in 1996. My wish list was to be able to go fishing, hunting, hiking, and camping with my sons, because they loved to be outdoors, and while it lasted, it was the most wonderful time. We had all of that time together in the wild of nature and worked with the Great Neck Vigilant Volunteer Fire Company, and because I kept an FDNY fire helmet I even volunteered a few times with the department at really big jobs. I loved everything I did in those years, from 1996 to September 11, 2001.

. . .

It's still baffling to me: How did I get to this point, after my son was taken from us? I think it started not long after 9/11. The mission at that time for me was him, Jonathan. . . . I still cry every time I think of him. . . . Happens every time. . . . Still, ten years later.

The site, on September 11 was where and when it started. Finding Jonathan was paramount, obviously, but as I have said many times, I do not want people to think that I and my buddies in the Fire Department were looking only for firemen. We were looking for people, and I was looking for my son, but anyone we found along the way was going to be a blessing to someone. It's a great way for me to think about the way things happened at the site. It took three months to find Jonathan, three months to the day. Of course I wanted to be there, but at the same time I didn't, and I guess the good Lord worked it out correctly. That evening I had left the site and gone home, and when I got the call I came back with my son Brendan. We did what you're supposed to do in the fire service: You carry out your own. So that little chapter ended right there. Jonathan was brought home.

We were blessed. There were only 174 bodies found whole, and after three months Jonathan's was a whole body, or what they considered a whole body. A week or two after that we found his helmet, and then a week or two after, his turnout coat. So were we blessed? We were totally blessed.

At the funeral service for Jonathan, I made a statement at the church, St. Aloysius, in Great Neck. I wasn't sure if I could get up to speak, but my family didn't have the vaguest idea of what to say either. There were so many guys there that had given of themselves—the guys who had come out of retirement. They knew they couldn't all come to the site, so what they did was to go to services and funerals—thousands of them went to hundreds of services and funerals. There is no way to comprehend that so many thousands of beautiful people went through all of that.

So I felt I had to get up and say something, because I wanted to honor them. I can remember saying, "We do a lot of clapping at all these services, and I want to acknowledge a group of people we need to clap for," and I gestured toward these folks. "These are guys who have been leaving their families and going to services. They knew they had to do something, as we all did, and so I'd just like to acknowledge them." And I can remember clapping for them, which was . . . I hope they remember that, because it was a beautiful thing. And when I was going to finish, I said, "I know my son Jonathan is in God's hands, but I really wish he was in my hands." And then I went and sat down. And I still don't know where that came from.

We buried Jonathan about two blocks from our house in a beautiful, beautiful cemetery in a spot on a little knoll, under the shade of a tree. But my mission was not over.

All the other dads were still there at the World Trade Center, and so I went back to work at the site for the long recovery period, and I was there for nine months.

The more time I spent at the site, the more I came to develop different points of view. I began to see how huge this great tragedy had been for so many people: the victims' families and friends; the volunteers giving up their lives to help at the site, handing out food and equipment; the construction workers skipping coffee breaks and lunches or dinners to get their work done; the police and fire departments' bosses watching out every second for the safety of the responders and workers. Seeing all this I realized that we needed to remember what had happened here in a big way. We needed to understand what hatred and intolerance can do.

So my first thought was steel. . . . Because it had become the most famous place in the world, I knew people were going to be asking for steel for 9/11 memorials. I don't know where that idea came from either. But I was able to capture a lot of steel with the cooperation of the Port Authority, who owned the site, which we then used for a major project of the Fire Department: to give a piece of that steel to the families of the 343 firefighters who had been killed. The Port Authority and I then did a major project to give out these pieces of steel to almost three thousand additional people, mostly 9/11 families. So, in a way, I didn't want all these people to forget.

Of course we'll never forget 9/11, but I really don't want people to forget the minutes, the day, the search, the recovery, the aftermath of 9/11 either. I want people to understand why 9/11 happened. So steel was one of those devices that would bring you right there. For when you touch that piece of steel, there's something there—you can feel it. So I guess that's how I started thinking about education, and that's how it continued.

Over the course of the months I spent at the site I began working with a number of family members. Marian Fontana was one, a young lady who lost her husband, Dave, from Squad 1. She started one of the many organizations created by surviving families of 9/11, all seeking to gain more information from the city, state, and federal governments about what was going to be built at the site, what kind of memorial was planned, and how big it would be, who was investigating the terrorists, who would compensate the families for the great loss of family income, and that kind of thing. There was much politics involved in the aftermath of 9/11, maybe too much. Marian called her organization the Widows' and Victims' Families' Association and asked if I would join, I guess because she knew I was spending so much time at the site. I told her I would love to join, but that I wasn't going to leave the site, as there were still many things that had to be done there. And so I became the eyes and ears of the WVFA.

A young lady by the name Jennifer Adams, a very competent woman who came out of an investment banking company, came in to organize things. A firefighter from the NYC firefighters' union knew that Marian needed some help and introduced her to Jennifer. Her company had left for Houston just shortly before 9/11 and wanted her to come along, because she is commendably brilliant, but she was in love with New York City, and so she stayed. She had been working in the North Tower on the eighty-sixth floor when it was hit. Jennifer had spent about three and a half months as a volunteer at the World Trade Center site, working on the corner of Liberty and West in a little white tent with many other volunteers, handing out coffee, hot chocolate, inserts for shoes, a warm word, a comforting shoulder, maybe some guidance. It was a very difficult place for anybody to be, but it gave her a pretty good understanding of what had happened at the site. Jennifer agreed to join us, but only for a few months, because she needed to work. We were able to pay her a minuscule amount of money at the end of each month, and that enabled her to stay on for almost eight years. We got our funds from banging on doors and calling on friends like the International Association of Fire Fighters. Family members helped us, because they knew this was an effort that was going to be vital for them and for everyone.

I think that Jennifer's joining us was simply meant to be—so many things have happened since then that cannot be coincidences. When she came onboard we saw right away what a godsend she was. She began by organizing our little WVFA completely. Early on she noted that there were many family organizations that were redundant and were conveying mixed messages, so she put eight of them together and created the Coalition of 9/11 Families. She was just relentless in her endeavors. She started a quarterly newsletter, which we still publish to this day. She built a database of some forty-five hundred family members. And then, after four years of work, she suggested that we step back and perhaps rebuild our own organization. "The Widows' and Victims' Families' Association" was proving to be a mouthful, so we decided to call it the simpler "September 11th Families' Association."

One day she looked out the window, pointed to Liberty Street, and said, "Why don't we lease that little building down there, and we'll make it a visitors' memorial center?" So I looked at Jennifer like, I don't know, as if she were an oracle, and so we discussed it. I said, "Jen, that's wonderful." We were given a very inexpensive space to share with a Lutheran organization— everyone was so generous.

That was January of 2004. Our little odyssey began in March.

During this whole period people were coming down here in droves, moving around aimlessly and wondering, *Is this the World Trade Center site?* There was nothing here saying that it was, except maybe for dubious street vendors selling 9/11 T-shirts and coffee mugs, so it was foolish to think that everyone who came to the site would automatically recognize Ground Zero. Hundreds of thousands of people have never been to New York, and what they saw was a hole in the ground. Nobody was out there to guide them, to help them, tell them the stories of that day.

Jennifer, meanwhile, had been paying attention to what I had been doing at the site. I had just stopped my part of the recovery work after many uninterrupted months, and I was no longer working as a retired FDNY member. At around that time I had begun to get calls from people who wanted to go through the site. It began when the Port Authority asked me to bring a group of reporters through the site. And I felt something there, when I did that. I was able to talk to people about 9/11. I cried every time I did so, but I was able to talk about it, and I saw the value of talking, and of being a firsthand storyteller. I started to walk them around, explaining that terrible day to them, trying to give them a sense of what really had happened. It was a natural thing for me. And, I had become a tour guide without knowing it.

Then the Fire Department asked me to take another group of reporters around. I can still remember vividly, walking through the site, with recovery work still going on, how a reporter stopped me, with a little bit of a smile on his face. He was watching one of the firefighters on the pile. "Did you see what that guy just did?" he asked. I said, "No, what?" The reporter said, "He just picked that shoe up and smelled it."

And I looked at this reporter and said, "Most guys are going to pick a shoe up and smell it, because it could have human remains in it. And that may be the only thing a family gets back." I had caught him off guard, and he now had a tear in his eye. But these are things that we did at the site. We were looking for parts of people, and we were looking for them in places that were hidden, because there were no bodies here. And they were hidden, in any place you could think of: a shoe, a sock, inside a shirt, in a two-inch void between two massive beams. Only 174 complete bodies of the 2,752 beautiful people who were murdered at Ground Zero on September 11 were recovered. There are still 1,222 missing.

A professor from Duquesne University, Mike Dillon, who has since become a very good friend, came to do a story. Someone in the city press office had asked if I would meet with this reporter, a professor, who was doing a story for a local newspaper in Pittsburgh. I don't remember the full content, but it was about me, the site, Jonathan, and the recovery workers. In it he gave me a title, "ambassador to the dead." When I first read it, I said to myself, *Is this good?* And then the more I thought about it, the more I realized that it was a good title, as our 9/11 dead need to be talked about and represented.

At the World Trade Center site thousands of people came to volunteer their services. In America the volunteer spirit is still very much alive, whether it is working as a candy striper at a hospital, helping kids read at a library, or being a volunteer firefighter in your hometown—75 percent of the country is protected by volunteer firemen. And this volunteer spirit was prevalent at Ground Zero then, and is present at the Tribute [WTC Visitor Center] today.

I have met many beautiful, wonderful people—my BWs, I call them— from every state in the union. They have come here, some during that nine-month recovery period, to do something, and they could not stay at home and do nothing. Those who could not come in person went out and collected money, equipment, and supplies, things that could be used at the site. It was so beautiful.

One couple from a little place called Phillipsburg, Kansas, which is about as big as a pinhead, came here four separate times at their own expense. On each visit they spent two weeks feeding us and cleaning up after us. The wife asked me, "After this is all done, will you come to speak to us?" I said okay, and they were ecstatic. I went to their little town not knowing what to expect. It was the first time I had really traveled to speak to a large group about 9/11. I went into the large and spiffy auditorium of their brand-new school, and it was overwhelming: The crowd was standing-room-only, hundreds and hundreds of young people and families. It was very rewarding to be there.

I spoke positively, and talked about tomorrow. I told them how my best friend had been taken from me on 9/11, along with eighty or ninety other good friends whom I had worked fires with. But my best friend was my son Jonathan, and although I couldn't bring him back, much as I wished I could, I had to do something for tomorrow that would make the world better. There was no alternative, as it was our sacred obligation to give all children the best that we could, and the most effective way to start was with an education about understanding the good things in our world. But to understand good, you had to talk about the bad—the horrors, the world wars, slavery, starvations, and 9/11—in a positive way.

I speak regularly now and say a lot of things that are very difficult for people to understand and hear. I talk about the men and women who worked at the site on their hands and knees every day to find 19,979 body parts. But then I turn it into a positive, something we can learn from. We can't hate. The people who did this, these are people who hate. They are fanatics. They come from what we now call radical Islam, as opposed to Islamic people in general. But if we're going to be afraid to talk about radical Islam, we must pay heed to the adage about history repeating itself. In fact, it has already repeated itself. It repeated itself with the underwear bomber, the shoe bomber, the guy who had a bomb up on Times Square at Forty-fifth Street, the attacks on the trains in Spain, the buses in London, and the hotel in Mumbai—every time you read or hear about somebody strapping a bomb on and walking into a crowd of people. How many more people have died since 9/11 because of this thing called "radical Islamic extremism"? Catholic churches were just bombed in Arab countries. A person walks into the crowd and detonates a bomb he is carrying, pulverizes twenty or forty or sixty beautiful people. How can you turn these terrible things into something positive? That is the challenge.

It's easy for us in this country to forget these things because we live in the lap of luxury. So I speak positively about what we can do. These young people are tomorrow's people, and if they don't understand history, then shame on us. Almost ten years later and there is still not a state in our country that has a curriculum to teach the history of 9/11—not *what* happened, but *why* it happened. Who did it? And why did they do it? If our educators aren't teaching, one day we're going to be very sorry.

Today there are countries that are very close to developing nuclear weapons, autocratic countries in which there is much unrest and turmoil, where change can occur overnight. Will these nuclear weapons fall into the hands of fanatics? Just think about the planning involved in 9/11. Would those planners stop short of dropping a nuclear bomb on Tel Aviv, Paris, London?

I've asked that question many times and have occasionally been asked, "Don't you think what you're saying is kind of radical?" And I respond, "Well, let me ask you one question, and then you tell me: On September 11, if these same nineteen terrorists had had the capability of bringing a dirty bomb into the center of Manhattan, would they have done it? Would they have detonated it?"

And what is the answer I get from these people? Silence. Because they know damn well the answer is yes.

When I got back from that trip to Phillipsburg I was called by people there who told me they were planning to come to New York with a group of high school students who had just graduated and asked if I would take them on a tour around the site. Although the site was already closed off to visitors, I said sure, of course. Jennifer came with me as I gave the tour, and, as she recalls, they were typical high school kids, all fidgety, looking around, [but] as soon as I started talking, everybody stopped and listened with a real intensity. At the end Jennifer realized this was something that was so important to those kids. They were going to go home with a totally different attitude—a good attitude, because we ended by discussing what we could all do for a positive future for our country.

Back at the 9/11 Families' Association office we talked about that experience, and Jennifer said, "Let's build on it. Let's do tours and change people's lives." So we went out and knocked on many doors. Governor [George] Pataki thought it was a fabulous idea and asked the LMDC [Lower Manhattan Development Corporation] to help us financially. We met with Mayor [Michael] Bloomberg, and he said, Great. We needed to raise at least $6 million to build out the Tribute WTC Visitor Center to what it is today, and we were able to do so with funding from the Port Authority, the Red Cross, and American Express. That effort started started in March of 2004, and by September of 2006 we opened our doors to the public. We're a nonprofit, so fund-raising remains a major challenge, especially with the current economic situation.

When we were first looking to build the Tribute Center, we assumed that the official 9/11 memorial that would be built on the footprints of the original towers was going to be many years away from completion and operation, so we conceived the Tribute Center as an interim memorial for visitors. But after many meetings with the people that we brought in to help us from the museum world, we realized that we were building something that was going to be out of the ordinary and not in the same vein as a typical museum or memorial. Just as I had been called the ambassador for the dead, the Tribute Center would become the ambassador for those people who could not speak.

We have trained over 390 guides—all volunteers. They come from the 9/11 community, which we define as anyone who lost a loved one, rescue workers, survivors who made it out of the towers, volunteers like Jennifer, and then the people who live and work in the area who watched that day and witnessed things that no one should ever have witnessed. Can you imagine being there to see those people who jumped from the two buildings? Who better to give a tour than this 9/11 community? They are the voices of the people who were murdered that day.

The Tribute Center is a person-to-person, I-was-there history. It is a sharing. Everything you hear, see, or read is testimony by people who were affected by 9/11. It is like a museum in that it has many artifacts and a historical collection of objects, but it also has living stories and living storytellers. The Tribute Center is open seven days a week, and our guided tours are held seven days a week. We limit the tours to twenty people, and do four and five a day.

When you enter the Tribute Center you see in Gallery 1 what the World Trade Center and the area were like before September 11, after which you follow a timeline that starts on February 26, 1993, the date that's forgotten by just about everyone: The first time the towers were attacked by radical Islamic extremists.

In the next gallery we start the timeline of September 11 and take you through the events of that day. You hear voices and see people who died that day. There are transmissions of the firefighters on their walkie-talkies as they are ascending the stairs in the South Tower—all those great men, all those powerful voices, doing what we as firefighters did every day before 9/11 and have done every day since. You'll see photographs of police officers like Moira Smith [see Jim Smith, page 128] and civilians coated with ash. You'll hear families talking about their loved ones. You'll see posters of missing people. You'll see a powerful five-minute video of what it was like to spend nine months at the site. You'll see my son's helmet and his turnout coat, which we were blessed to recover.

Jonathan's helmet and coat are now on display in Gallery 3.

Gallery 4 is the family room. Jennifer reached out to every family and asked them to send us one photo of the loved person who was lost, so as you enter the space your breath will be taken away. It's a very solemn, quiet place, with walls that are covered with beautiful smiling faces of all ages, colors, religions, and economic levels. And you will sense immediately that the only thing wrong with this room of good and decent people is that they are no longer with us.

When we leave Gallery 4 we want to change the experience and stress how tomorrow has got to be a better day. We want to brighten you up a little bit, so you'll see photos of workers hugging at the site, photos of spouses, lovers, family, friends. You then reach a little spot where there are tiles on the wall with drawings and sayings, the work of people from all over the world who went into a ceramics shop and made them to hang on a fence up on Greenwich [Street] and Seventh Avenue. Ten years later there are still four thousand of these memorial tiles on that wire fence; we have about four hundred of them at the Tribute Center.

On the opposite wall is a little origami crane, no larger than a dime, created by a young girl by the name of Sadako, who lived through the bombing of Hiroshima. She was two years old at the time, and eventually came down with leukemia from radiation poisoning, and died in 1955 at the age of twelve. Of course, like all of us, she wanted to live, and her dad suggested that if she fold a piece of paper into the shape of a crane, her wish might come true. It's a cultural belief in Japan. So Sadako started folding cranes, and because there was a lack of paper in postwar Japan, she carefully picked the labels from her medicine bottles. She made well over a thousand before she died. The family donated all of the cranes to the Hiroshima memorial except for five, which they kept as a remembrance of their daughter.

About two years ago Sadako's brother decided it was time to give the five cranes away, one to each of five continents to carry on his sister's wish that she could live, live in peace, and stop nuclear proliferation. For the continent of North America, her brother decided to give it to us, and we now have a beautiful little crane made out of brilliant ruby-red cellophane. It is so little but so hugely consequential in its power. The unique and telling aspect of this story is that the label Sadako used for our origami crane came from a medicine bottle that was sent to Japan by the United States to try to fight her cancer.

Because the cranes started getting smaller as death got closer, the crane given to us is one of the last cranes she made before she died. Here we are some sixty-five years later, and we still can't seem to find peace in this world. But this little twelve-year-old girl was smarter than most of us, having turned her wish into something tangible.

As you make your way downstairs you can look up and see over ten thousand origami cranes that were sent to the Tribute Center by schoolchildren in Japan, which lost twenty-four of its citizens, who worked in the banking industry, in the towers.

Downstairs in Gallery 5 are the thoughts we hope will provide the food for thought that will bring people to change. We ask visitors to sit at a long table filled with blank cards and answer the following questions:

How have you been affected by September 11th?
What action can you take in the spirit of September 11th, in tribute
    to those lost, or to help educate another?
What are your feelings?

More than two million people have come to the Tribute Center from more than 135 countries, and they've recorded their feelings and their advice in their own hand, in their own language. We now have over two hundred thousand cards. The world speaks here, from all countries, including Iran and many [other] Muslim countries, and they all speak with the same words. We must find a way to live with each other. We must find a way to stop hatred and intolerance. We must stop terrorism. These cards are stunning: They are poetic, and their words range from rudimentary to artful. It is a powerful place, with a powerful message: WE MUST LEARN TO LIVE WITH OUR DIFFERENCES.

So much good has happened since 9/11 that our tomorrows might well become better for all people throughout the world. For example, there have been thousands of scholarships established in memory of 9/11, and my son has two named in his honor. Many foundations have also been created [see the Jackmans, page 304, and the MacRaes, page 315] to relieve the suffering from tsunamis, hurricanes, earthquakes, and kids in need, with money and supplies sent in memory of 9/11.

There's a photo that was taken of Jonathan and me after the Father's Day fire in June 10 2001 at which three firefighters died [see Zack Fletcher, page 149], two from Rescue 4 and one from Ladder 163. Jonathan was by this point the second volunteer chief in Great Neck, and we were in his chief's car with his scanner on when we began to hear screaming in the background. We knew right away there was a problem: There had been an explosion, a wall came down, and three firefighters were missing. We drove over to the fire, and while Jonathan had his gear in his car, I was wearing shorts. On the way down the block we met a fireman from Jonathan's company, Squad 288. The guy was in a panic; you could see it in his face. One of the guys trapped in the collapse was from 288—Brian Fahey, who had just transferred to Rescue 4. John Downing from Ladder 163 was lost, and Harry Ford. Jonathan got his gear and mask on, and I told him, "Go ahead, do what you have to do. I'll stay around here and help wherever I can."

Forty-six Engine Companies had responded to the job, along with thirty-three Ladder Companies, sixteen battalion chiefs, and two deputy chiefs. All five Rescue Companies were there.

I then saw Dr. Kerry Kelly [see David Prezant, page 28] come running down the street. She saw me and asked, "What are they up to?" I told her three guys were missing, and she immediately tried to climb onto this pile of rubble where the wall had fallen out onto the street, burying someone beneath it. I yelled, "Doc, you can't go up there like that," because she had heels on and a skirt. But she is the daughter of a New York firefighter, and I could see the spirit. I said, "Doc, you're going to be more valuable down here," and just then Jonathan appeared and said, "Dad, I think we have Harry."

I then heard a voice, and it was Dennis Collins from Ladder 111. "Lee," he said, "what do you need?" I told him they might have Harry Ford, and to get a stretcher. I turned back and saw they were carrying somebody, and we got to a spot where we could transfer whoever it was to the stretcher. They brought him over, and it was Harry Ford. Jonathan knew Harry well, because they lived near each other, and because the rescue units and the squads are very tight. And I had known Harry for an eternity, as he was a longtime firefighter in Rescue 4, and we worked together countless times.

To look at Harry, he seemed fine, but he wasn't breathing, as he had been compressed far too long under the wall that had come down. We began rolling the stretcher down the street, and somebody was riding along on its rail, doing [CPR heart] compressions on Harry. The ambulance was at the end of the block, and when we got there we began clearing Harry's airway. As we loaded the stretcher onto the ambulance, a hand came out and pulled me in, and it was Jonathan's. Kerry Kelly was already there, and maybe an EMT. As soon as the door was closed behind us we started CPR. I can remember vividly Jonathan talking to Harry, and I was yelling at him, trying to get his brain focused. "Harry! Harry! I want you to hear me, we are working on you, and you better not die on me." Jonathan got a great airway going, Kerry was taking vitals, and I was doing compressions. When you do compressions you can feel the exchange of air coming in and going out of the lungs, and if you're trained you can actually feel the person's heart being compressed, like a heartbeat. I thought we were going all right and told Harry, "We're doing good, we've got great airway!"

When we got to the hospital we took him out, and it was there that the photographs of Jonathan and me were taken. We continued working on him in the emergency room for a while until the doctor said he could take over from here. But Harry had been crushed for so long that the air we had been giving him and the compressions weren't enough.

So Harry died, and John Downing died, and Brian Fahey died. Fahey was missing for a long time, but you could hear him calling on his walkie-talkie. But he was underneath the stairs, and no one could reach him or get down to him. He was Jonathan's friend from 288, whom I had met a week or two before at a convention. This was a very sad fire, and it is still baffling how all of this happened, the explosion, the wall.

Little did we realize that September 11 was only a couple of months away, and on that day everybody who came to the towers from Rescue 4 would die. And Jonathan, and everybody from the two companies in his firehouse, Squad 288 and HazMat 1, died, nineteen of them. Five Rescue Companies in the city responded that day to the World Trade Center, and because the alarm came in at the time of a shift change, men from both the night tour and the day tour responded with many of the companies. They rode heavy. Every Rescue Company firefighter there that day died. Five of the seven Squad Companies were there, four riding heavy. Every man in every Squad Company died except for one. Seventy-five firehouses lost men, and many of them lost every man working. There are 128 firefighters still missing. How can you comprehend that? There is no way to understand it. The New York City Police Department lost twenty-two great guys and a wonderful, heroic woman, Moira Smith. On any other day the deaths of twenty-three cops would be front-page news around the world. Port Authority lost thirty-seven of their police officers. I just cannot get over September 11: 343 firefighters killed. It's difficult to even say that. It makes no sense.

In the Fire Department we lose men every year. You can't expect to not lose men, because they serve a special and dangerous function that's needed in New York City. Especially in New York, where there is such a large fire load. We lost three men at the Father's Day fire, six men at the Waldbaum's fire in Brooklyn, thirteen men at the Twenty-third Street fire. But 343. You know, I still can't . . .

I don't know how to put the right words together. When I go into Gallery 4 at the Tribute Center I have the marvelous, God-given opportunity to talk not only about the people who died that day but also about our firefighters. I get to explain to people that what they did at the towers was nothing more than what they did every day before 9/11, and what they've continued to do to this very day. And that it's what they loved to do. And that they go into places where nobody wants to go. Few people can imagine what a wonderful opportunity it is to be a New York City firefighter, to work with the best of the best. Every one of us understands that it is the teamwork of the New York City Fire Department that matters: the training and the caring and the courage of everyone—these are the things that give every firefighter the opportunity to put himself forward at mortal risk to rescue another human being.

The Fire Department is filled with unique individuals, and Jonathan was one of them. When Jonathan first went into the Fire Department, I was still a Brooklyn firefighter. Jonathan came back a couple of times saying, "Dad, guys are talking about you and what you did, the boots I have to fill." And I'd say, "Listen, from this day forward, the boots you have to fill are your own boots, not mine. You do what you have to do at the job, and don't let anyone tell you you have boots to fill. Don't let them make me out of you." I said the same thing to Brendan: "You can't, and you shouldn't, go through this job as Lee Ielpi's son. You are Brendan Ielpi."

Firefighters are still firefighters, and 9/11 did not change that.

Brendan Ielpi

Brendan Ielpi is a New York City firefighter assigned to Ladder Co. 157 in Brooklyn. He was a probationary firefighter for just three months when the attack on the World Trade Center occurred. He responded to Ground Zero with other firefighters who had reported in, arriving there just after the second building collapsed. His father, Lee Ielpi, a retired firefighter from Rescue Co. 2, also responded to the site. Lee's son and Brendan's brother, Jonathan, and every man in his company, Squad 288, was killed in the South Tower.

For a while I didn't know if I would actually go into the Fire Department. I did four years of college up in Colesville[, New York]. The school was outside in the woods, so I got my bachelor's degree in wildlife management. I loved it, and I still do—I can't get enough of the outdoors, studying the birds and the amphibians. My first job out of college was at the fish hatchery and aquarium in Cold Spring Harbor, but I was only making nineteen thousand dollars. I really wanted to continue in that field, but it was hard to even make a living.

I grew up in Great Neck in a pretty big family. We had two sisters—an older sister and a younger sister—and Jonathan and I were in the middle. Jonathan was four years older than me. And we were a Fire Department family. My father, Lee Ielpi, worked at Rescue 2 in Brooklyn, and is known as one of the most highly decorated firefighters in the history of the FDNY. My brother, Jonathan Ielpi, worked for Squad 288 in Queens. And he also served as chief for the Great Neck volunteer fire department.

So it was a big part of my family, and joining the FDNY had always been an idea at the back of my head, but I guess I was a little rebellious initially, trying not to follow in everyone's footsteps.

Still, I always remember seeing how happy my father was with the Fire Department and how much he loved the job. Actually, he never even called it a job—[he] was always "going to play." Every once in a while, when I was younger, I would go visit my father at Rescue 2, but not nearly as often as my brother. Jonathan lived and breathed the Fire Department. His Friday night was not going out and picking up girls; it was the fire truck. And so my father and Jonathan really bonded through the job. For me the bond with my father was through the outdoors, fishing, and camping.

Seeing how much my father and brother loved the Fire Department made me believe that I could be happy there, too, and the FDNY was certainly a stable career path where I could make good money. So I decided to take the test and really make a push for it. I was carrying on the family tradition, carrying on my father's legacy through my time in the Fire Department. Knowing that I'd be able to put out fires for the next twenty-five years was exhilarating. I couldn't ask for anything more than what the Fire Department had to offer.

I started my training with the fire academy in May of 2001, and right away Jonathan began telling me what firehouse I'd be going to. I said, "Well, what about 111 truck?" And he'd say, "Number 157 truck. That's where you're going." He'd come over and tell me about how the night before he'd had an all-hands [all companies working a fire on the first alarm], so it was fun. I really looked forward to Sunday dinners at home during that time, sitting at the table and talking Fire Department with my father and my brother.

Jonathan started off in Brooklyn with Engine 214, Ladder 111, working the engine there, and then went over to Queens. And after about three and a half years on the job, one of his old bosses, Captain Murphy, opened up a new house—Squad 288—in Queens. He asked Jonathan if he wanted to come over, and Jonathan joined them in 1998. But his ultimate goal was to transfer over to Rescue. And from what I was told, he was pretty close to making it happen.

In 2001 Jonathan and I both had pretty busy lives. I had the fire academy and was just starting my FDNY career, and Jonathan had two sons, Andrew and Austin, and his wife, Yessenia, at home. Plus he had a second job, working with a friend of the family doing all sorts of handyman and carpentry work. Like most firemen, Jonathan was pretty handy. Actually, you could build a whole house with just the guys from the firehouse.

So while that year was hectic for both of us, we definitely hung out. Was it as much as we wanted to? No. We all lived in the same town, though, so even if we just ran into each other for ten minutes, we saw each other constantly.

I did eight weeks at the fire academy, and my first tour in the firehouse was on July 4, 2001. I was working on Tillary Street in Brooklyn as a probie [probationary firefighter], assigned to Ladder 110, Engine 207. Every probationary firefighter from our academy class was supposed to do fourteen weeks out in the field, seven weeks in the engine and seven weeks in the truck. And then we were supposed to go back to the Rock [fire academy] in the fall of 2001 for two additional weeks of training. That was the plan, but it never really happened . . . after September 11 we never went back to the Rock.

On September 11, I was assigned to Engine 207 on Tillary Street, in Fort Greene, Brooklyn, but I wasn't working that day, because I had a camping trip scheduled. And four of the guys in my firehouse who were working were killed.

On Tuesday morning I woke up and began packing my car to meet the guys for our trip. Then I turned on the news and, sure enough, the first plane had hit, and I was looking at floors and floors of fire. I can just remember sitting on my bed, cursing up and down that I wasn't at work. Because I knew Tillary Street would be there, across the bridge, right at the second alarm.

So I remember thinking, *You've gotta be kidding me. It's going to be the fire of the century. They're going to be talking about this fire forever.* And I'm still cursing up and down that I'm not there. I called Debra, my girlfriend, who is now my wife. She worked in Manhattan. I said, "Look out your window. Do you see the Trade Center?" She looked, and then you could hear her and everyone in the background: Holy mackerel, what's that? After I hung up the phone, the second plane hit. That's when for me it kind of changed from *Damn, I'm not at work* to *Maybe it's a good thing I'm not at work.* Because then the reality started to hit a little: No one was going to be high-fiving after this one.

So I called my father, who had just gotten off the phone with Jon, and he said he was heading in. I told him to wait for me. I drove to Great Neck and picked him up, and we drove to my firehouse on Tillary Street, which is just on the other side of the Brooklyn Bridge.

On our way there the first tower collapsed. We had the scanner on and could hear everything that was happening. There wasn't much conversation during that drive; we were just trying to get there as soon as we could. I can remember thinking that you don't see your father in a worried and panicked state of mind too often, and I'd never seen him like that before. He was truly, truly worried. He knows our job, he knows fires, and he knew how bad this was going to be. I could tell just by his demeanor that this was not going to be a very good day.

Jon had been at his firehouse, Squad 288, when he called our father. Whenever its doors were opened up, his house had a beautiful view of the city skyline. And that's what Jon was looking at when they were talking on the phone. He was saying, "Dad, you gotta see this, this is crazy." The phone started cutting off. And Jon said, "Dad, I'm going, they put [assigned] us on the box." And that was it.

So on the way in, we knew Jon was going. And then the buildings starting collapsing, and we could hear the sheer panic over the scanner. When we got to Tillary Street, the 11th Division was there, and my dad just jumped in a car with them. I couldn't go with him, because I had been on the job for only four months and had to stay with my company. I didn't see my father again for another five or six hours.

I wasn't at the firehouse for more than fifteen minutes before a group of us got in a car and started heading over to Manhattan. There were about eight of us, mostly senior guys, and we teamed up with an officer who took us to one of the command posts, or what they were calling command posts, right by the church on Broadway. We told them that we had a bunch of guys here and were ready to go.

By this point the second building had collapsed, and they just had us sitting around. We were all thinking, *What are we doing here? There are a thousand things that have to be done, why are we just sitting here? We can't sit here any longer.* Eventually the boss said, "All right, let's just go," and so we walked the two blocks to the site and started doing whatever we could do.

Jonathan was on my mind, but, for some reason, it took me a little while to really start to worry. I don't know what it was; I guess I just didn't realize how bad the collapse had been or comprehend how big and monstrous those buildings were. Guys were saying that the entire second-alarm units must be dead, but Jonathan hadn't headed in until right after the second plane had hit, so I was really thinking that he was going to be all right. A lot of guys were in the same hopeful frame of mind, because do you ever experience anything like that?

Once we got to the site and started looking around, though, the devastation became real. I saw bodies all over the place . . . people in the rubble . . . just dead bodies everywhere. I remember running into a few guys from Rescue 4, whom I'd known before I got on the Fire Department. And I said, "Hey guys, how you doing?" They just looked at me with a look that said, *Don't even ask us how we're doing.*

I don't know if it was my young mind, my innocence. I was only twenty-five years old then, and I thought I knew everything. I was so naive about the world. We were so pampered growing up—no war, no fighting. Everything was great. I'd never seen anything like what I was seeing on 9/11, and most people haven't. But I got to work. Whatever they told me to do that day, I did. That first day I just had to root around the pile with my hands, feeling for anything.

Hours later, at around 4:00 in the afternoon, I finally ran into my father somewhere in the pile. I looked at him and asked, "You find Jon yet?" He just looked at me, and he didn't say anything, and I knew exactly what he meant without his saying it. He managed to tell me that the chiefs thought they were all gone, trapped someplace. He said that he ran into a few guys from Squad 288, and they couldn't even look him in the eye. They started walking the other way, because they didn't want to be the ones to tell him.

I worked all through the night, until about 1:00 or 2:00 in the morning. I was adamant that I was not going to leave. If Jon was here, I was staying. I finally sat down and said, "I'm just going to sleep here."

But a couple of the guys talked me into going back to the firehouse to get some rest, and said we'd come back in the morning and do it all over again tomorrow. One said, "And we'll do it all the next day, and the next day, until we find everybody. So let's go." After they talked a little sense into me, a few of us made our way back to Tillary Street.

On that first day my dad got in touch with our family and told them that he and I were all right, and that we were just doing as much as we could. The only person I spoke to was Debra's mother, now my mother-in-law, to make sure my Debra got home okay from Manhattan. So I called her house, and her mother answered the phone, and that was the first time that I lost it. Reality really set in. I remember just crying, and she asked if everything was all right. And I just lost it.

The first couple of days at Ground Zero, looking at that pile, at that monstrosity, you would think that there had to be people alive in there. In a plot of fifteen acres, some people must have landed in the right spot. You'd find huge voids, and you'd think that hundreds of people would have to be in them, guys trapped here and there, with all their protective gear on. How could there not be *someone* alive in here?

You would be standing on the pile, and you'd hear someone say, "Shhhh, quiet." Next thing you know a thousand people were yelling, "Shhhh, quiet," until all of a sudden everyone was silent. It was amazing to see thousands of people being quiet and standing still together, just because someone may have heard something.

But after three or four days without finding anybody, I think we realized this was just not . . . this was just not happening.

At that point you start thinking logically. *What are the chances that anyone survived this?* You start thinking, *All right, they were in the South Tower, and they climbed down, and if they did a flight of stairs every . . . They were here fifteen minutes, and you have a videotape, and then they were here twenty minutes before the building collapsed, if they did one flight a minute, they were up twenty flights, then how do you survive this?*

No one asked me specifically what he could do for me. I think they all did what they could: Guys just being there for you and letting you vent. We were all dealing with so many people, so many families, and so many lives that it was really hard to focus on one specific person. From my own fire-house alone four were killed. So everybody knew somebody or somebody else's family who was in that pile.

The Fire Department went to a twenty-four-hour shift, with groups A, B, C, and D. So if you were the A group, you would work twenty-four hours, and then you'd have three days off, and so on. I did that for a week or two, and then I spoke to my father and the captain who was making up the charts. And the captain basically said, You come back here when you're ready.

I wound up spending a lot of those off days with my father at the church down by Ground Zero. But whenever I crossed the bridge, I saw the smoke. And on the windy days, the smoke would blow right across the bridge, and you could smell it. I thought to myself, *I can't just be sitting here. I need to go back there and help,* so I was only off for about a month before I went back to the pile.

After 9/11 I didn't see the rest of my family for the first three days. A friend of the family's was coming into the city, so he drove Jonathan's chief's car [the Great Neck Fire Department car] in for us. My father and I drove it back to Great Neck that night, and my dad parked it around the corner from my parents' house. I said, "What are we doing parking two blocks away?" And he said, "If I pull this car into the driveway, and the whole family sees Jon's car pull up in the driveway, they are going to freak out. I don't want the kids seeing it. I don't want your mother seeing it. Otherwise, they may think Jon's coming home, Daddy's coming home." I don't think Jon's kids saw that chief's car for months, simply because they would have believed Daddy's pulling up, Daddy's home. It was a long time before his kids were old enough to comprehend that Daddy wasn't coming home.

So we parked the car around the corner and walked the two blocks to see the family for the first time. It was pretty chaotic—a lot of crying, a lot of tears, a lot of speechless hugging. They all wanted to know what was going on at Ground Zero. It was extremely hard to describe. There were things I didn't want to tell them, and I wanted to keep hope in everyone's mind, trying to keep them positive, so that my mom and my two sisters and my nephews and my brother's wife could forge ahead. Meanwhile, in the back of my head, I knew what was really going on. The writing was on the wall, but I tried to be positive for everyone else.

My father went on the *Larry King* show, and I joined him. Three fire-fighters from another truck in Manhattan were also being interviewed, and one guy was talking about a firefighter from his house, saying, "We know he's in there. He's a big guy, a strong guy. And we know he's going to survive this."

When the interview was over, we all went back into the green room. My father sat the guy down and said, "Brother, you gotta face reality. He's not coming back." But this guy was in denial: "No, you don't understand." My father just said to him again, "You gotta face reality." And that was it for me. It was almost as if my father was telling me without telling me: *You need to face reality here, Brendan. Let's just hope we find Jon.*

And we did find him. For me, it was—I hate to use the word "bitter-sweet," but it was a good ending to a horrible, horrible story.

It was close to midnight, and I was very restless. I was getting agitated and thought, *I'm going to go to Great Neck, to the volunteer firehouse. Just have a cup of coffee and get my mind away from things.* So I got in the car and starting driving. At a point in the road where I could either take a left and go to the firehouse or make a right and go to my parents' house, for some reason I just said, *Let me go past my parents' house.*

It was almost midnight when I got there, and all the lights were on. I was thinking, *What are they doing up?* So I parked the car and walked inside. My dad was on the phone, and as he hung up. he said to me, "Oh, it's you already. How the hell did you get here so fast?" And I said, "What the hell are you talking about? I just didn't feel right. . . . I just needed to get out of the house." He told me that he had just been calling me because they had found Jonathan.

So I guess Jonathan had been urging me to hurry up and come get him.

My father and I drove into the city. One of the rituals that they always did at Ground Zero was to salute the casket as it came up, with the guys lined up on both sides of the ramp or the trail. But this time they had all the guys lined up before we even got there. So as we were walking down we passed between these two lines of men saluting. It was the only time I saw them do this, and it was done for my father. It was very impressive, and it was a heck of a way for the guys to thank my father and to show how much they appreciated everything that he had been doing down there.

We got down to the bottom of the hill, and there was Jon. They had him all packaged up in the American flag. My father knelt and had a short conversation with Jonathan, and then we picked him up, and they saluted us all the way back up the hill.

We found him three months to the day, on December 11. We had been at the site two nights earlier, when they found a couple of other guys from 288, and we knew he was there. I've said a few times that besides the birth of my son, December 11, 2001, was probably the greatest day of my life. It makes no sense that that could be a good day; it makes no sense at all. But I really mean it. I just remember feeling that the weight of the world had been taken off of our shoulders. We got him. We finally got the son of a bitch.

So we went to the morgue at the hospital, and they asked me and my father if we wanted to go in. My father said, "No way, I'm not going in." We knew what the bodies looked like after three months. We saw them every day; it wasn't a pretty sight. It's the worst thing you can possibly think of. All of a sudden I just felt that somebody needed to see him, someone from the family. So I went in there. They undid everything and took his coat off, and his back was facing me, so I didn't see anything. I just saw the small of his back, and the boxers he had on, and I remembered that he had a similar pair. And so I got to look at him real quick, and then they took from his pocket the Swiss Army knife that my father had given us both for camping when we were little kids, and that was the real . . . This was him. Finally something was over, and we had some type of closure, at least to this part of the story.

They put whatever Jonathan had in his pockets in a bag, and they gave my father the bag. I'm sure he still has it. The next day we had to pick Jon up to drive him to Great Neck. We had the whole police escort and everything.

The week of Jon's funeral, that Monday through Friday, there were six or seven others, so getting proper funerals and proper burials with ten thousand guys standing in line saluting the coffins as they went by was not possible. You were lucky if you got a couple hundred. Jon's funeral, fortunately, had a very good turnout. They had to turn plenty of people down at the church, and they were flowing out onto the street, with guys from the FDNY and also from the Great Neck volunteer fire department. It was gratifying to see the number of people who showed up. . . . How touching it was, and how Jon touched so many people. I saw that beforehand, but I guess I experienced it at a more personal level because it was at his funeral. There are lots of better words to use, but it was definitely a bittersweet ending to finally bring him home.

As my father gave Jonathan's eulogy, I remember thinking, *How can he possibly be up there right now?* Growing up, we were always in awe of him: Daddy, Daddy, Daddy. I felt the same after seeing everything he had done at the site for those three months, and what an impact he was making at Ground Zero. And to have seen the praise that he got from everybody: the mayor, the chiefs, the Fire Department, the governor. When I saw him up at the pulpit, I just thought, *Dad, you never cease to amaze me. How the hell are you up there doing this?* I know he'd been debating with himself whether he'd be able to do it, and he did it with such strength. It was just another day of my father being my father.

I didn't start thinking about the cause of 9/11 until later on. I think my head was in the mind-set of trying to help, and to bring as many people home as possible. I definitely cried for a long time, but I don't recall for the first month or two really focusing on the reasons for the attack. I had the mind-set at the site of *If we can just find somebody or something to have a little closure for one family every day, then it's a good day.*

When I started to think about the reasons behind it all, I felt a lot of hatred. Some people turn the hatred into a positive, and for others it remains a negative. I don't think I had hatred in a good way, unfortunately. But how can you blame someone for having that kind of hatred after something like 9/11? You can't.

Maybe one of the reasons why I get so angry is that we haven't come up with a solution to the issues. To me most of those issues stem from religion. And I don't really know if there is a solution. It doesn't make any sense to me that because you believe in a different God you have so much hatred for us. And because of your beliefs you kill thousands and thousands of innocent people. I have major issues with religion in general, because in my opinion, it's the reason for the majority of everything bad going on in this world. And it just makes no sense.

Growing up, we went to church every Sunday, and I was an altar boy. I went to Catholic school. I never minded going to mass then. But now it's different to me, very different.

Where was God on 9/11?

How do you let that happen? I know that it might not be the proper way to think, but how do you let something like 9/11 happen? If people pray and say it has meaning and consequence, and that everything will work out. . . . Well, it didn't work out on 9/11. So why? Why didn't it work out that day?

One morning, at around 3:00, I was on the pile with my father, just the two of us, and a priest came over with some woman pastor. He started talking to us, and you could tell right off the bat that he had a good frame of mind. He wanted to be positive. He basically was saying that we had to work with Muslims to end terrorism, and when were we going to do something about this?

I turned to him and said, "Father, no disrespect, but please go and tell all those Muslims, every last one of them, women, children, that I don't give a shit."

He looked at me then, and right in front of the woman he said, "Fucking right."

I was not shocked. Look, enough is enough. We need to do something about this, the Muslims and the murder that grows out of their thinking. There are lots of religious fights in history—the Catholics and Protestants in Ireland, and the Jews and Arabs in Palestine—but you don't see the Catholics and the Jews running around the world from New York to Spain to England to India killing people wholesale.

This priest meant it. So I said to myself, *People can think outside of the box a little bit.* He had feelings, and he was not going to patronize me and try to talk me in circles around the issues. But that poor woman pastor's face—she was shocked.

We can't forget about 9/11. . . . But we're getting complacent. All these tragic stories, and everyone's crying so they could try and feel what we've gone through—it's all going by the wayside. We're changing as a country. All of a sudden we want to back down the road of our history, to not be the tough guy we used to be. We were tough but fair. Americans were a decent people, but you did not want to mess with us. And now, for example, Iran has nuclear energy. If that is not a sign of America's weakness, I don't know what is.

We have to be careful about the Muslims. We don't want them teaching hate and separatism in their mosque schools. We have to stop homegrown Muslim terrorists. It's a shame for all the Muslims out there who are good-natured, hardworking people who mean no harm. But they brought it upon themselves. They're docile, afraid of their own religion and coreligionists. Where is their movement to stop terrorism, or to see women with equality, or to renounce jihad or Sharia law? The polls show that fully half of the people in the United States have unfavorable feelings toward Muslims. Why?

For me you're the enemy; I can't separate you. I don't know who's good and who's bad. Again, that might not be the right way of thinking, but how do I know? You can't tell if your cab driver hates you. So how do you categorize if your cab driver is in a terrorist group? You can't blame me or anyone else who experienced this murder in his family for thinking that way. You might say it's wrong, but if you were in my shoes, you'd do the same thing. I'm not saying it's right, but I think it is human nature to [want to] make people accountable—a brother I loved was killed by their thinking.

I am definitely not the same person I was before 9/11. I grew up a lot faster than I wanted to. I think that innocence was taken away from a lot of people. The things we saw, the things we did down there on those piles, the body parts, the carnage—you never imagined ever doing or seeing. It changed all of us. It was unimaginable. You couldn't in your worst nightmare realize what we did. And we were expected to get up every day knowing that we just had to keep on going as if it were just the next day. Well, it wasn't that easy.

And so religion has become a very big issue for me, especially since 9/11. Maybe it's also because when a firefighter goes about the job, he makes no such judgment. When someone calls for help it doesn't matter if he is black, white, Muslim, Jew, atheist, Spanish, Italian, Irish—we come and help. You're not given the right to judge who this person is.

All it really does is get me aggravated. You can sit around the kitchen table at the firehouse and talk about this all day long and get aggravated. But is there anything we can do to change it? Probably not, and so I try not to get myself too aggravated. I just try to help others, and do my best to raise my family, and that's it.

During the first three or four years after 9/11, I was not in a good place. I was pissed off at everybody. I really didn't care about anybody but myself, and if you didn't like it, tough. And it took a few years for me to start realizing that that's not what it was all about: *It's not about you, you can't keep doing this. You need to start growing up a little bit.*

People are going to move on in one way or another. But you go through different periods. As a family, I think we've done pretty well. Like any family, especially 9/11 families, we have our good and our bad, our ups and our downs. You do hear some real horror stories about families that have just been completely torn apart, or drifted apart, or don't talk to each other. So we're pretty blessed. The whole family is pretty tight. My sister had two kids, so that brought more closeness into the family, and she named her first son Jonathan. My sisters and I and the kids all see each other, and my mom babysits all the time. So in the last couple of years, I think I've been getting better.

When we're at the firehouse we can sit at that kitchen table and talk for hours. And we talk about religion, and someone says, "Well, who do you pray to?" And I tell them I pray to my family and friends. That's my religion. My family and friends. I pray to my brother. My uncle, my grandparents. My friends, my godfather. Those are the people I pray to and ask to watch over me. If I can hold them tight and treat them right, then I think at the end of everything I'm going to be on the right side of the street.

Sometimes it's tough being the Ielpi kid. I will never be able to shine my dad's shoes—it's just never going to happen. I do my best to carry the name, but I am who I am, and I hope that one day I won't be just the Ielpi kid, but Brendan Ielpi. Even though it's not easy, it is very satisfying that people respect you just because of your father's name. I had a lieutenant not too long ago say to me, "You're the Ielpi kid, right?" And then he congratulated me. I thought, *Are you kidding me? Get out of here.* And he shook my hand. I will carry on the Ielpi tradition as best I can. I definitely won't let my father down, and more important, I won't let my brother, Jonathan, down. That's for sure.

For me the memory of my brother is with me every time I go to work, every time I get on that rig. I have a few hundred buttons with a picture of my brother on them, and I always have one on my helmet, and I've gone through a few, but he's always there. And after every fire I clean him off, just wash the button real quick. He loved our job more than anything; it's all he ever wanted to do since he was a little kid.

People joke with me and say, "You know he's always going to watch over you when you're in the fire." Watch over me? He's right next to me. Jon wants to be going down the hallway with me, not watching over me. I caught myself staring at the button with his picture on the way to a fire the other day, and I was just talking to him in my head. That's the best way that I can remember him. I'm the only Ielpi left in the Fire Department. There are big shoes to fill here. I try to carry on the name and the tradition in a good manner, because it's pretty obvious that the bar's set pretty high.

Jim Smith

Jim Smith is now a retired NYPD police officer, but on the morning of 9/11 he was an instructor of law at the police academy. His wife, Moira, was a patrol officer assigned to the Thirteenth Precinct on Twenty-first Street, around the corner from the police academy, and she responded to the World Trade Center. Moira helped one person out of the South Tower to safety and had returned to help others in the evacuation when the building fell.

It's funny, but one of those things that's always indelible is when I first met Moira. I finished work one day and went to a place where I used to hang out, a bar on Barrow Street that a friend of mine owned. Cops would go there off duty. When I walked in, Moira was already there—the blond hair, the big smile, laughing, having a good time at a table with some other people. We were both transit cops at the time, and she had come into District 4 while I was out with a knee injury, so I had never met her at work. It was my first day back after four or five months out on sick leave. I walked over to the table to say hello to my friends. I was wearing a Yankees hat, and she looked up and grabbed it off my head and threw it across the bar—she was a Mets fan. And that was it. We were friends from that moment on.

In the beginning we worked a lot together, including the subway crash in 1991. I was off duty and waiting on the Fourteenth Street Station subway platform for a train home. There was a lot of work going on, jackhammering and that sort of thing, so I didn't even hear the train crash but just felt how loud it was. All of a sudden I saw Moira running, in uniform, and I chased after her. She had thought it was an explosion—two of my friends were actually on the train, transit cops who were working—and had put it out over the radio as an explosion, not realizing that the train at Union Square had crashed. We spent twelve, eighteen hours pulling people out of the wreckage there. The department gave Moira a medal for that work.

As a police officer, there was no backing off for Moira. She liked to have fun at work and wasn't always by the book. She was a regular cop like everybody else, but when it came time to do the job, she was there. A lot of friends of mine are great people, but when it came to being cops, they didn't always do the right thing. Moira always did the right thing, whatever the inconvenience or the danger.

We had a sort of Brooklyn wedding, all family and cops, and were living in Bay Ridge at the time. Unfortunately, Police Department policy was to leave it up to the commanding officer to decide whether a husband and wife could work together. There was a captain, now a chief, who told us one of us had to leave, even though we worked different units and hours—she was in street narcotics at the time, and I was doing anticrime. I'm still mad at that guy. He actually wanted Moira to go, but I got an opportunity to teach at the police academy, and I had always wanted to teach law. So I said I would leave, and a couple of weeks later I was in the academy. We were still in the building, so it was convenient, and we often went to work together.

I didn't have much background to be a cop. My older brother, John, had always wanted to be one, but I hadn't given it that much thought—I guess I wanted to be a lawyer. I went to college, and I played rugby, so getting my degree took a little longer than it should have—the broken bones, the partying. In my senior year, however, they were administering the PD test, and because I was going to school in Buffalo, my mother said, "If you take the test, I'll pay for the airfare."

I took the test on December 15, 1984, and only a month later they started calling. Back then fifty thousand people were taking the test, and the department was putting together huge classes because they were fighting the battle of the times. The economy wasn't that great, crime was rampant, crack was everywhere. It was crazy, and we were losing two thousand people a year.

On September 11, 2001, I was working the four-to-twelve tour, and Moira was doing community policing, which she figured gave her more flexibility with the baby, Patricia, who was two years old at the time. We used to do the switch-off to watch the baby, and sometimes even bring her to work and pass her off there, when I was at the academy.

That day she had to be in by 5:30 A.M., as some planned demonstration was going to be held in the Thirteenth Precinct, and she had to cover it. As she left the house she gave me a little kiss on the forehead and walked out the door while I was still in bed.

I got up with Patricia early in the morning, and we were downstairs watching *Winnie the Pooh* or something on a DVD. I didn't have the TV on so didn't have any idea what was going on. The phone rang upstairs, but by the time I picked up Patricia and got there, it stopped. Then a couple of seconds later it rang again, and it was my sister telling me that Moira had just tried to call me, and that she's down at the World Trade Center. And I said, "So?" She asked, "Aren't you watching?" I put on the TV then and saw what was happening.

I said to my sister, "Okay, they are probably going to need me, so I'm going to bring the baby over, and I'm going to go into work early." I was sure they would be calling people in. The first tower collapsed while I was getting ready, and it was then that I panicked. I raced to my sister's house—I think Patricia was in just her diaper—threw the baby to her, and drove in at ninety.

It was a mad scene trying to get onto the Long Island Expressway and into Manhattan. Traffic was closed, and you could see who the cops and the firemen were, trying to race in, beeping their horns and finally getting people to move over. I must have hit twenty cars and the rail a few times, but as I was getting over the ramp toward the Midtown Tunnel, I saw the second tower go down. And God—at this point it was terror.

I went directly to the Thirteenth Precinct, and as I walked in I saw a friend of mine was the desk officer. I said, "Joey, where's Moira?" And he said, "She's okay, we heard from her. Everything's okay." So I said, "All right," and I relaxed. A guy I trusted told me it was okay, so I went in, got dressed, and let them know I was here. They gave me twenty recruits, the biggest guys, and sent me to Bellevue Hospital. I figured we'd be moving bodies, and maybe help at the morgue, which is just next to Bellevue.

The precinct had set up a command post in the hospital, assuming they were going to be overloaded, which never came to pass. Nobody came in. There were some bomb threats, and we had to secure. My sister would call me and say, I haven't heard from Moira yet. I told her they told me Moira's okay, and that the cell phone antennas might be down. And then I'd call the precinct, and they'd say, Someone saw her over here or heard her on the radio over there, and I was okay. But this went on all day. At midnight we were finally relieved at the hospital, and by now I must have called ten times over to the precinct, and my sister had called me a dozen times. I went back to the precinct house and asked, "Do you know what Moira's doing?" And they said, "She's down at the pier." I figured she was going to stay a full tour, so I volunteered for another tour and took a bunch of rookies down to the perimeter at Fourteenth Street, below which everything was blocked off. State troopers were there, and soldiers, so we had some assistance. I made a couple of trips down to the site to deliver supplies, water, masks, and stuff to the cops down there, and then I saw the devastation. It was mind-numbing—completely numbing. At about three in the morning the Thirteenth Precinct car came up to me, and I thought I could see Moira sitting in the backseat. So I figure, *Good, Moira's back.* But it turns out it was Mary Young, a sergeant and a friend of mine from college who became good friends with Moira, and who was very similarly built. She came up to me and asked, "Do you know where Moira is?" I said, "You guys have been telling me all day that you knew where she is, and now you're telling me that you don't know where she is?" For all intents and purposes, that moment was the last time I was working for NYPD. I went back to the precinct, where I met one of the guys that I had trained as a rookie. He was now a sergeant, and he was just about to leave, in civilian clothes. He said, "What's going on?" and when I told him they couldn't find Moira, he got dressed again, and we took one of the cars and headed down Broadway. I found out then that Moira had driven the van, and knowing her, I knew she would have taken Broadway to get downtown.

We found the van, got in, and found her hat and memo book. And then I start finding other hats and memo books. I said, "How many cops are missing? And how many of these guys are unaccounted for?" We gathered up whatever we could there, and then we just started looking. For the next three to four days it was nonstop: hospitals; walking around the site; checking who was doing what. Who had seen who, and just trying to figure out where she was. The next six or seven days was all talking to people, trying to find out where she was and where she had last been seen. From the beginning I was hoping that she was over in some hospital in New Jersey with a concussion but okay. But it became clear a day or two later that nobody . . . Everybody who had gotten out was out. Anybody else . . . There wasn't even anything to pick up. The rubble was dust. The first photograph I saw was of a bloodied woman in a wheelchair, with EMS [the Fire Department's Emergency Medical Services] all around her. But behind her, in the background, was Moira's butt, and as soon as I looked at it I said, "That's Moira." I could tell from the bottle of water in her back pocket, and from the gun—she was one of the few people who still had an old .38. Once we saw that picture of her at the triage area, we had something to go on. We called up a number of the [NYPD] Emergency Service Unit trucks, as we had the truck numbers, and whatever else we got from that picture, to find out who had been where and what had happened to them. We tried to find out what happened to that woman in the wheelchair, to ask if she had seen Moira, and if they had any contact. And then the picture came out in the *Daily News* of her helping a guy from Aon out of the building. His name was Nicholls, and they didn't even have her name in that photo. So we had to jump all over the *Daily News* to try to find out who had taken the picture, and what were the circumstances. Basically, I guess, she had led him out and was photographed at the triage area. And then she went back in. A gentleman who at that time had been coming down the escalators later got in touch with me. He had spoken with her. It had to be early on, because she was directing people out with a flashlight, and he remembered her. He looked in her eyes, and she was like, Keep moving, keep moving, getting them out of the building. So I guess, from that point, the more seriously injured people started coming down, and that's when she took Mr. Nicholls out. And then she went back in, and what we heard was that there was a woman having an asthma attack on the third floor who couldn't go any farther. Moira went up to help take her down. That was the last information we had from the different sources.

And even that took months to find that much out. It was all very chaotic. The first week, when I was down there, it seemed like I couldn't find anybody in charge. Nobody. It didn't seem like anybody was doing anything. The frustration was deep. It penetrated deep.

Moira did not consider herself as special. Medals, for instance, were totally meaningless to her. She got one medal for the train wreck. Somebody had to write her up, as she wouldn't even put herself in for a medal. That was the kind of person she was. She wasn't doing it for medals; she did it because it was her job. She was without a doubt the kind of person who was there because she wanted to be a cop. She had always wanted to be a cop. She wanted to do the right thing. I did it because I had college bills to pay, and I needed a job, and this one was staring me in the face. I eventually came to love the job, but I didn't take it for the altruistic reasons that Moira did. For Moira it was just a simple matter of doing what you had to do. What you were trained to do.

After Moira was lost there was a rush of hungry media. The Police Department didn't give out my information but filtered requests; if they thought something was legitimate, they let me know someone wanted to talk to me. But mostly I refused. Joe Dunne, the first deputy commissioner, spent a lot of time with those of us who had 9/11 Police Department losses. Bernie Kerik, the police commissioner, never met with me. The first time I actually met him was at President [George W.] Bush's second inauguration. I had my daughter with me, and I wanted to go up to him and say, "Hi, I'm Jim Smith, and this is Patricia"—a deliberate introduction. Because every time we were supposed to meet with him after 9/11, while we were still looking for the bodies of our family, he blew us off. He'd be doing something else. He'd be on *Oprah* or a book tour somewhere, or changing this or doing that. He never even came over to say he was sorry but would send Joe Dunne, so Dunne was the guy who sat there and consoled twenty-three families.

Dunne is a good man, and I have a lot of respect for him. But his time was split, and I couldn't spend a lot of time with him. But we had John McArdle, the ESU lieutenant who was basically in charge of the site. I met with John daily at Stuyvesant High School, where he had set up an information post for us, and where they were doing the mapping. We'd ask, What are we doing? Where are we at this point? The guy was a straight shooter and didn't pull any punches.

We had two services for Moira, the first on her birthday, February 14. I had talked to McArdle, who told me that by this point they should be done—the whole area would have been excavated, and they'd either have found her or they wouldn't. I then made arrangements. If we hadn't found Moira by the time we had a ceremony scheduled, I wanted it to be big, for her family, and so I arranged to get Saint Patrick's Cathedral. The cardinal said the mass. The governor and mayor were there, and President Bush sent a letter. It was huge. About ten thousand cops showed up, a great tribute. I think we had four busloads of family that the PD shuffled around. I can't say enough about how good the NYPD people were.

After the memorial service, I drove down to Key West, where I had rented a house, and brought Moira's sister and my niece. My father came down, just to take a break from everything.

And then, early on the morning of March 22, I got a phone call from my friend Kevin, a guy I worked with in the Thirteenth Precinct. He told me they had found Moira.

The department brought my uncle down to the site. He was a detective fifty years ago, and about eighty-six, and they all helped take her out. They drove by the Thirteenth Precinct, which had a formation outside that saluted, and then took her to the morgue. That day we flew back, and I went down and met the officers who had recovered her and thanked them. She was found with a couple of firemen and a Port Authority officer, and they think it's possible they were all together in the lobby. This time we just had a funeral service at our local church. We had a month to plan it, and people came from all over the world.

It's a double-edged sword in a lot of ways. I knew early on that Moira was dead, and that there wasn't going to be a miracle. I don't think her family actually believed it until they found her body. A lot of them kept thinking she was going to turn up somewhere with amnesia, or whatever crazy theory they could hang their hat on. I remember calling my cousin, telling her, "We found Moira." And she said, "So, she really is dead." And this was six months later.

But it is nice to have her home. It was good to find her, to know she wasn't lying out in some field blown apart, or in little bits scattered all over Lower Manhattan. So many other family members didn't have that, and still don't have that. So that was important, that finality. There is no miracle. There are no mistakes.

The Police Department took care of me, treated me like a father would treat a son; 3:00 A.M. on September 12 was the last time I worked. I took a year's leave of absence, and the next five years they kept me at the academy, where I was assigned to employee relations.

I didn't get married for the first time until I was thirty-eight—I wasn't the commitment type. Since I have retired I remarried, and have a two-and-a-half-year-old son, with another one due. We are living in East Hampton. It was easier the second time, but I had to have been hard to get along with.

I was totally distracted, and for a long time I couldn't even read a book, and I was used to reading two or three books a week. That lasted about four years, and even now I pick up a lot of books, thinking, *Oh, this looks good,* and some of them I never open. I don't know if it's the inability to concentrate or a lack of desire.

I get a million offers to do things, and try to pick and choose what I think is going to be appropriate, to judge the balance between banging my daughter over the head with all this 9/11-related material and keeping Moira's name, image, and heroics relevant. I always ask, Am I doing the right thing or am I not doing the right thing? I try to play it how I feel. If I think I'm doing too much, I back off, and if I don't think I'm doing enough, I consider more. Also, I feel that no one is asking her sister, aunts, uncles, or cousins to do anything. They ask me, and so I do it for them too. I represent Moira for all of us. Not just for me and Patricia.

When Pope Benedict came, I got to meet him at Ground Zero. Then Patricia was given an award after the fifth anniversary, and her picture was in every paper around the world. When it was picked up in London, the British named her a children's champion. We were invited to London, and we went to 10 Downing Street and met the prime minister and his wife, who was actually on the charity that gives out the awards. Another time, Patricia met [Secretary of State] Colin Powell, and that's the kind of thing that I thought was appropriate for her: to travel and meet people, so somewhere down the line she can look back and say, This is what I've done. Because of her mother, these are some of the things that we've been able to do. This year we've been invited down to Pasadena for the Rose Bowl, where they are doing a 9/11 memorial float. There won't be a lot of chances to be invited to the Rose Bowl.

In thinking about 9/11 and Moira's death, I don't think I ever got to the rage stage. I was angry about a lot of things, but I knew I couldn't make it be about me. It couldn't be *Poor me.* It couldn't be *I'm a victim of this tragedy.* Rather than mourning Moira, I prefer to celebrate her. To celebrate who she was and what she did rather than commiserate about how she died. A tragedy would have been if she had been coming home from work at 4:00 in the morning and got hit by a drunk driver. The way she charged into those buildings time and again to get people out—that wasn't a tragedy. That was heroism, the definition of what it is to be a hero. I focused on that.

I never saw Moira as a victim—nobody did anything to her. She was where she wanted to be at the time she had to be there, and she did what she had to do. That doesn't mean these people weren't murdering savages, but she wasn't a victim. That poor guy having a cup of coffee on the ninety-second floor who got hit by an airplane was a victim.

Do I want to see these terrorists who planned these things go to their deaths too? Absolutely. Am I infuriated at Barack Obama, the president of the United States, and at Eric Holder, the attorney general? Absolutely. Because justice delayed is justice denied. I never understood the truth in that expression until now. Ten years have passed, and we haven't even begun the trials at Gitmo.

Family members started going down to Gitmo for the hearings. I haven't gotten my chance to go down there yet. They started hearings, and then all of a sudden, Obama wins the election, and the hearings are put on hold. Then they start talking about trying them like they are some sort of liquor store holdup men, up in New York City. They didn't drag Tojo to criminal court in Hawaii for the bombing of Pearl Harbor. Our president Obama wants to reduce the gravity of it, what they did on 9/11 and in other terrorist activities.

I have a big problem with discussions of Islam being a peaceful religion with just a couple of crazies in it. That's like saying Germany just had a few Nazis and everybody else was okay. But they still managed to kill a lot of people. Maybe not everybody in the Soviet Union was with the Communists, but they killed forty, fifty million people before it was said and done. And so while maybe not all of Islam is complicit, they allowed a lot of people to be killed without a huge Islamic cry of murder. And if these killers are unchecked, a lot more will die. We have to demand that Muslims stand up and say, This is not us, this is not our religion. The whole idea that we have to be politically correct when we're talking about some of these issues is so frustrating.

I'm constantly arguing with my friends—all good-natured arguments about politics. Why are police officers and military people more likely to be more conservative than the average American? I think it has to do with the fact that they see so much more, on a day-to-day basis, of the horror and the misery of people—people at their worst. We see the best people at their worst. You come to realize that not everything can be handled by throwing money at it, or giving people things for free. Sometimes tough love has to work, in foreign affairs too. Soft voice, big stick.

We need leaders with character that will enable them to be heroes. Is Eli Manning a hero because he took the Giants to a Super Bowl? I love the Giants, I love Eli Manning. I don't think he's a hero. He's a good quarterback, but we throw that "hero" term around, and it dilutes what a hero is. The Chilean miners who were trapped are lucky to be alive, and they certainly had the fortitude to withstand the sixty-seven days they were down in the mine. But what choice did they have? They didn't have much other choice but to try to survive. Well, we all survive. It's what we do every day. But every day cops go out there, and people like Moira, every day she went out there to do the same job, and whether it was the towers or the Fulton Street fire bombing or the tunnel or the Fourteenth Street crash, if Moira was there, she did what she had to do.

Moira was a woman who was one of the most fun people to be around. She partied with the best of them when she had the opportunity, but she was a person of character and morality who constantly put herself second to the good of others. If everyone walked around with that attitude, what a different place this world would be—if everyone thought about doing the right thing at the right time, not worrying about the consequences to the self. Moira was a person who had a husband and a child at home, her own family life, but she put it behind her to do what she knew to be the right thing. And that's what I try to tell Patricia. She's asked me, "Well, why did Mom do that?" I want her to know it was her, who she was, it was in her character. She was a better person than most of the people you're ever going to meet. Why? Because she didn't worry about herself. She did what was required of her. She had a sense of honor and loyalty.

She was just thirty-eight. No one is going to know that she had a young child. No one is even going to put together that she had a life, and that she was content and happy and loved living. It just doesn't say that on a plaque, and it's not going to say that on the memorial wall. It isn't going to say that she was on Sixteenth Street and Third Avenue when the [first] plane hit, and she went there with all speed to help people. The committee that was making the decisions about the memorial worked so hard to not have any sort of special recognition. They wanted to be socialist, that everybody was equal. But I don't believe that. Like I said, my heart goes out to the man who was sitting in his World Trade Center office having a cup of coffee, you know, for his family, but his death and Moira's death are two different things, and I think that should always be recognized. Moira was not just courageous. She was a hero.

Dan D'Allara

Dan D'Allara is the twin brother of John, who was an Emergency Service Unit (ESU) detective. John was assigned to Truck 2 and his first call that fateful morning was an order to respond to the World Trade Center.

In remembering my brother John, every question I am asked about his life begets another question. I have often asked myself, *Why did John do this or that?* The why is always answered for me by the first line of the medal the New York City Police Department gave to our family, the NYPD Medal of Honor, which reads: IN RECOGNITION OF AN INDIVIDUAL ACT OF EXTRAORDINARY BRAVERY PERFORMED IN THE LINE OF DUTY AT IMMINENT PERSONAL DANGER TO LIFE AND SAFETY. It is the "extraordinary bravery" that explains him.

John, my fraternal twin, was five minutes older. We were born in New York Hospital and grew up in the Bronx, on Allerton Avenue. We attended St. Lucy's School in the Bronx and Christopher Columbus High School on Pelham Parkway. We're twin brothers but exactly the opposite: John was more driven academically, I was more driven to get out in the world, play my guitar with different bands. John was at Lehman College and studied phys ed. He had a minor in biology. He also did some work at a Colorado university. He became a teacher, though he always wanted to be a cop. He had taken a few police exams and finally got called by the NYPD.

I was in the city working at a quarter to nine on September 11, 2001, in the decorator building on Fifty-ninth Street. Someone said a plane hit the World Trade Center. The first thing I did was pick the telephone up and call Truck 2; no answer. I knew they had already left quarters because my mother was listening to the police radio and she heard them leave. We're a police family; the day after the first Trade Center bombing, in 1993, I bought a police radio and have it going all the time. It's the best source of real-time information you can get. My brother likened my mother listening to it to the old tenement days when people would peek through the blinds. This radio was a big electronic window, and it wasn't unusual for me to call my mother and say, You got your ears on, Mom? What's going on here? What's going on there?

At that minute we became ordinary people caught up in extraordinary circumstances. Though I'm a fraternal twin, my twin experience on the morning of September 11 gave me such a strong feeling that John was there. Maybe it sounds too dramatic, but that really happened. I just knew that my brother John was down there. But I didn't know what was going on, what exactly he was doing. I called my wife, who was down on Forty-second Street and who was concerned about her brother-in-law, who was working down on Wall Street. I called Truck 2; John wasn't there. I called my sister-in-law, Carol, and asked, Where's John? At work, she told me. We were concerned about everybody downtown, as even uptown we could see the smoke.

I went into the Barney's store on Fifty-ninth Street and sat down just as the radio antenna of the North Tower was collapsing. I jumped out of my chair with a burst of anxiety. *Holy shit—John. Holy shit, holy shit.* I went back to my office and was confronted by my manager, who asked, "Where are you going?" I said, "My brother just got killed, I got to get out of here." And he says, Go back to your desk—you don't know that for certain.

I walked around a little, and then remembered a conversation we had had at my house. My brother had trained in antiterrorism [response]. He had just been in the subway, doing a test with a remote-controlled robot. Because of the sarin gas attack in Tokyo, the Police Department was looking at ways to disarm dangerous devices. John had said to me, "If anything happens in the city, get Angela, and get out as soon as you can, as fast as you can. They are going to shut it down." So I ran down to Forty-second Street, where my wife, Angela, works, and on the way there found myself on Lexington Avenue looking up at the Citicorp building. They then thought there was another plane inbound, and I said to myself, *Oh, my God. I've got to get away from this building.* Madison Avenue looked like a Godzilla movie: Traffic was jammed, as everybody was coming uptown. I got Angela, but she couldn't run for her life in heels, so we stopped to buy sneakers. My plan was to get to the FDR Drive, walk up the drive over the Willis Avenue Bridge, and get a gypsy cab to our home on City Island.

While all this was going on downtown, I saw people uptown doing their nails, like life was normal. A cab stopped in front of a building at Seventy-ninth Street, and a well-dressed woman got out, saying, "It's terrible, it's terrible." I asked if the cab driver would take us to City Island. "Yes, yes," he said, with an Indian accent. He was hysterical, and said he had been downtown, and the woman had begged him while people were trying to get in the cab. On the Bruckner Expressway I looked over my shoulder and could see the smoke. This cab driver was saying, "Who would do such a thing? I have only been driving a cab for three days here in New York. This is terrible. This is terrible."

We reached the City Island circle, where there's a turnoff to the NYPD firing range. The circle was filled with cars; the police had mobilized everybody, a level-five mobilization. The cab driver turned into the range instead of turning into City Island, and there I saw two cops with machine guns—AK-14s, just like my brother's. They pointed the weapons right into the windshield of the cab. I jumped over my wife and screamed at the driver, "You made the wrong turn. They are gonna turn us into Swiss cheese!" We backed out, and after stopping at a store on City Island I gave the guy a hundred-dollar bill and told him, "There's a lot of bad people in this world. You're not one of them."

I called my mother, and she said, "We lost John"—mother's intuition.

I knew John would be right in the middle of it; what I didn't know was that at that exact moment, when I felt that big rush of anxiety in Barney's, he was being crushed to death in the North Tower. At eleven o'clock a policeman from Truck 2 by the name of Steve Alter called and said, "John's missing, and we're sending a car for you." And they came and got me, my wife, my mother, and my father to take us to police headquarters. My mother later told me she thought we were going to the morgue to identify his body.

During that day I had called Father Peter Colapietro, pastor of Holy Cross Church, the oldest building on Forty-second Street. Father Pete had been a friend of our family's, and he married Angela and me on City Island. I left a message telling him that I didn't know what was going on, and that John was missing—maybe gone. When I walked into 1 Police Plaza [NYPD headquarters] on that night, Father Pete was right there, walking the hallways with the Police Department families.

. . .

My personal experience with 9/11 comes on three levels: I'm a 9/11 family member, a New York City Police Department line-of-duty surviving family member, and one of the fifty-plus twins affected that day. In a matter of 102 minutes I got clobbered, and, looking back, I didn't realize it at the time, but each of those experiences are different—particularly being one of the New York City Police Department line-of-duty survivors. As such we are used to the tragedy of line-of-duty deaths, and we remember every one of them. At the Police Department that night, many of those affected families were materializing right in front of me.

They had cots set up for us, and that night my mother and father and I slept at police headquarters. I left the next morning and returned that afternoon. Carol, John's wife, came down, but his children were much too young—they really didn't come to a lot of things, because they were too young.

Not only did I lose my brother, but the neighbors behind us, the Rizza family, lost their son, Paul. The people next to us lost somebody. In my neighborhood in the Bronx, you couldn't go too far without seeing someone who was connected to a 9/11 death. I lost friends. My brother John lost twenty-two coworkers, fourteen ESU cops, with whom I had become friendly through his relationships. All the ESU cops know each other and have a special closeness. There are only three hundred of them in the whole Police Department, and they all receive the same training out at Floyd Bennett Field [in Brooklyn]. My brother was at the stage in his career where he was a training officer. He had been on Truck 2 for fourteen years, on a lot of high-profile jobs on the Upper West Side, and had been at it so long I knew the people he talked about—people who trained him and whom he trained. So after 9/11 I started to put the names together with the faces on the list. The average Trade Center first responder was a young person. My brother John was forty-seven years old, and we were lucky we had him for forty-seven years. For some of the other 9/11 family members, who lost someone who was twenty years old, it was a real tragedy. Our situation was no less tragic, but we're glad we had him for forty-seven years.

Every family has a hero, but when you have a cop or fireman in your family, that's your hero. Our families suffered a very steep loss on September 11. Police officers and firemen give a blank check to the city as regards what they will do in the line of service, but it should not be normal for them to lose their lives in the line of duty. The public perception may be that when you have a job like that you have to figure that you may die, but it's not supposed to happen that way. We had never been worried about my brother's safety; 9/11, as they say on the job, was all asses and elbows, and they did the best they could under horrendous circumstances. My brother is an American hero for what he did.

But there's also the story of what he left behind. My mother was from the World War II generation, and she looked at 9/11 like, well, a lot of boys didn't come home from the war. That was her way of accepting it. My sister-in-law has her own challenges as a 9/11 widow. I think the two boys are now doing as well as can be expected—children are remarkably resilient. They are in high school: John is about seventeen, Nicholas about thirteen.

I describe the hurt as a pyramid: At the top are the kids, and then the spouses, and then the parents. Underneath are the siblings. Each category has its own dynamic. In December my company began asking, When is this going to be over? I'm sorry—family first. Basically, the last ten years for me have involved looking after the welfare of my mother and father and filling the void for them that my brother left. They say when you lose your children you lose your past and your future. For me, I lost every link to my childhood. That was taken away from me by al Qaeda, and I remind some of the police families that if those radical Muslims wanted to destroy American families, they did a really good job of it.

Lee Hong, my brother's partner, was assigned to me as a family liaison. We were down in the pit one day about two months after the collapse, and, of course, all the ESU guys were there. Soon a whole group of filthy ESU cops came up to me, and one of them said, "You're John D'Allara's twin brother?" They couldn't even look me in the eye, they were so sad. To relieve them I said, "I'm about two months older than him about now." They all looked at me, smiled, and said, "You've got your brother's sense of humor." Humor does mask a lot of the tragedy.

John had a great sense of humor, and I was thinking about this especially when Osama bin Ladin was killed by our brave military. My feeling was that I have an underwhelming sense of satisfaction, because the damage to my family has already been done, and maybe I'll read the book in twenty years from now. But you know what John would have said? He would have said something along the lines of Why would you bury him at sea when the Space Shuttle was all gassed up and ready to go?

Later, when I went down to Ground Zero, I was presented with a placement map of where John was. The Police Department knew where their people were, and NYPD Chief Esposito took me personally to show me why they couldn't get to him. Commissioner Joe Dunne and Chief Esposito—I cannot say enough wonderful things about the brass of the New York City Police Department and the way they handled us after 9/11, and subsequently to this day. When I talked to Joe Dunne it was like he was one of my family. These people have helped me through the worst times of my life—Joe Dunne, George Grasso, Father Romano. I've been told that thirty police officers have lost their lives because of post-9/11 illness. I can't imagine what the Fire Department is going through. I don't know how the other families got through it, those who didn't have near the support that we had. Because they often lose people in the line of duty, the Police Department and Fire Department have a system of support in place.

John was found on April 11, 2002, exactly seven months after the attack. I knew at that point that if we were going to make a recovery, it was going to be very soon. The night before, I saw on TV news a grappler [similar to a backhoe] working down at Ground Zero, and I remember yelling at the TV set, "Get that grappler off my brother." The next day I got a call from the Police Department to tell me that they were sending a car for me. I didn't ask for permission to leave work, as I didn't want to get into an argument with my boss. At Ground Zero I sat in the NYPD holding area, as they had asked us not to come down into the pit. There was a Pelco camera [a well-known high-resolution security camera] right there, so I was able to see exactly what they were doing. They made an identification from John's gun. As I sat there waiting with Father Romano, God bless him, he was telling me, "You know, they say that heaven is where you can drink all the wine you want and never get drunk, and eat all the spaghetti you want and never get fat," and he said that there was something really comforting about that. I laughed. Is that what heaven's like? Is that where John is? It was great.

They finally called us down to the pit, but we recovered very little. One of the things that my brother always told me was that you didn't have to lift the sheet up and look underneath: Spare yourself that. Maybe in the future I will go to the medical examiner's to see the pictures, but I can't now. We found just a little bit of a leg and a jawbone—there was no whole body—and I was given the flag they covered him with when they made the recovery. My family was honored because Police Commissioner Ray Kelly [see page 16] came down to help carry John out. It was very solemn. There is a story about a family member who went down to identify remains and was given a little box. He left the medical examiner's with a bag that he sat on his lap as he drove to the funeral home. I can understand that kind of sadness.

It wasn't until May 15, 2002, that we were told they had made a positive identification from the mitochondrial DNA, the original DNA cell from my mother. They took many DNA markers [from the family] but they needed something to compare them to. The first week we were all told to give samples to the Police Department—hair and toothbrushes of the victims to get the DNA matches. But we also had the gun found alongside the remains, with a serial number that made it John's.

John was at the plaza level. What happened? As near as it can be reconstructed, John was looking for a way out of the building, out of Tower 1. He and another man found a door, and they were able to leave. John then ran across the plaza and went under the overhang of one of the lower buildings, number 5. What I realize is that John was looking up and saw smoke and debris coming out, so he ran across the plaza, waving people coming out of Tower 1 toward him, including a police officer named Jimmy Hall, a Port Authority sergeant. At the memorial at St. Aidan's, Jimmy Hall came up to me and said, "Mr. D'Allara, I just want you to know I can honestly say that if it weren't for your brother, I don't think I'd be standing here talking to you." At 10:28, when that building came down, it came right down on John. The Police Department reports that there were four ESU officers killed on the street. Joe Esposito, the chief of the NYPD, must be given credit for giving an order holding everybody back, so the number of police killed was held to twenty-three: fourteen ESU cops and nine regular white-shield police officers. I have to believe the police saved a lot of lives—just look at what Moira Smith did.

We had held a memorial service on November 10 of 2001, and then had a funeral when we found his remains. Five thousand people showed up at the memorial, which was held at St. Aidan's in Pearl River. About three thousand people came to the funeral at St. Lucy's, so it was quite a turnout and quite a send-off for John, and I am very proud of the people who came to both. Law enforcement is a true fraternity in this country, and I met police officers from so many states. Contingents from the Boston Police Department and the California Highway Patrol came, and I got the biggest kick out of reading that the Niagara Falls Police Department came—it never occurred to me that Niagara Falls *had* a police department.

You know, you can never heal a broken heart, but you can learn to live your life around it. I want to memorialize my brother John as a hero. I don't know how to run a golf outing or start a foundation, so I did what I could— the street naming, for instance. I worked hard for that. So for the last ten years I tried to memorialize my brother's life: supporting the 9/11 families and giving effort to better the city of New York, to make it safer. Maybe God put me here on earth for a reason. I've done really everything that I possibly can, and it's all in an effort to heal and get to the next step. I think "closure" is a terrible word to use. Closure is like when your pet canary dies, and you know you'll get another canary. When you lose a family member there's never closure. There's a big something that you learn to live with—the 9/11 monkey on your back, which I don't like having. I hate 9/11; it just confuses things. I don't know that people look at you the same. If we don't stop to commemorate it, that day will be forgotten, but people like me, who live with it all the time, can never forget it. This is why it's important that I talk about it.

When you get knocked down, your first instinct is to try to stand up. I guess I've been trying to right the ship for ten years, but there's a lot of weight in that ship to right. I can honestly say, because of the recent loss of my parents, that my brother's loss is magnified even more. So now I tell my wife, Oh, when John and I were little kids, we used to do this. Or John and I planned this or that, or wore this or that. I've done things that felt right to me, and that's how I survived.

September 11 was a political wake-up call for me. I didn't vote for George Bush, but I had an experience with him that I will never, ever, ever forget, and that is the day that he came to New York and was standing on the fire truck with fireman Bob Beckwith. They assembled us and said that the president wanted to meet the Police Department families. We were led into a room in the Javits Center with seating for about three hundred people. George Bush came in with Governor Pataki and Mayor Giuliani and began walking around. I could not believe how personable he was. I witnessed history that day. I was standing there, and when Bush came up I said, "Mr. President, this is my sister-in-law Carol, this is a picture of my brother John—he was killed in the Trade Center, a New York City policeman." I asked him, "Would you sign the back of his picture, to John and Nicholas, his children?" As he was signing I said into his ear, Do what you got to do. This man turned to me and said, "Oh, I will." They talk about political promises being kept, and he kept his. And you know what? I took that as a personal promise to me.

The president had it right: He did not target Muslims, but extremist Muslims. I'm a New Yorker, and there are Muslims all over the place, and I've never had a bad experience with any of them. I don't believe in painting all Muslims with the same brush. Extremism is a worldwide problem, an ideological movement with extreme people hiding behind the Muslim religion. I've realized that these people are at war with us, and the building of a mosque down there [near Ground Zero] is just another front in that war. When I saw people in Muslim dress protesting on behalf of building the mosque, they were yelling at the 9/11 family members, calling them racist assholes. Those 9/11 family members, so wounded and injured, were being called by them *racist assholes*. I had to leave that demonstration there, because it was just very, very upsetting to me. I wish the American people could have seen what I saw down there at Ground Zero, the total destruction. I saw a woman cry so much, she was standing in a puddle of her own tears, crying over her lost daughter.

After 9/11, I heard a saying going around that a conservative is a liberal that has been mugged. I think I fit into that. My brother and I were twins, but we were exact opposites in politics. I was with the people on the East Side of Manhattan, and he was with blood and guts on the West Side. But he was right: He was a prudent American worrying about our safety. This is a war that's going to last a century, and I don't know how we're going to resolve it. Certainly in the world community, barriers have been broken down—for instance, those between blacks and whites, or between Catholics and Protestants—but this war will continue. It's very easy with the Internet and all the new communications to wage war against the United States in ways we never thought possible. We need strong laws, a sense of Americanism, to protect us from people using our laws against us.

·   ·   ·

John will live forever through memorials with his name on them. People will know. We have the story; we know what happened. I've done everything I possibly can to memorialize him.

We're such a great people, a wonderful, giving, understanding people, and we just have to protect our culture, our institutions, our way of life. They'll use our laws against us as they do in Europe. We're not like these other countries that endorse and cheer religious totalitarianism.

I don't know how we are progressing in America as a multicultural country. We should all want to be American. But we are broken down into factions of ethnicity, and everybody needs to be heard and represented. But we're American. America *should* mean a lot of different things to a lot of different people, but that meaning should be fundamentally American—free, fair, hardworking, and with allegiance to our flag and our law. My friend Mike, who runs the grocery that I go to, came here from Yemen. I see his kids now in the store; they're Muslim, and they're just trying to figure out who is going to win the next football pool. And what's more American than that? That's what America should be—with each generation they're more and more American.

Zack Fletcher

Zack Fletcher is a New York City firefighter, as was his twin brother, Andre. Both brothers played football for Brooklyn Tech High School, and also football and baseball for the FDNY teams, in addition to being volunteer firefighters on Long Island. Andre was killed on 9/11 while working with Rescue 5 in the North Tower.

My brother and I were actually fraternal twins, but probably only a handful of people would have thought so, given that we looked so much alike. We were born in Brooklyn in February of 1964—my mother didn't even realize that she was having twins, and when we came out, she named my brother Andre and my father named me Zackary, after my grandfather.

Mom is retired from the New York City Department of Social Services, where she was a social worker for about thirty-five years. She used to be in the field visiting foster kids, and then she moved up into dealing with the courts. My mother was proud of working for the city and had a sense of what was right and what was wrong. She was just trying to do whatever she could to help anybody out, any kids out. And she was always very proud of my brother and me. Mom gave us everything. She bought us everything we wanted that was within her means. We knew there were certain lines that we couldn't cross with our parents, and we did what we had to do to keep them happy. But also keep us happy. My mother was very instrumental in the way I am now. There was always a difference between Andre and me: I'm more like my mother, and Andre was in many respects more like my father.

Dad used to work for Prudential Securities down on Wall Street as manager for their mainframes. He was very proud of his job, and would always drum into our heads that if you want to get ahead in the world, you have to connect with the right people. We kind of blew that off— yeah, whatever, Dad. We listened to a lot of things he said, but we were more apt to listen to what Mom told us. Men from the Caribbean—West Indian people in general—have a sense that you have to have straight As in school. He used to put the belt to us and provide discipline. Dad retired some time ago, and unfortunately has dementia now. He used to smoke three packs a day, and that helps [bring on] dementia. He also used to drink a lot, and I would say to myself, *I never want to be a person who drinks and smokes as much as he does.* I can understand now why he did so, because of all the pressures that he had when he was raising us. Also, being a man of color back in those days, having to deal with the racism, was very, very tough. He stopped drinking only after 9/11. My mother tried to be patient, thinking that if she kept quiet it would go away. And I would say, Mom you're in denial. And you know, I would always be by her, and I would let her know, Don't worry if he gets physical with you, I'm right here.

But Dad had six ministrokes. They had to put a shunt in his head to relieve the pressure that was building up, and put a screen in his leg, so that no clots would come up to the heart. Very tough time. And dealing with him now is also tough, like another full-time job. The guys at the firehouse are always saying, Zack, if you need the day off or something like that, just give us a call and we'll cover your shift, no problem. They know it's tough too.

We grew up on Chauncey Street between Bushwick and Evergreen. In 1974 it was named the best block in the whole city—pretty good for an impoverished neighborhood. It was a beautiful block, almost like a little paradise within the jungle that surrounded us. It's like where I work now, my firehouse. They call it the eye of the storm, as it's in a nice part of Prospect Heights, but around us, everything is pretty run-down, with a busy fire load.

Mom and Dad both realized how hard it was out there, especially in the sixties and seventies, and they wanted the best for their children. So being that my parents were from Jamaica, they sacrificed to put us into private school. We went to Brooklyn Junior Academy—which is right around the corner from Engine 222—from kindergarten all the way up to eighth grade. We had to wear uniforms to school. When you're a kid, and you're at that age, you're very malleable. Often that's when you get formed into the type of individual that you will become. I remember the gangs, tough guys, and Andre and I wanted to be part of it, to be accepted. Back then, in the seventies, martial arts were big, thanks to many martial arts movies, and I wanted the excitement of joining a gang. One gang member, the leader, used to always come by and say to us, "You guys keep doing what you're doing." I think he was actually proud of Andre and me because he recognized *These guys are going somewhere. These guys are going to be somebody.* And he put the word out on the street: Nobody, nobody messes with these two. I asked to join, and he told me, "No, this is not for you. But if you ever need anything, just ask me." Of course we didn't realize the favor that this guy actually did for us. They were watching out for the Fletcher boys.

We excelled in our grades, and when we graduated, my brother went to Bronx High School of Science and I went to Brooklyn Technical High School. Our parents had also wanted us to learn music, so my brother and I took piano lessons at the Third Street Music School in Manhattan. As a result we had also been accepted at the High School for the Performing Arts and also the High School of Music and Art, very difficult schools to get into. I absolutely loved Brooklyn Tech though—great sports, and again I excelled in my grades. It was a huge school—something like seven thousand people—and it was intense; very, very rigorous; and competitive in academics and in sports. A lot of top people come from that school, and a survey showed 80 percent to 85 percent of its graduates are very successful. The trek for Andre was up to an hour and forty-five minutes each way on the train, so he figured, Why don't I just go to Brooklyn Tech? The fact that Bronx High School of Science no longer had a football team, and he wanted to play football, was another reason. He transferred in his junior year.

Andre and I both graduated with a Regents diploma in June of 1982 in a class of fifteen hundred. At around that time we left Brooklyn—my mother had gotten mugged for the third time, and she said, "That's it, I need to get out of here," and decided to move to Freeport, Long Island. We were used to the concrete jungle, and we moved to grass, prim suburbs, and the whole nine yards.

Although I got into American University in Washington, D.C., my parents didn't have the money to send me, and I didn't have a scholarship. So I had to pass on that. Andre and I went to New York Institute of Technology in Westbury, Long Island. My brother then went to community college in

Medford. I stayed for one year, paying for school myself and studying architecture, but then stopped going and started working. New York Institute
of Technology was very expensive, but I was making then more than enough
money to get student loans—you have to make a minimum amount of salary to get educational assistance. I decided to go to the State University of
New York at Westbury. I have ninety credits, and as soon as I get promoted
to lieutenant I will go to John Jay College of Criminal Justice to finish up
my degree. To be a fire marshal you need at least forty credits. For lieutenant you need at least sixty. To be a battalion chief you need a bachelor's
degree. The Fire Department will pay for these promotion credits with
grants. From Medford, Andre then went to SUNY Westbury and was in
the process of finishing up when the tragedy happened.

In 1987, when we were living in Freeport, we both became volunteer
firefighters, and were both gung ho about it. We just loved firefighting. We
got our EMT certifications. I got an AEMT [Advanced Emergency Medical
Technician] certification, which is one level below paramedic, and Andre
ended up getting the paramedic certification. We took the FDNY test together, and I got a 98.6 on the written part, but missed 100 on the physical
by three seconds. Andre got 100 on the physical, but he got 96 on the written, so when they averaged out the scores, his was three tenths of a point
higher than mine. So Andre was appointed to the job in January 1994, and
I got on in July in 1994—just six months apart.

We had no hooks, no "rabbis," to get us the choice assignments in the
busy companies. He went to Engine 297 for about three years, but in
the FDNY you can use your knowledge as your rabbi, and because Andre
was a paramedic and not just an EMT, he asked to go to the busiest EMS
engine in Brooklyn, 257. It is a big deal to be a paramedic, and the guys respected him because he knew his shit, pardon my language.

The law gives medical authority to whoever is the highest medically
trained personnel, and there were sometimes stubborn bosses, lieutenants,
or captains who knew better than to give orders to Andre. Andre knew
what he was talking about. There were times when bosses said, We are
going to do it this way, and Andre would say, No, we're not going to do it
this way. They would look at him like, Who the hell are you? Andre had no
problem telling a boss, No disrespect, Lieu or Cap, but this is my license
on the line. So just please do as I asked you to do. He would do it in a way
that didn't seem like he was arrogant. The lieutenant would be a little pissed,

but he'd do it Andre's way. And so Engine 257 won many medical EMS commendations because of Andre.

After that Andre wanted to get into a ladder company—he really wanted to get into Rescue. The one thing we would always talk about was, Okay, who is going to get into SOC [Special Operations Command] first? SOC was then looking for people who had some type of training besides mechanical skills, and because of his training as a paramedic, Andre had his way in. But still, getting into a Rescue Company is very, very hard, so he decided to go to the facility on Randall's Island where all the special units would get trained, or get refreshed in training. Andre did two years there, and once you did that you could pretty much go anywhere you wanted.

In 1999 the captain of Rescue 5 said, "Why don't you come to us?" Andre hopped on that offer in a heartbeat. Rescue 5 was off Clove Road on Staten Island, and he was then living in North Babylon, New York, with his wife and his son. He was really proud of being in a Rescue Company. I loved going over to Rescue 5 and spending time with them on my off days. I would have lunch with those guys, and they would say, Hey, Zack, when are you coming over to SOC? And I said, One of these days. Actually, the Fire Department doesn't like putting two members of a family in the same unit.

When I started my career out of the academy, after probationary training, I got assigned to Ladder Company 15 in Lower Manhattan. Now I did have a hook, but my rabbi didn't pan out. My girlfriend at the time was a detective in Freeport. She had busted an FDNY two-star chief for a serious traffic thing but let him go. He told her who he was and that if she knew anybody that needed a favor, just mention his name. She wrote his name down but lost the paper. So it didn't pan out for me to go where I wanted in Brooklyn. I went to Ladder 15, with Engine 4, down on South Street, just a few blocks from the World Trade Center, and was there for almost seven years. It is a nice firehouse, and a great company, but I wanted to transfer out of there because I wanted more work, more firefighting. But there was an unwritten rule that you had to stay in the first battalion, first division, for five years, because they couldn't get anyone to go there. I just had to get out of there, especially after 9/11, because every time we responded to a call and we passed by the site, I would have a minor anxiety attack. It was hurting me. I said, I can't stay here, and then the captain, and even Chief [Joseph] Pfeifer, said, Anywhere you want to go. I could even have gone to Rescue in honor of my brother, but I felt that it might be too much for the guys there, seeing my face and knowing Andre so well, and that he died there. So I said, Let me go to a busy Brooklyn company. So I chose Ladder 132.

Just before 9/11 Andre and I talked about developing a modeling and acting career. We used to see the Doublemint Twins on television and thought, *Hey, we can do that.* But we were always so busy doing everything else, we just didn't have time. But one day we said, You know what, screw it; let's just start, and we went to an agency. One of the agents looked at us, and he said, "Where the hell have you guys been all my life?"

"You guys are tall, clean-cut, handsome. Twins—for that in and of itself," he said, "you guys can go a long way." We were asked to go to California; everything would be paid for by the agency. This was two months before the towers were hit.

Andre and I weren't just brothers; it was as if he was literally a part of me. We did everything together. When he got on the fire marshals' list, I got on the fire marshals' list. [Fire marshals investigate the causes of all fires in New York.] Andre was posthumously promoted to fire marshal because, though he had been on the list, they had kept pushing the promotion back. It was the right thing to do, and generous of the department. So I am on that list now, and as a matter of fact, will be in the next class.

On the morning that Andre died, I was at my girlfriend's house. Andre had separated from his wife by then, and a little more than a year before he died, he had moved back in with my parents, though he would still go to see his son every single day. It wasn't official with the department and the city, and I kept telling him, make it official, just do the paperwork and file for divorce too. He was, I'll get to it, I'll get to it—always the last minute for everything. He had started dating, met someone, and kept going down to North Carolina to visit her. He called me from there two days before to tell me he was having a great time, and that he was coming back to New York on September 12.

At that time, though, he was trying to get as much overtime as possible, and Rescue 5 called him and said, "Fletcher, twenty-four hours overtime: You interested?" He would have to come back just a day earlier, no big deal. Now, I remember the night before, September 10, vividly. We were having some really bad lightning storms, and they closed down LaGuardia and

JFK airports. The only one that was still open was Newark, and they were accepting only half their flights.

Andre's flight from North Carolina to JFK was canceled, and they told him they would put him on a flight the next day. Andre was like, "Man, I want to do this overtime. I don't want to lose it." With overtime, you have to grab it when you can get it. He told them that he had to get back to New York, so they said, We can possibly get you into Newark, but you will have to hang over for five hours in Atlanta.

So Andre was calling me the whole day: "Zack, you think you can pick me up if I can get a flight in?" I said, "No, I'm not going to pick you up." And he's like, "Come on. You know, I do everything for you." He never did anything for me, but you know how brothers are. He knew I was going to break down; I love him a lot. So I said, "All right, what airport?" He said, "I'm coming into Newark." I'm like, "What? You expect me to drive from *effin'* Long Island all the way out to Newark?" I asked, "What time?" He said, "Midnight." I said, "Hey, you're *effin'* kidding me. You're fucking crazy. I'm not doing that." He's like, "Fuck you," and slammed the phone down, but called me back ten minutes later. "Come on, man, please, pick me up. I don't want to lose the overtime." And I'm like, "Damn." I'm shaking my head, and after going through this for an hour, going back and forth, I finally said, "Okay, but you owe me big time." I laughed to myself then. Well, at least Andre would be there in the morning to get his overtime.

I picked up his car to drive to the airport. He was wearing a spy coat, a trench coat, and I asked, as he opened the door of the car, "Who are you trying to be?" He looked at me, smiled, and said, "I knew you'd come for me." And I asked, "How did you know that?" And he said, "'Cause you're my brother." That made me feel good then—and now, too, so many years after 9/11. I said, "Just get in the car. Do you know what time it is?"

By now it was after midnight, so it was now 9/11. I drove to my girlfriend's house, gave Andre the keys, and said, "Be safe." And I added, "You know, you owe me a dinner." And he laughed, and said, "No problem." That's the last time I saw him.

The next morning I was in bed with my girlfriend. I did not even know what had happened. I had had a good sleep, a great sleep. Everyone remembers that day. It was so beautiful and warm, not a cloud in the sky. And I began to hear sirens—must be something going on. Turn the TV on, and

I'm like, What the . . . ? Andre calls me, "Yo, get to work man. They have a full recall, all off-duty personnel, everyone. A plane went into the World Trade Center." And I'm, "Get out of here." He said, "Zack, I'm not dicking you: A plane went into the World Trade Center."

My girlfriend at the time was a cop who was working downtown by Alphabet City. She was getting calls too, for off-duty personnel to report. So we got in the car and started in. The second plane hadn't hit yet, but I could see the smoke billowing, and I'm thinking, *Oh my God.* I knew my company was going to respond because Ladder 15 and Engine 4 were just a few blocks away. First thing I thought was, *How the fuck are we going to put this out?* I said as much to my girlfriend. An interior attack, way up there? This is going to be worse than any basement job I've ever been in— if we can even get up there. We might have to walk it. 'Cause who's to say about the elevators?

Andre was the type to fly in, no hesitation—which made him great for a rescue company. If he were a cop he'd shoot first and ask questions later. I was totally different. I felt, *Wait a minute. How are we going to attack this problem?* I actually started thinking then: *If this thing burns to compromise the structure, part of it could collapse,* and then the second plane hit.

So I told my girlfriend, "Just go across the bridge, put the blinkers on, and hit the horn." We had our badges and IDs out. There were police cars all over. They had closed the Brooklyn Bridge. I said to the police, "I've got to get to work. I'm at that firehouse right over there." He looked at our badges and said, "Go ahead." While crossing the Brooklyn Bridge I remember looking at the speedometer. I didn't realize I was going over ninety. That's when the first building fell.

In the firehouse I got my gear to make sure everything was good. Firemen from other areas were going to any firehouse available, grabbing coats and helmets off the rack, because this was a unique, once-in-a-lifetime emergency. I made sure I put mine to the side and waited for orders. Ladder 17 from the Bronx was relocated to cover my firehouse, and I went on a few alarms with them, which is when the South Tower fell. *God.* Then I was back in my firehouse, and a captain from another house came by, and said, "You're going to come with me—we're going down to the command post at the scene." So we started walking toward the World Trade Center. The sky was dark with smoke. By Hanover Square, thinking about the brothers, "I said to the captain, 'You know what? We have tons of extra air bottles [for the breathing masks]. Let me go back to the firehouse for them.' When I got back about eight minutes had passed, and the captain and I headed down Dey Street.

We then began to hear the rumbling of the North Tower falling. We were close, and it was the loudest thing I've heard in my life. We jumped into a building alcove—myself, the captain, and four cops in riot gear. When we saw all the debris, that huge cloud rolling our way, we just looked at each other bug eyed. We grabbed at each other, not even thinking; we just grabbed each other. We folded on top of each other and let everything pass by. If we hadn't moved fast, we would have been hit by the shrapnel and probably would have been dead. We were just a short block and a half away. If I had not gone for those air bottles. we would have been in the North Tower. We would have been dead. No ifs, ands, or buts. I know we would have been dead.

After the building came down, I was so glad I had my hood and a mask [a surgical filter-type mask]. It was as if time stood still. It was like a dream. I remember, I thought I was in a dream. Everything was in slow motion. Looking around, saying to myself, *This can't be real.* We went up Church Street, and I saw Engine Squad 252. Everything on the front of the truck burned to nothing, but everything on the back end was still there, though pretty beat up. I said to myself, *Nah, that can't be 252. That can't be a fire engine. I mean, this is not real.* I said to myself, *My God, this is unbelievable.* We then passed a car on fire. The captain saw a hose hooked up to a hydrant and said, "Open up the hydrant; do what you can with that car fire." I started spraying water, and I began to say to myself, *Why am I fighting a car fire? Putting this out ain't going to do anything.* Also, the pressure on the hydrants had completely dropped, so it was basically just pissing a trickle. So I'm like, *The hell with this. I'm not doing this. I gotta look for my brother.*

I knew Rescue was there. When we were coming in, my brother hit me up on the two-way walkie-talkie instant communications. "Rescue 5," he said, "is about to go through the Verrazano Bridge tolls." They were weaving their way in and out of all the traffic. Andre told me to get down to my firehouse and that he would meet me down there. I said, "Andre, I know you. Don't do anything stupid. Don't try to be a hero on this one. I'll see you there. I'll hook up with you." That was the last time I spoke with him.

After the South Tower collapsed I joined other firemen and did a search of the surrounding areas. The carbon monoxide level was extremely high, to the point that, even though I had a mask on to filter out a lot of stuff, it didn't filter the carbon monoxide. I knew that area and remembered large open spaces, and I was looking for those spaces, but it was all solid now, a mountain of debris. I remember thinking too that if they were in that pile there was no way that we would be getting them out. They were dead. I was getting a little overcome with the carbon monoxide, and I thought, *I can't stay here,* because I didn't have the right mask on. I needed a self-contained one. And then we were told to group up and to meet at the quarters of Engine 7 and Ladder 1 on Duane Street. They were first-alarm companies, and it's amazing how a firehouse that was so close, and one of the first at the World Trade Center, didn't lose anybody. I was just so happy for them. Some of the guys there saw me, and because my company works with them a lot, two of them came over and hugged me, like, "Man, good to see you."

I walked around looking for Andre, or anybody from Rescue 5. I saw Rescue 1's rig, but where was Rescue 5? Ground Zero was too big, and there was so much debris around.

A chief came, and after taking a roll call sent most of us back to our respective quarters. More off-duty personnel were already at my firehouse. I got cleaned up; I was full of soot: My ears were totally covered, my nose, and that smell. It's the worst feeling, as if you'd gotten slimed.

I didn't think that I'd lost Andre. I said to myself, *To have any hope you have to have a positive mental attitude.* I kept saying to myself, *Don't get negative. Positive mental attitude. If anybody had a chance, it would be those guys in Rescue. They are trained for that.* It's the Rescue guys who end up pulling firemen out when they get in trouble, so they must have known how to get themselves out. I was not thinking that they could have died instantly. I was just in a daze, almost on autopilot. My first priority right now was to accept that this happened. That's what we're trained for. *It can happen; I can't do anything to change it. But what can we do to alleviate any of the suffering? We can at least save some lives.*

Nobody said anything specific to me, but people were talking: "Man, seventy percent of SOC was decimated. They were working, and they're not here anymore, and nobody's heard from them." Not that they were dead, but nobody's heard from them. That's when people started thinking negatively.

When I got home, people were there waiting—some friends of mine, cops in Freeport and Nassau County, making sure Mom and Dad were okay. They hugged me, and they were like, "He's going to be okay, he's going to be okay." "You heard from him?" "No." "Okay," "Don't worry about it." And I guess it was just their positive attitude, so I said, "Okay, probably it's going to be fine." I was in denial.

But you know, when I saw the damage, when I was doing a quick search, the mountain of broken concrete and steel, I knew there was no way that anyone was going to find any survivors. But there's denial, wishful thinking. *No, no, no, they weren't in that pile. They are going to be okay.*

Every day my mother would ask, "Did you hear anything?" She was real upbeat. Dad was too. I said,"No, but, you know, they are Rescue guys, they're fine."

A week or so later they began sending people to make formal announcements. They would send a chief. I was at work in front of my firehouse, and a chief came up to me and said, "We haven't heard anything from them. He didn't make it." And I said, "What do you mean, he didn't make it? Nobody knows anything yet. I refuse to believe that. I refuse to believe that. As a matter of fact, get out of my face."

He understood the way I was feeling, and I went on, "No, he's fine. He's in Rescue. They're fine. It's up to us to find them. They rescue us all this time, when we're in trouble." I said, "Now it's our turn for those of us who made it to go after them. He's fine."

I told my parents that they were saying that he was dead, and I told them that I didn't believe it, that I believed that we were going to find him. My mother said, "Yeah, we're going to find him. We'll find him, honey." I held on to that. I honestly believed that he could have been wounded, or gotten amnesia. Ten years later, ever though I don't believe it anymore, there's still a small portion at the back of my mind that says there's still a possibility. Because nothing was ever found of him.

Over at Bellevue they still have a lot of body parts but just don't have the DNA technology to positively identify them. Some of those parts are so badly damaged that it's going to take some future form of testing to assess them. And so, until I get that confirmation, I'm not going to 100 percent believe that he's dead.

The professional fireman in me tells me that he's not coming back. I've accepted that, and that's what's helped me move on. A lot of the things that I've gone through and that I've strived to become are not just for me anymore, but for both of us. I'm living for both of us. It's one thing to be brothers and siblings; it's another to be twins. Twins often feel the same thing. But when the North Tower fell, I didn't feel anything—there was no feeling of separation. That's why I still hold on to that little hope.

Out at the Fort Totten Counseling Unit, we had the brothers' meeting, for all the guys on the job who had lost brothers. Right after 9/11 a captain said, "Hey, Zack, do you want to take a leave?" I said no; I thought I was just sad. I lost a twin brother, but people were like, Don't worry, we can handle it without you. I was supposed to have my vacation that October, but I kept putting it off. My captain kept saying, "Why don't you take a leave?" I kept saying, "No, I want to stay and continue to do this, to find Andre." He finally made me go out on vacation—I was on that high of working on autopilot. Even when I finally went on leave I was spending time at the site. I don't think I am very sick from working there, except for a little cough every now and then. What protected me was that I knew when the federal government was telling us the air was fine to breathe, they were lying, and so whenever I was down at the pile, I wore the respirator mask, as uncomfortable as it was.

When I officially returned to work after 9/11 and after my vacation time, I started to have anxiety attacks, and I'm like, "What's going on with me?" Lieutenant John Violi, one of my best friends, said, "Hey, Zack, you okay?" I said, "I don't know what's wrong, but for whatever reason, I'm having anxiety attacks, dizzy, panting, feeling weird whenever we'd pass the site." He said, "Zack, I'm putting you out, and I want you to call counseling." So I went on special leave for counseling. At first I didn't even tell them that I was still going down to the site, but I had to continue to be part of this situation, the recovery at Ground Zero. In the long run the counseling helped, but I was going crazy at home not doing anything, so in August or September of 2002 I went back to work, after nine months in counseling.

Andre and I never worked jobs together, because we worked in different boroughs. But on Father's Day in 2001, Harry Ford, John Downing, and Brian Fahey were killed in a collapse at a hardware store fire. Andre and I went to the funerals, and I remember at Harry Ford's I said to him, "You have to promise me something: If anything ever happens to me, or if I die doing this job that we love, you're close with Britney." That's my daughter, and Britney looked up to my brother as a second father. I said, "Promise me you'll take care of her as if she was your own daughter." And Andre looked at me and said, "Absolutely." But he added, "Then you have to promise me something too. If anything ever happens to me, promise me that you'll take care of my son, Blair, as if he were your own." I said, "Without a doubt, absolutely."

For Andre's service, I was supposed to lead the eulogy, but my sister-in-law didn't want me to do that. That devastated me. I pretty much lost it, and Dad had to hold me away from her. Since then there has been a dispute over visitation rights of my brother's family, and I've only seen Blair three times. But I'm not going to kill myself worrying about this—I'm not. I hope he'll come to realize what's going on. But it's tough on my mother, who prays about it every day, besides having to deal with 9/11. I don't even get to see my own kids, because I'm going through a control issue with my children's mother. It's tough, and that's the hardest thing for my parents. My mom has not been able to see Blair, her oldest grandchild, the only boy, and now my two daughters. Mom just turned eighty, and her own blood is not able to pay respects to their grandparents.

But I keep going, and try to do positive things. One thing that I take great pride in is that I'm one of the main post advisers for the Fire Department Post of New York Explorers, the one in Queens. [The Exploring program, which is operated with the Boy Scouts of America, gives fourteen- to twenty-year-olds a chance to work with firefighters.] I took it over, and it's given me purpose. I was a Boy Scout, and Andre was too. As a matter of fact, when Chief Cassano, now commissioner, found out, he was very honored. He said, "I have to come by and check out your post. You're doing a good job. Keep it up." It gives me a lot of satisfaction when I do community service. Twice a month we also do Meals-on-Wheels with the Explorers, and POTS, Part of the Solution, a community soup kitchen in the South Bronx. I know I'm not going to be able to change every single one of these kids; it's just not going to happen. But if I can turn just one kid's life around and help him to see that there's something better out there, it's all worth it.

I think I learned a lot about giving from the New York Fire Department. Our unselfishness. Our commitment. Our desire to always be there and never give up. Our bravery. Our courage. But more than anything, our unselfishness. I think that's probably the key word. I find all firemen are like that, the world over. I used to play with the Fire Department football team, The Bravest, and when we went out to Los Angeles County, the LA firefighters said to us more than once, We don't know what it is, but it seems that you in New York City have a bond and a love for each other that is not matched anywhere. The firefighters in New York City know who we are, and know what we want to be, and the other firefighters around the world want to be just like New York City firefighters.

Ken Haskell

Ken Haskell is a New York City firefighter, as was his father. Ken is an expert in rescue techniques and teaches this important lifesaving subject to firefighters all across the country. His two brothers, Tommy and Timmy, were also FDNY firefighters, and both were lost in the mayhem of 9/11.

My father was a marine. In 1969 he joined the New York City Fire Department, starting out with 35 Truck and then moving over to Ladder 174 in East Flatbush. He had an active firefighting career, but he had a minor heart attack in 1979, and so he retired. Afterward he started his own contracting business, which is how he supported our family, and my brothers and I basically grew up learning the trade. Working with my dad was an invaluable experience to me, for I learned so much from him. He died in 1994, but I still learn from him today.

Timmy was two years older than me, and Tommy was four years older than me. My mother and father had a big family to raise, five kids, all close in age—my sister, Dawn, is the only girl, and then there's also Kevin. Our father was very involved in our lives, in a good way. He was our coach for Little League and football and always taught us things. We lived on the water in Brooklyn, and he'd show us how to take care of a boat and drive it around the bay. He was very comfortable just letting us do our own thing, be ourselves. My father gave us guidance to be the man that he was, but it wasn't as if he ever forced anything on us. I think he would have liked to have seen us all join the marines, because we all knew what the marines did for him, but he never pushed it. It was the same with the Fire Department. His attitude was, Look, guys, when you're ready you've got to take these tests if you want the job. It's a good job. If you don't want it, it's something you can fall back on if whatever else you decide to do falls through.

I remember that some of my fondest memories as a kid were going to his firehouse for Christmas parties, and being in the city was always unique, but becoming a firefighter wasn't something that I aspired to as a young boy. As I got older, though, I saw that the people my dad employed in his contracting business were all firefighters he was working with. I was really struck by the bond they had with one another, and the work ethic every one of them had. Each guy brought something to the table. They all busted their asses, and their being guys from my father's firehouse really resonated with me as a kid. Working alongside my dad and those guys, and hearing the stories they would tell about the job they had the night before—who got hurt, who got burned, or something funny that happened in the firehouse kitchen—probably had more to do with my going into firefighting than anything. Besides, of course, the fact that my father was a fireman. As I got older it just became my natural progression.

I was actually a police officer before I was a fireman. The NYPD hired me, and I did about three years with the PD before I rolled over to the Fire Department. I worked in the Fifty-third Precinct and the Seventy-first, which are in the Flatbush and Crown Heights areas. I was part of the Street Crime Unit, where there was a lot of interesting work, and I was doing real well. But then the Fire Department called. I almost didn't leave, and the whole time I was in the fire academy I had some regret, thinking about how much I had enjoyed the Police Department. But my father was going, Are you crazy? Just give it some time. And once I got a taste of firefighting, I thought, *This isn't so bad*. I don't regret it at all. I love the Fire Department.

And my brothers, Tommy and Timmy . . . They were great firemen. They loved it too.

Timmy was more of a laid-back kind of guy. He wanted to be in Special Operations, and so he requested a Squad Company. Tommy was actually kind of a buff: You could rattle off a box number [an area] and he'd tell you what street it was on. Timmy loved being a firefighter, but Tommy wanted to go up the ranks. He would have risen higher up earlier, but they froze his list for two years. He was a rising star, no doubt, a superstudent. He was in the top five of every list—the lieutenants', the captains', and the battalion chiefs'. He wrote a ninety-five or better on each test. When Tommy was studying, that was his life for the year leading up to the test. Because I was so involved with the carpentry business, I never put that kind of studying time in.

I feel there's got to be some type of competence and fire experience prerequisite for a guy to get promoted. It shouldn't be enough just to pass the test and go out in the field to a fire. Most people can pass the test, but doing the actual work is a whole other ball game. Tommy was good at both, the tests and the work. One day we caught a job, a good fire in a three-storied frame building. We were on the floor above the fire, in the rear of the third floor, and the guys were having a bit of an issue with the water—a hydrant was shut down or something. The fire got out the windows underneath us, and it got pretty hairy. The chief ordered everybody off the top floor and out of the building because it didn't look as if the engine company was making any progress. No sooner did we hit the streets than the whole house lit up. We would have been jumping out the windows. So I'm thinking, *This chief is good, making that call, pretty heads-up.* When I got outside I could see that it was my brother Tommy, Captain Haskell, acting chief for that tour.

I said, "You just saved our ass."

And Tommy replied, "No problem, just go get a drink of water somewhere, rest up."

You know, a fire in Staten Island and a fire in a high-rise in Manhattan, they're two totally different animals, but Tommy was equally proficient at both and could get his head wrapped around either scenario. He was going to make a great chief. Tommy was very intense, almost to the point where it could be a little too much. My father always used to chastise him, saying, "Would you freaking lighten up, you're going to give yourself a heart attack." He was always busting his chops.

Before Tommy got promoted he went up to Squad 41 in the Bronx, after working in 332 in Brooklyn. It had been very competitive in Brooklyn, where they would race one another to be first in, and I guess Tommy bought into that whole act when he worked there. But up in the Bronx he saw that the guys were more relaxed and respected the response protocol. It really rounded him out as a fireman, and prepared him to be a good officer. When he got promoted he eventually went to Engine Company 82 in the South Bronx, where he served as lieutenant. After a year or two there he got promoted again, to captain, and he knew he would have been promoted within the year to battalion chief, but then 9/11 came.

On the morning of 9/11 I was off duty. I was working on my house, reconstructing my bathroom, and I was in Farmingdale buying the tile. It was about ten minutes to nine, and there was nobody in the store. My cousin Frankie actually owns the store, and I thought, *Where the heck is everybody?* They were all in the back office watching the TV. Someone said that a plane had just flown into the World Trade Center. I said, "Really?" I looked at it and said, "Oh, my God," and I thought right off the bat that it was a terrorist attack.

I was at the Trade Center in 1993. I was a police officer then, and remember thinking, and feeling strongly after that day, that they were going to try to attack that building again. So I said, "Son of a bitch." Then the second plane hit. I just walked out of the store and called my wife, who was at work, and told her I was headed to the firehouse. "Just be careful," she said.

I got to Brooklyn within half an hour—they had started closing the roads, but I was able to get through with my badge, and sailed right in. At the firehouse I thought: *What the hell do we do now?* There were about ten of us there. Right behind the firehouse is a bus depot, so we went there and told them we needed a bus to get to Manhattan. We threw all our gear in and started heading up Flatbush Avenue, stopping at Ladder 157 and Engine 255, Ladder 113 and Engine 249 to pick up more guys. The bus then was full.

We got to the Manhattan Bridge, which was one of my most vivid memories of the day—just the faces of everybody coming over that bridge. Flatbush Avenue southbound from Tillary Street was just packed with people walking out of Manhattan, all covered in dust. The first collapse had just happened. They were, I guess, the first group of people walking out of that dust storm. I'll never forget that sight. All of those people, half of whom didn't even have their shoes, who must have lost them running.

There were several hundred firemen on the Brooklyn side of the Manhattan Bridge waiting for orders. A chief was trying to gather everybody together and come up with a plan to direct us. There had been reports of a third plane coming, and of a secondary explosion, so I think they were a little apprehensive about sending us in. At that point everybody's asking around, Do you know so and so? Is he working today? We knew we lost guys. Obviously. I felt that because the buildings had collapsed, there were going to be multiple heart attacks too.

A guy I worked with, Brian O'Neil, came up to me and asked if I had heard about Daniel Suhr, a mutual friend of ours in Engine 216. I said, "No, what happened to Danny?" "He's dead." I said, "Oh shit. No." He had been struck by a woman who had jumped, as I later found out, just as they were headed into the South Tower. Ironically, his death saved everybody else's life in that company, because no sooner did they stop to get him out of that area than the building collapsed. And so they all survived.

I remember being very pissed off. I'd played with Danny on the FDNY football team, and he was just an all-around good guy. He'd just had a baby too. When I heard about Danny, that's when I determined, *We gotta get the fuck over there. Enough of this dicking around here in Brooklyn.* Five minutes later we were told that another command post had been set up on Broadway, right by City Hall. We got on the buses and, just as we were going over the bridge, we saw the second collapse.

After getting off the buses, we were walking on Broadway and all the dust and debris came blowing through. We had to find shelter until everything could lift. I think I waited for about an hour for some kind of direction and to find out what was going on. I finally got fed up and decided, *I'm not sitting here anymore.* I grabbed a little dust mask. They had been trying to get equipment gathered up at that time, piles of shovels and brooms and stuff in the streets.

When I got to Church Street, on the east side of the site, I was just dumbfounded by what I was looking at. Right in front of me an entire building, six or seven floors, was on fire. A firefighter was trying to get a hose line going on that, and I helped to stretch that line. Buildings, fire trucks, and police cars were all destroyed, everything burned. I remember how dark it was, even though it was about 11:30 in the morning. It was a surreal experience. I thought that if I were to imagine what a nuclear holocaust would look like, this was it: no color anywhere, everything ash and gray.

After working for a while, trying to get some water on building 5, I moved to building 7, the one that collapsed in the afternoon. Parts of it started falling off and landing in the street all around us, and I was thinking, *We'll be all right, it looks like a pretty well-constructed building.* But looking across Vesey Street and seeing that the entire World Trade Center was gone, I began to think that we should probably get out of here. Moments later building 7 collapsed, and the streets were filled with running cops and firemen. I ran east to the side entrance of the Woolworth Building.

When [building 7] collapsed I did not have a feeling of fear but just went right into work mode. I did start to feel a bit uneasy, though, when I saw that the radiant heat from the initial fires in the Twin Towers was causing problems. The Deutsche Bank Building and the building next to it were also on fire, and building 7 had just fallen. These were all huge buildings. Now I'm thinking that the structural integrity of the foundations of all the surrounding buildings was probably undermined from the collapse of the Twin Towers. *Shit, we're going to lose half of Lower Manhattan.* Every time one of these buildings goes down, it's going to compromise the structure next to it in a domino effect. We're a little lucky that that didn't happen. People say that if the Twin Towers had been built better they wouldn't have collapsed, but they took the impact of two jumbo jetliners, fully fueled, so it's a miracle they didn't fall right off the bat. Because the support columns were on the outside skin, they fell inward with the interior weight, floor by floor. It's pretty remarkable that there wasn't more collateral damage from the collapse.

I'd been thinking about Tommy and Timmy the whole day. When I'd left for the city I called [my wife] Genene and asked her to call Tommy's wife, Barbara, and my mother to see if she could find out if Tommy and Timmy were working. I didn't know if either of them was actually on duty that morning. I assumed Timmy was there, because even if he wasn't working, he lived in the neighborhood, in Tribeca, and his firehouse was not far away, on Greenwich and Tenth Street.

At about seven o'clock I made my way over to West Street, because I knew that's where the original command post was. I figured, *I'm going to find out if my brothers are here or where they might have been.* The chiefs at the command center would know.

The destruction down there was just gargantuan, and it took a couple of hours just to get over there. Every time you turned around there was something to do. I originally walked south and came up behind the Engine 10 Ladder 10 firehouse on Liberty Street to make my way over to West Street. There was a body in the street there, literally sheared in half. It's hard to describe what that looked like. Try to imagine someone lying on his side in water, so you could only see half the face, half the torso, and one arm. That's all that was left of this man, this victim. His eye was open, expressionless. It is impossible to imagine the trauma he went through. His face didn't have a mark on it, and I was kind of fixated on it. I just couldn't believe the condition of his body, and I was thinking, *How the hell did he end up two blocks south of the Trade Center?* He had to have been on the airplane and just flew out of the building. That thinking really got my blood boiling, and seeing him there, that pissed me off. A cop was there, next to the body, and he was going to wait with the remains.

I kept going until I got to the firehouse, and then tore through the place looking for an ax, a halogen tool, anything to work with. But the firehouse had already been pretty much raided. Chief Brian O'Neil grabbed me and ordered us up to the roof to get some lights set up. We did that and helped as they were trying to get a pumper backed up to the block to try to put some water on the Deutsche Building and on the pile of what was left of the South Tower.

It was now about 8:30 P.M. and starting to get dark, and it was still very smoky all around. Looking over toward the World Financial Center, I saw beyond the smoke that it was just a beautiful day, the sun beginning to set over the Hudson River.

I don't remember what company it was, but they finally got a ladder tower backed up right next to 10 House—Engine 10 and Ladder 10—on Liberty Street. They put the bucket up and started to put some water on the fire in front of the Deutsche Bank Building. There were three flagpoles there, and they were all kind of bent, listed over, and one of them had the American flag. As the bucket was going up, the firefighters stopped the water flow and swung over to the pole, picked up the American flag, tied it to the bucket, and then continued up.

Every so often there would be some visibility through the smoke, and as we watched the flag going up, it caught the light from the setting sun, which made it glow. It was a very patriotic moment, and I got renewed energy when I saw that. It was probably the most poignant moment of that whole first day for me.

I then made my way over to West Street, where everybody was asking, Hey, did you see so and so? I found a couple of guys who knew Timmy and I asked, "Is Timmy working?"

"Oh, yeah, I saw him," one of them said.

So I thought, *Oh, good.* And for seven or eight hours after that I went around thinking he was just around the corner, that I'd run into him at the pile somewhere.

I still hadn't heard anything about Tommy. To get to the command center I had to walk all the way around and through the Financial Center. The lobby there was like a ghost town. There was maybe a foot of that ash in the building, and all of the windows were blown out. A phone started ringing at a security desk there. I dusted it off and couldn't believe I got through when I called Genene. She told me that Barbara said that Tommy was working, but that she hadn't heard from him since she called the firehouse and was told that they had responded. *Oh boy*, I thought. I asked, "What about Timmy?"

And Genene said, "Timmy's working too."

I just remember saying, "I pray to God they weren't in there, because if they were in there they're dead."

I felt like crap after that; a lot of emotion hit me at that point. I didn't cry or anything, but I said, "I'm going to go; I want to get back to work; I'll call you later." She said, "Please come home tonight," and then repeating it. "I can't come home, Genene," I said, "Don't worry, I'll be all right. I have to get back to work."

At around one o'clock in the morning, I was still digging. We had recovered a few remains on West Street. Somebody came up to me and said, "You know, everyone from 132 is missing." I said, "I figured that." And Timmy . . . I already knew. I just had a feeling in my gut. I thought then that I needed to go home and tell my mother. I left the site near 2:00 A.M., somehow hitching a ride. To tell the truth, I don't remember how I got back to my firehouse. I made it to my mother's house by three o'clock in the morning. She was up, watching the news. I remember she stood up, just had this look on her face, as if she were hoping I was going to tell her something good.

I lost it. I gave her a hug. "What can I say, Ma? If they were there, it doesn't look good." I didn't want to say they were dead, but I knew they were gone, and I didn't want her . . . She was clinging to the hope that everyone was still just missing, and I wanted her to have that hope. I didn't want to dash that. I was honest with what I had seen, and what was going on down there. She just sat back down and continued watching the news. She asked me some questions, and we talked for a little while, until I finally said, "I'm going to go home and try to get a little sleep."

I got home at maybe 4:30 in the morning but couldn't sleep more than an hour. I was back on the site by 8:00 A.M. and spent pretty much the next forty-eight hours straight there. When I finally went home again, I again first stopped to see my mother. My brother Kevin was there, and he asked if he could work with me. He wasn't a fireman, so I said, No, you can't go;

it's too dangerous. He didn't argue with me, and Kevin and I always argued. We shared a room for twenty years, so there was sibling rivalry all the time.

But Kevin was certainly capable of doing the things I was doing, and I had to stop myself there. *Who was I to not let him go and look for his brothers?* So I picked him up the following morning, on Saturday. We went to my firehouse, and I gave him my extra set of gear. At that point they were busing guys to the 15th Division and would deploy them from there. Over the course of a couple of days I kind of figured out where each of them had been at the time of the collapse. I knew the Brooklyn companies were in the South Tower. I talked to some guys from Ladder 113 who survived the collapse, and they said that Ladder 132 had been right behind them, so they almost made it. I figured if they were in the lobby when that building collapsed, they'd have been cremated or were all the way down in the rubble. I'd heard that Timmy was in the North Tower, and Tommy was in the South, so I focused half my day on each pile of rubble.

One day we reached a really hairy spot, where there was a large void, almost a cavern, under the South Tower. It was like being in the barrel of a wave, and you could see the impression of each floor in this barrel, everything had been crushed so tightly. To me it looked as if ten floors had been compressed into a space of two feet, and it literally curved over us. The image brought memories. Growing up on the water, my brothers and I always surfed, and we all used to love to get that wave and get in the barrel, which was the highlight of any surfer's day.

I insisted that Kevin stay outside, as I didn't want anything to happen to him, and there was plenty for him to do on the pile. The radiant heat in the void was so intense that you always had to do a shuffle to keep your gear protecting you, to prevent parts of your body from getting too hot. To understand how hot that environment was, the only things there were either ash, steel, rebar, or concrete. Everything else was smoldering. If any paper landed it would ignite. We went about fifty yards into this cavern when it made a turn, and then got tighter and tighter, and everything was shifting. It was getting a little scary, and I thought that there was no way that anybody could be alive in here.

We were getting ready to come back out when one of the guys grabbed me and said, "The lieutenant wants to see you." When I came out of the void, my lieutenant, Frank, was there with a cell phone in his hand, and I just knew that look right away. I said, "Which one was it?" He said they found Timmy. I couldn't believe it. I couldn't believe they had found him in all of this. And as Frank told me that they found Timmy, I noticed a Bible sitting just off to my left, and Kevin was standing next to it. I don't know why, but I just instinctively reached for this Bible. It was a Gideon's Bible, I guess from the Marriott Hotel, and Kevin later took it and held it for the rest of the day. I thought it was so extraordinary that at the exact moment I learned of my brother's death there was a Bible close by. It hadn't been there before, because I would have seen it. The only thing that may have happened is that there were operations going on above us, and this Bible must have been dislodged from somewhere and tumbled down. But it was extraordinary, and I still have it. I have never been an especially religious person, but I do believe that there is a life hereafter, and maybe that was some kind of sign—my brothers letting me know that they are all right. That's what I choose to believe. That's what helps me tremendously emotionally. The thought that we will all be together again.

Timmy was in the North Tower, and he was in the lead team. He had worked the night before and was still in the firehouse when the first plane hit. He and a couple of other guys from the night tour grabbed some gear and headed down to the site. There's actually a quick video snippet of him going up the stairs of the North Tower. He made it up more than forty floors before the collapse. As his team was going up, they came across a man who was having a heart attack, so they stopped to help him out. They were actually going to evacuate him, but the staircase that they had come up was just not viable for that, as there were just too many people on it. One of the firefighters, Pat Murphy from Squad 18, found another staircase, which was hardly being used, but when he came back, Timmy was gone. He had left the man who was having a heart attack with a Port Authority police officer and told the officer something about a Mayday: A firefighter needed help a few floors up. Timmy ran to help him.

Pat and the police officer started to bring the guy down, which took them a long time, and just as the three of them got to the lobby, the building started to fall. The pressure that was created by the collapse generated a tremendous force of wind, which literally blew them off their feet and out onto the street. All three of them survived.

One of the guys who found Timmy had worked with both my brothers. He tried to describe the scene of the recovery, but I didn't need the graphic details, and my only question to him was, "Was he intact?" And he told me that he was. I said, "Then that's all we can ask for." I was grateful for that. He had been with other guys from the squad, so he wasn't alone, and there was some solace in that. Beneath them were civilians, and it was almost as if they had been sheltering them. I remember feeling just a tremendous sense of pride at the courage Timmy showed and the chances he took. He's heroic in every sense of the word. What is a hero? Firefighters are heroes. Guys like my brother Timmy, what they did . . . All those guys who were lost. They are the heroes. Firemen might do heroic things all the time, but you get to be a hero only once.

After I got the news about Timmy, I wanted to get home to talk to my mother. They were using retired fire chiefs to notify the families, so I knew someone would be going to the house. I wanted to be the one to tell her, to be there with her. Just after I got home, two real old-timers arrived in dress uniforms, there to break the news. I told them I already had and offered them a drink, but they just wanted to express their condolences. The way the department was making these notifications was tastefully done, but I just felt it should come from me.

We buried Timmy a few days later. I remember when I delivered Timmy's eulogy I was struck by how few people were at his funeral. When you think of a line-of-duty funeral, you usually think of a sea of blue fifty blocks long. But not that day. Except for Congressman Peter King, none of the elected officials showed up, which again was understandable, though unusual for a line-of-duty funeral. But Pete King made a point of being there, and I will never forget that. I know that he was busy with his work in Washington, and I felt a tremendous amount of respect and gratitude.

I'd never delivered a eulogy before, but my sister asked me to. The whole experience was so overwhelming: I would literally go to the site, dig all day looking for Tommy, and come home to go to Timmy's wake at night. Then back to the site in the morning. I didn't have a lot of time to write a eulogy, and I'm not known to be a public speaker. But I woke up the morning of Timmy's funeral and just started thinking of things I wanted to say. I didn't need to write them out, as I knew Timmy's life.

And at the end of my eulogy I said, "You know, we may find ourselves back here again, eventually, for my brother Tommy. But I'm not worried about Tommy, because wherever Tommy is, I know Timmy has his arm around him." I remember looking at my mother right then and, oh, my

God, this woman has lost two sons, and I couldn't imagine. The death of two brothers to me cannot compare to a parent's losing two of her children like this. My grief could not be near to what my mother must have been feeling. I was so very conscious of that.

I've always loved my mother. She is a beautiful and strong woman. I've never met anyone as strong as she, which was evident in the way she carried herself through all that grief. I'm sure I got from my mother the fortitude to move on from 9/11, to deal with my own great sense of loss.

We never found Tommy. I overhead some guys from Ladder 113 talking, and they said that Ladder 105 was right behind them, and Ladder 132 was right near them. They had to have been heading out of the building. Once I heard that he was down near the lobby, I knew that there was no way we would find him. The only reason we found Timmy was because he was so high up when the North Tower collapsed, and so he was basically on top of the pile.

All the news organizations and papers began calling us once they heard about Tommy and Timmy, the two brothers, both firefighters and both lost. I was busy at the Trade Center and didn't have time. The *Today* show kept calling and calling to interview me, and I kept saying no. But then we found Timmy, and I thought it would give me a chance to talk about my brothers, to let the world know what they had done, and so I agreed to it. Early on the Monday after 9/11, Matt Lauer showed up via video, and I was live on the *Today* show from Ground Zero. He asked me about my brothers. I told him that we'd found Timmy. I said I'd be spending the day working at the site, and then I'd be leaving to go to Timmy's wake that night. That's how I left the interview.

Right after the interview we found a girl. I remember seeing her arm sticking out in a void at the site. I jumped down and started helping another firefighter, who was digging at all the ash around her. She must have died from asphyxiation, as she was buried in a couple feet of ash with very little trauma, because the steel had sheltered her from any falling debris. She was young and pretty, though it was beyond the point where they would be able to have an open casket for her. She had a crust of dirt all over her, so I took a bottle of water I had in my coat and cleaned her face, just trying to make her presentable before the body bag got there. We put her in the bag and sent her on her way. It was such a poignant and memorable moment to have found her just after I'd been talking about finding Timmy and looking for Tommy. I was so grateful to get this girl to her family. It was a rare experience down there—rare that anybody would get any remains of a loved one back, let alone intact. She was the only intact body that I remember seeing down there. Everyone else . . . was body parts, fragments.

I have always been an optimistic person, and I was determined not to sit around and feel sorry for myself. I was thirty-two years old then, with two young boys, and I wanted to live my life. I knew this was an extraordinary event, and that it would be part of my life for the rest of my life. As much horror as I've experienced at losing Tommy and Timmy, there's been a whole other facet of the experience that I've been grateful for: the extraordinary people whom I have met over the last ten years whom I never would have met otherwise. I've been to the White House twice and met President Bush four times. It's surreal when I look back on it, knowing that I wouldn't have had these opportunities had it not been for 9/11—not that I wouldn't trade it all to have my brothers back, and everybody else back, and for the world to be normal again. I'm always conscious of the opportunities I have to do good, whether it be to help a wounded soldier or to find ways to keep the memories of my brothers, and of all the people that we lost that day, alive.

After 9/11, my family organized a golf outing in memory of Tommy and Timmy—The Haskell Brothers Memorial Golf Outing. We hold it the Thursday of every Memorial Day weekend. This will be our tenth year, and we've probably raised about $150,000 in total. We donate to the FDNY Fire Family Transport Foundation and the New York Firefighters Burn Center. And because my son Ryan is handicapped, we've donated money to a special needs event out on Long Island. This past year we also gave to a firefighter cancer support group.

The whole family comes down to help at the golf outing. It's always a great day. The guy who runs the golf course adores my mother, and so he gives us whatever we need. And then, following the golf, we do a dinner, which my wife pretty much runs, including the raffles. We have a keynote speaker every year, and we never know who it's going to be until that day. For the last couple of years we've also been joined by many wounded guys from the military, and I've asked them to speak, because I think they find it therapeutic. For the last three years each of their stories has been more remarkable than the last. You can hear a pin drop when they are talking, and that's not an easy thing to do when you've got a room full of 150 drunken firemen. But we truly understand the incredible courage that they've shown in their actions, and it's a great honor to have them with us.

One of the organizations that we love to support is the FDNY Fire Family Transport Foundation, which I am on the board of. We transport families when a firefighter is sent to a burn unit, or if there is a line-of-duty funeral. Before the attacks they only had two vans, but after 9/11, I heard about all these vans being donated. I said that's a really great cause and something good that we can do.

Since 9/11 the Fire Department has seen how much good Fire Family Transport has done, and so they've linked the foundation to the Family Assistance Unit. All the vans are privately donated, and each company handles the maintenance and provides fuel. The vehicles have FDNY markings, so they can be used in No Standing zones around hospitals. A van is assigned to a particular firehouse, and then it's up to the firefighters to volunteer to staff it. As well as making it a lot easier for families when firefighters get hurt, the foundation has evolved over the years, and we now also use these vans to help our wounded soldiers, which is helping build a unique relationship between the FDNY and the military.

One regret I have is not having joined the military—not because of what happened on 9/11, and not in a vindictive spirit. I'm grateful, though, that I've been able to work with Hope for the Warriors, which is one of our main charities for the golf outing. It's a big organization started by wives to support their wounded loved ones, and they're bringing in multimillions of dollars. They'll provide whatever wounded troops need, like building a house for a quadruple amputee who lives on Staten Island. Just this past year, we gave them fifteen thousand dollars.

I've met so many extraordinary people over the years, wounded veterans and military personnel, and I'm always struck by the fact that their character is second to none. Despite the trauma that these guys have experienced in their lives, they still have a positive attitude, and their patriotism, and all the wonderful things you want to see in an American. I find these guys truly inspiring.

To be able to impact somebody's life in the ways we've been able to with the money we've raised is the greatest thing, as is the opportunity, even after a decade, to get together once a year and have the golf outing, a day when all of us spend the day talking about Tommy and Timmy. Each year I continue to hear new stories about them.

This is the way I've chosen to live my life post-9/11, but others have taken different routes. Just look at what Lee Ielpi's done [see page 98], truly extraordinary things—starting the Tribute WTC Visitor Center at Ground Zero, speaking about 9/11 all over the world. Guys like Lee are unique in having the strength to do the things they do.

Since 9/11, I've always wanted to be around like-minded people. When you experience trauma in your life, it's very important that you're around good people. Some family members affected by the tragedy have taken up conspiracy theories, blamed the government for everything, and were just bitter. Others have kind of crawled into a hole, or they've latched on to political issues that have just paralyzed their lives. I do not want to be that kind of person. You control your own destiny, and if you are around misery, you're going to be miserable.

I always say that my brothers were the first casualties in the war on terror. And here we are, ten years removed, and we're still fighting that war. As we become further removed from 9/11, one of the biggest emotions I feel is frustration that people fail to remember what we all went through. What happened to "We Will Never Forget"? I don't want my children to experience what I experienced. And they will if we're not brave enough or honest enough to address the real issues. I just hate to hear a politician get up and talk about the beautiful, peaceful religion of Islam. Well, maybe there's a small minority who've perverted the religion and espouse hatred, but they're still using that religion and their beliefs to attack and murder innocent people. We need a leader with the courage to address this for what it is, and to resolve it. This is not a problem that we can wish away; the only solution is going to be a military solution. The world that our children are going to grow up in is going to be a very dangerous one, and I don't want to see that for my kids. I don't want them to shed as many tears as I have because of terrorism.

I remember going to the christening of the USS *New York*, which has five tons of the World Trade Center steel built into its hull. The story of how the ship came to be, and the fact that the name was available again for a ship at that time in history, is pretty extraordinary. I was thinking about my father, who had died in 1994, and what he, as a marine, would be feeling on this day. After meeting the captain of the ship, I thanked him for his service and told him, "My father was a marine, and I don't think there would be anything he would want to stand for more than what we're standing for right now."

I don't know if you want to call it retribution for those who took Tommy's and Timmy's lives, but that that ship is a warship that is going to go out on the seas of the world and do incredible things—it's really in the spirit of the way those cops and firemen sacrificed their lives on 9/11.

These days when I'm not working at the firehouse, I support my family with a second job, in the trade my father taught me. I used to own my own contracting business, but it got to be too much with two jobs—it was just easier for me to go work for somebody else. My wife, Genene, works as well. So many of my friends now are out of work, losing their jobs. I've always had the ability to support myself because of the skills I have, and I really hope to pass them on to my older son, Kenny. He's a lot like I was when I was I young: good with his hands and very inquisitive—maybe a little smarter, though. I have two boys: Kenny's eleven and Ryan is nine.

Ryan was born right before 9/11, in June of '01, with a host of medical issues. He had a condition called craniosynostosis, a premature fusion of the skull bones. The skull is actually made up of six different bones, six different sutures in your head. In the first year of a baby's life those bones are very pliable, which is the body's way of shaping itself. The head's growth is actually dictated by your brain's growth. The bones in Ryan's forehead had fused prematurely, so his brain grew [in] the only place it had room to move, which left him with kind of a cone-shaped head. He wound up having seven operations. On top of all that he had some other problems, and then 9/11 came. So I had a big challenge.

Ryan's baptism had actually been scheduled for the week of September 11, and we hadn't given him a middle name. But then my two brothers died, and since our son Kenny already had the middle name Thomas, we decided to give Ryan the middle name Timothy. We postponed the baptism, because I was down at Ground Zero, and it wasn't until maybe six weeks after September 11 that we finally had him baptized. I remember calling the city to try to get his birth certificate changed, to have Timothy added, because we needed the documentation for the church to baptize him with that name.

I was told it would take six months, so I just explained to the guy what I was going through. And he said, "I'm sorry, buddy, you can have it this second." So we got him a middle name, and we baptized him Ryan Timothy Haskell.

I probably didn't deal with 9/11 as directly as I would have had my son Ryan not been sick. Most of my energy from 2001 to 2003 was devoted to his health. We almost lost him more than once. The things we went through with Ryan then, coupled with losing Tommy and Timmy, made this an incredible time in our lives. There probably was a certain amount of strength in me already, to be able to handle what I did, strength that came from my parents. I've just always been somebody who could see things clearly, see them for what they are, and just deal with the problem—whether it is a fire in Brooklyn or my son in an emergency room. Ryan is a very special kid. He's handicapped, mentally retarded, probably as a result of the craniosynostosis and all the trauma he had with his skull. But he just smiles all the time. He doesn't have any physical limitations other than he just doesn't do things as well as a normal kid would. And he has an attitude that has just inspired me over the last nine years. He never cried, never complained. Obviously there was pain involved, but he was so strong through all the surgeries he had to get, almost as if it were just a matter-of-fact thing to do. I realized a lot of my own strength from watching my son. Just the way he handled things. He is the one, really, who got Genene and me through it, and it brought us closer together too.

Tommy and his wife, Barbara, had three girls: Megan, Erin, and Sara, who is a senior in high school now. We're very close with Barbara and the girls—we talk and see them all the time. We're very fortunate to still have Tommy's girls so actively a part of our lives, as some families have been torn apart. It's real sad. I know some of the lost firefighters whose parents had to take the spouses to court to get visitation to see their grandkids. The guy who was killed might have been the glue that kept the whole family together, or kept a particular relationship together; perhaps the in-laws didn't like the spouse or vice versa. But the thing that really breaks my heart is seeing his girls hit all these milestones without Tommy being there. I remember when Megan was moving up from elementary school to middle school, they had a father/daughter dance, and she called me up and asked that I take her, which I was honored to do. I tell you, that got me. When I got off the phone . . . I hardly ever cried before, I don't know why, I didn't feel the need. I was impacted by 9/11 tremendously, but the two times I actually did cry, both were with Megan.

The first week after 9/11 everybody was at Barbara's parents' house, and because I was at the site pretty much the entire time, my mother asked me to come home and just have dinner with everybody. They were tired of watching the news and wanted to talk to me and get a sense of what it was like down there. When I finally was able to go over to Barbara's parents' house, Megan, who was eleven at the time, came up to me and asked, "Did you find my dad yet?"

"No, Megan, not yet. But I'm going to find him for you."

And she said, "I need you to find him for me."

I said, "I will, Megan," and I just had to walk out of the house. I went to the side of the house, and it just hit me like I had gotten hit by a freight train. I sat there alone and cried for like five minutes. Realizing the loss had already come to me that day—being at Ground Zero on 9/11, seeing the destruction, I knew Tommy wasn't coming back. But seeing it through Megan's eyes just killed me. And then doing all these things with Megan over the years that Tommy should have done—you know, it's just tough.

The exciting part of living in that post-9/11 world is getting to watch Tommy's children grow up. Megan is driving now. Tommy had this old Mustang, an '86 Capri, that was his baby. He kept it under a cover in the garage, taking it out only on nice days. Tires with like thirty thousand miles on them. Barbara thought about selling it after 9/11, but I suggested, Let's hold on to it. Megan was always talking about it, thinking it was going to be her first car. So when it was time to get her permit, she wanted that Mustang. But that car is superfast, so I told her she would not be driving it for a couple of years. First get a car and bounce it off the walls and whatever you're going to do, and when you become a good driver, when you become comfortable, then you can start driving the Mustang. So she's driving a Honda Civic in the meantime.

My brother Timmy, on the other hand, had not started a family yet. He had had a girlfriend for two or three years, a woman named Gabrielle, but they weren't married or even engaged. She was young, a young woman with a difficult personality, and the family found it hard to get along with her. When Timmy was killed, Gabrielle wound up getting the federal money from the Victim Compensation Fund, probably close to $1 million. In the long run that was pretty much the last we have seen of her, and I guess she went on with her life.

Tommy's girls are stronger than they even realize. I don't think they'll ever take anything for granted, as most kids do. But I'm hopeful they won't see any more trauma in their lives. Their innocence was taken ten years ago, and they were forced to grow up quicker than they had to. Barbara is also not the same person she was prior to 9/11. She has had to learn how to be without Tommy, how to do more things on her own, and I think she was much stronger than she knew. When somebody loses a father or a husband, when a loved one is murdered in such an extraordinary event as September 11, I think it forces you to become a different person.

Tommy's family has always loved ladybugs, and Barbara and the girls said that whenever they see one they think of Tommy. I thought that was sweet and kind of funny and really didn't think anything more of it.

Then, in December in 2001, I went back to work. The Fire Department had told me to take some more time off, but I felt that I needed to work, to try to get my life back to normal. I got transferred to Ladder 175, and on one of my first calls there we pulled a really big fire—a three-story frame house with fire on the second and third floors, blowing out every window but one. I grabbed a portable ladder and put it up to that one window on the second floor. I'd done the same thing at many other fires, but this time, at the tip of the ladder, I suddenly felt apprehensive. It was like a clairvoyant moment, and something was telling me not to go in there. My senses were on overload, but I climbed in anyway to make a quick search of the room. I found the bed and felt my way around the room, and there was no one unconscious.

But now, rather than find the door and go into the hallway and on to the next room, as I normally would for a full search at a fire, I just stopped myself and turned around. I turned around and said something like, Tommy said get the hell out of there. I went back down the ladder, and as soon as I stepped off it, the fire flashed out of that window, and part of the parapet on the front came down and wiped out the ladder I had just been on.

Afterward I was sitting on a stoop across the street, reflecting on what just happened. I reached for a bottle of water, and just as I was bringing it up to my mouth, I saw something on the top of my hand—a ladybug. Right away I thought, *Thanks, Tom.*

Michael Burke

William "Billy" Burke, Jr., was the namesake of Deputy Assistant Chief of Department William Burke, a high-ranking officer in New York City's Fire Department. He followed in his father's footsteps and entered the FDNY. Billy, a captain, was lost in the North Tower on 9/11. His family today refers to him as Captain Billy Burke, FDNY, which is the way he liked to describe himself. Billy was one of six children, and his younger brother Michael describes his peregrinations through the clouds of New York politics in trying to memorialize his hero brother appropriately.

We were raised in Plainview, Long Island, around forty minutes outside of the city, and we kids had very little concept of what my father was doing in New York City. He never told us why he joined the FDNY. He never really talked to us about his job, never came home and told us about any fires or exciting runs they had had that day. He would talk about the South Bronx, his experiences with the people there; he'd talk about the community, the poverty. I think he had a strong sense of social justice. It might have just been innate in him. My father was first-generation American, and my mother was as well. His parents, our grandparents, were old, both in their eighties. They were ordinary elderly people, Irish immigrants. They went to church on Sundays, but religion or social justice wasn't something they brought up or spoke about.

My father came out of the big war, put a year in at Fordham, apparently didn't like that much, and then didn't do a whole lot of anything for a year or two, taking whatever jobs he could get. When he got the Fire Department job in 1949, he got married and started a family. We were not a small family, six kids in all. There are two girls—Elizabeth is the oldest and Janet is the youngest—and then there are four boys in the middle—Billy was the oldest boy. Chris and I are twins, and then Jimmy. Very balanced. And the blue eyes were the oldest and the youngest.

We were always a Fire Department family, but much different from other department families. My father didn't have work paraphernalia around the house, and he didn't wear anything that was particularly Fire Department, which I guess was not as common as it is now, because they didn't have all the sweatshirts and stuff back then. I could probably count on one hand the times we were in the firehouse when I was growing up. If we were there, it was only because he was going to see his parents in the Bronx and had us with him while stopping by the firehouse for some reason or another.

When my younger sister, Janet, was in seventh grade, she made a little doll in her ceramics class at school—a little go-go dancer with blond hair, blue eyes, and pink skin. Seeing it, my father thought of the children who would hang around his firehouse. And he knew that a little Puerto Rican girl was having a birthday, so he asked my sister to make another go-go dancer, but one with dark hair, dark eyes, and dark skin. I can still see him wrapping it up in a shoebox, tying it up, putting a lot of paper in it. He was really careful with it. He took the train then, as he usually did. And just imagine it: Here's this deputy chief going to the South Bronx and bringing a doll to this little girl. I always remembered that. In fact, I ended up marrying a black Puerto Rican girl, and when we were first dating I used to look around her apartment to see if the dark-skinned go-go dancer ceramic doll was there.

My brother Billy was a chip off the old block in many ways. He was an FDNY captain, and there was no doubt he would become a chief like my father. He was good-looking, witty, charming. You could say life was pretty good for him. Because he also lifeguarded at the beach, in his mind was: *I save lives for a living.* And his running joke was that he used to sign all his letters: Hero Billy Burke. He put it tongue in cheek, but it was pretty accurate. There were one or two instances in which he got hurt and was treated, but, kind of taking after my father, he didn't bring that up. He never told us about it. I remember one fire that he was proud of when he was with 11 Truck, on the Lower East Side. He and another guy, Leroy Smith, saved people on the third floor. There was fire beneath them, and still they were able to get them down in a very difficult, hair-raising situation. There was an article about it in the *New York Post*, along with a couple of photos, and he saved those papers. He had a bunch of papers like that. When I met Billy's lieutenant after 9/11, he told me, "I wish I had put him in for a citation. . . . I should have put him in and the other firefighter."

Billy had worked in a firehouse right down from La Salle Academy. My father had actually graduated from La Salle Academy too, and was the captain of their basketball team. They won the Catholic Eastern Seaboard Championships when he was a junior, and they went back to the play-offs when he was a senior. My father had saved the newspapers that covered the stories of his team and shared them with us as kids. It's kind of funny that we knew all about his success in basketball, but we didn't know all about his success in the Fire Department. Well, we did know what his responsibilities were. We knew he was of high rank, a deputy chief. We didn't know he was the commander of the 6th Division in the South Bronx.

On 9/11, I was working at the Sheraton Hotel, the big one on Fifty-second and Seventh. My wife, Wanda, was also working there—it's where we met, actually—on an early shift that Tuesday, so I dropped her off at 6:00 A.M., driving in like we did every day to get to work. At the time we were living in the black Latino section on Commonwealth Avenue in the Bronx, the same kind of neighborhood my father had worked in the South Bronx. I was off that day.

So on 9/11, I dropped my wife off and then drove back home. Our son, Josh, was home sick from school that day, and Wanda called right before 9:00 A.M, to check up on him. She then said, "Oh, by the way, turn on the television; a plane hit the Trade Center." I looked out the window, and it was a beautiful, clear day, so I'm thinking, *How'd that happen?* I hung up the phone and turned on the television, and there it was on the first station: ten floors of the North Tower, smoke pouring out, and I thought immediately, *The only thing that could have done that is a jetliner.* It had to have been hijacked; it couldn't have been an accident. It would have taken a hijack on such a beautiful, clear day. Somebody had to have flown that plane intentionally into the building. But . . . you know, it was unbelievable. Your mind couldn't comprehend it. Couldn't accept it.

On the TV station that I was watching the newscaster was saying that people were calling in and reporting that they had seen the plane fly overhead and hit the tower. They were reporting it as a private jet, a chartered jet. So then I thought it was a private chartered jet and debated with myself whether it was terrorism or not.

But then Wanda called back. She had just gotten off the phone with my brother Billy, who had called the hotel looking for me, thinking I was at work. They passed the call to Wanda, and she was in a state when she reached me, you could hear it in her voice. This is a tough woman, my wife— you're talking about a black Hispanic woman, a single mom, who had raised a son before we married. So to hear the fear in her voice was scary. Billy had told her, "We're under terrorist attack. Get out of the building, get out of the city. Go home." And I was like, "Where was he calling from?"

She said, "I don't know. He sounded like he was out on the street some-where." "Mike," she whispered, "I could hear it in Billy's voice, I could hear the urgency in his fear. And that scared me."

For Wanda to have heard fear in Billy's voice, that was a hell of a thing. And that's when the second plane hit.

I didn't know it at the time, but Billy was calling from the firehouse. And he'd called other people who lived in New York from there.

And then my younger sister, Janet, called from Florida and said, "Mike, do you see what's going on?" I was like, "Yeah, sure." And she asked, "Where's Wanda?" I said, "At work." And then Janet asked me what I was going to do. Like everyone else I had to think. *What to do?*

How was Wanda going to get home? She couldn't get on the train, for fear of bombs. She was in Midtown. If they hit the Trade Towers, then they were gonna hit Midtown too. Then they reported that the Pentagon had been hit. . . . You could see smoke coming from the Pentagon. They didn't even know what happened there. You didn't know what to do.

I was watching a reporter on TV who was downtown. And as the first tower collapsed, he reported that a third plane had hit. That's what he thought. He was running for his life; the cameraman was running; every-body was running. There were people passing by and were screaming, "A third plane has hit. A third plane has hit!" I was at home in the Bronx, and my wife was in a war zone. And that's when I told Wanda to get out of the hotel—now. She was saying that nobody in the hotel knew what to do. They were all sitting around there crying and making calls. They didn't know what to do.

So I said to her, "A captain in the FDNY has told you to evacuate the building. Get out of the building." So that's what she did, and started walk-ing up Madison Avenue. I told her to go up Madison, because I figured Fifth Avenue was more well-known. If they were gonna hit an avenue, it'd be Fifth. She was in good shape, so I knew she'd be okay walking a long dis-tance. Once I knew she was walking, I got on my bike to go down and meet her. Wanda's older son, Louis, who was about nineteen, was home, and so he stayed there to watch Josh while I headed out.

I rode down the Bruckner Expressway service road into Manhattan, and from there I got a full-scale view of the skyline. By the time I set eyes on it, all you could see was the white smoke of the towers, and I wasn't sure what that meant.

On the service road there was no one—no cops, nothing. So I biked along the Bruckner Expressway, which I was familiar with because I used to run it when I was training for the New York City Marathon a few years back. It was about ten miles and took me right through the South Bronx, past St. Jerome's Church, where my parents were married, Intervale Avenue, where my father worked the fires, and over the Madison Avenue Bridge. And that's when I started to see the people marching up like refugees. I was stunned. It was just: *Wow, this is New York City. This is America. This is happening.* I remember thinking, *Well, we're at war. We are a different world now than we were a half hour ago, and it was . . . This is the world now. That was then, this is now.*

My sister Janet had told me a reporter was saying there were eight more planes, so I fully expected more planes to drop into New York.

At the time Wanda had a cell phone, but I didn't, so I would stop on my bicycle whenever I saw a pay phone to call her. Then I would call home to get the messages, hoping that someone would have called about Billy. Wanda and I planned to meet at Marcus Garvey Park, and when I got there I couldn't find her at first. The park was . . . Wow . . . There was this stream of people, thousands, who had just walked up from downtown. Everything and everyone was so frantic. The day was frantic.

By now I knew that both towers had collapsed. In my mind I was visualizing a partial collapse—chunks of the towers the size of a city bus. I knew the towers. I once worked not far from them and used to walk over there at lunch. Those buildings were so big that if a piece the size of a city bus fell from the hundredth floor, you couldn't possibly outrun it, because your perspective would be all off. How dangerous that was.

And then I saw Wanda, who had her back to me, and there was that instant sense of relief, knowing that she was alive, such an emotional thing. Now I began thinking of Billy. Wanda saw the look on my face and asked, "What's wrong?" I said, "Billy's down there."

I got home late that day, eight o'clock, and spoke with my younger brother, Jimmy. He had spoken with Billy's girlfriend, Jean, who said that Billy had called her from the towers.

"I'm okay," he said. He told Jean to call our sister Elizabeth in Syracuse and let her know he was all right, and for her to call the rest of the family: "Tell everybody I'm okay." And that was just after 10:00 A.M.

He was in the North Tower.

So that night I was with the family, and I was talking to my brother Jimmy on the phone as we were watching everything on television, looking at the ruins. And as we were staring at the screen, we both realized we hadn't heard from him. Billy was the type who called, and he hadn't called. I said, "Well, if he's down there, if he is, how's he gonna call, anyway?" He'd have been too busy doing something else. So hell, it wasn't a sure thing; you know, it wasn't a sure thing.

Then there was the rest of our family, my mom and other siblings. I guess I spoke with Janet again; I don't recall. And my twin, Christopher, went over to Elizabeth's up in Syracuse, and they were watching TV together, hoping to get word from us, or from Billy. We were all communicating, but none of us had heard from Billy yet.

The next day everything changed. I drove into the city to look for Billy's firehouse, Engine 21. I wasn't sure exactly where it was, because he had just started there as captain five months before 9/11. All I knew was that it was somewhere around Fortieth Street on the East Side. I got stuck in a massive jam by Grand Central Station. There was a bomb scare, I heard on the radio. I just gave up and pulled over into a parking spot. I don't know what street I was on, somewhere on Park Avenue by Grand Central, but it was a spot no one should park in. So I wrote on a piece of paper: "I'm looking for my brother, Captain of FDNY, ticket if you must, please don't tow." I left it on the dashboard, and I took off.

I found a pay phone and called my brother Christopher in Syracuse to ask him where the firehouse was, but he didn't know. Then he told me that he was watching the news, and four firemen just walked out of the pile. "They were down at Bellevue," he said. "Go there, get down there." At this point I was on Thirty-eighth and Second Avenue, so I wasn't far away. I was halfway down and began thinking, *Things just don't happen this way. It's a nice dream, but things don't happen this way.* But I went down there anyway.

There was a big crowd outside of Bellevue, and so many pictures everywhere—pictures of people whose families were trying to find them. There were a bunch of people holding the flyers, and family members crying, being interviewed by newspapers, holding up the pictures, hoping that somebody would see them. I managed to speak with a woman at Bellevue who had this great big book, and I said, "Billy Burke." And I asked about the four firefighters. She said that those four guys had just been working at the site today, and fell into a pit down there, and they were fine. But nobody had found anybody yet. I looked at the flyers again, seeing those family members. It was so sad.

I left Bellevue and somehow stumbled upon Engine 21, which was on Fortieth Street between Second and Third avenues. After speaking to a couple of the guys there, I became the point man for our family. Plus, I was the one who lived closest to the city.

I remember calling a general number given to me for the Fire Department. You were supposed to call this number for any updates, hopefully, on survivors. I would call and ask these FDNY guys on the phone, "Billy, Captain Billy Burke?" And they knew Billy, knew who he was. Still missing.

There was another guy I wanted to know about, a good friend named Quinn, who was with Engine Company 55. I asked about him as well, and they didn't have any information. And this was maybe a couple of days later. I knew one man had been found, the only survivor from Engine Company 55. His brother, who is also a fireman, found him in the cafeteria at Bellevue, maybe forty-eight hours later, sitting there, still covered in the same dust. When one of the towers collapsed, he ran, and was the only one in 55 who survived. It hurts to remember that story.

Jimmy came in frequently to help with the whole search. And our sister Elizabeth came down from Syracuse. I remember Liz and I walked around the city. We went past Union Square Park, which was filled at the time with flowers and memorials. It was hard to see all those things, reminders that we were missing Billy.

It was a gradual thing for us, my siblings and me, to realize that Billy was gone. And it was probably an individual thing rather than a singular moment for all of us together. After twenty-four hours, I knew, no matter how busy, that he would have gotten to a phone by then. Billy . . . Billy would have called. At first we were like everybody else. We went on TV. We went to the family center that they had set up on Lexington Avenue. I called all the hospitals in the city. Then I saw a story about a guy who was taken to a hospital in New Jersey. So I called up the hospitals there.

Billy was the oldest boy in our family, second oldest overall. Elizabeth may have been his older sister, but Billy was the oldest brother, and he filled that role completely in terms of making our lives miserable. He was also somebody we looked up to and depended on. He was the point man for us to my father, and that was a big job, you know, growing up. It was a complicated thing, to deal with my father, especially as teenagers. The classic butting of the heads. Billy took the grief. He was the guy who got most of the grief, and he kept it. We took the leftovers, but he took the brunt of it. There were just clashes—as if a competition was going on between my father and Billy. Ten years later my brother had such admiration for our dad—and reverence. I found some letters that they had written back and forth, and it was interesting to see how special their relationship had become. My dad giving Billy advice, talking about the job—there was real communication and mutual respect there. You would never have predicted it from those teenage years.

As kids, our experience with the Fire Department happened on special occasions, such as at a New Year's Eve party or on St. Patrick's Day. The firefighters would come for a barbecue, or we'd go to a picnic—that was a big thing, the firemen's picnic. We saw the reverence that they paid to my father. That was a big influence on us when we were growing up, because you could see that even when you were ten, and it really affected Billy. We grew up with the idea that firemen were the greatest guys in the world. That was the line in our house. And my mother would quote my father in a playful way, imitating him, saying, "Firemen are the bravest and the greatest." All in good fun. But I never really appreciated the truth in that statement until after 9/11.

What we learned when Billy died, what we lean on, is the idea that he left this legacy: Billy was doing what he wanted . . . what he loved. He was following in his father's footsteps. It was so important to him, living up to that ideal. It was not just an ideal but a fact—the entire culture of FDNY. I think that was the comforting factor for us. There was nowhere else that Billy would have wanted to be on September 11 between the hours of 9:00 and 10:30 A.M. than where he was.

Had Billy not been there, had he not been working that day, his company would probably have been wiped out. I remember telling people, "Had any of his men died and he survived, I would have had to go down to his apartment in Stuyvesant Town and nail the windows shut." It would have been very difficult. We know that Billy always put his men first. And that's the thing we lean on, that's what got us through in the days afterward, and the months afterward.

I want to see the firemen get as much attention today, as much appreciation, as they received in those days and weeks after 9/11. And they got a lot. The city would stop for a fireman's funeral. The city did just that for Billy's. Fifth Avenue was stopped; people stopped walking on the streets out of respect. I remember the east side of Fifth Avenue was filled with pedestrians, and the west side was filled with firemen from all around the city, and the world.

The attention the firefighters received in the media, the papers—it was real and genuine and deserved.

We went down to Ground Zero not too long after 9/11. My mother, my twin brother, Christopher, and his wife came in, and we went to the site. We took the subway there. We clowned around. Mom was taking pictures of us, as if we were out-of-town tourists. We got to Broadway, which was as close as they let people go. You could look at the facade remnants, and you could see the damaged sphere.

But as much as everyone appreciated the way the press was turning the firemen into saints, we also knew that ultimately you looked at the character of the person. Me, I never cease to be astounded by what the firefighters did that day. And I think that's what got the country through it. That's what got New York through it. Thinking about it, I guess that was a big part of what got me through it in those days: Their courage. Their character. Their humanity. Their sacrifice. What those 343 firefighters, 23 New York police officers, 37 Port Authority officers, and 3 court officers left us is a memory of uniformed courage.

I called my friend Quinn and spoke to him maybe two days after 9/11. I'd known this guy since high school, and I could always make him laugh. I began talking to him and trying to get his mind off of what had happened. But I knew at some point I'd have to get to it, and I asked him what had happened, and he started talking about it. He said, "Mike, they were falling out of the sky, and they were exploding," and his voice broke. I leaned on that display of character and humanity to get me through. And I think that's what each of us did.

Keeping this huge and historic courage in mind, it wasn't until the early spring of 2003 that I heard about and got involved in the plans for the memorial. By that point the discussion about how to commemorate 9/11 had been going on for a year already, which surprised me. I couldn't imagine people sitting around in conference rooms the previous spring talking about this. But they had been, and the first thing we heard was that they weren't going to identify the firefighters in any way on the memorial. Which was wild to me—totally disrespectful. My brother's identification would just read "William F. Burke, Jr.," rather than "Captain William F. Burke, Jr., Engine Company 21." Well, that doesn't tell any of the story.

We could see that the memorial officials were going to exclude the heroic sacrifice that our country had embraced, that our world had embraced. We were getting invitations from France; 9/11 families were being invited to Ireland. The world had embraced this sacrifice, and there was a reason for that. It wasn't just out of kindness, or that it was just the right thing to do. I think everybody understood what the first responders had done. But the people running the memorial did not: first Governor George Pataki, and then the people running the LMDC [Lower Manhattan Development Corporation]. When I found out that they weren't going to honor and commemorate that heroism and sacrifice, I was sure there had been a mistake.

I had gotten an e-mail from one in the 9/11 families, who was in opposition to identifying the firefighters and police officers, urging me to work against this. *This is a misunderstanding,* I thought. So I e-mailed the guy back and said, "You know, you have to understand how important this is for these guys. They went down there as firefighters and police officers to help. This is who they were."

It's very weird that the naming procedure became so political. After 9/11 Governor Pataki insisted on referring to all those who died as heroes. Sometime in October 2001 I remember hearing a woman say, "Everybody's talking about the heroes. My sister wasn't a hero. She was sitting at her desk when the planes hit." She was sitting at her desk, but we have to remember her. And we do not honor her memory if we don't remember that she was sitting at her desk. This woman, whoever she was, shouldn't be remembered as a hero. That's diminishing the meaning of her death. Of course there were some heroes among the victims—many men and women. As [Mayor Rudy] Giuliani said at my brother's service in Saint Patrick's Cathedral, "There were civilian heroes we will never know. They perished with everybody else."

There was an article in *USA Today* that basically asked: Who got out of Tower 2, and who didn't? Most of the people who did get out of Tower 2 were those who had a view of Tower 1. They saw what the hell was going on, and so they ignored the radio speakers telling them to stay in their offices. There was a man on the ninety-sixth floor of Tower 2 who looked out his window. A man in a brown suit was standing opposite him in Tower 1, the window smashed out, his tie flapping in the wind. The two men made eye contact, and then the poor soul in the brown suit jumped. That's when the guy in Tower 2 took off—he evacuated and lived to tell his story. A story of wanting to live. A story very different from that of the first responders, who went in to die.

The first memorials had actually already been created by the families, posted by the families. These were the memorials on our streets and in our parks, little groups of candles and flowers and photographs of loved ones. Each photograph in those little memorials gave details on the personal characteristics of the person, whether it was sex and age or tattoos and jewelry. And, of course, the floor he or she was working on. When I saw those flyers for the first time, there was still a desperate hope to find them. We, the families, did believe that some of them would be found. We looked at those photographs, at the photo of a man who had been on the 102nd floor, Tower 1. We did not know that he had jumped. We found out slowly. He was able to make a call, left a message at home, saying, "I love you. Remember me and that I love you," and then he jumped out of that building. But in the photo he's still sitting with a smile, looking at you. The terror of that, knowing your loved one was now gone. It's pure and spontaneous and genuine. These memorials were embraced by the people on their own, spontaneously, without any input from politicians or their cultural experts. Now they were going to subtract all of that personalization. This we couldn't have.

George Pataki and others who were referring to everyone who perished on 9/11 as heroes were and are wrong. I thought I was politically astute, but I learned otherwise. I thought Pataki would have done the obvious thing, but he did not make himself popular with the 9/11 families of the first responders by refusing to make any decisions, by just going along with the volume of the loudest argument at the moment.

But Mayor Giuliani was meeting with the families of Ground Zero to discuss the issue, and I thought that could help, because at the time Giuliani was the man. On November 12, 2001, there was a conference at the Sheraton Hotel for the FDNY family members. The city had the medical examiner there and a few other people to talk about the recovery of remains. I just watched what was going on, and it was a hell of a thing. These women, mostly the widows, were beyond distraught. They wanted their loved ones, their husbands, brought back to them. They had heard that there were entire bodies at Ground Zero, and they wanted the city to get them. Meanwhile, the medical examiner was saying that hundreds of thousands of tons had dropped on Ground Zero, and he presented a graphic medical explanation of what happens to a human being who is hit with eighty-five floors, each floor weighing four hundred thousand tons. It wasn't very helpful—it was insulting, and the crowd was about to lynch the guy.

Giuliani then walked into that conference room and just took control of it. The people there had such faith in him, because they knew that he meant what he said. I had always liked Giuliani, but Billy had loved him, because of how he had turned the city around as mayor. He told everyone at that meeting, "Here's what we're going to do," and they believed him, because they had a reason to.

What I wanted was simply identifying by rank, department, and company all of the first responders. Among the 9/11 family members there were a few who had a casual and sort of philosophical opposition to listing ranks, companies, and departments. They didn't want anybody identified. Because so many hundreds were lost from Cantor Fitzgerald—658, to be exact—they didn't want people from the company identified, because, they complained, it would end up being a Cantor Fitzgerald memorial.

In my family we felt a sort of Irish anger, a sense of injustice, that someone was cheating and denying what we believed was right. We knew what was important to Billy: his responsibilities and his rank. The job was everything to him, as it is to all of them. To be a firefighter, to be a captain, a chief, a lieutenant—that's who they were. You cut the guy open to see his heart, and you saw Captain William Burke, Jr. It's hard to explain, and I didn't really appreciate it until after 9/11 either.

The memorial at this point is just two large square voids, each side with fifteen feet of falling water and about two hundred trees to symbolize the rejuvenation of life, as the jury described it. There will be a wall around each void, about chest high and slanting toward you, and the names will be engraved on these walls. I believe they are going to put family members together but not distinguish them in any way as such. There will be no ranks or ages listed, so the young children on the hijacked planes will not be seen as children. You will see a woman's name and you will not know she is a four-year-old girl. You will see the name of Mychal Judge and not know he is a priest, and the name of Timothy Maude and you will not know he was just fifty-three and a three-star general in the U.S. Army. The memorial creators tell you to go to an information kiosk, but how will you know to go there? They are purposefully denying actual history. There's not going to be anything in the memorial that will speak to the attacks, to testify to what happened there.

The museum is going to be underground, and they advertise that it's going to be a big rock. The memorial foundation returned from storage to the site the last beam, and made a big deal about it, inviting all the press to take pictures. So the beam has come back, but the damaged Koenig's Sphere, which sat in the plaza between the towers, is not coming back. The only reason the beam is included is because it's going in bedrock, which means it's going underground. The rationale behind keeping the museum and the beam underground is to keep all evidence of the attacks out of sight to the memorial visitors. The jury said there could be no artifacts from the World Trade Center, or any 9/11-related artifacts, included in the memorial itself, in order to protect the integrity of the design. Any artifacts are to go belowground, out of sight. "Protecting the integrity of the design" were the words of Michael Arad, the designer of the memorial. I spoke with Michael and told him that family members would like some authentic artifact, like the Koenig's Sphere, returned to the site. He winced and said that would be didactic. I had to look up the word "didactic," meaning that it would tell us what to think as we were standing there.

The design of the memorial was supposed to be a democratic process, but the problem is that it became too democratic. It should have been given to the cultural artists and thinkers, who would know what the hell they're doing—then maybe we would have gotten a decent memorial. Some protest that the last thing we need is elitism. But in fact the competition and the process were a beauty contest. The memorial design was not the choice of a democratic system, but of a handful of political leftist and elitist appointments. This was a jury of eleven or twelve people deciding from over five thousand memorial design entries worldwide. Why this jury? Why these people? Who picked them? Those are questions we should have been asking.

All eight of the original designs that were picked embraced abstraction and minimalism; none of them recognized the attacks. The then architecture critic of the *New York Times* praised the memorial, saying it was ambiguous and narcissistic, values that are precious to the jury. In April of 2004 *Art in America* magazine praised the design because it doesn't acknowledge the attacks. *The New Yorker* said the design might trigger a dream state in which we could wonder.

Nobody talked about the human beings who must be remembered, whose families are suffering. Everyone was looking at the Vietnam War Memorial as a model, a minimalist but gargantuan gravestone.

I met with Michael Arad, who was living in the East Village in September 2001. On 9/11 his wife was working on Broad Street, and he rode down to meet her on his bike, just as I had ridden to meet my wife. They escaped the cloud and went uptown. He said he spent his time after the attacks riding around Manhattan, getting a feel for things, which was what moved him to enter the contest and moved him to create his design. But he never said he went down to the site, never went down to Ground Zero. In his design he never confronted the attack itself. All he did was confront people's expressions, their fears. He went to Washington Square Park at midnight, maybe two or three days after the attacks. He said people were gathered there holding candles, and nobody spoke, and he said it was very powerful and moving. Manhattan is a tough place to feel at home, and as a foreigner from Israel, he had never felt connected to it. But now he felt a connection, and one between strangers, which is hard to find in Manhattan. And that I think is true. But is that what our task is at Ground Zero?

A couple of days after 9/11 my wife and I heard that they had set up a family center at the South Street Seaport, and that you could go down there and identify your loved one. The word was that they were going to have bodies there. I imagined floors of bodies and body bags, which they would unzip. *All right*, I thought. *This is what I'm going to do. Identify the body.* But it was nothing like that. Everybody was prepared to do anything they could to help. There was a monk there, and people speaking in accents you couldn't ever recognize, and they all couldn't have been more helpful. But it was not what we went there for, so we got back in the car and started driving. Across town, on Sixth Avenue at about Eighteenth Street, both sides of the street were lined up with people, hundreds of them, standing and holding candles. That's all you saw for blocks. And they were silent. It was a spiritual, spontaneous thing, and they had all come together. It was a hell of a thing to see, and I'm happy to have seen it, to have experienced it. But you know, that's just a memory. It is not a way to commemorate 9/11. We have a greater task at Ground Zero than to simply commemorate feelings.

I was at work one day when my brother Chris called, telling me to turn on the radio. NPR [National Public Radio] had a panel of cultural community people talking about the memorial. They were taking call-ins, so I phoned and told them I was the brother of a 9/11 FDNY captain. The panel had been praising the memorial for its abstraction, its ambiguity, and how everybody could take home his or her own meaning of the day. I criticized it for exactly that and said that there should be more to the memorial than the art. There was nothing there to speak to 9/11. And one man said, "Well, do we want the memorial to be a history lesson?" As an example, he cited the Vietnam War Memorial as being a successful memorial.

I was prepared for this, and I had a response: "The Vietnam War Memorial is not a viable model for what we want to memorialize at the World Trade Center. You cannot use as an example a memorial in Washington, D.C., that commemorates feelings about a war fought on the other side of the world. You can't replace any authentic artifacts in Washington. None of the battles of Vietnam were fought in Washington, D.C. You didn't replace any of the authentic artifacts. You didn't replace a fire helmet, or a police badge, or a stockbroker's wallet. None of the names on the Vietnam memorial died right there in Washington."

I hope I convinced them that Ground Zero is the *site* of the attacks; people died right there.

We wouldn't go to Auschwitz and remove the death camp remnants and artifacts in order to better express our feelings or make it a more unique place for mourning. Our task at Ground Zero is not to make it a more unique place for mourning or, as Arad says, a place to think about the absence in our lives caused by these deaths. In other words, Arad's abstract design basically states: It's not about Captain William F. Burke, Jr., and what he did that day. Or how, and why, he died. Or about anybody else who died there. Or about 9/11. It's about us. And it's about Michael Arad.

But we have a greater duty. If you want to make an abstract 9/11 memorial somewhere else, you can do that. There are plenty of them across the country. Right now the national September 11 Memorial at the World Trade Center site is nothing more than two crying pools, which does not accurately display the great heroism and the great tragedy of 9/11. We can never forget what happened that day; we need to remember. Right now it is a memorial for thinking and reflecting; it is not a memorial for remembering.

I remember the first time I saw Billy's death certificate and saw that the cause of death was homicide. Thinking about those nineteen Islamist terrorists or Khalid Sheikh Mohammed, thinking about those who killed my brother is part of what drives me to stay involved with the 9/11 issues at hand. My sisters went down to Guantánamo Bay, and in that courtroom they got to look directly at Khalid Mohammed. You have daydreams about what you'd do if you had the opportunity to get revenge, that sort of thing. You want to hold the Islamists responsible. How difficult it must have been for my sisters to look Khalid Mohammed in the eye.

There is a failure to understand and to learn the lessons of 9/11. Look at Major Hasan from the Fort Hood massacre. They knew that he was a fundamentalist; they had plenty of evidence, and they did nothing. Nothing. Prior to 9/11 a field officer reported to his superiors that there were five Middle Eastern men who were learning how to fly an airplane without learning how to take off or how to land, and they said, They have a right to learn how to fly. And this is all due to political correctness, the same kind of correct politics and cultural ideals that come out of the New York thinking about 9/11. It's a certain mind-set, an agenda, a cultural and political power that is so hard to go against.

I do think a lot about Islam. The majority of Muslims worldwide criticized the building of a mosque so close to Ground Zero, so you can see that there are moderate views among them. However, fundamentalist Islam [often called Islamism], jihad, and submission to Sharia law are such a big problem that I think they don't want to face it. It's not something Muslims want to confront. It's a scary thing, but it seems nobody has a solution to it.

I don't know much about Islam, but I met a man recently whose sister was working for Cantor Fitzgerald on the 104th floor of Tower 1 of the World Trade Center. He said she called home and told her mother that the smoke was getting really bad, and then said, "I don't think I'm going to make it."

Her brother then said to me, "I'd like to think that the smoke got her, but I don't know that she didn't jump."

There was a third guy with us who had worked in Saudi Arabia, and he had nothing good to say about Islam, speaking of it in vile terms, with venom. He told us the attack on 9/11 was an act of war, and we had to fight it now.

The two of us looked at each other, both thinking this guy was kind of over-the-top. But here we were, two family members, neither one of us were bleeding-heart liberals, who did not feel this strongly about Islam. We didn't want to forgive and forget, but neither one of us wanted to be over-the-top either.

I haven't heard any family members hate Islam, but what's interesting is that the building of the mosque at Ground Zero is making people hate Islam and Muslims more than the attacks did. The 9/11 families weren't holding Islam accountable for the attacks, but now, when people don't act properly in response to something like this, a mosque that is seen as an insult, it is held against them.

Sometimes I ask, What have I accomplished? I've spent so much energy and time on this, on the memorial and commemorating 9/11 properly. But at this point the memorial is not going to acknowledge the attacks, so I feel as if I haven't accomplished anything. On the other hand, Billy's rig, Engine 21, is going to be part of the museum. I was on the museum committee with Commissioner Cassano, and with his strong support we were able to make that happen. Kids are going to come here for generations and see that fire truck and know Billy's story—how he embodies the heroism and the sacrifice of that day.

My family just deals collectively with our memories of Captain Billy Burke and what he did that day. And we do things independently, too. My brother Christopher recently wrote something for a Syracuse paper about the mosque issue, and how our politicians don't know that Ground Zero extends as far as the dust fell. Wherever that dust landed, that's the sacred ground. When Christopher was telling me about what he had written, he got very emotional talking about Billy, so this was one of those times when the emotion comes out. But I guess that's how we've dealt with it.

We're all working hard at preserving what Billy would have wanted. He was a history buff and had a superior knowledge of the Battle of Gettysburg, where we lost almost eight thousand men in 1863. I've got pictures of him down there on that field of battle. He had bookcases filled with things. His favorite figure from the Civil War was General John Buford, who was the first to engage Lee's forces. He taunted the Confederates with his small number of men, and he forced them into the best strategic place for Meade to fight Lee. Billy was really impressed by that. His admiration was genuine and not just a romantic idea. He understood what they did, and the importance of conveying that forward in history, and preserving it, for our own progress. A free society progresses by remembering the sacrifices for our freedom that were made in the past by ordinary people. And so that's the way our family thinks: Preserving the truth, and not some image of an autocratic mayor and of an inexperienced architect. Preserving the truth . . . I know that's what Billy would be doing. And that's what the Burkes are committed to doing for our brother.

Talat Hamdani

A New York City teacher, Talat Hamdani is a widow and the mother of three sons. One of them, Mohammed Salman Hamdani, was killed on September 11, 2001. He was a New York Police Department cadet and a certified emergency medical technician who responded to the attack on the World Trade Center when he saw the smoke while on the way to his job as a lab technician.

It was in May of 1978 when my younger brother came home and said that the American embassy was giving out business visas. He could not leave Pakistan because he wanted to stay with my mom, who was a widow. My husband, Salmeen, though, had always been an ambitious man, and he wanted to go to a foreign country so that he could prosper. We both had good jobs in Pakistan—I was a second-grade teacher with the government, and he was the manager of a battery company—but we still lived hand to mouth, even though we did not pay any rent because we lived in his family's place. So he applied for and got a visa. There were no savings for a new start in America, so a couple of weeks later we sold our motorbike and our refrigerator, the only two valuables we had after three years of married life. He cried when his motorbike was sold—that was his baby.

It was, I think, in June of 1978 that he arrived in America; I joined him on February 3, 1979. Our son Salman was then thirteen months old and wasn't walking yet. Later, his two younger brothers, Adnaan and Zeshan, would say, "You're an immigrant." And they did it to me also, because they were born in America and we weren't. That's the American attitude, and I'm glad they have it. It was funny, but it's not a crime to be an immigrant.

We lived first in Greenpoint, Brooklyn, which was a nice neighborhood then and is nicer now, though more crowded. Salmeen, of course, needed a full-time job to support our family and found one at the Blood Brothers company in Mamaroneck. It was a wrecking company, automobile parts, and that's where he worked for five years.

We went fishing a couple of times with Mr. Blood, and Mrs. Blood was a nice lady. We never discussed who was what religion or anything political—that was never a consideration before 9/11. In 1983 Salmeen started working for this Yemeni guy, Ali, in a store on Manhattan Avenue in Greenpoint, and purchased half a share in it. It was a small store, a deli and newsstand, selling newspapers and magazines, Lotto [tickets], cigarettes, soda, beer. We already had two children, Salman and our second son, Adnaan, and it was around that time that my youngest son, Zeshan, was born. When my husband first had the idea to buy the share, we didn't have the money. So I said, What to do? I took all my gold to Ali's wife, and said, "Here, keep this. Whatever you say our share in the store is worth, when I give you that money, you can give me my gold back." She is such a wonderful person. She said, "No, Talat. You take your gold back. I trust you will give me the money."

In 1986 Salmeen bought the entire store. Only eight years after coming to America he owned his own business. He set a great example for our sons.

All my boys grew up in Greenpoint, and all three of them went to St. Cecilia's, a Catholic school. I sent them there because I went to public school all my life, and I believed in the discipline of the parochial schools. Adnaan is four years younger than Salman, and Zeshan is eighteen months younger than Adnaan. Salman was the tallest of my three boys—a very tall, handsome man, with everything to live for. But the trinity of my sons is broken now.

Salman used to get beaten up in the neighborhood when he was around seven years old. So my husband said, "This is not right. I can't be there protecting him every day on the streets." So he put him in karate school, and they taught him self-defense. Salman told me, "Mama, I'm supposed to tell anyone who challenges or threatens me that I know karate, so don't mess with me. And if they don't listen, then I can hit them back." Which he did. That helped him to become strong and independent.

One day when Salman was in the fourth grade he came home and told me he didn't want to go to St. Cecilia's anymore, because all the kids were saying to him, "You're not Catholic, you don't belong here." It was because he would not go to the church. I had spoken with the nun who was the principal, and she had had no objection, and suggested that Salman could go up to the principal's office for that period. I went to St. Cecilia's again and apprised the principal of the situation. She said, "Don't worry, I will take care of it." A week later Salman came home one day and said, "I need the Koran to take to school, because the teacher told us to bring our book of faith to show everybody." They had all different faiths there, and there was no problem. Years later, I think this is what this nation needs now: a discourse on diversity of faith and tolerance. It's ironic that Salman experienced his first lesson in tolerance at such an early age

Salman went on to become a police cadet, even though he wanted to become a doctor, as the main profession in my family was medicine. Apart from your academic standing, when you apply to medical schools they want to see your extracurricular activities. So joining the NYPD and getting an EMT license added some points for him, as did studying abroad and doing volunteer hospital work. So when he applied to medical colleges, he looked good on his résumé. We also had a family friend, Elijav, who was a NYPD sergeant and a military veteran, but Salman would never let me ask for any help.

Actually, I don't remember getting anything for him after his ninth birthday. Even when he graduated, and I told him I wanted to throw a party for him, he said, "Well, you can have it, but I won't be here." So I asked, "Why don't you let me celebrate something for you?" He replied, "I'm not proud of it. When I'm proud of doing something, I'll let you know. Then you can celebrate for me." He had very high values, and was a humble person. Very humble. When our friend Elijav died, he was buried under the American flag. Salman said, "That is an honor, Mama, and that is how I want to go." And that is how he went when he was finally laid to rest in April 2002.

He was also very compassionate. He would bring home sick birds and nurture them, and he would help people out. One day we were walking in Manhattan, and there was a car on the street with two ladies in it who had been in an accident. He pushed people aside and wanted to know what was going on. Mostly because he was an EMT, it just came automatically to him to respond. He did not need anybody's command to tell him to go and do such a thing. His values and his personality enabled him to see other people's pain. He could see them hurt, or in the hospital, and I think he felt their pain. When he was a teenager he stopped eating meat, and once when he saw me eating chicken, he said, "One day a chicken is alive, and you're eating it now." He became a vegetarian—that says a lot.

In September of 2001 Salman was in his final year of the police cadets.

It was a three-year program, and he had applied the year before to medical schools. He had not been accepted, which happens to many students, and so he reapplied in 2001. He told me that if he did not get accepted again his aim was to get hired as a detective in the NYPD. As a cadet he worked out of different locations, including housing in Manhattan and a center near Queens College. He got paid by the hour by the NYPD, so he used to put in time over the weekend and evening to maintain himself. He also became a certified EMT and worked for one year with an ambulance company in Manhattan and in Brooklyn. By 2001 he was looking for a better job and got an offer from a pharmaceutical company, but he didn't want to work there, explaining, "I want a job that will lead me to medical school." So in August 2001 he took up a position as a protein lab analyst at the Howard Hughes Medical Institute at the Rockefeller University. He brought home only one paycheck.

For me September 11 began as a normal day, a normal Tuesday. We were in Bayside, where we had lived since 1989. I remember saying to Zeshan, "It's a beautiful day, crisp." I left about 7:15 A.M. with Zeshan to drop him off at Queens Community College, and I went to my school, Middle School 72, for work. Salman took the number 7 train to Manhattan and usually left home between 8:00 and 8:30 A.M. Because the train runs aboveground through Queens, he must have seen the towers burning. I used to pick him up from that train every day. He would call me on his cell phone—"Mama, leave home now"—but that Monday, September 10, he did not call: He had left his phone at work. So on the morning of 9/11, he had no cell phone during his commute to the city. I know he would have called to say, Turn on the television, look at what's happening. And maybe if he had called home, we would have told him not to go there. That's the whole thing: There's a time and place. You know, also in death.

When I came out of my eighth-grade class for a break at about 10:20 A.M., I saw the other teachers huddled in the hallway, and I thought, *Oh, maybe this is to see how the school is performing.* So I went over to them and heard that they were talking about the towers burning and falling down. This couldn't be right. I remember that moment saying to myself, *This couldn't be right. This can't be right. Let me go and call home.* So I went to the phone and I called my husband, and he was screaming his head off that the Twin Towers had been attacked, and they had fallen, and there was burning, and Salman is there. My Salman was there. I said, "Salman doesn't even work there, why would he be there? There is no reason for him to be there." Then he exclaimed, "Oh, the second tower is falling!" I said to my husband, "You are fine, and Salman is fine, too, you are both fine." And the second tower fell while we were on the phone. Months later that's where they said they found his remains. Under the North Tower. Why did my husband feel that he was there? Maybe Salman called out to him. I don't know.

At school they asked for volunteers to stay until all the students were picked up, so I left later than usual and got home about 4:30 P.M. We tried to contact Salman, but his cell phone was going straight to voice mail. My husband sent his brother to check out Salman's workplace, and when he returned he told us that Salman had never reported to his job that day. That was disturbing, for him not to report to his job, and then for him not to call home after the systems went back up. But that day we were not worried. I called Adnaan at SUNY Binghamton and told him *vhaijan* hadn't come home. That's what Adnaan called Salman—*vhaijan*, big brother. I said, "Don't worry," and everybody in the family figured that I wasn't worried, but then the whole night passed and no call came in. So the next morning Salmeen and I went down to his job, and Salmeen couldn't stop crying.

From that Wednesday morning Salmeen did not stop crying until he died. Even in the hospital, when he was dying, the staff asked me, Who is Salman? I asked why, and they said because every night Salmeen asks for Salman. They were best friends.

So Salmeen and I went to the Howard Hughes Institute, and we told the security guard there that we were Salman's parents and had come to re-trieve his cell phone. He got the phone for us, and then said that he had a friend in the FBI and would ask him to look for Salman. We asked him what to do, and he told us to go down to St. Vincent's [Hospital]. That's where all the injured and the dead bodies were being transferred, and we might be able get some information there. At St. Vincent's we found a very long line, and they told us to go and look at the list of the injured and dead that came out every three hours. We waited over two hours on the line, and Salman's name was on neither the injured list nor the dead list. So then we came home and made flyers with Salman's photo.

On Thursday we somehow ended up at the armory on Twenty-fifth Street. Everybody was outside with pictures and posters looking for their loved ones. We were told to give our DNA sample there and to report

Salman missing. We gave our name and address, his name and description, and whatever information we could provide. For the next ten days we searched for him, asking if anyone had seen him, but people did not remember, with so much powder and the dust that had come down that day.

They had given us a list of 150 hospitals where the injured had been sent, and we did go visit a few in Queens and one in New Jersey. We thought he might not be able to speak due to an injury, and we might find him somewhere. But he was nowhere to be found. Still, there was hope. Hope gives you that drive to keep moving forward in life. We have to have some hope.

Then, at the end of September, a man came to our store and said there were many people who had been detained. This gentleman used to work for the MTA [Metropolitan Transportation Authority], and he said that officials were asking about Salman. He said he told them, "I know this young man. He grew up in Greenpoint." He knew our family because he used to work at the hardware store. He was Pakistani, and he said they didn't ask him out of the blue: They were asking questions at the MTA, where they said that if anyone knew Salman Hamdani, to step up. And then he told me, "Maybe your son did not die over there, and you should write to the government and ask where your son is." So we wrote a letter to President Bush.

Why were they asking about Salman? I think it was because of his first name, Mohammed. Yes, definitely. I had told Salmeen not to name him Mohammed, because one day he would have to pay a price. But he didn't agree with me, and said, "Well, he should be part of our people's everyday faith and nationality." It is difficult to survive in any society with the name Mohammed, but he did not understand that. It's just politics. Another factor may have been that Salman had not put in hours with the police cadets for about six weeks before 9/11, but that was only because he had just started his job as a lab researcher at the Howard Hughes Institute.

Twenty-five days after 9/11 we decided to go to Mecca to pray to find Salman. Before we left I said I was going to call the morgue, because they were telling people on television to come and identify their loved ones. It took a lot of courage for me to make the decision to go and look at the dead bodies, but I said, "If I am going over to Mecca to get an answer whether he is alive or dead, let's look at the dead bodies; if he's among them, then I don't need to make the trip." Just for my own satisfaction I called the number the armory had given me. I don't know if I misdialed, but they asked, "How did you get this number? Why are you calling here?" I explained that I had been given this number by the armory for information if I needed to investigate my missing son's case. I gave him Salman's name, and he said, "Oh, he is a Pakistani?" I said, "Yes, he was born there, but he is an American." And then he said, "But he is also claimed by the British government—why is that?" I told him my sister came from Britain—maybe she had given his name there. He asked all sorts of questions about Salman—what he was wearing, what he looked like—and later that evening we got a call from another detective, asking questions.

On Saturday, when Salmeen and I were going into Manhattan to the morgue, that detective kept calling us: 'Where are you now? Are you going there? What are you doing?' But when we arrived there, it was the Red Cross; there was no morgue; there were no bodies to be identified. So why did they send me there? I don't understand. I wanted to see the bodies. And all the hospitals I called gave me the same statement: We have fifteen victims; fifteen patients came in. We cannot give you their names, but your son's name is not on our list. And you are not allowed to see anybody to identify.

No other parents had to go through what we had to go through. It was horrible. Such a great injustice. You give your life, try to save your fellow Americans, and then this nation goes after you, calling you a terrorist.

On the day we were leaving for Mecca—October 12, 2001—a *New York Post* reporter came to talk to me about Salman and what he had been doing. He asked me, "Oh, your other son is the president of the MSA [Muslim Students Association] at Binghamton?" Adnaan was the president that year, and he was running for the secretary of some other organization.

That put my antennas up, and I said, "I don't trust you." While he was sitting there a reporter from the *New York Times* called, and then one from *Newsday*. I asked them, "What brings you back to my house so many months later?" Something must have happened to bring all the media back. One of the newsmen, from the *Daily News*, told me there was a flyer at the NYPD with your son's name on it, asking anyone who knows Mohammed Salman Hamdani to come forward. I still have the flyer.

Despite this we left that day for Mecca. And the next day, October 13, the story hit the media that our family had gone to Mecca to pray for their

son—except for the *New York Post*, whose headline was MISSING—OR
HIDING?—MYSTERY OF NYPD CADET FROM PAKISTAN, by William J.
Gorta and Simon Crittle. The implication and insinuation was that Salman
was linked with terrorists and was seen at the Midtown Tunnel at 9:00 A.M.
that day. After the funeral, much later, in April, I was watching New York
1 News, and the banner that ran at the bottom read: MOHAMMED SALMAN
HAMDANI, WHO WAS THOUGHT TO BE A TERRORIST, WAS A HERO.

After we returned from Mecca two weeks later, on October 25, 2001,
it was amazing: Calmness had descended upon us. Stepping into that
mosque in Mecca was so peaceful. We needed that to get out of the grief.
When we came back, everybody said we looked relieved. We were not
unhappy, not so much in depression.

While I was over in Mecca I had a very significant dream. After performing the ritual of the Omra I went to sleep with a prayer asking God
to just tell me whether Salman was alive or not. When I woke up at 5:30 in
the morning, at the call of Adhan, I was in the middle of a dream in which
I saw my family all standing around, and I asked my kids, "Where is
Salman?" And he was standing outside on the road, outside the mosque
near Mecca, and he was wearing his red shirt with his crew-cut hair. He
had a pole in front of him and was looking at the ground, and he was very
sad. And then I woke up, and I felt he was there, at Ground Zero.

It's very hot at Mecca in the daytime, so what they usually do is go to the
mosque in the evening and stay all night long, and then they sleep in the
daytime. So I went to sleep, and when I woke it was around 3:30 P.M.,
the call of the Adhan in the late afternoon. But what was amazing was that
the dream that I had in the morning [had] continued. This time Salman
had joined us, and he had a shopping cart and was going shopping. I took
that as an omen that he was alive: He would come back and join us. I figured that ten hours had passed between these two dreams, and that ten
meant that something might happen if I wait ten weeks, ten months, then
ten seasons. But nothing happened in ten weeks, ten months, or ten seasons, and now it's the tenth year. This September will be ten years, and
something has to happen this tenth year. Maybe. Maybe I will have a grandchild named Salman. Adnaan told me that he believes that Salman's going
to come back as a grandchild.

When we were in Mecca we got a call saying that Congressman [Gary]
Ackerman's office wanted to contact us about Salman. When we came back

we met with him, and after a few conversations he was sure that there was nothing wrong with our family, and now we are very good friends. He also made us write a letter to [Attorney General John] Ashcroft, saying that Salman might be with ICE, Immigration and Customs Enforcement. I said, "Why would he be with ICE? He's an American citizen." [Ackerman] said, "But he wasn't born here." The dividing line is whether you were born here or not. And so in November we wrote a letter at his suggestion. When he was satisfied that nothing was going on, he did not deny it: He led us to believe that Salman might have been detained. So the hope was still there that one day he would come home—a lot of hope. Even if Salman had been detained, at least he would be alive. I wanted my child back. I didn't care where he was as long as he was alive. Because a child is a child.

In the third week of January 2002, we received a form letter from the White House: Thank you for reaching out to the President, we are forwarding your inquiry to the FBI. A letter from the FBI arrived five days later which said, We only investigate criminals, so if your child is involved in a crime, then we can help you.

After all this time, two officers came to our house on March 20, 2002, at 11:30 P.M. Salmeen and I were the only two at home, as Zeshan had gone to California that day and Adnaan was then at Syracuse University Medical School. The officers said, We are confirming that your son's remains were identified through DNA at the Twin Towers. Here is the medical examiner's number; you should call them right now. My husband just fell to the floor right there, but they were adamant: Go get the phone and call the ME. I said, "You know what, officers, thank you very much. You have done your job. You can leave now." And they did not have the decency to tell my husband, before giving this bad news, Have a seat, we want to talk to you. They just came in and blurted it out. I found that to be very crude, crude and unprofessional. Then I said, "Nothing is going to happen now. If he is dead, he is dead."

I gave Salmeen some medication to help him sleep, and the next day we went down to the medical examiner's office. They had a big file. They said they found his lower body part, from his waist down, and thirty-four pieces. And so I said, "Why did it take you so long? When did you find it?" The ME said, "The third week of October—October 23 and October 26." He explained that they had to match each body part with my husband's DNA, and then with my DNA. It didn't sound very convincing. I waited a long time—four months. DNA comes back in two weeks.

So I said, "Who is to say that these are the remains of my child? I want to have my own DNA testing done." He had a file in front of him, which he pulled toward himself and said, "Go get yourself a lawyer." He was very defensive. My mother-in-law was there and asked, "Why are you becoming so defensive? All we are asking is that you convince us that our boy is dead. And if you are trying to help [us] understand the situation, you are not doing the right thing." He said, "You have two options, Mrs. Hamdani. You can take the remains and the death certificate and do whatever you want with it. Otherwise, it will remain with us, and whenever you are ready, we will have it. If you want to have someone do your own DNA testing, it will have to be done in front of us."

I had to inform my family, who came to attend the funeral: Salmeen's brother, my brother, my sister from England. I knew the media would come up to my door again, once they heard Salman had been identified, so the next day Salmeen and I went to California to visit my sister. We took the remains. The funeral parlor handled it, and we went there the day before the funeral. There was a casket, but I don't know what was in it. We were told not to open it, because there was nothing in it to see. And they gave us his jeans. The jeans were his. One of the legs was missing from the knee down, and one leg was there. And one sock. But those were his jeans.

Even if he had been ten, twenty, fifty miles away, he would have gone down there. That was him. He was a bone marrow donor—that we found out after his death. I knew he gave blood twice a year at Queens College. He was very giving.

Having it confirmed that Salman's remains were found at the World Trade Center redeemed his reputation: Salman the police cadet, and Salman the EMT.

Not long after 9/11, I went to a memorial event. Someone there questioned me about Salman being a member of the NYPD cadets, saying that I was lying about my son's affiliation with the department. After that I wrote to Commissioner [Ray] Kelly, because I don't have any badges or a shield number, so there was no proof that he had been a cadet except for his paychecks. I asked him to give me a shield or something that would vouch for the fact that he was a cadet. So on the first anniversary Commissioner Kelly invited us to One Police Plaza, where they gave us a shield that said CADET on it, in Salman's honor.

In 2009 the NYPD honored Salman. Police Commissioner Ray Kelly gave us an award that says in tribute:

Hero Tribute
The NYPD Muslim Officers Society
Recognizes the Sacrifice and Heroism of
Cadet Salman Hamdani
on September 11, 2001

————➤◆◀————

With honor and appreciation
presenting this award to the Hamdani Family
First Annual Scholarship Dinner May 7, 2009
Ahmed Nasser
President

That year I got a package from the 9/11 Memorial about where Salman's name would be placed. There is a designated spot for the FDNY and NYPD members, but his name would not be placed there: It would go with the persons who worked there [at the World Trade Center]. So I wrote and called them and told them his name should go with the NYPD because he was a cadet. The gentleman I talked to said, "You know, Mrs. Hamdani, we did not get his name from the NYPD list." I said, "Yes, I know. But if you want, I can get you information that he worked with the NYPD, and they did give him a funeral in April 2002." I was finally told, "Oh, Mrs. Hamdani, your son did not get an award from the president. That's why he cannot go on this list." Can you believe that? To go onto that section for the NYPD, you have to get an award of heroism from the president? [Mrs. Hamdani is here referring to the Public Safety Officer Benefits Act, first enacted in 1976, a cash award that is given to the next of kin in the event of a line-of-duty death. It is $315,764.]

We had to move forward in life; we had closure. And from that point onward we tried to go back to our normal lives. After the funeral Salmeen went back to his store. I went back to teaching. Adnaan got married in the summer of 2003. It was a nice summer, happy times. But then I got into three automobile accidents, the last of which, in December, was a head-on collision, which left me disabled and unable to go back to work. Salmeen's health worsened. He went through a series of medical tests, and the doctor told me that it was very important that he have a colonoscopy. The doctor explained that Salmeen had a complicated medical situation because he had a heart condition and was also diabetic. Salmeen refused to go for a colonoscopy, and in October 2003 had a stent put in his heart, after which he developed pneumonia. At the beginning of 2004 he went back to Pakistan because his uncle was sick. When he returned on February 19, he went straight to the hospital, and that was it: He had cancer, and it had metastasized to the brain. I believe it was because of his depression, and that 9/11 was the origin. It just wore him down, and all of it started overtaking his immune system. He was very down, and he died July 24, 2004.

That was a very bad blow, and just left a vacuum within our family. First their brother dies, and my three boys, these brothers, were very close. And then their father dies, and I have to step up into his shoes, to be a father as well as a mother. I had to make sure these boys were taken care of. When their father died Zeshan was nineteen and Adnaan was twenty-one. All of us were in a very deep depression; nobody was really functioning anymore. We wanted to move away from Bayside.

It was a very rough time in 2005 and 2006. Adnaan was at the State University of New York at Binghamton during the time of 9/11 and then he went to Syracuse University for medical school. When his father was in the hospital for five months, though, dying of cancer, Adnaan came home. After that experience, and with two and half years of medical school under his belt, he said, "I don't want to be a doctor anymore. I won't have the strength to lie to a patient, knowing that he is going to die in ten days or a couple of weeks, Mama." So I told him to take time off, and after that he stayed at home for two and half years, doing nothing. I told him it was time to get back. He had a wife, too, having married at a very early age. At a friend's wedding in December 2002 in Pakistan, he met the girl and proposed. It wasn't arranged; parents cannot pick a partner for American children. When the girls are educated it is very difficult to make an arranged marriage anymore, especially if the girl is independent and able to support herself economically. The only reason she wants to get married is if she falls in love.

Zeshan tried to go back to college three times, but he just could not perform. So we all moved to Long Island in October 2006. It was tough for me; holidays and whatever had to be taken care of, and everything was on my shoulders. But my boys were there for me, and I thought I was there for my boys. However, I don't think I could have carried it without my siblings, my oldest sister especially. All three of my sisters are doctors. The eldest one is a psychiatrist in California. She is about ten years older and takes good care of all of us. Of course there was a lot of anger after losing one loved one in 9/11 and then another loved one to a horrible cancer. Young or old, losing someone from your core family is like a part of your body, and your soul is ripped away.

Then I became very sick and almost died. I was cleaning the deck in the backyard with a poisonous solution and the pressure nozzle came off. The solution went straight in my nostrils and I got chemical pneumonia. Zeshan had come home that day, by chance, and a few hours later I said, "I can't breathe, take me to the hospital." My oxygen level was forty-seven, and they said I had to have a lung biopsy, which revealed that my lungs were damaged. They then said that I would not come out of it, and if I did, I would need a lung transplant. But then I made a remarkable recovery—it was a miracle recovery. That was last June, in 2010, so now there is still just the three of us—myself, Adnaan, and Zeshan. Adnaan is now doing his medical residency at Syracuse and is in the emergency room department. He finds it very challenging, and he likes challenges. Zeshan is going back to college. We all suffered; we all suffered a lot.

We try to be happy. Even considering the climate at the time and what we as a nation went through, I still feel our trust was betrayed. I remember thinking it was as if America had been raped at that moment. And now, what happened during the ninth anniversary, with the Muslim center going up and all the Islamophobia that grew around it, there was all of this hatred again. There was so much hatred, discrimination, and bigotry that reared its ugly face to the nation.

When I was in the classroom teaching my eighth-grade class after 9/11, I gave them a lesson contemplating what comes to mind when you hear the word "terrorist." The top answers were Muslims, or Islam, or also bin Laden. But now I've gone back to teaching, and a fourteen-year-old in my school actually called me a terrorist, based on my Muslim faith. When 9/11 happened he was only five. How does he know all this? His parents and our society. And our media. Children at that age echo what they hear. So that truly concerns me, because this is not something like fighting communism.

This anti-Islamism is directed against one of the largest faiths in the world. As President Bush said, We all need a good faith. There are some people on this side of the Western hemisphere who are fighting for a good faith. Many people over there in al Qaeda are fighting for a jihad. So if you look at it from that perspective, I think that most people who are religion-minded, whether they are Muslim or Christian, are in their minds fighting a religious war with one another. We are paying the price for jihad—especially those of us who live on American soil, who have been living here for years and as citizens. I am of the first generation, but there are many other Muslims who are second, third, fifth generation living here. I do think the Arabs are paying more than the Pakistanis and Indians because of their race, because bin Laden was Arabic, from Saudi Arabia and Yemen, and his mother was Yemeni. But we are all paying a price.

Why are we being held responsible for the acts of a foreign terrorist organization? They don't have ties with any nation or state, and they have distorted my faith, our faith, in the name of Islam. People living here, Muslims who were not terrorists, also died on 9/11. We are paying our taxes, going into the military, serving our nation, our country. Even if not a single Muslim American had died that day, it's still not right to hold a whole community convicted based on its faith.

So how do we educate the public? My neighbor asked for a ride to her church one day, so I said, "Okay, I'll go with you." And I ended up going a few times, and it was very nice. They have different activities, and they know I'm a Muslim. I volunteered to go with them to distribute church donations. They go to poor areas, and they give out food and clothes as a way to reach out and help these neighborhoods in need. And that's what I think the Muslim communities, wherever they are in America, should be doing more of. Immediately following 9/11 there was—and still is—a lot of talk about the mosques breeding terrorists. So people are keeping an eye on the mosques. No such thing is happening, there is no anti-American talk going on in any mosque. At the mosque I attend in Queens, they don't talk about any politics at all. Before 9/11 many sermons were given in Arabic, and a majority of the students don't understand Arabic, so they are also given in English. They have Sunday schools, but what they need to do more of is to reach out into the community and show them we are Muslim Americans, and we are here for you as your neighbor.

Things are happening now, interfaith dialogs and so on. There is still segregation in the mosques, women sit separately and men sit separately, and I don't know when that will be resolved. Another thing is to have discussions at the university level to debate mutual tolerance. The media also plays a very important role in disseminating knowledge and directing the heart of a nation, and so far the media has not been fair. CNN does studies on different ethnic groups, and needs to do a similar project and show the American people the different faces of Muslim Americans who are contributing members of society. How often do you see a Muslim face on the television? There are scientists. There are people in the military. There are people in the private sector who are very successful businessmen. There are people in the education system, teachers and educators. Bring them forward and show that they are normal people.

A national debate opened up this last year: Who are the Muslims, and why are we being ostracized? I asked one 9/11 parent, who also lost his son, "Do you think that your pain is greater than my pain? So much so that you are willing to advocate cutting off the religious freedom of an entire community and throw this nation back into segregation along religious lines, instead of uniting this nation and healing and moving forward?" That's what we need: to move forward together as a nation.

I want people of all nations to remember my son Salman as an American, and as a hero who gave his life saving his fellow Americans. Without the thought of faith, race, and ethnicity, he sacrificed for all. He and the other people who died that day were killed not because of their faith or race or ethnicity, but because they were Americans. America was attacked that day for American values. Salman's legacy is to represent those values—of liberty, democracy, and freedom of speech and religion, to practice the faith of one's own choice without any discrimination. This is a great nation, and I'm very proud of it. And so was Salman, proud to be an American.

Toni Ann Carroll

Toni Ann Carroll lost her husband on 9/11. He was a firefighter assigned to Squad Company 1 in Brooklyn, and he responded early to the attacks on the World Trade Center. It was a late marriage for both, and Toni Ann was grateful that she had finally found the love of her life. After losing her husband, Toni Ann went through years of suffering, both physically and emotionally. She is only now starting to find happiness again.

It was 1995 when I first met Pete, when he came and painted for me. Painting was his side job, when he wasn't firefighting. I had heard his name years before through some connection of sorts, but we had never met. I initially hired a different painter, but he was a little expensive. My cousin called and said, "Toni Ann, there's this guy, Pete the painter, who works in our development. Try him; he's more reasonable." I called Pete, and he came over for an estimate, which was fifty dollars cheaper than the other guy. So I hired him.

I was working in Manhattan at the time, as executive legal assistant in a maritime law firm by the World Trade Center, and my mom stayed and chatted with Pete the entire day while he painted the room. When I came home she said, "What a nice guy that Pete is. But he's had a life like you've had."

My first husband left me with two children when I was very young, only twenty-five. Then I remarried at twenty-nine, and my second husband was very controlling, so I got out of that relationship. Pete had similar difficulties with married life. He had been married twice as well. So I guess we had a past in common.

When he came back to be paid he saw that I had fractured a few of my fingers and gashed up my arm from a Rollerblading fall. Pete was very concerned and asked, "Oh, my God, what happened?" I told him, and he felt so bad. But that was it. I paid him, and he left.

Pete stopped by again the next day, but I wasn't home. My daughter, Dana, spoke with him. He had flowers. "How's your mom feeling? Please tell her to call me." But he had so many problems, and was going through a divorce, that I didn't want to get involved, so I didn't call him. But then he called me and came by again. My father was outside gathering the mail, and he said, "Hi, I painted for your daughter. My name is Pete, and I just wanted to know how your daughter is doing." My father told him that I was doing okay. And Pete said, "Well, please tell Toni Ann I was asking for her."

My father said, "Hold on, Pete the painter." And he came inside to get me.

I said to my father, "Oh, that jerk? What does he want? Tell him I don't want to be bothered." And that was it.

In the meantime, he had split from his second wife for good. So I finally gave in and said yes when he called and asked to take me to dinner. And from that day forward it was like we were the best of friends.

Pete would take me out to dinner, oh my God, almost every night. When we'd finish dinner, he'd say, "Thank you, Toni Ann."

I'd respond, "Why are you thanking me? Thank *you*, Pete."

He would then say, "No. Thank you, for your company."

By 1998 we were engaged, and we were married on February 17, 2000, in St. Lucia. We got married on the beach, and it was really beautiful. Then we came back home and had a little ceremony and dinner with a wedding cake and all, with the family.

This was the third marriage for both of us, and there's an old line about marriages that goes: The first is for because you don't know any better, the second is for money or looks, and the third is for love. And it was that way for us. We were really in love.

People could see our love—it was like that. Pete's captain gave his eulogy at the funeral, and in it he said, "I've never seen Pete with such a smile on his face until he found Toni Ann. He came to work every day with that big smile, and he couldn't wait to go home to her."

There were a few who made comments about how we had only been married for nineteen months when Pete died. But the others who could see what we had would say, It doesn't matter if it was nineteen months or nineteen minutes, the love that they shared was so strong that it's immeasurable.

Everything that Pete and I did is just a memory now. Everything was just beautiful. We would take walks at night, and constantly talk, with never a lull in conversation. And it wasn't just the wedding that was memorable—it was those smaller moments, like just taking a ride to visit his dad, a retired NYPD police officer who lived up in Neversink, New York. He had prostate cancer and was very sick. Pete was so happy, because he did not see his dad often, and when he met me, I used to love to go there. He enjoyed that.

Pete had called his dad from St. Lucia on the morning of our wedding, and he was so nervous. His dad said that he couldn't have picked a better woman, and that he was going to be very happy. I didn't meet his mom, because she had already passed away. But I loved his dad. I really did.

On Monday, September 10, 2001, I went to a tattoo parlor and had Pete's name put on my lower back—just a no-frills tattoo that said PETE. When I got home he told me not to uncover it, because it needed to heal, but I said, "I really want you to see it." When I showed it to him, he actually got tears in his eyes. He picked up the phone and called the tattoo parlor where I had it done, and he made an appointment for that Thursday to have my name put on him the same way. But he never made it in, and the tattoo artist was so touched by the story that he decided to give free tattoos to firemen after 9/11. If they wanted their shield or their company patch put on, he was doing it for nothing.

The next day was Tuesday, September 11, and Pete was going back to work at Squad 1 in Brooklyn. That was a tough job. Before 9/11, I had been pushing him to take the lieutenant's test, but he said, "I don't want to leave my house and be jumped from here to there. I just want to stay where I am." At one point he transferred to Squad 288, HazMat 1, in Queens, as he wanted to be able to teach HazMat eventually, and there he could become an expert at it. But he missed Squad 1, and so I said, "Your happiness is what matters." And so he returned to Squad 1 in Brooklyn, and he was a first-rate firefighter for nineteen years.

That Tuesday morning, Pete left for a day tour. I was sleeping upstairs, exhausted from a long weekend and not feeling well. At the time I was on medical leave because I had been very sick in 2000. I had fallen off my bicycle while we were on vacation at the cranberry festival in Cape Cod. It was a very bad fall, and we should have gone to the hospital. I was cut up, and the bone was sticking out of my leg—it was really bad. Pete took it kind of lightly, because he had seen so much gore in his life as a fireman that it didn't seem like a big deal to him. I got an infection from the gravel and dirt and developed fibromyalgia. I was critically ill, bedridden for five months, and Pete literally had to carry me around. I also had herniated disks in my neck from the fall, for which I had to have surgery in 2004.

So at 7:15 A.M. he kissed me good-bye. I said, "I love you," and he said, "I love you too"—that was our thing.

He went downstairs, where my daughter, Dana, was eating Cheerios, getting ready for her first day of school as a senior at St. John Villa Academy. She said, "Where are you going?" "I gotta go to the firehouse." She said, "Stay home. Mommy doesn't feel good." He said, "I can't." And he wasn't usually affectionate with the kids, but that day he kissed Dana good-bye, and left.

After I got up, I and my son, Anthony, were getting ready to go to the mechanic. I was trying to use my cell phone, and I had no service, and Anthony said that his phone didn't have any service either. And so I thought, *That's weird*, and turned on the TV. We saw the first plane hit the World Trade Center, and I said, "Oh, my God, do you know how many people just died? Anthony, do you realize what just happened?"

I got on the phone and called Pete's firehouse, but the phone just rang and rang. Finally someone picked up: "Squad."

I said, "It's Toni Ann. Where's Pete?"

"Toni Ann, I can't talk to you right now. Pete was one of the first. He was driving. He's gone; he's there."

Anthony and I went to the mechanic, and as my car was being inspected we were watching TV in the shop. We saw the second tower fall, and at that point I felt like that was it. He's gone. Pete's gone. And we cried.

My father was supposed to have a meeting at 2 World Trade that day, but it had been canceled. He and my mom were still going to the city for some reason, though. Anthony was getting worried that something may have happened to them too, so when they walked into my house later that day, we were so happy and relieved to see them.

My mom immediately said, "Pete's not working today, right? He's painting, right?"

I said, "No, Mom. He's there."

Oh, my God, he can't be there. So that's what happened that day. I watched the towers fall.

Then it was night, and still nothing. No word. I heard from no one.

I called the firehouse again that night and finally spoke with one of the guys, Timmy Rogers. He said, "Toni Ann, don't be too optimistic."

And I said, "What do you mean? What are you telling me?"

He said, "Just what I'm telling you. Don't be too optimistic."

For the rest of the night everyone was calling for Pete: his father, his sister, his brother, his kids. His two older kids from his first marriage, Nicole and Michael, had come over to my house.

Pete had four kids in all. Nicole and Michael were around the same age as Dana and Anthony; from the second marriage, he had two little boys, Peter and Christopher. It was Christopher's birthday that day, on September 11. He was turning six. I was saving Christopher's birthday gift that we had bought for him.

Later that night the phone rang, and it was little Christopher on the line. He said, "Is my daddy dead?"

And I said, "No, Christopher, Daddy's not dead. Who told you Daddy's dead?" "Mommy keeps saying that Daddy's dead."

I tried to tell him that Daddy was helping people to get out of those buildings.

Two minutes later the phone ran again, and it was Christopher's older brother, Peter. "Toni Ann," he said, "Mommy keeps saying that Daddy's dead."

I said, "Peter, Daddy's not dead. All right?"

And all of a sudden their mother got on the phone with me and said, "He's fucking dead! You understand? He's fucking dead!"

I only found out later that someone had forgotten to change Pete's contact number, so they called his second ex-wife that night and told her that they had found him. And that's why she told me he was dead. She didn't like me at the time, but I realize now that it was a traumatic thing for her as well, and maybe that is why she reacted the way she did.

And she kept saying, "*He's dead!*" But I didn't believe then.

The next morning there was still no word about Pete. And my father kept saying to me, "Don't give up hope." And my brother: "He may be under the stairwell." No, nothing.

On September 13, they finally came to my home. I was sleeping on the couch, still waiting. My boss, Simon, had come over. Even though I was on medical leave, we were very close, and he was truly there for me after 9/11, taking care of me, because I was not in a good place. The bell rang, and Simon went to answer the door, and it was like out of a movie.

Simon told me, "Toni Ann, you have to come here."

I got up and saw the two men with black suits. They flashed their badges, and one said, "Mrs. Carroll, we found Pete."

"You found him?!" I was so excited. My face lit up, and I said, "See, he wasn't killed. He must have been under a stairwell." But then I looked at Simon, who was crying. I asked him why he was crying.

Then one of the two men said, "We are so sorry."

I said, "Sorry for what?"

"You will have to make funeral arrangements."

And I collapsed in hysterics. They had to carry me to the doctor's office and tranquilize me. And that's what happened when I realized that Pete wasn't coming home.

I had to determine where we were going to have his wake. I remembered, when we went walking one night, Pete said, "You see that funeral home, that's been there for years. It's a family-run business. And you see this church? I love this church. And I want to be cremated." These things stuck in my mind. So I knew what Pete wanted. When his father suggested we bury him, I said, "No, I know he wanted to be cremated." He had told another friend the same thing, so he was cremated.

The funeral was held on Monday, September 17, 2001, at the Harmon Funeral Home in Staten Island, followed by a mass at Blessed Sacrament Roman Catholic Church. At the funeral home we had a traditional wake with a casket. I was told that they found him intact, but they wouldn't let me see him. I wanted to open the casket, and they wouldn't let me. They just had a photo of Pete on top of it. And in my nerves, I tried to pry open the casket. I began to lift it, and they had to pull me off.

I wanted it open. I wanted to see him.

And everyone was saying, You wouldn't want to see him. Remember him the way he was.

I never saw so many people in my life as at his wake. I used to say to him when he would have to go to a wake, "Why do you have to go?" and he would say, "Because they are firefighters," and "Out of respect." I couldn't understand why he had to go to each and every one, because he didn't know these people, and then I'm in a chair and these firemen are coming up to me, and I said, "Did you know Pete?" "No, ma'am." And I said, "Oh, my God. Now I understand." And I cried, because I had never really known what it was all about. And I got to experience it.

The older children came to the wake with the first wife. I didn't want the second wife there after the way she had spoken to me on the phone on September 11. I said her kids could come in, but I wouldn't let her in. She came after-hours and put some pictures on the Peg-Board. They both came to the funeral, though. I was distraught. People had to dress me. I remember having Pete's dress cap on.

The years following 9/11 were a difficult time for me.

Pete wasn't originally supposed to work on the eleventh. He switched his tour with someone at his firehouse, one of his best friends. We were very good friends with this fireman from the squad and his wife. After 9/11, I would go out to dinner with them, and he would never look me in the face. I couldn't understand why. Finally, after three years, he looked at me and said, "I have to say something." He was crying. He told me, "Pete came to me in a dream, and it was so real, and Pete said, 'I want you to grab her, and I want you to look her right in the eyes and tell her everything is going to be okay.'" And that's what this fireman did. A grown man crying. And his wife was hysterical. She said, "I'm so glad he finally did it. He couldn't face you." He then gave me this big kiss, and I guess it helped him come to terms with it. He felt so guilty that Pete lost his life for switching tours.

I thought for a while that Pete had been found intact. My mom finally told me that he wasn't: He had been severed. I was in hysterics when she told me this. Later, I got a letter from the city medical examiner. So I called up the medical examiner's office. I was by myself in the house, sitting on my bed, when I phoned. I said, "I'm calling about Peter Carroll. I got a letter from the medical examiner saying that if the person wasn't intact to contact the office. And that you've been looking for me. For what reason?"

"Oh," she said. "We found a body part of your husband. We found his heel. And he's also missing the top portion of his head."

Well, I just went into hysterics again. I called the Fire Department, and they came to the house to try to console me. It was like 9/11 all over again. I had to cremate another body part, and now I have two urns. I spread the ashes from one of them. I wanted to give the second to Pete's son Michael, because he had asked for it. After the fifth anniversary of 9/11, I met up with Michael, who had become a firefighter like his father, and I saw him in uniform. He held his arms out to me, and we exchanged phone numbers. I thought things would be okay again. After that he didn't talk to me anymore. I tried calling him to say that I wanted to give him the ashes and he wouldn't accept my phone calls.

And then, in 2006, the medical examiner called again, while I was in the middle of a birthday lunch in Atlantic City. They had found the top portion of his head. Everyone at the lunch was then crying with me. I called up the funeral home again, and they told me, "You can't keep doing this to yourself. I'm going to have to step in, Toni Ann, because we have already given you two urns, and this is just not healthy for you."

What happened was that we waited until December, and then accumulated whatever we had and put it into a single urn. The urn is in my bedroom now. And I also got back his wallet and his wedding band, which they found. The wallet has our wedding picture in it, and ten dollars and twenty-five cents. Pete always wore his wedding band, so I feel blessed to have gotten those items back.

I was so angry for a while, because Pete had said he would never leave me. I know it wasn't his fault; he was killed. But I was angry, because I had finally found Pete after all these years of being miserable. I was left with two babies to raise on my own. Then I remarried and made another mistake. So many empty years before Pete, and then, finally, I find my soul mate, and he's taken away from me. That can make a person bitter. But it wasn't Pete's fault. It wasn't anybody's fault except Osama bin Laden and the terrorists'.

I went through a depression, and I was hospitalized in 2006 for about ten days. I couldn't find happiness for years—you know? I just couldn't find it. And it wasn't until 2006 that I was able to go on with my life a little bit more and let go. I was suffering from depression and post-traumatic stress syndrome. And that's when I think I snapped out of it, when I learned I had post-traumatic stress.

After the hospitalization I realized that Pete wasn't coming back. I used to look at people and think they looked like Pete in some way. It's so hard. There is not a day that goes by that I don't think about him. Still. I have a handyman who helps me out, and Dana says that he smiles just like Pete. You still relate people to him. It just doesn't go away. It doesn't go away.

I'm not like some of the other widows. I lost $517,000 in 2007 when the market had a big downturn. I was awarded $680,000, and I lost $517,000—almost my entire settlement—from a person who was highly recommended to help people. I saw it coming, and I wanted to jump ship, and he wouldn't take me out of the funds. And yes, the market did crash. So I'm not a millionaire. I never was.

Most people I meet have this preconceived notion of the "9/11 widow." The first thing they think of is money. I didn't lead an extraordinary lifestyle; money didn't change me. If I could have Pete back, that would be my first wish. I didn't care about the money. I didn't marry him for money. And I found it upsetting that they had to put a price tag on someone's life.

Healing is different for everyone after 9/11. For me, one of the things that helped was a letter I received from a woman, Ruth Rossi, who worked as an attorney for Morgan Stanley [on 9/11]. Ruth had seen Pete's picture up in a gas station in Neversink, which was hung as a sort of memorial, because his family was known around town. And when she saw his picture she recognized him by his eyes, because he wasn't in gear. She knew those eyes and said, "That's my fireman." So she asked who the parents were and got the address and wrote a letter to his father. And then his dad had called me and said, "I have a letter here. It's from a woman that Pete saved on 9/11. And she wants to get in touch with you." I have the letter she wrote to me framed in my home. And she wrote to me about exactly what he had done—how he led her to safety and saved her life.

Ruth had seen Pete standing in front of the rig, because he was chauffeur that day. She said she had frozen when she saw the blood that was splattered and body parts and bodies in the plaza, and it was Pete who went to her and put his hand on her shoulder and turned her away from it all. She looked at him—she remembered the sad look in his eyes—and he said, "Ma'am, you don't have to look out there. Look at me and I'll lead you to safety, we're going to get out of here." And she said he escorted her out and went right back into the South Tower. And then the tower came down.

As Ruth ran across the Brooklyn Bridge, she wondered if her fireman—that's what she called him—had ever made it out.

Sal Cassano called me last year and asked me if I wanted to meet Ruth. She came really to thank me for giving up Pete to save her life. It was a very touching meeting. My son was there with me, and she was with a battalion chief, a woman who was friends with Sal. The four of us just huddled together and cried.

Ruth had to leave Morgan Stanley shortly after 9/11, because from their new location in New Jersey she could see the site across the river. And she could not look at it anymore. So she gave up her job and moved to Maine.

I met someone back in 2002. His name was Pete also, and he helped me a lot. He was very kind to me, but I wasn't ready for a committed relationship then. I just couldn't commit, and I felt guilty. I felt unfaithful. But this past year he came back into my life. He asked me to marry him, and I said yes. He's a good man, and he understands when I talk about Pete.

So I'm moving on in life. It's just a little harder to move forward when you're not well. My fibromyalgia was actually Lyme disease that turned chronic as of last year, so it's as if the Lyme disease is taking over my life little by little by little. Hopefully they'll find something to help me get better. I can't take antibiotics anymore. I just had the gallbladder taken out, and so the stomach became so badly inflamed that I cannot take antibiotics anymore. So I just have to be thankful for each day. The only thing is, I live each day in pain.

I love life, yes. And if I had at least my health, I'd be happier. Because if you don't have your health you have nothing. I have to say that. You could have all the money in the world, but if you don't have your health . . . So I don't really know what's going to happen.

I asked Pete to send a sign that he was with me: *Send me a quarter.* I want to find quarters. I don't want to find pennies, nickels, or dimes. How often do you find a quarter? It's more special, because it's not that often. Well, now I find them constantly, and in the weirdest places—in the basement, even on top of the cuckoo clock. It's just amazing, how little things happen.

One day we'll be together again, but for now I'm trying to move on with my life here.

But you know what? It's all in God's hands.

John Vigiano

John Vigiano is a retired captain in the FDNY. His reputation within the ranks of the city's firehouses is that of a very professional, experienced, and reliable manager—a "great boss," as many refer to him. Throughout his career he worked in the busiest fire companies of Brooklyn, including the legendary Rescue 2. He and his wife, Jan, had two sons: John, thirty-six, a FDNY firefighter, and his brother, Joe, thirty-four, a NYPD police officer. Both brothers responded to the World Trade Center on the morning of 9/11, and they died in the line of duty.

We are a police and fire family. My father joined the Fire Department in 1937. He was a very interesting, talented man. He could draw, and illustrated most of the training material that the department used. I can still see a huge picture of the MSA mask [an early smoke mask]. He drew the whole thing and labeled all its parts, like something you would see today in a catalog.

My mother and father divorced when I was seven, so I never really had a father. I didn't know him, other than that he worked in Greenpoint, was a handsome fireman, and took me to the circus, the rodeo, and *The Last Alarm*, the firemen's show they used to hold in Madison Square Garden. Maybe that was the mustard seed that was put in my head about being a firefighter.

I lived with my mother and my grandmother. Back then there was no such thing as alimony checks. A fireman was probably making $2,000 a year, so every month my father would send a green money order for $18.75, and every month I would take it to the delicatessen, where the owner would cash it and take his $0.75 out of it. We lived in a poor man's brownstone, a frame building laid out like a brownstone, no heat, one bedroom. So I would sleep in the living room.

When you grow up without a lot of frills, and everybody's the same, that's normal. Today they call it dysfunctional. It's not dysfunctional but just the way it was. Everybody was struggling. It was a different code. I grew up in Bedford-Stuyvesant, a predominantly mixed area. I didn't have any problems. You judged a guy by how many sewers he could hit in stickball. There were no parks. Our football was a newspaper rolled up and tied with a string. At Christmastime someone would get a football and think, *Wow, that's the cat's meow*, until the asphalt beat it up. It was a good life.

One day, when I was fifteen and hanging out, a couple of guys said, Why don't you come with us to the National Guard? National Guard, who are they? Soldiers. You get to carry rifles and shoot guns. I said, You're kidding me—that sounds like fun. So I went down to the armory, and I said, I want to join. It's amazing what you can get away with. Because I had some of my father's art talents, I created a birth certificate, not a problem. The hardest part was making the seal, but I found a way. It didn't look good, but it was raised. I brought it down there, some sergeant looked at me, and asked, "You're eighteen years old?" I said, "Yes, sir."

I was assigned to 10th Company, 106th Infantry Regiment, Heavy Weapons, at Camp Drum. In the daytime I got to run around in the woods blowing things up, but at night I had, like, twenty godfathers making sure I didn't smoke, drink, or get into trouble. I never told my mother. When I brought my seabag home with all the army clothes, she asked what they were, and I told her that I had won a chance to go to a camp through the Herald Tribune Fresh Air [Fund]. I said, "Because they knew we didn't have any money, they gave us all these old army clothes." She bought it the first time, but when I came back with a corporal stripe she got wise to me. But she never said anything, and I had a good time in my two years in the National Guard. So I was now eighteen years old, and all I wanted was to be a marine. My mother said, "You've got to graduate high school." And I said, "Yeah, yeah, yeah." I never graduated.

I think it was about my tenth week in boot camp that my DI [drill instructor] called me into his hooch, which is never a good thing, and I got a little bit of a bouncing around. He was screaming at me, and the junior DI was screaming at me, calling me a liar, a traitor, for what I had done to their Marine Corps by being in the army. I asked how they found out—nobody had told me about fingerprints.

After two years in the Marine Corps I was looking for something to do, and took a test for the Police Department and a test for the Fire Department. I went to visit my father at the firehouse—the last time I had seen him was the night I left for Parris Island [the Marine Corps training camp]—and told him I had taken the test for the Fire Department. He said, "Good, good, and I hope you make it." We sat and talked, and he introduced me to a couple of the young men that were there. I got on the Fire Department list, and because they called before the Police Department did, I said, "I'll be a fireman."

I went to probie school, and my father came to the graduation ceremony. My mother had left when I went into the Marine Corps—I don't know where she went—and my grandmother had died, so my father's being at graduation was a pretty special day, and his coming in uniform made it even more special. And my wife-to-be was with us. He was proud that I was a fireman. We talked a little about the job, and he asked, "Where would you like to work?" I said, Where he worked, and he said, "Well, right now I'm driving the chief in the 36 Battalion, which is in Greenpoint."

I said, "Pop, to be honest with you, I'm probably gonna screw up, and if I screw up, it's on me, and if I do something good, it's on me. I don't want somebody saying, You did it because you're Vigiano's son. I want people to come to you and say, You're Vigiano's father." He said, "You're a hairy little son of a gun." I told him I didn't know what "hairy" meant, but that's the way it was going to be. I told him, "I love you, but I don't want to work with you."

My father had good friends in the job, so I was assigned to Ladder 103, East New York. I had a very good Fire Department career—there were maybe three days or five days in thirty-six years when I wasn't happy. Probably the worst day of my life before 9/11 was when a fireman died in my hands. You know, I never forgot that. I was a lieutenant in Rescue 2. I was actually holding a mask on this firefighter in the emergency room in Kings County [Hospital] while another firefighter, who happened to be a Special Forces medic, was doing the chest compressions. A few firemen had been brought in, plus the normal collection of bodies in an emergency room, and by the time the team got to him, he was dead. It was Bob Goldman. That wasn't a good day.

Our boys, John and Joe, were good sons. Whatever we asked them to do, they did. Jan got them started in Cub Scouts real early, at seven or eight years old. When they were eight, I began to coach them in baseball and football. When they were ten years old, Mama said, "Now you've got to take them into Boy Scouts." So I became an assistant and took whatever job they gave me. When the scoutmaster quit, they asked me to take over, and I ran it like I did in the Marine Corps. The scouts are a takeoff of the military—learning skills, leadership, what you're made of, and learning the role of rank.

For the next eight years I saw each of my sons grow from boy to man. When John was ready to make Eagle Scout—I think he was close to sixteen—Joe was shy of about four merit badges, and he asked his brother, "Why don't you wait, and we'll make it together?" And not only did John wait, but he helped Joe get the merit badges. They both made Eagle Scout the same night, and I don't know if that happens very often.

Joe would come with me to the firehouse, and the firemen adopted him. He was as big as some of them that I had working for me, and he used to wear the guys' boots. Lee Ielpi [see page 98] would teach him how to light up an area when we were doing extrication training. He looked like a little mini fireman, and would say that he was going to be the next generation.

For his thirteenth birthday I brought him to Rescue 2. We bought a big chocolate layer cake with "Happy Birthday" written on it. But Lee Ielpi was there and said, "We're gonna give you a better cake." So he took a milk container and cut windows out, cut the bottom out, and put it on top of the candles. He lit them, and fire started coming out of the little so-called windows. "You got to put it out, Joe," Lee told him. They gave him water. So he put the fire out, and the cake was saturated. We had a soggy birthday cake, but it was a good day.

But at seventeen he began dating a young girl whose father was a police officer, and the guy talked him into taking the PD test. We drove him to the test, and I told him, "Joe, go in and do your best, and when you finish, meet us at the Van Wyck Diner." Just one pencil, that's all he had, and he said, "No problem, see ya." I'm watching him go in, this seventeen-year-old kid, with a group of men. He was a good size, but he was still a kid. So my wife, Jan, and I walked to the diner and were on our second cup of coffee when Joe walked in. I thought, *This is not good*, figuring, all told, an hour and ten minutes for a three-hour test. I said, "How'd you do?" He said, "I aced it." He took out a piece of paper, and we looked at the numbers. I said, "It's a good thing you didn't break the pencil." He said, "I did, but the guy next to me had a lot of them, and he gave me one." So I asked, "Well, when are they gonna give you the answers?" "I think tonight. They're gonna be on the radio." I said, "You know, Joe, if you fail the test, it's not the worst thing in the world. It's an experience. You're gonna take another one down the road—maybe the fireman's test. They're all pretty much the same." He said, "I'm not worried, Dad."

We went home, and he got dressed up to go out with his girlfriend. Calls me up about 11:30. "Dad, I got 110 on the test." I said, "How did you get 110?" He said, "I did the extra credit." After the numbered questions they had a couple of reading comprehensions, then one with a diagram in which you had to pick out certain things, and he got them all. So I said, "So you're seventeen and you're on the list." He said, "I'll be in the first class." They later called him up and said they couldn't take him until he was twenty, so at twenty years and two days old, Joe was a New York City police officer.

John was in college at the time and said to Joe, "You're an idiot. You should be a fireman." But even when he was a cop, Joe was heavy into the Deer Park Volunteer Fire Department. He had joined when he was sixteen, and he was on every team that the Deer Park Fire Volunteers had. He loved the fire service.

John wanted to finish college at Stony Brook. When he started there, I said, "Since you're not going into the military you've got to learn to be on your own, and living at home would be an extension of high school." So we agreed, and he lived on campus. Then, in 1984, I got diagnosed with throat cancer. I didn't tell the boys, as I didn't think it was something they had to be burdened with. Joe was a senior in high school, and John was taking his final exams in college, so I said, "Let him get through school, and then we can let him know, and Joe too." But after all the tests were over, Jan told them. They came to the hospital and realized what all the secret meetings had been about. John was upset, really upset, but Joe handled it better.

A firefighter from my company would volunteer every morning and another every night to drive out to Long Island with the chief's car, pick up my wife, take her to the Sloan-Kettering hospital, and then bring her home. They did this for three weeks, and not one person got overtime, not one person complained. I got to see every member of the company every day. When the radiation started, the department had Ambulance 4, which was in Manhattan, pick me up here in Long Island, drive me to Sloan-Kettering, and then bring me home. Two of those guys also owned two successful restaurants called Donovan's. They said, We're not using the Fire Department cars, so would pick me up in their Cadillacs, back and forth, for thirty-six treatments. When it was all over I wrote and I thanked the Fire Department for what they had done, but told them about the Cadillacs. The department said we have to get something to take care of the families, and an old, broken-down FDNY chief's car won't do. And that was the start of what is now the FDNY Fire Family Transport Foundation with comfortable vans.

Cops and firemen are like Spartans and Centurions. At every family dinner Joe would shoot off something, John would counter, and I'd be in the middle, the arbiter. They might get a little heated, and Jan would step in and say, "It's over." But on other nights it got exciting, arguing, Who does more work, firefighters or police officers? Jan stopped that too. But then I took it to another level when I started teaching the use of the Hurst tool [widely known as the Jaws of Life, an air-compression tool that can lift up a bus or cut through the doors of a car] around the country and took John, who as a firefighter was learning the tool, with me. And Joe said to me one day, "What about me? I'm not an orphan. I should go with you." I said, "Joe, you're a cop." He said, "I'm an *emergency* cop. I know more about those tools than John." I said, "I'll take you, but John's in charge." John loved it; he got to order his brother around. But they were both excellent instructors, which I had seen in the Boy Scouts. When John became an Eagle Scout he was my senior patrol leader, and I used to watch him counsel other boys. He just had a knack about him. Joe watched him, learned, and developed his own technique. They became quite successful when they moved into this instructing world with me. Joe and John were the glue that brought everything and everyone together.

So I watched them grow from little boys to young men in Boy Scouts, and then I got the opportunity to work with them as men in the world. I don't think you can measure that, and there isn't a father alive who can say he had a better life. Ours together was cut short. Yes, we banged heads, fathers and sons, and more than once I told them, "I'm not your friend. I'm your father, and there's a line you can't cross." But man, I had nothing but good times with them for the thirty-four and thirty-six years that those boys were on earth.

On the morning of 9/11 Joe was working the day tour so he could be home to lead his son's Cub Scout troop. John was just going off duty when a guy called in and said his child was sick, so John said, I'm here, I'll stay. I was shaving when the phone rang, and it was Joe, in Truck 2 of ESU [Emergency Service Unit]. He said, "Dad, turn on the television. A plane just hit the World Trade Center." Sure enough, Channel 5 was doing a bulletin, a report that a plane had hit. They were thinking it was a Piper Cub, and Joe said, "No, Dad, it's not a Piper Cub. I'm on the West Side Highway, and we're heading south right now. From the column of smoke, this wasn't a Piper Cub." I said, "All right, Joe, be careful." "Okay, Dad," he said. "I love ya."

That's how we ended our conversations every time I spoke with my sons. I spoke with John the night before, I spoke to Joe en route, and the last words I said to each were, "I love you." Every time you get on that fire truck, you can die. Every time. I gave this advice to both my sons: "Don't ever leave your house pissed off at your wife or your kids, because you don't know if you're going to see them the next day." I said, "So no matter what the gripe is with your wife, your girlfriend, or your children, put it aside. Hug them. Kiss them. Take it up the next day. Because the last thing that you want to re-member is that you hugged them and kissed them."

We can think about 9/11 from different points of view. Chief Dan Nigro [see page 1] looked at it from the command standpoint: Here were two huge buildings with many floors of fire, hundreds of people getting killed, so, tactically, what were they going to do? The chiefs knew you couldn't fight a high-rise fire like you fight fire in a tenement. In a project fire the heat was incredible; in the World Trade Center, you had a minimum of ten or fifteen floors being fed by jet fuel. Holy . . . God. I can't imagine the temperature.

Just two months before 9/11 John had called me up and said, "Dad, can you call the chief of department [Peter J. Ganci] and ask him to put Tom Haskell [see page 163] in my company?" I said, "John, I'm retired. How am I going to ask the chief of department to transfer somebody to your com-pany? Those days are over." He said, "Dad, he's great, and he worked with you. We've gotta have him." I said, "I remember he was a fireman, a big guy, but I never knew he was the captain." So Tom Haskell was the captain the day of the attacks. He accepted the temporary assignment, but since he was on the list to be a battalion chief, he refused a permanent transfer.

Now, when they pulled up in front of the South Tower, they looked up and knew they were gonna get their ass kicked in this building; there was just no way you were going to hide. And nobody hesitated—they all followed him up the stairs. Watch the films. You see the fear in some of these kids' eyes; you see that they didn't really want to go, but they didn't stop. How do you measure that if you don't talk about heart, training, desire, courage? It's not just one quality. Those kids all showed what they had. Tactically, if I had been a lieutenant or a captain at that time, I wouldn't have hesitated. Once I was in the building, though, up close, the realization would have kicked in that we didn't belong there. I've been to more than a few fires in my career where I found, *This is not a good spot; now it's time to make a retreat.*

The people coming out of those buildings that day were men whose families relied on them, women who just went to work, your wife, your daughter, your niece going shopping—the people we were sworn to protect. When you saw them you knew there were more people in there, but you didn't know what situation they were in. You forgot about the fire; you forget about what was going to happen. *I gotta get those people out.* And that's what they did. Firemen are no different from cops. When they saw thousands of them fleeing, they knew there were more—there was always one more.

I never saw the fire. Chief Dan Nigro never saw the fire. Chief Pete Ganci never saw the fire. Chief Peter Hayden never saw the fire. What did they see? Tactically, they saw victims, people. The firefighters weren't there to put out a fire. They could have stretched all the hose in the world, but they weren't going to put out that fire. But they were going to get people out, and they did—thousands. The sad commentary is that we actually trained with high-rise procedures.

That day I watched the coverage on television, saw the impact of the second plane crashing into the South Tower, the column of smoke. I had to leave the house for a minute to run to the store, and on the way home flipped the radio on. The building had collapsed. I said to myself, *High-rises don't collapse. Floors can collapse in a high-rise; buildings don't collapse. Never. No high-rise has ever collapsed.* At home I put on the television and watched the second tower come down. I was dumbfounded.

The phone never stopped ringing. Because I knew that Joe was there, I tried to call the firehouse but couldn't get through. I called a friend of mine who's a dispatcher and said, "You gotta help me out." And he said, "Let me see what I can do," and then he called me back and said, "Don't worry about it, 132 relocated." I said, "Okay, that's a good sign." They didn't relocate. They went right to the staging area.

They sent a car to pick us up, to go to One Police Plaza. After thirty-six years as a firefighter I would have assumed that the Fire Department would take care of us. The Police Department I knew only as a peripheral thing, but now I saw how strong it really was, looking at it tactically. Streets were closed; policemen were everywhere, and not just traffic cops but armed policemen. And every place you went, there was a checkpoint. I said, "We're in a war here." We got to One Police Plaza, and they take us into the auditorium where a few tables had been set up, where people were sitting there and waiting. My daughter-in-law Kathy, a police officer, arrived, and had already been up to Truck 2.

Nobody knew what the hell was going on, and then Commissioner Joe Dunne came in and said, "I want to keep you informed. Coffee and some doughnuts will be here soon." They were assuming people weren't going to leave, so we camped out. It must have been two o'clock in the morning, and there were still ten families there, and nobody knew what to do. The Police Department didn't know what to do. Twenty-three NYPD officers were missing, maybe killed. At any other time this would have been front-page news for months all around the world. So we were walking and talking, and the adrenaline was flying. Joe Dunne came back in, and people were swarming around him. He came over to me and said, "Mr. Vigiano, can I speak to you? Most of these people have no idea what's going on, but you do. I want to ask you a favor, to explain to them how people survive in building collapses. About voids. About water. Food." He said, "We want to try and keep their hopes up." I said, "I didn't even see the building, I just saw it on television." But I spoke to the people there as an officer experienced in emergencies. But one father of an officer just wouldn't let go; he wanted results. I said, "Look, I got two kids in those buildings. They're tough kids, physical kids. If there's a void they'll find it. There'll be plenty of food, because it's an office building. There's water, because they're putting out fires. Water pipes break. There's water fountains. There's plenty of air. You can last a long time in that environment." I said, "We just have to dig them out. It's going to take time."

At about two o'clock in the afternoon my daughter-in-law said to Joe Dunne, "I want to go to the site." Joe said, "Okay," and asked if I was going to go with her. They had a motorcycle unit drive us over to the site.

When we pulled up and I looked at that zone, I knew right then and there that there were no survivors. There were no survivors. There was no way anybody could be alive in that building. They had already gotten Jay Jonas out [see page 52] and all those peripheral people on the eleventh; this was the twelfth. Kathy walked the entire perimeter, questioning cops. She knew most of them because she worked the Seventy-fifth Precinct. I was right behind her; I'm just looking. Back at One Police Plaza Joe Dunne got ahold of me and asked what I had seen. "Well," I said, "I can't make that speech to these people anymore." He said, "That bad?" I said, "I really think so."

The next day, the thirteenth, Truck 1, Emergency Service Unit, picked me up and took me to their quarters, where they gave me a pair of boots, a helmet, and some clothes. We went to the site and started digging, and they took me into some tunnel—probably one of the subway tunnels— and it was scary. We were poking around for about an hour but didn't find anybody. When we came out I watched the anthill with a thousand people picking stuff up and filling buckets. I walked around a little bit more, talked to firemen and some cops, and got back to 1 PP around seven o'clock

By now they had brought in army cots and were serving breakfast, lunch, and dinner. They were trying to make it hospitable, but we were still in an auditorium. Joe Dunne again came up to me and said, "I'm going to ask you a favor, Mr. Vigiano. I have a friend, Dennis Duggan, who works with *Newsday* and wants to do an article. He's a friend of the Police Department, and he's the only reporter I would ask you to talk to. Would you consider an interview?" I said, "Do you want it?" He said, "Yeah." I said, "Okay." Duggan was a real gentleman, and the headline of his piece was TWIN TOWERS, which ran with photos of both boys.

Up to that point at One Police Plaza we hadn't been allowed to see TV or read the newspaper. They were sheltering us. Because I had been at the site, I was the voice, so fathers would come over and ask me questions, and I'd say, "They're working hard." At around eleven o'clock each night kids from the ESU would come in, filthy, dirty, and would give us an update: We were digging here. We found this. We had a void. Most of the people had no idea what they were talking about. But everyone was getting information from the site.

At the end of the following day I got back to 1 PP around eleven o'clock, and Joe Dunne says, "I have another favor to ask. We want to get you people in a hotel. This is not good; you can't stay in an auditorium." I asked, "Well, what do you want me to do?" He said, "Where you go, they will go.

But they are not going to leave here as long as you are here." I said, "I answer to Jan. You convince her. If she says go, we'll go; otherwise we'll stay here."

He said, "Mrs. Vigiano, I'd like you and your husband to go to a hotel. We're going to take care of that. Would you please go?"

She said to him, "I have two sons probably sleeping on concrete tonight, and you want me to sleep in a hotel? That ain't gonna happen."

Well, this six-foot-five-inch police officer was speechless. He got me outside and said, "Are you kidding me? You've got to convince her. Beg, do whatever it takes." I said, "What, do you need the floor that we're sleeping on?" "No, no," he said. "We want you in beds, with a shower. Police headquarters is not a place to live."

I went back and talked to her. I said, "Mama, my back is killing me, these army cots are not doing me any good. I need a shower." She gave me a look that said, *You wimp,* or words to that effect, but finally agreed, and Joe had us escorted to the Roosevelt Hotel before we could change our minds. The other families followed.

At 6:00 A.M. a police officer would be there to pick me up and take me back to 1 PP for breakfast. After breakfast I'd be out the door and down to the site, and I'd come back to 1 PP around eleven o'clock and stay there until twelve o'clock, when they would take me back to the hotel. This went on for two weeks, when Kathy told us that our grandson was waiting for us. He wanted to see us.

So we made a deal: From now on Mama would stay home and I would stay at the site until Friday night. On Friday I would come home, wash clothes, have dinner with Jan, and then go back in on Sunday afternoon. I did this until they closed the site down; that was my goal.

At the site I just sat and listened to the radio. But I had my binoculars, and as soon as I heard that a body had been recovered, I put everything in my bag and walked down to be part of the honor guard. I had the honor of being there when they found my son Joe in October. He had been on the thirty-eighth or thirty-ninth floor in the C staircase. I know this because the NYPD emergency service had it on their radios. They had everybody pinpointed, because the ESU cops all had a chip in their radios indicating where they were. We were one step away from that modern technology in FDNY.

I had the honor of escorting my son to the morgue. I didn't get to see him. They asked me if I wanted to, and I said no. The picture I have of my son is not the picture I'm going to see there. I saw what those buildings had done to the human body, as I had recovered a few of them. I remember finding one fireman with an open pocketknife right next to him. He didn't die suddenly but had to open that knife to try and cut his mask off, and he didn't succeed. And we saw him five, six weeks later, and it was like watching a Stephen King movie. I didn't want to see that with my son.

They never found John, and why they never found him was a matter of tactics. The man in charge had to make a decision: One pile they were going to leave, the other they were going to work on. Two things destroy DNA, fire and water. The South Tower, where John was, burned and burned and burned, and to put it out they used water, water, water. So any remains that may have been found, no matter how small, were lost.

On the twelfth of November they closed the site and locked down the city when Flight 587 crashed in Rockaway and killed 260 people onboard and a few on the ground. Afterward everything got back to normal, but they did not reopen the site. They planned to reduce the forces there to twenty firemen and twenty cops, and Mayor Giuliani had agreed to have a meeting at the Sheraton Hotel with the family members to discuss the manpower reduction: We don't need them because the situation is under control, all kinds of crap. So that was the agenda.

Giuliani prefaced the meeting by saying, "I have to go to another meeting and can only be here for a few moments, but Commissioner [Thomas] Von Essen and Deputy Commissioner [Lynn] Tierney will answer all your questions." The medical examiner was there, as was Sal Cassano [the second ranking fire chief and now fire commissioner]. Each person on the podium made a presentation, and the deputy commissioner said that because of the size of the tragedy, in which 343 firefighters perished, the Fire Department was overwhelmed.

The mayor was getting ready to leave when this young lady sitting just on my left, who was there with two big men, went up to the microphone. They recognized her, and she said, "I want to address this to the Fire Department. Do you know what overwhelmed really is?" She said, "Overwhelmed is taking care of six-month-old twins and telling a three-year-old girl that her father will never come home. That's what overwhelmed is." She sat down, and you could have heard a pin drop. I looked at her and thought, *Holy crap. She has three kids; she looks like she's only about thir-*

teen. We later became very good friends, and it turned out that the two men who were with her that day were her brothers, both of whom were firefighters. Her husband had been killed.

Giuliani now started to field some questions. I waited my turn and said, "Mr. Mayor, I have a question to ask you, and a question to ask Mr. Von Essen. Can you tell me why the site was closed today?" And I swear, Giuliani didn't know. He looked around as if for some assistance, and then, being the astute politician that he is, said, "Well, you know, John, the men and women have been down there nonstop for two months. It's Veterans' Day. We figured they needed a break to regroup themselves." I said, "I beg your pardon, Mr. Mayor. What is Veterans' Day? Macy's going to have a big sale? It's not a holiday. We don't celebrate it like we celebrate Easter or Christmas." I said, "If there is anybody in this city who knows that the eleventh hour of the eleventh day of the eleventh month is when the Armistice was signed, it is the firemen. Firemen do not leave because it's a holiday. There are still men missing. How can we leave?" He said, "You have my assurance that the site will never be closed again." I said, "Mr. Mayor, I know that, because I'm going to be at that site every day. I'm going to be there every holiday. And I'm going to hold you to that."

I then said, "My second question is to Mr. Von Essen. Tom, you pride yourself in saying that you worked in a very busy truck company in the Bronx. From what I understand, all busy truck companies critique after a fire." I said, "You've just had the world's biggest office fire, and you haven't critiqued it yet." Sal Cassano then got up and said, "We have been discussing this at length." I said, "Sir, I can give you the names of three men who were there when the building came down, and nobody has spoken to them. How can you critique without talking to the witnesses?" Man, I got their attention with that.

Not long afterward I was at Macy's with my granddaughter at the union's Christmas party for the kids. Mayor Giuliani said hello, and then Von Essen came over and asked, "We still friends?" I said, "Why wouldn't we be friends? The PD offered us police cars for all the families. Did you get my message about the police cars?" He said, "Yeah, but we gotta take care of our own, John." "Taking care of your own?" I said. "Does that mean taking trips to Hawaii? Is that taking care of your own?" He said, "What are you talking about?" I said, "Your chief of the special operations companies is leaving Tuesday for Hawaii with a bunch of family members. We haven't found Ray Downey's [the chief of special operations who was lost on 9/11] body yet. And he's going to Hawaii. Why? Does he have trouble sleeping at night the way we do? Does he wake up at night in a sweat? Does he cry over stupid things? Does he have to stop his car when he's driving because he's crying and he can't figure out why? If he has those symptoms, then maybe I should go with him." He said, "Are you sure about this?" I told him, "The problem is, Tom, it's your command. He works for you. I'm retired—how come I know about it?" He said, "Well, he's not going," and before he left Macy's he called that chief and told him he was not taking that trip. Three days later we found Ray Downey. The trip was canceled. People on the trip came home a week early from Hawaii.

At the funeral for Ray Downey that chief came over to me, but I walked away from him and have never talked to him since. I later found out that there were a lot of guys who went on trips while we were still digging. What kept me going was that I had two pretty good kids who were good men. They were brave, they were good family men, and I would assume they were very good husbands. They were great fathers, and for me to be anything less than that would be a dishonor to them.

After Joe died, one of the police chiefs asked me if there was anything I needed. I said, "You know, you could do me a favor. Joe has a whole bunch of medals, and I have no idea what they mean, and I have three grandsons who may ask me one day. Could you give me a list of what he has and what they mean?" "Oh yeah, no problem, we can take care of that." So, four months go by, I forgot about it. And I assumed he forgot about it. After six months I got a phone call: "Mr. Vigiano, what you asked for, it's being worked on as we speak, and we'll get back to you shortly." I said, "Wow. How difficult could that be?" Another couple of months went by, and I got another phone call. "Mr. Vigiano, would you and Mrs. Vigiano care to come in to Commissioner Kelly's [Police Commissioner Raymond Kelly] office at your convenience?"

At One Police Plaza, we went to Kelly's office, and the NYPD chief of department, Chief [Joe] Esposito, my wife, and I just sat there. I had known Ray Kelly a long time, and finally said, "Thank you very much for inviting us, but it's a long way to come for a cup of coffee." He laughed and said, "Well, you asked for something, and I wanted to give it to you personally." He took out a box and said, "This is for you and Mrs. Vigiano." It was a shadow box [a special case that protects against light damage] with Joe's name, and it held his badge, the ribbon they wear for the Medal of Honor, and the combat cross. Then he handed me a booklet, in color, with the Police Department shield on it. And it was a record of Joe's career: The medals he got, how he got them, and what they meant. And I looked at it and said, "I don't know what to say." Kelly said, "There's one for each of your grandchildren, so now you don't have to share it."

My son Joe had a remarkable career in the Police Department, and before he died a producer named Rob Port had filmed a documentary on the ESU featuring him. At their first meeting Rob was sitting between Joe and his partner, siren blasting, as they were heading to Harlem. Rob asked, "Where are we going?" It was a gun run—somebody with a gun. They gave him an NYPD Windbreaker to wear. By the time they pulled up, the operation had been neutralized: Whatever it was had been taken care of. They took Rob into this tenement, where there was blood all over the floor, blood on the landing, a couple of people killed, and a guy in handcuffs, deranged, on drugs. Rob's eyes were like egg yolks, sunny-side up. One of the cops said, "Now you're going to see what kind of world we live in." Just after this, they started filming a series called *E-Man*.

But 9/11 occurred, and twelve of the sixteen or seventeen men who were in *E-Man* were killed. The producers said, There is no way we can capitalize on those men's lives. I said, "Wow, to see all those cops—and I knew most of them— it would be a shame if their voices weren't going to be heard." But then they found out that one of the officers had a brother, a firefighter, who was killed—*Newsday* had called John and Joe Vigiano "the Twin Towers." So Rob asked me if we would be interested in a film about my sons. I said the decision was beyond me: I had two daughters-in-law, Kathy and Maria, and five grandchildren, Nicolette, Ariana, Joe, Jim, and John Michael, who had to be considered. I told him my wife and I would go along with it only if my daughters-in-law and my grandchildren agreed. So Rob contacted both of them, and they said if our mother-in-law and father-in-law want to do it, we'll do it.

The producers had a lot with Joe, but they needed film and photos of John, so we supplied them with everything. Through the magic of editing, they put together a short documentary called *The Twin Towers.* My sons were boys of action, and you can see it in that video. You can see what

Joe's made of: I'm the first one in. I got to be the first one in the door. And John was a very aggressive firefighter. On 9/11 they were doing their jobs the way they were trained.

So, fast forward. We left the Sundance Film Festival and were past the first hurdle, and a few months [later] get a call asking if the family would like to come to Hollywood. I said, "For what?" "For the Academy Awards; it's one of the five nominees." So in 2003 a lot of firemen and cops all rented tuxedos and flew with us to California. On the red carpet a lady with a microphone goes, "And here we have . . . ? Who are you?" Nobody knew who we were. Our seats were all over the place; we couldn't even sit together. I was with my two grandsons up in the mountains someplace. My wife, Jan, was with one of my grandchildren and my daughter-in-law down below.

When it was announced that *The Twin Towers* won, boy oh boy, it was bedlam.

Afterward we were in limousines, going from party to party, and everybody was looking at us again, Who are they? Here's this beautiful blond lady with handsome grandchildren. Rob was showing us off. We had a few cops with us too, so we had a super time.

The next day Rob came to the hotel and found out that the Oscar doesn't float. Cops took it for a swim in the pool, among other things. Oscar doesn't drink—can't hold his liquor. It was a good time, and Rob became part of our family. Oprah wanted us to go on her TV show. I called Rob and said, "This is your world. Where do I go?"

So you can see how our lives changed. Joe Dunne, who was the first deputy commissioner, put up a wall around us with the press, and the only ones that got in our house were people that Joe Dunne approved. That's why we got mostly the anchor people, and we met some very good people. I still kept my guard up, because of my training from the Fire Department about not trusting the press, but I have to say, the people that we met in those months were kind, very much like Boy Scouts.

In that period my family had become everything to me, and then a friend of mine got me involved in going down to Norfolk, Virginia, with two of my grandsons to sail back home on a navy ship, the USS *Shreveport*. Wow, our grandkids and I loved that. Then, in 2003, a woman from City Hall asked if I would be part of a USO [United Service Organizations] trip going to Iraq. One woman would be going representing the Port Authority, another the corporate world, and I would represent police and fire.

When I got there, in Iraq, and saw how those soldiers lived and what they were doing, it was like an epiphany. I came home and went back into my routine, until I got another call from the woman at City Hall. She said, "You've seen them in their element—would you now like to go to the hospital and see some of them that were injured?" In December of that year, I, Bill Butler, and Dennis Oberg [two other FDNY firefighters who lost their sons on 9/11] went to Walter Reed Hospital, and it was a typical grip and grin, well orchestrated and well run, a photo op for this, a photo op for that. But that's not my world. As the group was heading in one direction I noticed a kid in a room by himself, so I went in. Marines usually have tattoos saying SEMPER FI, and when I walked over to the kid I saw that he had one. "What's a marine doing in an army hospital?" I asked. He said, "I was a marine in the Gulf War, got released, and since there was no marine reserve, I joined the National Guard." So I said, "That's the reason, dummy, that us marines never get shot—only stupid soldiers." He laughed, and I sat on his bed, shooting the bull. I didn't see Undersecretary [Paul] Wolfowitz walk in behind me with his general aide, who stood there listening. I told the soldier about my going into the National Guard at fifteen, and then into the marines, and said that he had done it the opposite way, but that he was dumb and got shot, and I didn't. He laughed. I gave the kid a T-shirt, kissed him on his head, and I got up to leave, saw Undersecretary Wolfowitz, who looked like the school principal who just caught me. I said, "How much of this did you hear?" "We heard it all." "Well," I said, "they can't do nothing to me now anyway," and I started laughing. The general asked, "Why would you leave an infantry unit to go into the Marine Corps?" I said, "Did you ever check out our uniforms? We get the women after us." Everyone laughed at that.

As we were walking down the hall to catch up with our group, Undersecretary Wolfowitz says, "Could you come back, and bring more firemen with you?" I said I was certain I could, and they asked that I come with no more than ten, which would be broken up into two groups of five, so as not to overwhelm the patients.

Since then those trips down to that hospital, which I make every three months, have been my therapy. Commissioner Sal Cassano gives us a vehicle, and the Fire Department gives us the diesel fuel at the firehouse. We drive down, we take all of the outpatients, the corpsmen, the chaplains, the doctors, and any family members to a pub. Anything they want to eat or drink is on us. Next morning, we go to Walter Reed, and then to Bethesda, and we bring them FDNY hats and shirts. We just sit and shoot the breeze with these kids, and they love it. They all know when the Fire Department's coming, because they all wear Police Department shirts: Look what the cops gave us. And now I'm taking my grandsons down there in two weeks. My daughter-in-law thinks it will maybe stop them from wanting to go into the service. I honestly think it's going to be a push to get them in. But we don't know.

Whenever you feel low, and like it rained and you just washed your car, or, Oh, damn, the wind just blew your hair away, think about the kids who have been shot up. Brendan Marrocco has no arms, no legs. I walked over to him, asked what he did, and kissed him, telling him, I'm a fireman, I kiss everybody. I started talking, goofing around, now we're friends. I met a kid two years ago who looked like our newspaper delivery boy; half of his calf had been shot away, and they were debating whether to save his leg or not. He had just finished running one hundred miles in Florida to raise money for special operations marines.

I just showed my wife a letter. I gave a kid in the hospital a pin, one of those little pins I keep with both my sons' photos on it. His mother called me, then wrote me: Can I buy a pin? My son lost his, and he's petrified that he can't find it. I told her to just send me her address and I'd send one. He was blind in one eye and wanted to join the Fire Department as a paramedic. Where do these kids come from? Seeing them, their strength, is my adrenaline.

When I moved into this house, I was a young fireman, struggling, working two jobs, going to school. My wife was working. We were driving an old beat-up car. Some forty-odd years later we're still in the same house, with different furniture and a newer car. We eat out more. I haven't changed. I could probably own a Jaguar, a Cadillac, a Lincoln, any of these things, if I wanted them. It's not me. I am what I am.

Before 9/11, I expected to spend my retirement playing golf and chasing grandchildren and watching my sons get old. We would save as much money as we could. *One day*, we thought, *they would benefit from that, and their lives would be better.* Both the boys were struggling, John more than Joe. Every two or three weeks John's car would break down, and I'd go to the gas station, drive him home, and then go back to the gas station and tell the guy, Fix whatever has to be fixed, give me the bill, and just tell my son you had to change the wires, and charge him twenty-five dollars. And we did this for a couple of years. That's what I expected my retirement to be like.

September 11 changed everything. Everything. My sons were such good people that we had to maintain their standards and stand up for them. I would never get involved in any of the controversies, the angry issues around the 9/11 hearings and the memorial. There are a few family members who always refer to the murder, the murder, the murder. Maybe it's because of my affinity toward the military, but I believe that this was our Pearl Harbor. This was an act of war, and the people who were killed that day were the first victims of that war. I always felt that my sons were doing their jobs as a policeman and as a firefighter, and that they were killed in the line of duty. I never used the word "murder," but I can understand why people do so. The people who were murdered were the ones in the planes and buildings, who were killed with box cutters, by crashing aircrafts, fire, and collapse, victims trapped in an environment that they had no control over. These people were victims. When I meet people related to them, I talk to them, and I end the talk by saying, Your son, your daughter, they were victims, my heart goes out to you. My sons went to work to save your son, your daughter; they were heroes. Some people don't like to hear my honesty.

Understanding that caused me to stop going to a therapy class out here on Long Island. The therapist asked us to bring a photo and story about our lost loved ones. So each person got up with his photo and told a very moving story. I said to my wife, I think I screwed up. I brought a classic picture of my two kids: There's John the firefighter holding a police shotgun with a cigar in his mouth, Joe the police officer, a cigar in one hand and a firefighter's Halligan tool in the other. And neither one smoked.

Does losing them hurt? You bet your ass it hurts. There are days when I don't want to see people. I have a nice patio. I go out there and I read, a lot. If there's a real bad day I get in my car and I go to the beach in the winter. Jan does the same thing. My therapy every day was being at the site, seeing unbelievable things by young men and women who gave everything they could, to try and make sense of what happened.

Debra Burlingame

Debra Burlingame, an attorney and 9/11 activist, is the sister of Charles Frank "Chic" Burlingame III, the pilot of American Airlines Flight 77. On the morning of September 11, 2001, terrorists hijacked his aircraft and crashed it into the Pentagon. During the hijacking Chic died fighting for the control of his plane and the safety of his passengers.

To understand how my family felt about Chic's career choice you have to know a little bit about my dad. My father was first of all a career military man, and was in the service for twenty years. He was air force, so it was all about airplanes.

In some branches of the services—for instance, in the navy—the family is left behind during an overseas deployment. But in the air force the family goes with you, so our formative years were spent on military bases, on them or near them. My mother was nineteen years old when she had her oldest, Chic, and was twenty-three when she had her fourth and youngest, me. Because she had so many children in such a short period of time, we were not only close in age but were a tight family who helped one another in our learning and relied on one another as companions. When you live on a military base, everything that happens away from the base is on the outside: The park's on the outside; job's on the outside; school's on the outside. And as a child, you very much have the feeling that you're in a special, closed, very safe community.

From the time Chic was a very young boy, I can't remember him really wanting to do anything else but be connected to flying. In fact, one of the photographs that I most cherish is of him with the first airplane he ever built—from scrap lumber he found in the alley behind our house in England. He was six years old, and its wingspan was bigger than he was. He not only built this rather complicated plane, but on its wings he painted the letters U.S.A. Here he was in England and already hoping to be an American military pilot.

That's what he wanted to be. All four of us siblings had aspirations, and were encouraged to have them. I thought all kids were like that, that all families focused on each kid, and said, "What are you going to be when you grow up? What will your contribution be?" And we rooted for one another. I found out much, much later in life that that's not the case among many people. Chic's grades were good, and he was an Eagle Scout, played the trumpet, was in the French club and the Key Club. He also played in the Annapolis Drum and Bugle Corps. But knuckling down and studying was something he had to really force himself to do, because he was an action kid. I have a tape recording of my father interviewing him, during which they get into a sort of argument because Chic wanted to get a car. He was then a junior in high school, and my father wouldn't let him have one, saying, "You go through a set of tires on that bike of yours every month, so I'm afraid of what you'd do to a car." So he didn't get a car until he was a senior.

Chic wanted to go into the air force because of my dad. He focused on that, but he ended up not getting an appointment, which devastated him. You can get a congressional appointment or a presidential appointment, and Chic ended up getting a presidential appointment from Lyndon Johnson to the Naval Academy. I think he got the appointment because our father was retired air force. Although he had no influence, it was something that stood out on Chic's application.

When he finally got the acceptance at Annapolis, we were all not just proud but greatly relieved, because he could be a pilot and that's what he wanted to do his whole life. We, his siblings, were emotionally invested in that with him. When he got emotional, we got emotional. And when he was joyous and deliriously happy, we were too—it was that way with our family.

I will never forget taking him to the airport for his flight east to Annapolis in '67. I was thirteen, a ripe age to be so in awe, for to me he was a man, a full-grown man. When I saw him in his uniform with his classmates, those cadets were like gods to me. He really thrived at Annapolis, and his whole thing was, he wanted jets. He didn't want to just fly, he wanted *jets*. He wanted fixed-wing, and he wanted jets. We sweated with him till he got there, but he just excelled in the cockpit. He got a degree in aeronautical engineering, and [he] ended up as a carrier-based pilot on the *Saratoga*, a ship built, I've come to learn, at the Brooklyn Navy Yard. So it was ironic for me to go to the Brooklyn Navy Yard as a board member of the World Trade Center Memorial Foundation.

Chic was the guy who was always stuffing suggestion boxes. He was like that in the military. He was certainly like that at American Airlines, where he got a job after a brief period working as an engineer at Lockheed. He really believed in writing letters of advice to presidents of the airlines. He was an inspiration for me, because he was confident that one person could make a difference. It was simply in his nature to try and improve a situation. And he loved people, the kind of guy who was always crossing the room to introduce himself to strangers, but not in a self-promoting way. He made people feel at ease and so was very much loved by his peers.

I remember having to fly shortly after 9/11. I was living in Los Angeles at the time, after almost thirty years of living in New York, as I had lost both my mother and father recently and wanted to be closer to my family on the West Coast. Plus, I was starting my own production company. I had to fly back and forth quite a bit in those first days, and initially it was very difficult for me, because I was on American Airlines flying back and forth to the scene of the crime. I actually had to fly the very flight number that Chic flew on 9/11: Flight 76 to Dulles and Flight 77 back to LA. The crews on those planes all knew Chic very well, and they would come over to talk to me and tell me great stories about him. My brother Brad just can't fly on American anymore, because he looks a lot like Chic, and he can't take it. A flight attendant came over to him once, put her hand on his face, and said, "Oh, you look so much like him."

When the first plane hit, I was asleep in California, as it was just before 6:00 A.M. A few minutes later my sister-in-law, my brother Mark's wife, called me from Pennsylvania. She said, "Debra, I'm sorry to wake you, but you need to go put on the television set right now."

My legs swung out of bed and I was holding the phone as I walked over to turn my television set on. I asked, "What's going on?" And she said, "Just turn on the TV." Of course, there were the smoking buildings, and they were playing the tape over and over of the second plane hitting, and I was in . . . I was shocked. I kept asking, "What's going on, what's going on?" She said, "A plane hit the first tower." And as I was watching the second plane hit, I reacted to that with her. It was just an utter and complete shock.

I said to myself, *This is my hometown.* The last Mother's Day that I had spent with my mother, who had died ten months earlier, was at Windows on the World [a high-end restaurant on the 106th floor of the North Tower]. It was just a completely surreal, disorienting, shocking experience. I knew that it was terrorism. I knew too that this was beyond just a terrorist incident: We were going to go to war. Of course I know now that while I was staring at the television, Chic would probably have just been killed—a little after 9:00 A.M. American Airlines Flight 77 left Dulles International Airport in Virginia at 8:10 A.M. and crashed into the Pentagon at 9:37 A.M., killing all 64 on the aircraft and 125 inside the Pentagon building. Chic died on the plane before the crash, when his plane was breached.

But interestingly, when I watched that morning I never thought of Chic, because this was in New York and Chic flew out of Dulles. What I did think of, as I watched the replay over and over, were the pilots. Not understanding how the attacks happened and how the cockpits had been commandeered, I had an image of the pilots up in the cockpit and was just thinking, *Oh, my God, those poor pilots. Those poor pilots.*

I had been a flight attendant for seven years, and I spent a lot of time up in those cockpits talking to those guys. I knew the procedure on airplanes really, really well. A grave worry went through and around my head, because when you see a plane that has turned like that it can only mean an emergency. Chic used to say the first person at the scene of an accident was the pilot, because the plane noses in.

A friend of mine called whom I had flown with as a flight attendant with the former TWA. She asked me if Chic was involved. And I said, "Oh, no. Chic flies out of Dulles. Chic wouldn't be in New York." Looking back, that didn't even make sense, because those planes weren't necessarily from New York. I had no reason to know where those planes came from; I wasn't thinking logically at the time.

For the first forty minutes or so of that day I, like everybody else, was reacting to 9/11. I didn't know that I was about to become personally involved. All I knew was that the video of that plane hitting, United 175, made me feel so awful for the families, and for those crew members and passengers.

I thought it would be an incredibly horrible thing for those families to have to live with for the rest of their lives. It's bad enough to know someone had died in a horrific thing like this, but to have to see it and to live with it? It's an image that you wish you could erase but can't.

I then got the call from Brad, and at first I didn't understand what he was saying, as he was just screaming. And I said, "Brad, I don't know what you're saying, I can't understand you. Please, please calm down." And it still didn't hit me; I still didn't know. And what he was screaming was "It's Chic! It's Chic! It's Chic!" Over and over and over again.

I said, "What do you mean? What do you mean?"

And here's the horrible thing: Someone we know in aviation told us that the second plane to hit the towers was Chic's plane. In the confusion, no one knew where the planes were. Chic's plane was scheduled to depart at 8:10 A.M., rolled out at 8:20 A.M., and turned around sometime after 8:50 A.M., after which they lost it. They had no idea that it had turned around and actually sent out a search-and-rescue team in the vicinity of where it went off radar. They still thought that the second plane hitting was Chic's plane.

The Secret Service called Chic's wife, Sheri. Then Chic's best friend, Tom, who had gone to Sheri, called my brother Brad and told him Chic's flight was involved. I immediately got on the phone and called Sheri's house to talk to Tom, who was also a pilot with American Airlines. I said, "Are you sure? How do you know?" Tom just said, "They know, Debra."

I just didn't want to accept the fact that it was Chic's flight that hit Tower 2. Here I was, thinking about those poor pilots and their poor families, and now I'm realizing that I was talking about my brother and me.

I'll never forget that it was Jim Miklaszewski at NBC who reported that a bomb had just gone off at the Pentagon. *Oh, my God*, I thought. *All hell's breaking loose.* And then that switched to a small plane, and then that switched to a larger plane, and it wasn't until the afternoon that we found out that it was American 77, Chic's plane, that had hit the Pentagon.

There was only one cockpit voice recorder that was recovered—the one from United 93. The recorder on Chic's plane was analog tape, so it was destroyed. We pressed really hard to get confirmation of that, and finally saw a picture of it, and it was rubbish in the fire. The data recorder from United 93, however, told us a great deal: when the cockpit was breached, and how long the fight would have lasted inside the cockpit for my brother.

As a former flight attendant, I can tell you that it would have been very easy for them to get in. We also know that they had done a lot of rehearsals and research on test flights: which airplanes would have the lightest loads; which day of the week would be most advantageous. The cockpit door was open when they went in, and I think it must have happened when the flight attendant got up to get the pilots their coffee. Remember, they positioned people in the first row of first class, so that when they saw the flight attendant open the door, they would be right behind her. On United 93 one of the flight attendants got pushed into the cockpit, and you can hear her on the cockpit voice recorder begging for her life. The pilots knew they were going to kill her. I believe that all of the flights were taken over in the same way.

Unlike so many 9/11 families, we knew what had happened that day. Although the focus of the reporting was mostly the Trade Center, it all felt very much a part of the attack that had killed Chic. All of it was connected. And I felt very certain that the people who did this had all conspired together, so every revelation of reportage in New York felt very much a part of the attack that killed my brother.

Then, when I heard how many firefighters had been killed, I literally collapsed in my living room in LA. I remember taking my daughter to the firehouse on Eighty-fifth Street in New York, when I was pushing her in a stroller. The guys would all *ooh* and *ahh* at our little curly-blond-haired girl. So we felt a connection to the Fire Department: They weren't off somewhere in some remote location but were right in our neighborhood. . . . So that was a horrible thing.

There was a point when I remember feeling very grateful, if you can believe it, and lucky that Chic's plane had hit the Pentagon and not the World Trade Center. At least we knew where he was that day, somewhere in that mess at the Pentagon. We didn't know what we would get back in terms of remains, if anything, but we knew where he was. To this day, when I see people holding up flyers with descriptions of missing family members, with their wedding pictures, smiling faces, and vital statistics, I understand how harrowing it was for them, not knowing. I understand the denial and the hope in their hearts on 9/11. When the husband didn't come home that night, and the next night, and the next night, and the next day, they had to hope that he was still alive somewhere—maybe unconscious, maybe not knowing who he was. You hold out hope until there is confirmation.

What is ironic is that we had such special connections to the Pentagon. Chic had spent seventeen years as a reservist there. He had volunteered for the Persian Gulf War, had reactivated during [it], and had worked at the Pentagon. We all lived on Bolling Air Force Base there in Anacostia in Washington, D.C., and my dad was at the Pentagon all the time. So for his plane to crash there, where we had all this history, was bizarre—like having it crash in your backyard. It was a building that was extremely familiar to us, and on top of that, his plane went right over Arlington, where my parents had just been buried. It was all very bizarre.

I never would have understood how important remains are until we got them for Chic. We got them at the end of November, and he was identified through DNA. It was a gift, because we couldn't have buried him at Arlington without those remains. We could have chosen a columbarium, and he could have had a marker someplace, but he couldn't have a grave. That too made me appreciate the true nightmare and anguish that World Trade Center families have gone through with respect to the remains issue. My parents were both buried at Arlington National Cemetery, and Chic was the one who arranged for their burials. My father was a chief master sergeant—the first person, I believe, to get that rank—and was buried with honors, the full military funeral that Chic always wanted to have. Chic wanted to be buried properly at Arlington, and the very idea that that wouldn't be possible because there was nothing to bury would have added to the trauma of having yet something else taken away from him—first his life, and then his proper burial.

Chic's wife, Sheri, had a rough time. She is a very private person and wanted to be out of the limelight and stay in her house. I begged her to talk to the *Washington Post*—begged her, please, because we were trying to get him buried at Arlington, and they wouldn't let us. Chic was a retired naval reservist captain, and because the space there was filling up with World War II veterans, Arlington had created an arbitrary rule that retired reservists had to be sixty years old to be buried there. Chic died the day before his fifty-second birthday, so a media campaign to get them to relax the requirement was important. Sheri finally agreed to talk to the *Post,* and we got Chic buried there. But she was never really the same. Sheri was an American Airlines flight attendant but never flew again, and became reserved, and stayed mostly in her home.

When strangers ask me what I do for a living, I really don't like to answer that question. But really, what I am now is a political activist. I never thought I would be one, for I'd always considered a political activist to be a troublemaker. Most Americans were touched by 9/11; they know that their world changed. Of course, people went back to their lives, their jobs, and their mortgages, but I never went back to my normal life. I want to help get the message of 9/11 out, so through the next years I'll be trying to figure out how to do that.

I started getting politically active when, in March 2004, I wrote an op-ed, my very first one, for the *Wall Street Journal*, titled OUR 9/11. It was me basically saying to a small group of 9/11 family members, Hold on: 9/11 happened to everybody, not just you. The piece was a response to the controversial Bush campaign ads that appeared in February of that year, the ones that were cast in Hallmarkish golden tones, reminding people that we'd been through all these terrible things and asking where the country was going. They featured something like three seconds or less of Bush at Ground Zero, and some family members came out against them really hard, basically saying that was a slap in the face of families with victims. One family member was quoted as saying, "I'd rather vote for Saddam Hussein than for Bush."

And I became enraged by that.

I knew that so many of our members of the armed services had signed up because of 9/11, and were already dying in Iraq, and here was a 9/11 family member saying, I'd rather vote for the leader who is killing our guys. I thought it was incredibly ungracious and insensitive to our military families, of which I had been part for much of my life. And I thought of many of Chic's classmates, because when he died his peers who had stayed in the military were at the height of their careers: one was in charge of the Fifth Fleet; one was in charge of the Sixth Fleet; and one was in charge of the Seventh Fleet. Later, another led the battle of Fallujah.

I was also outraged because I saw how magnificent the American people had been on 9/11. I don't think I could have gotten through it all were it not for them. I felt it was very small of these 9/11 family members to belittle our country this way, so I wrote the op-ed piece, basically saying, We've all had this collective loss, but when you go out and do this, you do not speak for me. And you have to have respect for the military and their families. And when you consider that 9/11 images are now appearing on coffee mugs and postage stamps and place mats, I think your outrage is selective. Let the public decide the president, not you.

After that piece appeared, the press saw that someone was speaking out and then started coming to me for comment, and very, very slowly I ended up involved. I believe I was asked to join the World Trade Center Memorial board because I was viewed as someone who would push back against 9/11 families who were already very focused on Ground Zero and what would be built there. I think the Lower Manhattan Development Corporation, which is responsible for rebuilding the site and for the memorial, wanted to marginalize the families, to push them aside. They thought, *Here, this woman's great. Her brother died at the Pentagon, but she's a New Yorker. We'll bring her on the board and she'll help us. She'll be someone who'll be a buffer, push back.* Of course, it didn't work out that way. One of the things they planned was an International Freedom Center, and I became one of the people who wanted to tear that idea to shreds, because it would have been, with its histories of events with no relevance at all to 9/11, a horrible thing to put there.

That was a real education. Ultimately, all of this comes down to their successful PR campaign versus your successful PR campaign and fighting for control of the narrative. I also learned how things are run in the city by the political and cultural elites. I also butted heads with other 9/11 family members with respect to the 9/11 Commission and the war in Iraq, for I was viewed as a "Bush defender" and a "Bush girl." The truth of the matter is that I was, and have always been, a Democrat, and quite liberal. But for me and many Americans, 9/11 was just a game changer. It redefined the world; now all bets were off. No longer could I rely on the *New York Times* to tell me what was happening. I don't trust the *New York Times*, because much of what they reported was inaccurate. I am now reading primary source material, and when I want to know what is happening, say, in Iraq, I read the bloggers in Iraq on the ground. Their information was better than anything from the networks or CNN. And I started writing.

I was on everyone's list of family members who got information. When the Bush ad was aired, I received an e-mail that was a protest of those ads. It was funneled to everyone through a 9/11 families listserv, but it was signed by a woman who I noticed was from Fenton Communications. I thought, *Fenton Communications, that sounds like a PR firm. If this is such a grassroots family thing, what's a PR firm doing here sending information through the 9/11 families group?* I investigated, and it turns out that Fenton Communications is a liberal PR firm, with clients like MoveOn.org and 9/11 Families for a Peaceful Tomorrow. I thought, *Oh, my God, the woman who signed this e-mail organizing family members is not even one herself.* I called her up and said, "Who's the client on this Bush ad protest?" "Oh, it's MoveOn.org." And I thought, *Holy crap. This isn't being organized by legitimate 9/11 families but by the anti-Bush opposition.* I later found out that the woman who worked at Fenton was a former Al Gore staffer. So much of this is political, and the families were just being used. I was outraged enough to do another *Wall Street Journal* op-ed.

And between the writing, being on the board of the memorial, and all my other activities, I was really sort of stuffed into this kind of odd job, unpaid, where I was involved in all things 9/11.

I got involved in issues involving homeland security matters regarding immigration. I got involved with our national security policies, and with the terror project, trying to get corporations to divest their pension investments, mainly pensions with companies that were investing or doing business in Iran. I campaigned for George Bush in the 2004 election, and though I'd never been involved in a political campaign in my life, I felt that he had to get elected for a second term or that Kerry was going to dismantle everything, not just the war in Iraq, but the Patriot Act and all of the vital, necessary antiterrorism tools that had been put in place. I did tons of radio for the Bush campaign, and then I spoke at the Republican convention, an incredible experience. Remember, I'm still a Democrat, and I sort of still self-identify as a liberal Democrat, but everything to me was national security and 9/11 and stopping these bastards from doing it, or worse, again. And that's still what I'm all about. Stopping them, and educating the public about their threat. We've now gone beyond the dangers of aviation to considering the dangers of all the terrorist acts that they can do. They must be stopped. There must be a new awareness about the life-and-death dangers of the Muslim Brotherhood and Sharia law. Americans need to be educated about these threats to their future. They need to wake up to these truths. And I hope we actually are ready to stop them, because they're vastly embedded. You know, it was emotional to hear of bin Laden's death, and it was a great moral victory for America. But I also think of my brother. He was a military man, and he would still be angry at what was done to all his passengers and crew. We still have a long way to go.

Mosques in America are not part of a higher church order like the Vatican. They are privately owned; there's no oversight, either religious or governmental. The mosque in Washington, D.C., was taken over in 2004 by the Wahhabis. Wahhabism is the more extreme school of Islam. It's a big mosque and Islamic center, and when they had money problems the Wahhabis swooped in and took care of all monetary issues, and now they own the mosque. This is the danger for the moderates, to be forced out by the fundamentalist radicals. They build a mosque and everyone is happy, for these are peaceful Muslims, but then they can be taken over.

The Muslim Brotherhood was founded in 1928 in Egypt as the Society of the Muslim Brothers. It was revitalized in the 1950s, and then came to the United States. Since 1962 the Muslim Brotherhood has determined to bring down the house of the infidels from within, with what they call "settlements." The settlement process is embedding within all our institutions: education, military, government, culture, and media. They're big on educating youth. Many of the Mideast studies departments in our universities are funded by the Wahhabis.

I do not believe I could have gotten through any of this without my own faith. I know that there are people who have no faith, and I think they must suffer from it. My parents gave me that gift. They made sure that I had a good education, but they also made sure I was clear on the power and importance of faith. I actually have had enough time to get myself together, and have really come to learn that I am a strong person. You learn who you are through an experience like 9/11: You sink or you swim. And I was touched by faith. There was a lot of anguish over losing Chic.

I was furious, so full of rage. I'm still angry, and not just about what happened to Chic. I've sort of reconciled what happened to him, and the shock of that has over time been absorbed. What doesn't diminish is the arrogance of those who want to continue killing to advance their determined idea of world supremacy. It's such an outrage, and I can't walk away from it as long as it's still out there. If people say, Oh, are you doing this for your brother? I say no. I'm never going to get my brother back. I'm doing it for your brother and all the other brothers and sisters who are still alive. And the husbands and wives, the sons and daughters.

One of the things we have an obligation to do in the next decade is to put a pin in the balloon of this whole idea of multiculturalism. This has gone so far off the rails, taking the country in a direction that is unfortunate and dangerous. How do we bring people back to basics, back to how this country was founded, and to why we must remember our founding documents? If you study those documents—the Declaration of Independence and the Constitution—their language is so specific, and every word is so powerful. To me, it's heartening to see that people are going back, and they are actually reading the Constitution—it takes only seconds to find it on the Web. The more you read the Constitution, the more alarming it is to see what our government's been doing.

I started out as a grieving sister, and I then underwent an extreme education. I've got a room in my house which has a big wall that is filled with nothing but primary source material. I stay up late at night doing this research. Since 9/11, thousands of innocent civilians have been killed or maimed in terrorist attacks—Madrid, London, Bali, Amman, Moscow, Istanbul, Beslan, Jerusalem, Fort Hood, Mumbai. The Department of Homeland Security says that there have been forty-three homegrown terrorist plots to attack America since 9/11. When I think about walking away from this, I remember that the enemy is still plotting. They never sleep.

To expand, Muslims are using our values of freedom of religion and freedom of speech—freedoms that do not exist in Arab countries—as both their sword and their shield. We have to blast away at the educational and political elites in our country and remind them they were willing to tear Marxism apart [and] analyze what it was and its evil social destructiveness. We've had the benefit of scholarship analyzing every -ism, every political ideology under the sun, but not Islamism. Ayaan Hirsi Ali, the courageous activist who fled Islam, does this analysis with great moral drive, but to her detriment. She must now live with bodyguards, the price she pays for being a truth teller.

We have to persist in saying a nonreformist Islam is a way of life aimed at destroying all of the Western principles we live with—our very way of life. When they call us Islamophobes, it just rolls right off my back, because I know that it's aimed at shutting us up, but also because I know enough secular or reformist Muslims now who are standing with us and saying, We support you, because if you fail we will have no place left to go.

There is a collision down at Ground Zero about this mosque—a direct collision between two competing First Amendment rights: freedom of speech and freedom of religion. Politicians have been citing the principle of the separation of church and state to usher in an imam who is promoting Sharia, a legal system which demands the absolute *absence* of separation of church and state, and which has zero tolerance for other religions.

Magazines like *Newsweek* and *Time* publish cover issues that call America Islamophobic and then wonder why Americans are not buying their magazines. They lecture us with moral vanity about multiculturalism and scold us about how we're a bunch of narrow rednecks.

Where is our future bringing us? It's not just the implications surrounding shifting populations of huge numbers of Muslims in the world. It is the threat of the most sought after weapon of choice. What happens when Iran gets a nuclear bomb? I remember when I worked at Court TV, one of my colleagues covered the 1993 World Trade Center bombing trial, but I was not very interested in that case. So while I understand not being interested in all of the scare about terrorism, after 9/11 I think we cannot afford to ignore the reality in front of us.

In the cold war we had something called "mutually assured destruction." We do not have that deterrent today. Islamists don't identify with nation-states; countries are either a part of the nation of Islam or not. The mullahs rule. People wrongly believe that Ahmadinejad controls Iran, when it is definitely the ayatollahs. I believe that Iran would detonate a bomb in Israel in a heartbeat, knowing that they could lose a million of their own people. That is a culture totally alien to our Western society, which cherishes life and individual conscience.

The whole point of radical Islam is to supplant Western law with Sharia, to turn the United States into a part of the worldwide caliphate. They are working to institute accommodations to Islam, and that is occurring in many countries without anyone's truly realizing it. If we object to this, we're cast as bigots and racists.

I was fascinated by the preacher down south who wanted to burn the Koran. He was demonized for exercising free speech, but after all, a book— even a Bible or a Koran—is cardboard and paper, not the actual living, breathing Prophet. It is an insult to Muslims, yes, but the insult isn't as deeply wounding as putting a fifteen-story mosque up in the air where all those bodies fell as dust. More than eleven hundred people were never found in that place, not even the smallest body part, and so they were in that dust. Burning a book does not compare. Somehow burning the Koran was viewed as a despicable thing, and *people were going to die because of it.* The press just accepted that insane equivalency as some new moral norm. No one questioned whether people would actually kill over that.

While Mayor Bloomberg was defending Imam Rauf's freedom of religion, where was the liberal media pointing out that the mayor created a phony spin? No one, absolutely no one, suggested that this imam did not have a legal right to build a mosque. The mayor, I think, does not understand the grave insult to so many good and decent families.

This is the kind of battleground that we're going to be seeing in the next ten years, based on the speech issue. Our Founders complained about newspapers too—the press was the bane of their existence. But they defended it and fought for it, because they understood that if you don't have freedom of speech, the republic crumbles. It is the first and last bulwark against tyranny. If we can't preserve our country, if we can't name and say what's wrong . . . Think of it: The *New York Times* will publish classified national security measures aimed at protecting us but won't print the Danish cartoons that mock a religious figure. This is a form of cultural suicide. Freedom of speech is the battleground now. As it is said, not to speak is to speak, and not to act is to act. Let Muslims speak, but with transparency of motive, history, and religious belief. And let Americans speak as well in this way. Americans know who they are, and they know what this country stands for. They know what they want to leave for their children, and they will fight for it. This is the thought that gives me hope, that I rely on, to honor all the good my brother Chic gave to the world.

George Siller

George Siller is the second oldest brother in the family that created the Stephen Siller Tunnel to Towers Run, a nationally known and annually televised race that now attracts more than seventeen thousand runners each year. The event was created to memorialize the heroic run of firefighter Stephen Siller, who ran through the Brooklyn Battery Tunnel with full gear to join in the rescue efforts at the World Trade Center on 9/11, where he lost his life. The foundation the family created, online at www.tunneltotowersrun.org, is a not-for-profit charity that supports injured firefighters, burn centers, disabled veterans from the Iraq and Afghanistan wars, and the children of those veterans in need.

We're a very close family. My father was adamant about us being close all our lives. There were seven of us: Stephen was the youngest; Frank, who was about six years older, was the second youngest; then my three sisters—Regina (we call her Gina), Mary, and Janis—and then my brother Russell. Stephen was sort of a gift to us all. After so many children my father used to say that if another one came along, it would have to be an immaculate conception. We, the older ones, were packed together, a bunch of kids, and we couldn't appreciate one another. We were like puppies fighting for the milk or the bone or whatever. And now we had a child that we all appreciated. It was like having a toy in the family. He was such a joy. He had a great personality. I think part of that was he had a great audience, for we all thought he was so funny and smart.

My mother and father were both very religious. My father belonged to the Third Order, which is like [being] a lay Franciscan priest or brother. He loved everybody, and he was a very generous man. Both my mother and father would go to mass every day during Lent and Advent, and we actually read the Bible at suppertime, until everybody in the family was laughing so much that my father would get madder and madder, and finally he gave up on it. He wasn't a religious fanatic, but he lived a religious kindness. To make a living he sold religious articles: first communion and confirmation sets; little prayer books; rosary beads. His business would go south because he was often ill, and the people who worked for him would help us out. But in our family we have never cared about money. We never had it growing up, and we don't feel like it's the important thing in life.

We all grew up with a sense of service. My brother Russ went in the VISTA service, where he met his wife, Jackie. All my sisters became nurses. My sister Mary was a nun initially, but she left [the order], married, and now has three kids. My mother and Mary actually went to nursing school together. My mother was fifty years old at the time, and they became nurses together at St. Vincent's Hospital in Staten Island. I became a registered nurse as well, later on, with the GI Bill. My parents were also very generous, and they taught the same generosity to all of their kids. When we made a bet for a dollar or something—maybe on the World Series, since we were massive baseball fans—if we won, my parents would tell us, You can't take that money. But if we lost, they would say, You have to honor that bet and pay it. Why we ever bet, I don't know.

Our parents passed away a year apart, my father from a blood clot after surgery—he had bad circulation in his legs, and diabetes—and then my mother, from cancer. My mother was sick the whole last year, and Stephen used to come home from school and find her balled up almost in the fetal position, because with stomach cancer it was the only position she felt comfortable [in]. She didn't want the lights on in the room, and so he lived a sad and depressing life during that period. Even before my mother passed away, all the brothers and sisters had been dedicated to keeping Stephen occupied and happy. But it was a terrible way for a child to live—he'd just lost his dad, and now he had to deal with a mother who was dying.

Most of us were in our early twenties to early thirties when our parents passed away, but Stephen was still a child: eight and a half when my father died and ten when my mother died. And so, besides losing our parents, we had to deal with bringing Stephen up. We felt that Russell and his wife, Jackie, were the best to raise Stephen. They had no children, and also Russell was the oldest. We all had families already. Russell could give Stephen all-around attention and dedicate himself to bringing him up.

Russ and Jackie live in Long Island, so after our mother died, Stephen was moved from Staten Island to Rockville Centre.

When our parents died, we didn't feel sorry for ourselves. We felt sorry for Stephen. I cried a little at the funerals, obviously, but I never really wallowed in my own self-pity. It was poor Stephen. That's what we all did, and that's how we handled 9/11. We felt sorry for Stephen's children and his wife, Sally; not for ourselves. Over time, though, we have come to feel sorrow for ourselves, but I guess we hide it by feeling sorry for the other people. Put others first.

When Stephen was older he eventually got an apartment on Staten Island, not far from me, living on his own, in a basement apartment. He ended up marrying a girl named Sally Wilson, who lived one block from where he grew up on Staten Island. He must have met Sally a few times when he was a kid, but nothing had registered. He wanted to have kids because he wanted with Sally to be the parents he did not have growing up. He was determined to have a wonderful family life to make up for some of that sadness he had experienced. Stephen and Sally started their family with Jamie, and then came Olivia, Genevieve, Jake, and finally Stephen, who was around nine months old on 9/11.

Stephen joined the Fire Department because he had such a connection with people—he loved them, and he loved being around them, and he loved the family feeling. The Fire Department gave him that feeling of family, being with the guys, the teamwork thing. He was so sociable that he'd have a thousand friends, no matter where he was. In fact, at his funeral, almost every person who came told us he was Stephen's best friend. He made everybody feel that way, being so gregarious and warmhearted. He never slept; he would go to everything—any family or friend event you could think of, he'd be there. We called him Mr. Multiplicity. He did five things on the Sunday before 9/11, one of which was calling me up asking if I wanted to play some golf. All of a sudden, on the fourteenth hole, Stephen says, I gotta go. And that's the way he was. He was probably supposed to be someplace else the whole time. Then he came back to my house to watch *Band of Brothers*, the HBO miniseries, and after the episode ended, Stephen said he was going to come over every week to watch the rest of the series with me. So we made plans to do that, but, of course, we never got to.

His desire for the Fire Department was unstoppable. That's the word to describe the way Stephen went about everything in his life—unstoppable. I'm not sure where that determination came from. He did always love John

Wayne. All the athletes he admired were tough guys—like Lawrence Taylor, Bernard King—and his favorite baseball player was George Brett. In fact, he drove across country to see George Brett's last game in Kansas City. He made everything, did everything.

In sports, he never met a shot he didn't like. He had a great arm and could really throw, in both football and baseball. He was a little erratic, in that he'd make an unbelievable diving catch at third base, but then throw it over the first baseman's head at a hundred miles an hour. He was so competitive, so determined. And he brought that into his work. Maybe a month or two before 9/11 he fell through a floor into a basement filled with water. There was nobody in the building, and I said, Stephen, you gotta think. But he was gung ho: gung ho about his job and about his family. He gave so much time to each niece and nephew. I don't know how he did it. My son George said to me at Stephen's funeral, "I thought I was the only one who had a special relationship with Uncle Steve." But all the cousins were saying how Uncle Steve showed up for this and made it to that. I didn't even know about it at the time, but Stephen was helping my son Greg, who was playing college football. Greg went off to college as a tight end, but when he tore his ACL [anterior cruciate ligament, part of the knee], they wanted him to be an offensive lineman, which meant he had to bulk up. Stephen would go and work out with him at a park down the block here. I never even knew they were working out together, as Stephen was doing stuff with him while I was at work. When Greg had his first football game in college, at the University of New Hampshire, Steve planned to come up with me to see the game. But then a fireman died, and he had to pay his respects. Stephen told Greg, I'll make the next game. That was the Saturday before 9/11.

My brothers and I had a regularly scheduled golf game, and on 9/11 we had plans for a golf outing in New Jersey—Frank, Russ, Stephen, and myself. We used to play almost every month, but then we could only manage to get together a few times a year. We were pretty excited about that day, because we knew what the weather was going to be like—perfect. Ironically, every time we went golfing we'd try to get Stephen to leave early, or get some guy to pick him up early, so he could get there on time. But that day we didn't rush him because he was working the night before. And like Stephen, we usually tried to get the golf in and then go to work, but that day we all decided, let's just take it easy and really enjoy ourselves. It could be one of the last good days of the golf season, that kind of thing. So Frank, Russ, and I planned to meet at Frank's and to wait for Stephen. But Russ stopped first at Sally and Stephen's house on the way, and Stephen called Sally and said, "Tell the boys I'll meet them at the golf course, There's something going on at the World Trade Center. I'll meet up with them later." He didn't know then. And that was our last phone call from Stephen.

Stephen had a shortwave radio in his car, so he would hear whenever there was a fire somewhere. Even on his off days he would go to a fire, and sometimes would drive to check it out when he had his kids in the car. He had already left the firehouse that morning and was heading toward the Verrazano Bridge on his way to meet us when he heard on the radio what was going on and turned around. He went back to his firehouse, Squad 1 in Brooklyn, and his crew had already gone. They lost eleven guys.

They wouldn't let anybody through the Brooklyn Battery Tunnel, so Stephen left his truck at the Brooklyn entrance and ran through the tunnel. Frank and I later got a call from somebody from the Police Department saying they found his truck there, and we then tried to retrace how it all had happened. We later learned that halfway through the tunnel Stephen jumped up on Engine 239, which was stuck in all that traffic, and after taking a six-foot hook from them started running again. When he took the hook he told the guys, I'll meet you there. We went over to that firehouse, Engine 239, where we found out that someone had seen him on West and Liberty streets. That's the last place that we know for a fact that somebody had eyeballed him.

I had seen the fire at the World Trade Center before I left for Frank's house, and like everybody else, I thought it was either an electrical fire or a small plane that actually hit it—like what had happened at the Empire State Building. So it didn't really register with me at first that it was a ca-tastrophe. But at Frank's house I said, "Turn on the TV—there's something going on." And then we got the call from Sally telling us that Stephen would meet us later. So Russ joined us, and we sat there and watched it. When we saw the first tower go down, it was like, *Oh, God.* We spent a good part of the time saying to ourselves, *There's no way he could have made it in time.* To rationalize it. He couldn't have made it there from Brooklyn. And then we kind of slowly realized that Stephen would have found a way to get there. We spent the next day or two waiting for a phone call. Well, they didn't find any part of him. But we had a burial anyway, because his wife and family wanted that ritual, those prayers. Stephen's grave is on Staten Island, right down the block from here in St. Peter's Cemetery.

Why did this happen? Why? In 1993 there was a bombing, and every time I would see the pictures on TV I'd get mad. Of course, for 9/11—I've watched it a million times—I have more of a feeling of disgust than of anger. Or a feeling of desperation. Why? Why did this have to happen? Why did Stephen's children have to grow up without a dad after he ran in to help people? I . . . and, I think, our family . . . pushed our energy toward trying to make the world a little better, but there is always that *why* question. I feel like the reason that these terrorists hate us so much is envy, and you can't stop people from being envious. And jealousy. And like many people, I feel that a respect for life is not there. It's unfortunate. I think that until they have something to lose in life people have less respect for life. If you have a beautiful house or a wonderful family or whatever, then you think twice, but if you're living in a cave in the middle of Afghanistan, you're not really giving up much, and that's the reason you're easily brought into this martyrdom. I believe they have nothing to lose. And they have a lot of anger, and are easily swayed.

I was in a daze all of that day. Frank said, "I think we lost our brother." I kind of felt it that day, but for five or six days afterward I figured somebody could live in a hole or something, like when a mine collapses. So many people on Staten Island had a relative or friend who was involved in 9/11. We spent a lot of days sitting around Sally's house, hours and hours, and bringing the food in. We all kept trying to keep the kids occupied, [not] sitting there, waiting. Very anxious.

Sally is just a remarkable mother. She held up better than I thought most wives could possibly do. Not that she wasn't totally upset, worried, but she had five kids to keep her mind focused and occupied. In a way, for that situation, children are a blessing, to keep you busy. It also helps that we have a very big family. If we went out to dinner and everybody brought all their kids and grandkids, I think the reservation would be in the midfifties. I have a Christmas brunch every year, and depending on who shows up, we have from forty to fifty-seven now. I've never really counted them, but they can all be counted on.

At Stephen's funeral there were tons of people outside the church, and as many inside. It was very moving, almost presidential in a way, with all the firemen lined up. Mayor Giuliani came to the wake. I don't know how the heck he made all those things, but he was really, really wonderful. Lifted everybody he could. And Governor Pataki's wife was there, and other officials too. It was a good funeral, if there is such a thing.

My brother Frank is a take-charge guy. And he was already working in his head the idea of starting a foundation and what it would do. Not to knock golf outings or dinners, but when those things were brought up, I said, There's a million of them. I'm involved in sporting goods, and we do a golf outing every other day. We wanted something unique. Then one of Stephen's friends, Billy Todd, suggested, "Why don't you just retrace what he did?" So Frank called me up and said, "Billy has a great idea, don't tell anybody. I don't want anybody stealing it."

Fortunately, Richie Sheerer was a fire dispatcher years ago, with my cousin, so he knew our family a bit. He kindly led us to Rudy Giuliani, who was instrumental in getting us up and going. After that it just snowballed. Once we decided it was going to be a run, we had to go to all the agencies for approvals. Frank did most of the legwork; I went to a few of them. We had a meeting in my dining room, fourteen or fifteen people, here in Staten Island. My next-door neighbor works for the New York City Marathon. Another friend of ours, Nick Navarro, is a firefighter and also the starter at the New York City Marathon. It turns out that Nick went to St. Peter's High School a year or so ahead of my brother Frank, and my brother Russ was teaching as St. Peter's at that time, so Nick knew and respected Russ. We had all these people to help us out. We wanted to get it done by the first year, but we went into one meeting where they weren't very nice to us, and after 9/11 it was surprising how some city officials went right back to the official stuff.

Now, though, they couldn't be nicer to us. I'm sure they have a million requests every year. Those same officials told us a few years later that they left that early meeting saying, "These Sillers are crazy; this isn't going to happen. But we'll try." After all, for this race to happen they had to close the tunnel, part of Brooklyn, and part of downtown Manhattan. That's about 1.7 miles of very expensive real estate. Altogether it's about a three-mile run. We honestly shocked ourselves when it all actually developed.

There was a headline in the *Daily News*: He Ran from the Tunnel to the Tower. So I said, We'll call it the Tunnel to Towers Run. I knew in my heart it couldn't just be called the Stephen Siller Run. It's bigger than that; Stephen was bigger than that. So Frank's idea became an event where we honored all of the firefighters and police officers and all the civilians killed that day.

In fact, the first year we had the names of all 2,974 people posted on a sort of Vietnam wall, set up near the finish line. Then we had the firefighters' banners of the 343 lost firefighters that they wore at the race.

The first year, 2002, we actually had the race end in the tunnel, but over the years, with so many people running, we have had to put the finish outside, coming out of the tunnel. So it's really snowballed. Every time we get frustrated with the many things we have to deal with, we also see all the good that comes out of it. It makes Stephen's life mean something. Everybody in the family gets involved in some way. But it is really the brothers and sisters. The kids give out the shirts and things like that. But the determination is with the brothers and sisters.

My sisters all went out and got restaurants to donate food for the race. We have so many people who donate food that it's almost like Jesus with the loaves and fishes—I'm talking about ten thousand, five thousand, two thousand servings of food from some really nice restaurants in Manhattan. We receive a tremendous amount of help in this effort from FDNY firefighters, who cook thousands of hamburgers and hot dogs. Initially, people didn't charge us for a lot of things, but as time has passed, they have businesses to run, so now we're paying for most of the food. My brother Russ has a lot to do with the writing of the PR material and press releases. My sister Mary is very good with the graphics and the writing too, so we kind of pulled it all together. I got the Web site going, which we needed the first year because there were so many people wanting to register other than by paper. And the Web site has taken over now, to the point where we do more registering online than we do by mail.

The Tunnel to Towers Run is held on the last Sunday in September. We had approximately fifteen hundred the first year; last year there were about twenty thousand. For volunteers, we have seven hundred firefighters, with a flag and a banner for each one, and about fifteen hundred civilians, so there are over two thousand people there before the runners even start. We also have a lot of spectators, because so many people come to see their family members or friends at the finish line.

All along the actor John Turturro has been helping us out, and most years he has been our emcee at the run, if he can make it. My brother Russ taught his brother Nick Turturro, and John has an apartment near Squad 1, where Stephen worked [in Brooklyn]. He has been emotionally and physically involved from day one. He also narrated a PBS film about our family called *For the Love of Their Brother.*

As far as the causes the run supports, we knew right off the bat that we wanted to help out children who had lost one or two parents, because Stephen himself had essentially been orphaned. And because Stephen had been involved with the Firefighters Burn Center in Manhattan, we wanted to support it. Over the years we've also gotten involved with the Staten Island Burn Center. When my sister Regina was younger, she worked at the New York Foundling, a Catholic orphanage, so she and I went to the Staten Island New York Foundling building to check it out, to see if we could help out. It looked like something out of Dickens's *Oliver Twist.* It was an old, decrepit, crooked building. They needed new heating, so we went down and looked at this furnace, which could have been from the *Hansel and Gretel* house, so ancient it was ridiculous. The windows were all old and creaky. We sat down with the New York Foundling and said, basically, there is too much to do here, but maybe we could buy you new furniture so the kids feel a little better about their lives. We bought a bedroom set for all the rooms—new beds and dressers. After some time they came to us with a suggestion. They planned to knock the building down and rebuild it, and they wanted us to be part of a capital plan separate from our foundation. We agreed. We didn't take from anything we raised at the race, but instead solicited politicians, businesses, and banks. They eventually constructed a new building and called it Stephen's House. The front door is shaped like [one from] a firehouse.

We also got involved with the military, initially aligning with the Freedom Alliance, which is run by Ollie [Oliver] North and his group. Recently we have been trying to help a local military kid, Brendan Marrocco, who lost all four limbs, by building him a house adapted to his needs. Through a fund-raiser we've raised enough money to do that. And we're expanding now, thinking of helping out two other soldiers from the Afghan and Iraqi wars in St. Louis and in Chicago. We're going out to St. Louis to coordinate with the fire department there, and a lot of retireds, some active chiefs and captains, and regular firefighters are taking part. It is evolving. Lisa Bender, a teacher from North Carolina, called me up and said that she wanted to put a Tunnel to Towers race on in Wake Forest, which is now sponsored by the Franklin Academy there. They do a beautiful job. They feel what happened in New York happened to all Americans.

This year Gold Star Mothers, the military moms, want to put on Tunnel to Tower races all over the country, and we're negotiating with them to try to figure out how to do it. It is a way for communities outside of NYC to do something meaningful to remember 9/11.

There is also a segment of the race called Brother for Brother, a name my sister Gina came up with. Firefighters from every state take part in the race, so we put three guys from each firehouse together, and whatever their combined time is, the top three get money sent to their local burn center. We even have 150 London firefighters who come each year now, and [they] have become buddies with New York firefighters.

The fire commissioner, Sal Cassano, has been instrumental all along. He's been our right-hand man in taking care of problems. He's been a very reliable and sensible friend, and has smoothed out wrinkles for us a number of times.

Where will we be in ten years? I don't know. But with friends like Sal and the thousands who help the Siller family get this done, I think at some point in time we will be a much bigger foundation.

It took all of us siblings to create this event in memory of Stephen, and many a time we say that Stephen could have done it all by himself. He must be laughing, seeing how much work he left for us and how he continues to control and run our lives even in his death. I have given it my all, and every year I reach a point when I'm tired, and then a point when I become very excited. It's taken its toll, but it surely has its rewards.

I've often seen the beauty of what we've done. When a house is built in my brother's name and is going to help children for a hundred years—there is nothing like it. You know that it's made a difference. The military things we do are so important. We see needs and we try to be responsive. A lot of 9/11 families, together with our organization, have sent down fifty tractor trailers full of things to New Orleans to help them out. We helped build a firehouse in New Orleans. We've done so many things that surprise us. We're just blessed that we're able to do it. But no one does anything by oneself.

And we all try to remember that the more you give, the more you get. There is a saying: "Brother, while we are here, let us do good." That's the name of our foundation: The Stephen Siller, FDNY, "Let Us Do Good"

Children's Foundation. We say the prayer of St. Francis before each meeting, as St. Francis has been the focal point of our lives. Sometimes we have as many as five hundred people at a meeting, and I've never seen one person be upset about praying, because it's such a beautiful prayer. It's religious but it's really more about just being good to people.

Prayer of Saint Francis of Assisi

Lord, make me an instrument of your peace,
where there is hatred, let me sow love;
where there is injury, pardon;
where there is doubt, faith;
where there is despair, hope;
where there is darkness, light;
and where there is sadness, joy.

O Divine Master, grant that I may not so much seek
to be consoled as to console;
to be understood as to understand;
to be loved as to love;
For it is in giving that we receive;
it is in pardoning that we are pardoned;
and it is in dying that we are born to eternal life.

You know, a lot of people are just good in their bones. Sal Cassano, for instance, didn't come to the first run as an honored guest. We knew who he was, as he was a high-ranking chief, but he registered just like everyone else and came to run to support us. We have a mass the Saturday night before the race and Sal comes to that service.

The firefighters are always so impressive. The first weekend after 9/11, many members of my family drove over to Squad 1, Stephen's firehouse, at around midnight to say a prayer for him. The guys on duty were so kind to us, and the one person that really struck me, in retrospect, was Mike Stackpole. His brother, Timmy, had died in the Towers just after being promoted, and after going through years of rehab after being burned badly in a fire. Mike was consoling us, helping us, without ever mentioning that his own brother had been lost, which I only found out afterward. You don't ever forget people like that.

So many people have told us that they use the run as an excuse to go down to Ground Zero. They can't go there just to have a look, but they'll go to honor the firefighters and experience catharsis—a little better-ness. You're never going to be perfect after 9/11, you're never going to get back to what you were, it's never going to be the same, but you have to get on with your life. In our case, we're not walking around wallowing in our grief and crying about Stephen, but we still care. We're still proud of Stephen.

Stephen was somebody who was a hero, but he was a voracious reader and a very intelligent kid. He could have been a top guy on Wall Street or wherever. He had it all. Personality, brains. But he also had an incredible caring for other people.

My son made the high school basketball team, and at his first game he made his first shot, a two-pointer. I looked over at my brother Stephen, who had come with me, and he had a tear in his eye. I said, "What are you doing, Steve?" He said, "I know how much that meant to him." That was so kind-hearted and caring. It's what brought him to run through a tunnel knowing that he might be running to his death. That's what made Stephen truly remarkable: He had time to think about it, to think about his family. And he still charged in.

> our family has stayed strong from those days of the dust
> there has been plenty of sorrow, too much pain for all of us
> why did God take him from us that way
> it's just too high a price to pay
>
> —George Siller

Jay Winuk

Jay's younger brother, Glenn Winuk, was a lawyer whose office was just two blocks away from the World Trade Center. He was also a volunteer firefighter/ emergency medical technician (EMT). On 9/11 Glenn followed his instincts and ran into the South Tower to help, and was lost when it fell. Jay Winuk was instrumental in creating the September 11 National Day of Service and Remembrance as a lasting memorial for all those who were lost on 9/11, and to his brother. The Web site he cofounded, MyGoodDeed.org, is a testament to this memorial day.

My family, at least my generation, originated in Brooklyn. In 1961, the same year Glenn was born, our family moved to Jericho, Long Island. For much of his career my dad was in sales and management in the electronics components industry. At some point he gave all of that up and bought an automotive repair shop, and he made a successful go of that. He was also an inventor of sorts—a great mind, very bright. He invented a battery-operated burglar alarm that you could affix to your door, a device to water hanging plants, which sold very well for him, and a certain kind of innovative paper clip.

Glenn and I spent a lot of time together, because we shared a bedroom all those years growing up in Jericho. A happy coincidence for us was that most of my best friends had younger brothers who were also three years younger than they were, and so there was a lot of kinship between my friends and Glenn and his friends. Ultimately, Glenn went to the same undergraduate college as I, the State University of New York at Oneonta, where we overlapped for a year, which was very nice. Oneonta lost, I think, seven alumni in 9/11, and an artist that the university contracted with built a mini–Twin Towers there in tribute to the alumni that were lost. It is very moving, and overlooks the whole campus.

All through college, and later, at law school—he went to Hofstra—Glenn was a volunteer firefighter in the Jericho Fire Department, along with my brother Jeff, who is five years my senior and was eight years Glenn's. We had an uncle who had been a firefighter in Brooklyn, and who had died on the job. He was such a hero to us—it was so exciting to have an uncle in that job. We had another uncle who was a cop on Long Island, and that too was exciting. I think Glenn took great inspiration from both of them.

Firefighting was Glenn's passion. The alarm was always sounding, "beep, beep, beep," and he or Jeff would be off. He was always very enamored with fire and rescue, police, and, a little, the military, but it was the excitement of firefighting that caught his eye at a very early age. Whenever Glenn set his mind to something, he really went all the way with it, becoming kind of obsessed. He was a black belt in karate, and as a Cub Scout he got as many badges and gold stars as he possibly could. I remember speaking at the second memorial service we had for him, in October of '01, which his law firm held at a beautiful synagogue in Manhattan. I talked about how Glenn would write away to Johnson & Johnson and other medical supply companies asking for free samples of bandages, tape, gauze, and other supplies to put in a homemade wooden first-aid kit that my father had built for him. He would have been happy to be a career firefighter, but I think he had bigger aspirations financially, and wanted to be more intellectually stimulated. Ultimately, he was able to do both: become an attorney and maintain a firefighting career.

Glenn began his law career at Haight Gardner, which is world renowned for its maritime legal work. They merged with Holland & Knight, and Glenn became a partner there. When he really took on the responsibilities of being a partner, he had to reduce his activity as a firefighter. He was living in an apartment building at Thirty-fifth and Park Avenue, but most of his best friends were still on Long Island, and several of them were still in the Jericho Fire Department in one way or another. So on many weekends he would stay at my parents' house, go to Hofstra's law library to do some work, fight fires, do his laundry, and have a nice hot meal from my mom's kitchen.

He had many friends who were FDNY and NYPD, but particularly FDNY, in part because some of the guys were also part-time firefighters in Jericho. Interestingly, he has since been recognized by the FDNY Honor Legion for his actions on 9/11. They tell me that he's likely the first volunteer firefighter ever to be so honored.

I remember the night of September 10 well. I spoke to Glenn, as we usually did several times a week. We didn't see each other as often as either of us would have liked. Although we were always together for the holidays, or I'd have lunch or dinner with him in the city, we both had really busy lives at the time of his death. On September 10 I went to New Jersey to pay my respects to somebody who had died, from our hometown of Jericho. Marty Schwartz, the father of one of my best and oldest friends, was for decades a member of the Jericho Fire Department, and, like Glenn, had at some point been a commissioner of the Jericho Fire Department. Glenn was going to go the following day, and so he called me when I got home to ask for directions and to tell me he was disappointed that he couldn't have gone with me. He had arranged for flowers to be sent, which, of course, arrived on September 11. So the last time I spoke with him was the night before, to discuss the passing of a firefighter.

On the morning of 9/11 I was in my home office in Mahopac, New York, running my public relations company, when I got a phone call from a friend. "Did you see what happened downtown?" he said. "Turn on the television. A plane just crashed into a building downtown." I turned the TV on in my office in time to see the second plane hit. I knew that Glenn was already at work that morning. He would be running down there, as he had in '93 when the Trade Center was attacked.

In September 2001 he was still at the same office building he was at in 1993, which is 93–95 Broadway, just a block and a half from Ground Zero. When the towers were hit by those planes, Glenn did what firemen do—he ran to see if he could help. I later learned that he was still in his apartment on East Thirty-fifth Street getting ready for work when the first tower was hit. He was on the phone with his girlfriend at the time, and he saw what I had seen on the TV. He ran downstairs, passing the doorman, and jumped into a cab as the doorman said, "Don't go down there!" At his office he helped with the evacuation of the two floors that Holland & Knight had at the corner of Jay Street and Broadway. He then borrowed some rescue equipment from the guys who were evacuating his building: a mask, gloves, a first-response medical kit—Glenn was also a certified EMT. And he started running west on Jay Street toward the South Tower.

Meanwhile, the rest of us were watching this like everybody else was watching it, not thinking the worst, and of course not imagining that those buildings would come down. Just that here was my firefighter brother, responding again, in all likelihood. Calling him at work got us nowhere, because everyone had left that place, as well they should have. And so there was no reaching him at his home, on his cell, or at work. Still, I talked to my parents, and none of us was freaking out about it yet, not knowing what was to be. But then the hours started going by, and he still hadn't called any of us, and none of us was able to reach him, and the day started turning into night. I guess we all started thinking, *Well, there's no cell phone service down there or he's just so busy with triage or whatever it is. It's unusual, but okay—let's not think the worst yet.* But as we were watching the news reports, the mayor was saying what he had to say, and we learned more, and of course we began to think then, *Well, maybe he's wandering around somewhere. Maybe he got knocked on the head.* We were thinking what everyone was thinking. We were hoping.

I started calling around to the hospitals that night, and the next morning, all through the next day. Getting in touch with the authorities to do a missing persons report over the phone, giving them all kinds of information. We recruited a friend of Glenn's and mine, John, a real estate attorney with whom we grew up in Jericho, to go down to the armory, which is where I think they were doing all of the missing person's paperwork in the beginning, before we set up on the computer, and he sat with a detective while I was on the phone giving him information to give to the detective so we could file Glenn as missing.

My parents were probably no more or less panicked than I was at first, but the panic increased as time passed, and then really escalated. These were two parents who had raised two firefighters, whose sons ran into dangerous situations, and so they had confidence that both were able to handle themselves. Both Glenn and Jeff had had a lot of close calls over the years—every firefighter does—but they came home. Everything changed when those buildings came down. Over the next few weeks our house became the Ground Zero for our family and friends, the clearinghouse. It was where people called to check in if we knew anything, or could they do anything for the family, or what was the latest information from the authorities.

My wife, Carolyn, and I went down to Glenn's office. There was no electricity in the building on 95 Broadway. Because of its proximity to the towers, they had all evacuated, and the law firm had set up shop in the Roosevelt Hotel [in Midtown]. The place was a military zone. We searched

Glenn's office at Holland & Knight to see if we could determine what he was wearing. Did he take his cell phone? Was he wearing his watch? Did he leave his suit jacket and just run there in suit pants? Did he have his wallet with him? Anything we could do to try to piece some of it together to help the authorities potentially to find him.

This was a very unusual thing to have had to do, and I don't know what I would have done without Carolyn's help. I talk often with people about the nature of this kind of death. It's always tragic when somebody as young as Glenn, who was forty, dies. But to be missing, and then ultimately to be determined to have died in this way, is very unusual for several reasons. It was a murder, and it was a murder that was a mass murder, and a very public murder that continues to have a ripple effect throughout all of our lives today because of the changes that 9/11 resulted in. This is something extrapersonal in the very public loss of a sibling, which is now part of the fabric of our society. And to have that glimmer of hope for several weeks, that question of life or death hanging over you, is also very unusual. If someone dies of a car accident or an illness, or is even murdered, you know it right away, one way or the other. But in this case we were still hoping that he was in some air pocket five stories below ground level. So it was a very strange month or so until the mayor finally said, This is no longer a rescue operation; it's a recovery. Actually, Chief Dan Nigro [see page 1] made that transitional decision. And then we started figuring out how to plan a funeral with no body, and the things that go along with that.

The first time I ever publicly spoke about Glenn's situation was just days after 9/11, to a group from Holland & Knight, and I think in some ways it was meant to be comforting for them, and a kind of connection between our family and Glenn's colleagues, that we were in this together in many ways. And certainly it was comforting for me.

Glenn had worked at this law firm for more than a dozen years, and I knew by name the people that he worked for and the kind of business he was working on, but I didn't know his colleagues. I know many of them very well now. These were the last people he was with, the only people who could give me information about what his last minutes may have been like, or provide any of the pieces of the puzzle that was wide open to me: what he did, or what he was thinking, so that maybe we could figure out how to get him back, for it was not determined that he was dead yet. They thought my brother was wonderful—every day he'd try to go out of his way for somebody. They told us stories of the friendship that came with working with him. It was great for Carolyn and me to hear. It gave us strength, and comfort. Over the years since 9/11 Glenn's partners have been nothing less than filled with compassion and altruism and generosity, and they have been extraordinary in helping us with this traumatic event and this loss.

A few days before it was announced that this was no longer a rescue operation, I got a call from my uncle Lenny in Florida, the uncle who had been a police officer. He advised that we really needed to start thinking about this, that Glenn was not coming back, that we should plan a funeral and prepare our parents—that we had to be realistic. Glenn was not going to make it; none of them was going to make it.

I said to him that I appreciated his advice, and I understood, but until the authorities officially told me that it was over, I had no reason to rush. And he respected that [while] being a good uncle and preparing me for the inevitable. I'm grateful for that.

A few days later Mayor Rudy Giuliani and the fire and police commissioners said that no one was going to come out alive anymore. On October 14 we had a memorial service for Glenn in the Jericho Jewish Center, just a little more than a month after he was lost. It was the temple where all three of us, my brothers and I, had our bar mitzvahs. My parents still live in Jericho, and so there were many people in the community who came, friends of our family. It was the right place. We sought the advice of my cousin, Debbie Stein, who is also a cantor in East Hampton, and my mother's brother, who is an ordained Orthodox rabbi. We had to face the prospect of, Do you have a funeral without having a body? And if so, how do you do it? So it was a matter of religious law and customs to address now. The service was led by the cantor we all grew up with, who did a great job. There were about six hundred people there, and there would have been twice as many had we not asked the law firm not to overwhelm the building. There was no way we could accommodate everybody who would want to come. Ten days later Holland & Knight was going to have its own service in the city, but all the people closest to Glenn came, and all the senior people from the firm, and it was really very special that we had them. Someone from the firm spoke, some of his best friends. Some from the Fire Department where Glenn volunteered spoke, and, of course, family members spoke. It was beautiful.

We decided to follow what we had learned from the example of families from the Holocaust, which was to fill a pine box with possessions of Glenn's that represented different elements of his life. Law books, Cub Scout hat, toy fire trucks, an army truck, some stuff from his bar mitzvah, a lot of his karate belts—about two dozen different things. My son Justin was just four years old, and we had him draw some pictures for his uncle Glenn, illustrations of what Justin's view of this event was. We had been counseled by a professional, who advised us that it was a great way for very young people to handle dealing with this kind of trauma.

Ten days later Holland & Knight had a memorial service at a beautiful, very old synagogue in Manhattan. I also gave a eulogy at that service. There were hundreds of people from the firm there, including people from their other offices. And there was a choir. The service was very moving, and both services were so rich with such great tributes to my brother.

We sat shiva, the Jewish tradition of sharing grief in the home, at my house in Mahopac. This, by the way, was contrary to one of my Orthodox uncle's points of view, who felt that the custom is such—or maybe the religious law was such—that without a body you can't properly have a funeral, and therefore you can't sit shiva, which I respected. And so he did not attend, which was okay. We needed to go forward with something, and we went forward with what we felt was right.

We sat shiva for several days, and hundreds of people came through our house to express their love and support and offering, asking, "What can we do?" Over the course of two months, September and October, family members were flying in from all parts of the country, and it was just an extraordinary outpouring of love. And this love was so needed, so important. Again, it was not just a normal death but something that the whole country and the whole world was thinking about. And people who were directly affected, either because they were family or friends or colleagues of somebody who died or was thought to be dead, this love by others was connected to the funerals, wakes, or services.

To this day I am amazed at my parents' strength. It's not a forced or a false sense of strength. They're not, and were not, trying to be stoic. It was just them, the way they are. There were times they would break down and cry, and there were other times when they could be part of gallows humor that sometimes eases the pain. You know, this was their baby, the youngest of the three. This was the one who still hadn't gotten married, who hadn't had children yet, and who had barely gotten to live his life. And so it was and remains devastating for them. It would be that for any parent, I am sure, and yet they attended all the services—the park dedications, the service at the bronze wall, and the tributes on Long Island. If there's something to be done where Glenn is being honored, and they are able to be there, which is more difficult now because it's ten years later and they are both facing health challenges, they gather the strength to do it. And they have found ways to continue on, to enjoy their grandchildren, to go out for a meal.

You never know how you're going to handle these things. I think I deal with Glenn's death in a very different way sometimes than they do. I spend a lot of time trying to get national recognition for his heroism, using his story to inspire others to do good. That's a very public endeavor, whereas my parents chose to deal with things a little more privately. You have to do whatever works for you. They are very supportive of everything that I, his law firm, and the Jericho Fire Department have done in Glenn's honor.

In late March of 2002, they found Glenn's partial remains. There was a period of time there when they really weren't finding many more remains, but then, when they removed what had been the makeshift ramp to get trucks up and down to the site, they discovered more. Many of them were first responders, and that's when they found Glenn. I got a phone call from someone in Glenn's fire department saying, "Look there's nothing official, but we got a phone call from Ground Zero last night from somebody who has a connection to the Fire Department, who said that they found Glenn." That's an extraordinary call to get. At about ten or eleven o'clock that night my doorbell rang, and it was the Police Department giving me the official word. We did not have to wait to identify Glenn's partial remains through DNA or his dental records. The fact is, they found a portion of his body that had his wallet, and in the wallet was his Jericho Fire Department credentials.

They found more of Glenn in the subsequent days, and the additional remains were with the medical examiner. Interestingly, it was almost as if there were two case files, and it took some time for them to realize that the remains in Glenn A were linked to Glenn B. We now had to make a decision as to whether to have those additional remains go to the site of the memorial at Ground Zero, where other remains, both identified and unidentified, would be held, or whether to go through the process of returning to the cemetery.

Just when you feel that you are getting through it, you get another noti-
fication. I knew it could be coming for two reasons: One, they continued
to advance the technology, so that it was now possible to identify remains
that they couldn't identify before, and second, because you had to make a
decision when you filled out the paperwork initially, whether you wanted
to be notified. And we did want to be notified. Our view was, I think, that
we wanted to make Glenn as whole as we could. And when his remains
were then found we had another decision to face: What do we do with the
pine box with his possessions in his plot? Dig it up, take it away, and put
the coffin with his remains in it? Do we put it on top of the first coffin? What
would the cemetery allow? Again, this was a highly unusual circumstance,
and in the end the cemetery worked it out so that we could open up the
gravesite, leave the first box in place, and bury Glenn's remains atop the box.
That's the way it stands now.

Glenn's colleagues at Holland & Knight later worked very closely with Chief
Harry Meyers of the FDNY to sponsor a beautiful bronze memorial wall
on Liberty Street. It honors the 343 firefighters who gave their lives on 9/11,
and it also honors Glenn. I know that it wasn't an easy process to get things
going there back then, just in terms of various city regulations, and particularly in the face of the difficulties across the street at the official memorial at Ground Zero. I went out to the studio in New Jersey where the clay
modeling of the memorial was being finished. That's when it became very
real for me. To see it up on a wall in this studio in clay, essentially being
born, was when it hit me just how significant and magnificent it was going
to be.

The most memorable thing to me about the dedication of that memorial
wall was some of the family members—mothers, in particular—were coming up to me and our family, thanking us for giving them a place to go.
There are one hundred twenty-eight firefighter families with no remains
at all, and Ground Zero is their burial place, their cemetery, and just across
the street is this beautiful memorial. I don't know that I or our family
deserve any thanks for that, but if Glenn served as the inspiration, then
that's very gratifying.

That memorial wall is now part of the walking tours given through the
Tribute Center on Liberty Street. Together, the Tribute Center, the memorial wall, and Ground Zero itself tell a very important part of the story of

what went on that day. Every September 11, which is always a very bitter-sweet and full day for me, I have various responsibilities, but I always pay my personal respects to Glenn and all the others by attending some of the ceremonies in the morning and getting back there at night, whether it's twelve midnight or two in the morning, to just kind of "degrief." It's usually a very stunning scene to see late at night, with the wall all lit up with sometimes as many as a hundred people standing there. There's usually a long row of candles on the ground, stretching all fifty-six feet of the memorial, artwork that children have left about 9/11, and firefighters standing at attention—and all kinds of flowers. In some ways it really brings you back very immediately to the events of 9/11.

I also wanted official recognition of Glenn by the United States government, which initially was not forthcoming. He went into the World Trade Center as a firefighter. He was part of the rescue operation, and yet the United States of America seemed to have a problem formally designating him as a first responder. I also wanted a lasting recognition of his inspirational act and the actions of so many others, first responders and non–first responders, at the scene—not one that would be sponsored for just a few days but for months after, to help rebuild the city and the country and our national spirit. To me that was the best thing that I could get involved with if I was going to get involved with something to honor my brother, because it directly reflected the way he lived his life—not just as a firefighter, but as an attorney, and as an extraordinarily good Samaritan in his everyday life.

I got a phone call one day a few months after 9/11 from a friend of twenty years who lives in California, David Paine. A lot of native New Yorkers who have moved elsewhere felt a little disconnected: This tragedy happened in their city, even if they were now far away. David wanted to do something, and explained that what had moved him most was how people had responded. He was aware that the New York Mets had donated a day's pay to the New York Police and Fire Widows' and Children's Benefit Fund. David suggested we make 9/11 a day of service. It was a lofty goal, but it seemed right. We were all aware of what was going on around Ground Zero, how everybody was pulling together in a way that had never been seen in our country before, with the possible exception of Pearl Harbor. David had already been doing some work on it, and we put our heads together. Now, a decade later, September 11 is a national day of service in the United

States, with millions of people participating. It's one of those really wonderful examples of how a simple idea can turn into a major thing.

The seeds were sown early in 2002, and President Obama signed it into law as part of the Edward M. Kennedy Serve America Act in April 2009. All throughout that period millions of people had been participating in this grassroots initiative, which just grew and grew and grew every year. The notion is very simple: Mark September 11 to engage in some form of good deed. It could be in an organized way or in some self-directed project. You want to buy groceries for your elderly neighbor—great; it counts. You want to donate blood, or write a big check to a worthy cause, or donate clothes, or do something that is part of an organized thing, walk for breast cancer, or whatever it might be, or do some volunteer work within your company—that sounds terrific. Whatever it is, get out and do something appropriate and meaningful to mark September 11, to remember those who perished.

And so something good has risen out of the ashes of Ground Zero. The fact that it ultimately became a matter of law is terrific, as it has given an added boost to the initiative. People from all fifty states and from 165 countries participate in one way or another, even if it's just visiting our Web site MyGoodDeed.org.

David and I have had much public relations experience, so we know how to get the message out. We have had extraordinary press coverage. There were some PR people on the board who were friends, along with other family members, and we were able to spread the word and build support for it—not only support for it but participation. We had the great help of a lobbyist/attorney in Washington, Fred Dumbo, who worked the halls of Congress and set up meetings for us. There's not much political about this project—it's about as safe a spot as you could find. Just mark that day by doing something good for somebody else.

The first thing we did was to start meeting with the members of the 9/11 organizations, because we felt that if it didn't make sense to the 9/11 community, then it was not going to make sense to anyone else. And we got unanimous approval from all of the few dozen leaders whom we approached. Then Senators Hillary Clinton and Chuck Schumer and Congressmen Peter King and Mike Ferguson endorsed us and helped.

You don't have to be a 9/11 family member to know how 9/11 changed this country—almost completely for the worst, right? Think of the airport security issues, how we deal with other countries now, how you walk into an office building, what your kids have learned about the way of the world. There's very little, unfortunately, that hasn't been touched by 9/11. It's part of the reason that we're involved in two wars, and so the economy of our country is negatively affected. It's pretty much across-the-board negative. And of course it's negative at its core, because nearly three thousand people died. But there have been some good and inspiring responses to 9/11 too. Former New York Giant George Martin, a Super Bowl champion, lost a few neighbors in New Jersey and wanted to do something. When he learned that thousands were now sick, and some [were] dying as a result of their service, and that proper funding wasn't there for them, he wanted to help raise money and awareness, and so [he] walked across the country to raise money. Extraordinary. So 9/11 has become a special call to action for many people who are looking for a way to be generous, community-minded, or simply caring. That's promising, I think.

I know that there are some things that are terrible and unfair about all of this—that nineteen guys and whoever was supporting them could have had such a huge negative impact on the world. It's horrific; there's no justification for it, and there's no way to fix it. The part of me that is the sibling of a firefighter, though, knows that Glenn knew that he was taking a risk every time he went on a call, whether for a car fire or a burning building. That's part of what you buy into being a firefighter. While his circumstances were extraordinary in that he was not FDNY and didn't have to run into that building, the fact that he chose to makes him very heroic in my mind. He had the skills, guts, and the wherewithal to go there and to try to help people he didn't know, people who were in danger. It's all the more reason why we have to take care of our firefighters, our police, and anyone who is in the rescue business. The job they choose is to put themselves at risk for others who can't help themselves.

I hate having lost my brother; I hate it every single day. But it would have been more bearable if it wasn't the result of terrorism. This was not an accident, not fate. These were people who went out to kill people. There's no way to get your arms around that, for there's no sense to it at all. While Glenn ran in, there were many in the towers who did not make that choice, who did not know that morning when they went to work that they would be facing life-threatening danger.

During the time when we were battling for federal recognition of

Glenn's firefighting line-of-duty status, I met Governor [George] Pataki one morning at Ground Zero. The governor had signed a New York State law that designated Glenn's as a line-of-duty death, and [him] as an active firefighter on the day he died. I thanked him for that law, and he talked to me about how meaningful firefighters were to him, that his dad had been a volunteer firefighter too. Not long ago I met Vice President [Joe] Biden at Ground Zero, and he talked to me about the rescue professionals who showed up at the scene when his family had had a horrific car accident, in which he lost his wife and two of his children. The first thing he said to me was how personally indebted he was to firemen and policemen and those folks for saving the life of one of his children at the crash. I think if there's one good thing that's come out of 9/11, it's a greater national appreciation for firefighters and police. And that's a good thing, because they are really among our greatest heroes.

I think it's amazing what volunteer firefighters do. Of course they don't get paid, so it's very altruistic. I know the training that my two brothers received was extraordinary. In many ways I wonder if the firefighters of Long Island have training that is better than, or matched by, that of any fire department in America. Maybe they don't go to as many fires, and so maybe there's a lot less on-the-job training, so therefore they have to do an extraordinary amount of coursework. All I know is that none of the volunteer firefighters I met through my brothers were slouches in any way. It is like an exclusive club, but so is a big city firehouse. I've really come to see this in the years since 9/11. They have a fraternity that's very aggressive about what they do, men and women. They have to have relationships that make the difficult and the dangerous tolerable. I don't make the distinction between career firefighters and volunteer firefighters, for many of the volunteer firefighters I know are for the most part also career firefighters. All of these men and women are balancing their regular jobs and their families with being firefighters. It is not a job for them, and yet they treat it as if it were. They do it for their communities, and it's hard work, a lot of risk, and time spent away from their families What these volunteer firefighters sacrifice for their communities truly is impressive, and I'm proud that Glenn was a part of that.

Akiko Takahashi

Akiko Takahashi lost her father, Keiichiro Takahashi, when the Twin Towers fell. Twenty-four Japanese citizens died that terrible day, and Keiichiro, a Long Island resident and New York banker, was one of them. By 9/11 he had advanced in his profession to become the senior vice president of Euro Brokers, which had offices high up in the South Tower. Keiichiro's greatest love was spending time with his wife, Harumi, and their children: his son, Hiroyuki, who was living and working in Japan, and his daughter, Akiko, who was at Tufts University on 9/11. He was very excited about his plans to retire from business when Akiko graduated from college. Now, in honor of her father, Akiko volunteers, giving tours and sharing her story with others, at the Tribute WTC Visitor Center.

My parents had just moved from London to Los Angeles when I was born. I've never lived in Japan, and we moved to New York when I was two. We have been serious about preserving Japanese culture within our family, and so my parents sent me to Japanese school on the weekends all through grammar school. I learned to read and write there, and I don't have any trouble getting by when I travel to Japan.

We actually spoke Japanese in the house all the time. I was not allowed to talk in English, and even when I spoke to my brother in English, my mother would tell us to stop. We used to always watch Japanese TV, Japanese news in the morning, and then the movies. My friends were always surprised that I hadn't seen some of the classic [American] eighties films. We were very sheltered, culturally sheltered.

I went to a public high school, East Schreiber High, in Port Washington. It's not that big—a little under three hundred kids in my graduating class. Port Washington is on the water, and is a very pretty town. I think that's probably what drew my dad to the town. There's a dock you can walk along. It's nice.

I spent a lot of time with my family, especially with my dad, who was often home. I had a lot of friends whose dads were doctors and always at the hospital or on call, and they didn't work regular nine-to-five, Monday-through-Friday jobs, like my father did. Now I appreciate more that he was home so often. It was great that he was there. He helped around the house. He helped my mom prepare food or helped with the dishes after dinner. He did a lot of puzzles, and I'd do them with him.

Our family was a close unit, and we did a lot together. I was really lucky that way. We would take two trips every year—to a beach during the winter, and in the summer we would go to Europe. I remember all my Japanese friends would always go to Japan for the entire summer, and growing up I was a little bit jealous of that, because I always wanted to spend my summer in Japan. But my parents wanted to go to Europe.

Now I'd take Europe over Japan any day, and I'm really grateful that we took these trips. When I was in sixth grade I had to give a history report, and my assigned country was the Netherlands. And so my dad planned a trip there, which was great.

When I was growing up, my dad was definitely the good cop. My mom was definitely the disciplinarian. He never yelled at my brother and me, never raised his voice. I remember one time I had a class project to make tepees, because we were learning about Native Americans or something. I had to make a diorama and was having trouble with it, and my dad began helping me. But he ended up doing it for me, and then my mom got so mad at the both of us. He always liked helping out.

I had no idea what my father did for a living, to be honest. I knew he worked for a bank, and traded something, but I had no idea what. It wasn't until I had to fill out college applications and list my father's occupation that I asked him. He finally said he was like a money broker, in currencies. My dad never really talked about work much.

My dad started at Mitsubishi Trust, which sent him to London and Los Angeles, and then New York. We would move every couple of years. The company wanted to send him back to Japan, and to move to another place in Asia a year later. But he didn't want my brother and me to keep moving so often, so he actually left that firm and joined another company that promised he would not have to relocate from New York.

My brother recently moved back to Japan. He's seven years older than I and works for a record company. My mother has moved to Midtown, just twenty blocks from me. She sold our house in Port Washington after I graduated from college because it was a big house and she was there all by herself. I think it's a lot better for her in the city, and she keeps herself busy there. She volunteers at the Metropolitan Museum of Art once a week. She's in a choir group. She has practice and concerts. It's good.

My father's company, Euro Brokers, lost sixty-one employees that day. I think they were on the eighty-fifth floor, so they were right around the impact zone. Sometime after 9/11 they invited all the family members to visit the company. I got to meet the other employees, and it wasn't until then that I really understood what my dad did on a daily basis.

On the morning of 9/11 everything changed. I was at school at Tufts, in Boston, and just starting my sophomore year. It was the first week of classes, and I had an 8:30 macroeconomics class. Most of my friends were in the class with me, and I remember commenting on what a beautiful day it was. Boston is only four hours away from New York, so their weather is pretty similar, and the skies were just a gorgeous blue. The class was about an hour long, so it didn't end until 9:30 or so.

I had no idea what had happened during that hour. I had to stay a little longer to talk to the professor, and at the same time I kind of heard people talking about a plane hitting the World Trade Center. My first reaction was like, What happened? A plane? No one would imagine a big passenger plane. I just thought it was a single-engine, a small, single-pilot plane, an accident. The kids who were talking, they had no idea, no details of what kind of plane it was. They didn't know if anyone had gotten hurt.

When I got back to my dorm I went to my friends' room, because I knew they would understand what had happened. I tried to call my dad, but he only had a work phone and no cell phone, and all of his office lines were dead. I couldn't get in touch with him. And so I called my mom, who hadn't heard from him either. My father had been in the North Tower in 1993 when the first bombing happened. My mother said, "He lived through one attack. I'm sure he's fine. He'll come home. He doesn't have a cell phone. Don't worry about it." And I just had a really bad feeling. I don't think my mother ever thought he would die. She was concerned, but not too worried.

September 11 was a really long day. I had a friend whose dad did a lot of business in the World Trade Center, and she was worried, trying to get in touch with him. I remember just trying not to think about it. But every single news channel had it, and after a while they showed some of the people jumping out of the buildings. My brother was in Japan at the time, and I remember him later saying, "I just hope Dad wasn't one of the people who jumped, because, why would you do that?"

Now, as I think about it, that whole day, that week, and probably the whole next month is kind of a big blur.

For the first couple of days I stayed at college. But on Thursday, the thirteenth, my friends drove me home. I didn't know what was going on, and I just wanted to go home. We crossed the Whitestone Bridge going to Long Island, and we could see New York City from the bridge. I looked over and saw the smoke coming up from the World Trade Center. Every car on the bridge slowed down to look at that, and it was eerie. I had seen it on TV, but seeing it in person was different, horrifying. My mom was so grateful to my friends for driving me home, because there were no planes, no trains, no way for me to get there. It was so good of them.

My brother, Hiroyuki, was on the first plane out of Japan. I don't remember what day that was, but he was on the first flight out. He almost couldn't get on that flight, because of all the journalists from Japan who wanted to cover the Ground Zero story. The flight got booked up, and a family friend got into an argument with whatever airline it was, saying, "This is ridiculous. He's a family member. You need to give him a seat over a journalist." So it was good to have him home.

We went to Pier 94 to fill out all that paperwork you had to fill out for missing persons, to submit DNA samples, and to file the police report.

One of my father's coworkers, Brian Clark, actually escaped from the towers and was interviewed by the local newspaper. I read the story and saw he worked for Euro Brokers, so I called the journalist for Brian's number. I asked Brian, "Do you remember seeing my dad?" But they worked on opposite sides of the floor, he hadn't seen him, and so he didn't have any information. I was so disappointed. I remember just trying to call anyone. Looking back, it was probably insensitive to call him, for he probably didn't want to talk about it. Imagine, escaping the World Trade Center.

For the first few days I kept up with my schoolwork, my assignments. But I realized I had to ask myself, *Do I take the semester off or do I go back to school?* There was so much uncertainty at that point. We still weren't sure if he was alive or not. They were still looking for people at Ground Zero, so I had hope. After a while I decided to take the semester off. One of the classes I was enrolled in was actually about the Hiroshima atomic bomb. I remember reading some of my class assignments, stories about people who had gone into work in Hiroshima like any other day, and the bomb dropped, and their world was turned upside down. I had to read a book about it and write an essay, and I remember comparing it to 9/11. I just saw so many parallels. I actually never got a chance to retake that class.

On the day we went to Pier 94 to fill out paperwork and give them the DNA samples, you couldn't walk five feet without someone coming up to you and asking, "Do you want to talk about this? I'm a social worker, if you need to talk," and I just remember thinking at that point—I had just taken Intro to Psych—that I was going through the natural grieving steps, the whole anger and bargaining process. But now, looking back, I don't remember being angrier than normal. I remember thinking, *Why? Why me, and why my family?*

I have never used the word "murdered." I just feel that America wasn't at war against al Qaeda. I guess my father was murdered, but I never say that word, and I feel for some reason that he was an unfortunate victim of al Qaeda trying to send a message to America. Maybe for some it sounds like the same thing as murder, but I don't know if I like using that word. In our family we actually don't talk about it too much. While I do kind of blame Osama bin Laden and al Qaeda, part of the reason I might not use the word "murder" is because murder, to me, is when someone is targeted specifically, and I don't think my dad was targeted as a person. He just worked there, although I do think he represented what al Qaeda was trying to destroy.

My dad was an immigrant, and he actually died as a Japanese citizen. He was trying to get American citizenship. He had a green card, and I think he represented the idea that everyone comes to America and tries to make a living for himself. He represented the American dream and what America stands for, like freedom. My dad wanted my brother and me both to grow up to have an American education, and I don't think he liked Japanese society too much. My folks moved from Japan when they were about thirty, so they spent most of their adult lives outside of Japan. So I really do think my dad represented the American dream, and that's what al Qaeda attacked.

. . .

They recovered my dad's body very quickly, in the last week of September. Two police officers came to our house and told us that they found him early in the morning. They told us that his body had been severely damaged, that it had been burned, and in water, and they recommended that we not look at it. So I have no idea how intact it was. I like to think it was pretty much intact. I've never verified it, but it's probably pretty easy to do so. There were fewer than three hundred intact bodies recovered, and I always consider my dad to have been one of those. We were able to have a service for him around the first week of October. At that time I had no idea how lucky, relatively lucky, my family was, that they recovered his body.

I've met people who had only an elbow or another small part of their loved one recovered. I can't imagine how hard that is. I think finding my father helped me, because it happened at the end of September, so I was able to kind of start the process of closure earlier than most. You know, you start accepting the reality, just trying to move on.

We had had hope, but then I had to accept that my dad had passed away at the World Trade Center. We had him cremated, and we buried him. I was able then to start the healing process.

There was a gentleman who passed away at the World Trade Center whose name was Keiji Takahashi, and my dad was Keiichiro Takahashi. Because the names are so similar, a lot people mixed them up, and we would get things for Keiji Takahashi, or the other family would get things for Keiichiro Takahashi. Part of me still kind of thinks that maybe they mixed up the DNA, and the person that we actually buried is Keiji Takahashi. I don't know if they found Mr. Keiji Takahashi, and because of that, sometimes I think that maybe my dad's still out there alive. I just sometimes feel that he became something like a dissociative figure and just picked up and moved to another city and set up a whole new life. You know, he never had that option beforehand. And I know that that's unlikely, but it's a small hope. But for the most part, I have accepted that he's not going to come back, ever.

One of the things I think about when I go into the Tribute Center is that I had a very sheltered childhood. I didn't really have many worries. My biggest worries when I awoke on 9/11, since it was the beginning of the semester and I didn't even have to worry about tests, were getting my reading done for class, or what party I was going to go to that weekend, or what I was going to wear. Typical college issues. But after 9/11 that all changed, and my worries became, *Okay. Well, how is my mom going to take care of herself?* She didn't work, and my father was the provider for the family. More important, *What is she going to do for health insurance?* Then there was the filling out of paperwork, getting a death certificate, and the whole beneficiary payouts for the life insurance. My mom speaks English, but for something like going to Pier 94, she'd rather just have me take care of it, because my English is better. And I remember thinking, *I don't want to do it.* Or my dad had been paying for my tuition, so I was fortunate in that I didn't have to take out student loans or work during college. But then I realized, *Oh, I guess I have to start working.* I remember thinking that I had to grow up pretty quickly, and I guess at nineteen most people think they are grown-up already. But I wasn't grown-up yet, and it was a dramatic shift. My mom had been taking care of me, but now I felt as if I had to take care of her, and I felt that dramatic shift.

The Euro Brokers people were amazing—they were so helpful. They did everything that they could to make it easier for the family members. They actually provided health insurance and life coverage. That was the biggest thing I worried about, because it's so hard to get health insurance. They were also very supportive and set up a fund in which one day every year all the brokers give up their commissions and donate it toward the Euro Brokers fund for the families [the Euro Brokers Relief Fund]. They also held a service for the sixty-one employees they lost.

But after 9/11 it was hard on my mother. I think it was the first time I saw my mom cry. She has really supportive friends. She always had friends in from town, always over talking and supporting us. I think we had people over almost every day just for company, to make sure we were eating. And one of our family's friends came and stayed with us for about a week. My mom doesn't really like talking about it. I don't think she has gone down to Ground Zero. We get invited to go to the memorial every year, and she's never gone down there for that. Even for the memorial.

I think she's actually doing okay. In addition to moving into the city, one of her greatest assets is that she has a group of good friends who are very supportive. I'm sure she gets lonely sometimes, but I don't think she's depressed or anything. I think she's dealt with that.

One of the things that changed for me is that I now think often about how glad I am that my dad was in my life. Right after 9/11 one of my friends who had lost her dad to cancer said to me that she was so happy to have had him. I had never thought about it much then. It was hard for her to come to this point, but she was just really glad that he was a part of her life, because she had all these memories of him. But I think about it now a lot, and I'm just so glad that my dad was a part of my life. Going to Europe, or walking through town with him, I'm just glad he gave me the opportunity to be exposed to these things. Of course, I had those days where I was mad at him for something or other, but that quickly fades away. You don't even think about that.

My dad was a very calming presence. I always felt safe when he was around. It's also that the whole world was a lot safer and secure when he was around. I miss that so much. And it is hard to think that he's not going to be around for milestones.

At my high school graduation, he took a million and one pictures of me walking up, getting my diploma, and walking back. He was so happy doing that. I was just thinking about my college graduation—he wasn't there. When I get married, he won't be there for that either. I wish my dad could have seen how well my brother turned out and what an amazing person his wife is. It would have been so nice if they could have met each other.

For the most part I don't like to think about how my dad might have died. We have no idea where he was or what he was doing. He was in the South Tower, but we don't know at all if he had tried to get out, or where he was at the moment he died. I was thinking about this recently: He died all alone. It's an awful way to die, to be scared, and by himself. I always think about that—an awful way to die. He probably knew he was going to die, he was alone and scared, and it's just . . . I don't really want to think about it. I don't know if I've integrated that. I don't know . . .

I definitely am surprised that it's been ten years. It feels like it went by really fast. There's an absence still felt, and I don't think it's ever going to go away. Holidays are hard. When my brother got married, I definitely felt it. But it doesn't feel like ten years.

I think I would have changed a lot even if my dad were alive—just growing up, going to college, getting a job, all that stuff that has happened regardless. But I think sometimes that my life would have been more complete with him here. When I think about the past ten years, I think, *What have I accomplished that I'm most proud of?* I guess I'm independent, and my mom isn't supporting me, which I think is good. I think my relationship with Mom has matured. Because my brother went to school in London, he wasn't around much, so we weren't close at first. But now we talk more often. In the last ten years my relationships with my family and my friends have changed for the better. While some of it would have happened with or without 9/11, after 9/11 it became so important to have good relationships. And to find meaning in things.

Another thing that has changed for me is that I started to do volunteering at the Tribute Center. I wanted to do volunteer work, and part of the reason I chose the Tribute Center, a major charity in New York City, is that I was looking at the New York City government Web site, where they have all the charities listed. You can go through what you're interested in, and the time you have that is available, and Tribute came up. So I wanted to remember 9/11. I don't want to forget or ignore it; I just want to be a part of it.

When I found out that you actually give tours and talk to people about your experience, I was like, *What am I going to say?* I thought, *Just how would I best honor Dad's memory?* I kept thinking about my dad and being part of the American dream, and I think the decision I came to was that we all need to be sending out the message of hope. And so that's the message I wanted to send in honor of my Dad. I'm about to turn twenty-nine, and I've never had to deal with anything but losing my dad. I thought that getting older would help me to deal better with not just losing my dad, but losing my dad like this, in 9/11. I remember I only got through it because I received so much support, not just from my friends but from random strangers—when people came to our house and dropped off food, whenever I went to the Pier 94 and social workers would come and talk. I had one friend who was friends with a volunteer firefighter in Buffalo, and he wanted to come down and volunteer at Ground Zero. He just wanted to do something to help. Yes, there are people out there who don't care for others, who could care less about my dad, or what the terrorists did to my family, or what they did to everyone else, and all of those families. But there are a lot more people who want to help out, a lot more good people than bad ones. The message that I want to send, and why I joined Tribute to speak to those visitors to Ground Zero on our tours, is really peace. The world needs peace. And that's what I wanted to do, to honor my dad.

The first time I did the tour, I started out as a support person. I didn't actually give the tour, but I made sure people kept up with us, and I also gave a five-minute speech about my own story in the middle of the tour. At first I wasn't sure what to expect. I wasn't sure what kind of people would be on the tour, what their reaction would be, or why they wanted to take the tour in the first place. In training you were prepared for people who just want to talk about, maybe, terrorists, and how to take it into that direction. Or how to talk about whatever is going on with the war in Afghanistan or the war in Iraq, and take it in that direction, but not so much remembering 9/11. And so I was thinking, *I hope I don't get a bunch of people who just want my opinion on the war.* I was a little bit nervous at first, but then I did the tour, and nobody has asked anything about Iraq. They have just wanted to know our own 9/11 stories, the lead tour guide's and mine. I was so touched by that.

I can't believe these people come to us, out of all the things to do in New York City, but they take the time to learn more about the World Trade Center and 9/11. And they listen to me, about my memory and about who am I. We get to chat with the visitors, and they are so pleasant and supportive. A lot of people, I can see, are just silently praying. They might say, I didn't know your name or your dad's, but I was praying for you.

When I started doing the lead tours and had to talk, and give all these facts—when the World Trade Center was built, how many floors there were, how many elevators there were—I was nervous, because I've never really done public speaking, and I'm not good at it. And I was nervous that I might mix up facts and my words. But everyone has been reassuring. They are interested, and they haven't grilled me. They thank me for taking the time to give them the tour.

My tour takes only about an hour and fifteen minutes at most, because I talk and walk really fast. There's a firefighter who's a tour guide who rescued one of the last guys out of the building. He goes into a lot of detail, and he probably takes about two hours. It's just an amazing story.

When I first started volunteering I sometimes felt a little bit selfish, almost. I wasn't going out mentoring kids, or trying to make a cancer patient's life better. I was just giving tours and talking about my dad. But then it came clear to me that giving the message of 9/11 is giving the message of what happens when people are intolerant. The people that are on the tour come away with the idea that war and hate aren't the answer.

I am also on the junior board of Tuesday's Children, an organization that helps and mentors children of 9/11 and others affected by global terrorism. I think it's hard for any of us to lose a parent under any circumstances, especially the kids who lost a parent on 9/11. Many kids today of course probably don't really remember that day, for it's hard to grasp its enormity when you're three. So I think it's a great organization, and I am glad I am able to help.

My father was just fifty-three. He had a full life ahead. My parents looked forward to not having to take care of the kids anymore. When I was a freshman my mom and my dad took a trip together to Washington, D.C., just the two of them, which they hadn't done in ages. They were looking forward to that simply because they hadn't done that: taking a trip by themselves to just reconnect. Usually they would always include my brother and me.

I feel our country is getting worse. You're always hearing about terrorist attacks, more attacks and more intolerance. My personal belief is that the mosque shouldn't come to the World Trade Center. I think they have every right to build a mosque. Islam is a religion of peace—it's just a small minority who advocate violence and become terrorists. It's not like Muslim equals terrorism. But I just feel like people are growing more wary of each other, more distrustful. We hear about more terrorist attacks, or read how the government thwarted an attack, or about the screening at the airports. I know these things are supposed to make the world a better place. But I sometimes feel like they're not.

When I was in elementary school there was a camp for kids who were Palestinian and Israeli. When they went to camp together, they realized that they're all just kids who actually have a lot in common. They could get along, and they became friends, and they didn't understand the whole Israeli-Palestinian conflict. Kids are more tolerant, and if they are exposed to one another, maybe this won't be an issue. They will all be friends. I guess we have to teach tolerance to become more tolerant. And our politics in America—[we] don't really seem to be getting along. I think it's kind of bleak.

I just hope that people will always remember 9/11. Remember the tragedy. The outlook is bleak, but if people remember 9/11, they will have hope, and make sure it doesn't happen again. I hope . . . I hope so.

Ray Habib

Ray Habib is a docent volunteer at the Tribute WTC Visitor Center, where he gives walking tours of the Ground Zero site. His wife, Barbara, worked in Midtown as an executive with Marsh Inc., a subsidiary of Marsh & McLennan Companies. On the morning of 9/11, though, she was at a meeting with senior members of that firm at their World Trade Center offices. The firm lost 295 employees and 60 contractors that day, including Barbara Habib.

I was a former teacher of health and physical education at Bishop Ford High School in Park Slope, Brooklyn, where I had started right after college. The wife of a coworker of mine worked for Marsh & McLennan, where she was a managing director in the aviation division and was like a superstar with the company. She knew Barbara very, very well. In those days Marsh had a pretty big expense account, and my buddy's wife had access to the Madison Square Garden box that Marsh rented for the year. It happened that there was an oldies concert, and my buddy and his wife had extra tickets, and said, "Ray, why don't you come by?" It was not a setup; Barbara and a few of the other Marsh employees happened to be there in the Skybox too. We chatted a little. She was living in Staten Island at the time, and I was working in Staten Island at the time, so there was some common ground. By the time the concert was over I thought I had made a little bit of a connection.

I followed up with my buddy, What's her story? And so on. His wife did not want to introduce me to her, but finally she did, and gave me Barbara's number. So we talked, we went out, had a few dates, and it all went well. Barbara had gone to Kingsborough Community College in Brooklyn, but college really wasn't for her. She stepped right into a position with Marsh and was so dedicated and hardworking an employee that she had a great potential for advancement. She stayed with the company, had a number of different promotions, and rose to a position of high responsibility. After two years we moved in together, and two years later we were married. Barbara had been married previously, but it was my first, and I was forty-two, so a little bit late in life to get married. We were going to have one of these big, grand extravaganzas, and she was all for it. Maybe if I had been ten years younger we could have put it together, but we ended up having a small but very nice church wedding at Our Lady of Angels Church. We were both Catholic, and a good friend of mine who is a priest came and officiated at the service. We had the reception at a small restaurant in Staten Island. Funny thing, it was actually pouring rain on our wedding day—like buckets. The minute the service was over the rain stopped. All sunshine. We had four years of a wonderful marriage. Some might not consider that a long time, but for me it was a lifetime.

We were living in Staten Island and decided we really preferred to live in Brooklyn, so we bought a place on Ridge Boulevard in Bay Ridge. We renovated it for seven months and actually moved into the apartment the week before September 11. We had everything ordered—furniture, lamps, rugs, everything—and on September 10 spent our first night there. She made her first pasta meal. We enjoyed it—good food, new furniture, an apartment we loved, a kind of milestone in our marriage. And then, the next day.

At Marsh, Barbara was the office manager. She was the aviation administrator and tied up all the policies and contracts that they had, and so she was crunching numbers. There were times of the year when they were really working lots of hours, so she didn't have a lot of free time for travel and leisure. But that was the plan. She had been with Marsh for almost thirty years, and she was now ready to start traveling.

She worked in the corporate office on Forty-forth Street and Sixth Avenue and just happened to be visiting the Marsh offices at the World Trade Center on September 11. They had planned to bring together all the administrators from all the different departments within Marsh—aviation, general insurance, property, and casualty, whatever they were, the people who had the numbers, I guess. It was a nine o'clock meeting, and all the managing people were gathering at the North Tower, on the ninety-ninth floor. Barbara was never the type to be late, and normally she would have been the first one out of the house, taking the six o'clock bus from Staten Island. In this situation, of course, she was only going to the Trade Center from our first night in Brooklyn, and now that we were living in Bay Ridge she did not have that long a commute. I had to go to Staten Island to work, so I was the first one out. I worked for a hotel company there, and we were getting ready to open up another hotel that Hilton had bought. The Inn had scheduled a Fire Department inspection that morning. The Fire Department guy wasn't coming until 9:30, but the Fire Department is always early, so I was actually sitting in my office when the first plane hit at 8:46.

I knew Barbara was at the Trade Center when everything happened in the North Tower. I only learned exactly where she was later on, because the company was able to confirm it. They had offices on the ninety-third through the one-hundredth floors, which is directly where the plane hit. Marsh & McLennan lost 295 employees and 60 contract workers—everyone who was present in those offices that day.

When the first plane hit, I left my office and went to the site of the inspection to meet the fire inspector. By this time, the second plane had hit and all of Staten Island was in turmoil, as no one knew what was going on. I tried to call Barbara on her cell phone. After the first plane, all I was able to get was her voice mail. From then on, though, I kept calling and got nothing. Word spread like wildfire that Ray's wife was down there, and of course people I know kept calling: Ray, did you hear anything, did you hear anything? And no. Nothing. So I went about my business, doing what I had to do, though it's not as if I was even able to get off Staten Island, since everything had been shut down by 10:30. I could not go anywhere. It was just a waiting game. There was no communication.

Barbara was very close to my mother, who lived in Bay Ridge. She was about eighty-one at the time, and so I wasn't going to be saying anything before I knew something concrete. I knew that if there was a way for Barbara to contact me she would have. I had an open mind; I didn't know what was going to happen until I went home. Actually, I thought that she was going to, somehow, get home that night. I really did. My best friend, who worked in the World Financial Center, took the ferry over and came to my office, just because he wanted to be with me. He had lost a cousin, and they lived on Staten Island. The owner of my company was very supportive, and we did what we could. He said, Come on, we'll go out to dinner. I still had possession of the home in Staten Island that we had moved out of, so I went there, as I couldn't get over the Verrazano Bridge to Brooklyn. My buddy stayed in Staten Island with me, and since there was no furniture, we slept on the floor.

I kept thinking, *She will find a way, just stay positive.* I kept listening to the news, hearing the reports. But no word anywhere.

When Barbara didn't come home that night, the harsh reality was setting in that I shouldn't expect her to come home. Relatively soon afterward—when I had to start filing paperwork, when I had to go down and get the death certificate and give them an authentication confirming that Barbara Habib was at the ninety-ninth floor of the North Tower—it got more and more real. Looking back, I saw that the contact of the first plane had been between the ninety-second and ninety-ninth floors of the North Tower, and nobody at that point or above survived. But I didn't realize that until I received the official letter, probably within two weeks, which was the first real confirmation in black and white that Barbara was gone.

There was a perpetual numbness that went through me from the time it happened throughout the first year. Numbness to the point that I dealt with everything, and I was prepared, since I was not going to find anything worse. I dealt with all of the business things that I now had to face. If I became overly emotional I wouldn't have been able to deal with it. Although there was just the two of us, I knew there was a lot involved in tying all the ends. And so I was taking one day at a time. Whatever happened I was going to just go through it. I went to work that day and every day after. The worst time was when I was not active.

When Marsh had a memorial service at Saint Patrick's Cathedral, maybe a month or six weeks afterward, I'll never forget, that was the one day that was the most emotional for me. I tried to keep it together, but being in the church with all the Marsh people, and people making speeches and seeing everybody, walking out of there was the most emotional I got. My buddy's wife was with me, you know. And a few other close friends were with me and . . . you know . . . Yeah, that was bad.

The funeral that I put together was the most personal experience of all. I gave the eulogy. Her friends, her company, were there in force. It was attended by well over three hundred people, half of whom I didn't know. Mary Ann, my buddy's wife, gave a eulogy, and her oldest brother spoke a little as well. It was a full high mass. The Daughters of St. Paul were there, a group of nuns that Barbara and I had gotten to know through my employment in Staten Island. They had a convent there, where we went. They sing like angels, and they sang the mass for Barbara. They put together that mass card for me, and I could see they were heartbroken as well.

The day I had my mass for Barbara it was hot, and my mother was in attendance and had an episode of chest pain. She turned pale as a ghost, but it passed, and she was fine. She hosted people at the house after the service and cooked all the Middle Eastern stuff that she did so well. The day after the Mass, my mother suffered a major heart attack, and so my time was spent dealing with all these things going on with Barbara, and also dealing with my mother being in the hospital—alive, but barely.

At that point, I hadn't attempted to go down to Ground Zero at all. The first time I went to the area was when they were having a memorial service and the city invited people down. It was a Sunday, might have been October 28, and I'll never forget that day, because it was the day that my mother was actually going through quadruple bypass surgery. So when they finally decided to do the operation, it ended up being the same day that I went into the city for the first time.

It was supposed to be a memorial interfaith service. Andrea Bocelli was singing, and they were going to have a Muslim leader speaking too. But the thing that hit me so dramatically was the crowds of people hawking their wares. It was upsetting because, Hey, folks, this is not a tourist show. This is where a terrible thing happened. It offended me, and it got me a little bit angry. But you know, I've come to accept a lot. Giving tours as I do down at the Trade Center, I now see that it's a major attraction for tourists coming into the city. So I aligned myself with that.

But the first time going to the site, it was emotional. We sat there among people who were obviously family members, and I got to talk to a few people and asked, How are you holding up? But I wasn't the type to really share too much. I remember the smell of the burning steel was still pretty clear.

It was a tough day overall. Thankfully, my mother survived. The operation was a success, and she went through rehab, and is now ninety-one years old and still going strong. I had a good strong foundation with my parents. My father passed away thirty years ago, but I saw what my mother went through raising five children and watched her work ethic. My father was a worker, and maybe we never really got along when he was alive, but I think I've become more like him than any of my brothers. He was always the hardworking type, and that's how I am because I continue to work. In the long run we don't know how we are going to turn out, but our parents will be the major factor.

I was amazed that there were so many women whose husbands had passed away on 9/11, and a lot of them were just emotional basket cases. They were, I can't go on, I just can't, I can't do it. And what do you say? Okay? Take your time, whatever it is. Marsh was phenomenal in terms of support. Marsh and the city were like rocks of Gibraltar. They were there for all of us and made the process easier. Whoever would think that you would have to file for a death certificate? Marsh did that all under the tent on Pier 94, I think it was December 16. There were organizations like the Disney Foundation and so many others that were there to offer you Christmas gifts.

But still, it all took its toll—Barbara, and then my mother. I was down to 157 pounds, very light for me, a mess. But again, I worked every day, so that shell that I had was not often pierced, except at times when I had to sit around and dwell on it. I hadn't really talked about what happened to anybody, except to my best friend. But then I met someone, eight months after everything happened. She was someone I could talk to about it, and we wound up developing a pretty strong relationship that lasted right up until recently.

When I started this relationship, I had to open up again. I had to live life again. I wore my wedding ring for the first eight months. When I met this person and followed up and asked for her phone number, she had noticed that I was wearing a ring. She said to a mutual acquaintance, This man's married. What nerve does he have to ask for my number? So, there was a bit of a lapse until I was able to actually get her number, as my friend had to explain what had happened to me. When I started seeing her, I was unaware that she already knew about Barbara, but when I took her out to dinner for the first time, I didn't wear my ring. And I did tell her about Barbara.

Everybody handles his grief in different ways. That's how I handled it: I just went on. If Barbara and I had had children it might have been worse. There are pros and cons for getting your life back together. All I know is what gave me the most strength during that period was knowing that during our time together Barbara had given me strength. According to my buddy's friend, Barbara had gone through a marriage that was not good. She was also very close to her mother, who had passed away. All that had happened in the year before we met, and she was pretty much down in the dumps and not going out. Actually, that night of the oldies concert at the Garden, Mary Ann had to convince her to join: Come out with us Barbara, come on, come out, just get out. And, luckily, she came out, which is why we were able to meet. Although Barbara had gone through a tough time, so many people told me that when we started dating, and eventually got married, that she was at the happiest in her life.

And then there is fate. I'm a big believer in fate. Why did I go that night? Who knows? Why did they have the concert that night? Why did Barbara go? What if she'd decided she couldn't go? But we were there, at that fated moment, and we locked eyes. That locking of eyes, a ten-second glimpse with that little gleam, gave me the green light to say, you know what, pursue it. So if fate brought me into her life for that period of time, it turned out to be good—good for her and good for me. I'm happy with that. If I die tomorrow, that's probably the best thing that I did, that I was there to bring her out of an unhappy life, and I was able to change it by making her happy.

I have a letter that is important to me, even though I never got to meet the woman who wrote it. It says, "Dear Ray, You don't know me, but I worked with Barbara for many years before. When she told me that she met someone I thought it could not have happened to a nicer person. And I hoped it would work out for her. And so I was overjoyed when she wrote about your marriage and the plans for the new condo. I don't remember a time when I knew her that she was as content. You made her very happy, you know."

I started at the Tribute Center in 2007—my training class was that January. I didn't know anything about the Tribute Center or the important work it does until I received an e-mail from Lee Ielpi [see page 98]. He must have had a list of the family members, and it was actually the second one I received. The first time I don't think I paid much attention to it—fate closing doors. I don't want to be identified as having lost somebody from 9/11. That's not my identity; that's not me. It never will be me, but it is something that I'll accept. Sometimes I'm introduced to people with the comment, Well, you know, he lost his wife on 9/11. Hello, excuse me, is that necessary? But that's what it has brought. Somehow people want to touch or be close to everybody who lost anyone there. But I don't think that any one person's death is more important than another's. If you died tomorrow in a car crash, you wouldn't get this same type of attention. But the reality for 9/11 families is that you do, because this was such an unbelievable attack, unusual and historic.

But I read Lee Ielpi's second e-mail more closely, and I said, Okay. You know, I believe in volunteering. When I was a teacher for ten years at Bishop Ford High School I volunteered for the local ambulance corps. I did my four hours a week. When I got a nine-to-five job, I stopped doing that. After Barbara died I was just working and active with tennis and with my tennis club, administrating and doing all these other things for the club, but here was a chance to get back into volunteering. When I decided to leave my company after everything happened, because I just didn't want to work those crazy hours involved in real estate anymore, I was looking to volunteer somewhere. But the things I looked at never worked out to be anything meaningful. Tribute looked as if it was going to be meaningful, so I accepted the invitation.

I went down and was interviewed by the volunteer coordinator, who said, We'd love to have you join us, and I then went through the training class. There are leads and supports who give groups of twenty to twenty-five people an hour-and-a-quarter tour throughout various stops around the World Trade Center site. The lead does most of the talking, giving an introduction, telling a little bit of the factual background, why they built the buildings, what had happened that day, and so on. And then the support person speaks for about five minutes, giving his or her personal story. For the first year I was just a support person, getting a feel for what this organization was all about and giving my five-minute speech about Barbara. I talked about where I was that day, and how I first tried to call her. I didn't go into any gruesome detail, except I did mention that I was one of the lucky ones who was contacted by the coroner's office, which actually identified positive remains of Barbara. So there was proof that she was dead and not missing somewhere. The whole purpose of the World Trade Center walking tours is different from what you might get on a double-decker bus tour, in that you hear a personal story, a true account from people who were there, whether they survived, whether they worked on the rescue effort, or whether they lost somebody. It is those personal stories that have drawn people in and bring them to listen very intently and identify with others who went through it. This is the education that Tribute's cofounders, Lee Ielpi and Jennifer Adams, always talk about.

The first stop is right outside the firehouse of Engine 10 and Ladder 10, on Liberty Street, just opposite the actual World Trade Center site, and then we move on to the firefighters' memorial, the beautiful bronze plaque that depicts a reenactment of the day's events. Then we go into the World Financial Center, where everyone sits down in one of the buildings and has a great view of the actual site itself, and we talk about the day of September 11. And this is where we introduce the personal story. Most of the people who are on those tours are not native New Yorkers but visitors from all over the country, and all over the world. Many relate their own experiences on 9/11. And then we walk all around the site, pointing out what occurred at different times of the day.

After doing the tours for a year as the support person, I said, You know what, I could take the lead, and the Tribute Center pushed me to do so. I prepared my presentation, and they worked on it a little bit, and then I did my first tour. And I think I did a pretty good job. I've now completed four years at the Tribute Center, doing maybe three tours a month, both lead and support, and I'm happy to have that flexibility. Tribute does four tours [a day], Monday through Friday. So that's eighty people a day, Monday through Friday, and weekends are packed. That's a total of around a thousand [people] a week. There have been over two million visitors in all so far. If I wasn't part of Tribute, I don't think I would know as much as I know. When you're doing a walking tour, you have to know what you're talking about, almost every aspect of it. Although I'm no expert, at least I know what went on.

I've heard some of the support people, when they come and tell their stories, like the miracle on Stairway B, and the firefighters who were trapped there [see Jay Jonas, page 52]. Visitors keep telling us we must tell people to never forget. Some actually say they'll never forgive. I don't add that.

Do I blame somebody for Barbara's death? You know I've never really looked at it that way. I believe I'm a good Catholic. I went to Catholic grammar school, Catholic high school, and I even taught at a Catholic high school for ten years. Do I believe that there's a reward afterward? Yes. Do I try to go to church every Sunday? Yes. If I don't, I'm not going to lose any sleep over it. So I follow the Golden Rule. I don't hurt people. You treat people nicely, the best you can. I've been ingrained in the traditional faith.

Do I turn the other cheek? Is that why I'm not blaming somebody? No. Who am I going to blame? I'm not blaming the entire group of Muslims. Are the people who did it representative of their religion? I don't think so. People did what they did. People who take the tour sometimes use the term "murder." "These people were murdered." "People were murdered." I'm not looking to make it a dramatic thing, so I don't say, "murdered." They died. They aren't here anymore. What is it going to accomplish to bring anger up? Is it going to bring people back? Is my wife coming back? Should I be more angry? I don't know. Maybe I should be more vociferous in my protesting. But that is not me. You can only be true to your own self.

I am still at work these days, now with the Brooklyn Navy Yard, doing the leasing. The navy yard is a three-hundred-acre complex, three and a half million square feet of industrial space, 98 percent fully leased, even in this economic climate. I enjoy it, because I'm dealing with people and out in the field looking at spaces. Tenants come and go. It's perfect for me; I love my work. With the Victim Compensation Fund and her own company retirement plans and options, Barbara has given me financial stability; I don't really have to worry about the future. I just wish that she could be here to be able to enjoy these benefits. So I try to give back as best I can. I do my work at Tribute. I do as good a job as I can with my navy yard job. I've become the president of my little tennis club in Brooklyn. That's what I have. Am I out traveling the world? No. Will I? I don't know. Maybe. If somebody comes into my life again, like my last relationship, which lasted for eight years, who knows? We did have great times. We did travel all over, but it just didn't work out. So what's my next chapter? I'm waiting to see. Fate.

I do not want to be known as Ray Habib who lost his wife on September 11. I was a teacher, I was a good husband, and I've done good things with Tribute and good work at my tennis club. That's how I want to be remembered: You know, He was a good guy. Nothing more, nothing less. And so, September 11 was something that was thrust upon me. I didn't choose to be part of it, but the fact is that it happened and I am part of it. I'll accept it, I'll absorb it, and I'll do everything that I can to continue to deal with it.

Robert and Barbara Jackman
and Erin Jackman

Robert Jackman was a bond-trading executive with the firm of Bear Stearns. He and his wife, Barbara, raised three children on Long Island—Ross, Erin, and Brooke. At 8:46 A.M. on September 11, Brooke was working on the 104th floor of the North Tower of the World Trade Center. Because of Brooke's love of literature, her family created a foundation in her memory to concentrate on literacy programs for children in need. Her sister, Erin, is now the president of the Brooke Jackman Foundation. Since this interview, Robert Jackman has passed away as a consequence of a long illness, bringing further profound loss to the Jackman family.

ROBERT: I was at work on 9/11, running the municipal bond–trading desk for Bear Stearns at Forty-fifth between Park and Madison. My son, Ross, was working downtown for J.P. Morgan at the time. Brooke was in the World Trade Center, working for Cantor Fitzgerald.

BARBARA: I was on a golf course on Long Island.

ROBERT: We always had our [computer] screens up at Bear Stearns, and this thing comes across. At first you can't believe something like this happened. And then everybody's calling. We had direct wires to Cantor Fitzgerald.

I remember, when Brooke got the job there, saying to the guys I knew in the municipal department, guys who had maybe thirty years in the business, Take good care of my little girl. They were all nice, and that day I got a couple of them on the direct wire. Obviously they didn't know what was happening, what was going on.

BARBARA: Someone came out on the golf course to tell me they had gotten a call. I ran inside and saw everybody in front of the TV screens. My first instinct was to run into the city. I was in my car for about ten or fifteen minutes when I heard on the radio that there was no access. I remember just driving and I ended up at the police station not far from our house, telling them to call Cantor for me. I needed to talk to Brooke. And they were very nice and wanted to escort me home. They obviously knew. So I went home and just waited. My sister and brother-in-law came over, and before I knew it the house was filled with people who had heard. Most of them thought it was Bob who worked at the World Trade Center, never realizing it was Brooke. She'd only been working there three and a half months. She'd recently graduated from Columbia, and this was her second job. She had gone to Oyster Bay High School and graduated sixth in her class.

ROBERT: Excellent student.

BARBARA: My son-in-law and my daughter Erin were teaching at the time at PS 111 on West Fifty-third Street. Erin dismissed the kids when the parents came trying to get them and then ran to my husband's office on Forty-fifth Street. Ross, who was working in the building practically next to the World Trade Center, walked uptown. It took Ross a very long time after watching the building be evacuated, as he didn't want to leave the scene because he was waiting for his sister to come down. He had just gotten married a month and a half before. It was a terrible situation. They weren't going to let him stand there. . . . People were pulling him away.

ROBERT: They didn't want anybody hanging around down there. And Erin and Ross came up to the office, and we just said, Let's go search for her. I don't remember what the hell happened, but we just kept looking and looking and looking. I just remember passing all of the hospital triage units that were set up, and the thing that stuck in my mind was that they had all these doctors and nurses standing around doing nothing. There were no people. Nobody got out. It was almost like a Woody Allen picture or something. You know, What's wrong with this picture? And all these people waiting to help, and the victims . . . Being there was difficult for everybody because it wasn't long before you realized that nobody could have survived that.

BARBARA: And then they started the process of going from hospital to hospital to look for Brooke. The next morning I took the railroad into the city, and we went to the armory downtown. We went all over, looking for the list to see who was safe and who wasn't.

ROBERT: There were a lot of cruel things on those lists. There were names that were reported safe, but they were gone. My daughter's name came up. I got probably hundreds of phone calls. Everybody saw her name and thought she was okay. We created a poster, and my nephew, who was teaching at a high school in the city, would ride around on a bicycle posting them, because you couldn't get around.

BARBARA: As a matter of fact, not long ago a young woman from California sent me a poem. She said she was one of the artists commissioned at the time, and what she wrote about in her poem was Brooke. She had seen the poster of Brooke all over the city, and it was just haunting her.

Brooke lived on Twenty-eighth and Second, so every night on her way home from work she would go into the Borders bookstore [nearby]. Books were her passion, and she'd sit there and browse, looking for quotes and jotting them down. There was a candlelight vigil at the Kips Bay Borders, which put up a sign FOR OUR FAVORITE CUSTOMER.

About ten days afterward we went back to the armory to check the list. [Mayor] Rudy Giuliani was there. And I was at the table and I was checking her name, and he turned and said, "Nobody is alive." That's how I found out. He felt terrible. . . .

ROBERT: He didn't mean to say it the way it came out. . . .

BARBARA: No. He took our family, the whole extended family, in and sat with us for about forty minutes. That's when we learned it was over.

ROBERT: Actually, in his book there's an article about that meeting.

BARBARA: His book *Leadership*.

ROBERT: Also, Brooke's phone call that we didn't actually receive was one of the last phone calls from the World Trade Center that got out before the systems went down, according to the FBI. She was semicontrolled but sobbing, on the 104th floor.

BARBARA: They were in the northwest corner. They took off their shoes to break a window to breathe. . . . They were all together. She left that message at our home. And the last seconds of the message were, "We love you, bye." And then she remembered where I was and she called over to the golf club. The switchboard operator there really had no clue. . . .

ROBERT: Everybody lost somebody that day—people we had met over the years, some very nice people. "Sorry we're in the same club" and "Sorry we had to meet this way." Nobody wanted to join this club. It's a heart-wrenching club.

BARBARA: Brooke had actually called the night before. We had an apartment in the city at the time. So the night before, I'd gone out to Long Island, because I knew I was going to be playing golf. She called me about ten o'clock, and I told her I was getting ready for the holidays [Rosh Hashanah began at sunset on September 17 that year], and I had gone food shopping. Then she told me that she wasn't going to stay on Wall Street. She had been declined by the Berkeley School of Social Welfare. She knew she could get into Columbia but had failed to try there. She said then, "There's something I've been saying since the beginning: There's more to life than making money." And that sort of summed her up, the type of person she was.

I guess I believed that she was alive, that if anyone could get out, she'd get out. Not realizing that none of them could get out.

ROBERT: Brooke was in really good shape. She walked all over the city with her backpack. In our foundation now we give away book bags, and that's basically for her. She walked around with this backpack, with books and notes. She always was reading a book. I think she read a book a day, or parts of one. She always had notes. We cleaned out her apartment afterward, and in all the books we picked up there were notations about something she wanted to look up or remember. She was unbelievable.

BARBARA: Oh yes.

ROBERT: We were afraid when she was growing up that she'd be a complete nerd, but she was very well-rounded. And I think most of the kids that she went to school with would consider her a true friend. There must have been a thousand people at the service in Oyster Bay that September. After everybody in the family spoke, people came to shake our hands, express their condolences. This young man came up, a Sikh, and said, I have to tell you a story about your daughter.

BARBARA: And he had waited on line to tell us, for the longest time.

ROBERT: And he said what happened was, when he came into the school, because he was different, people wouldn't associate with him, talk with him, but Brooke did. Because Brooke did, he was accepted. She was that way; it didn't matter.

I think for us, and the process of healing, it's necessary to keep Brooke's memory alive. Keeping her alive will help us. I think, on occasions, *What would she do?* Brooke was outgoing, but she wouldn't want to be described like that.

BARBARA: She was way too humble.

ROBERT: She would always take the backseat and let somebody else take the praise. She was good at a lot of stuff, but reading was a great passion with her. When she was in camp in the summer, I am sure she would be under the blanket with a flashlight reading at night. And when the two older ones, who are a year apart—Brooke was the youngest—were studying for the SATs, sitting around the kitchen table, she'd help them with the words. And she was five and six years younger. She had a fantastic memory, basically a photographic memory. And when we were thinking about how to keep her memory alive, we knew it had to be something connected to literacy.

BARBARA: She wanted to go back to social work and work with children. Somehow to combine the two. It was during the first week that we started the Brooke Jackman Foundation. We have a wonderful family, and they began working at it, and a lot of close friends wanted to do something. I remember that they mentioned at the memorial service that there would be a Brooke Jackman Foundation.

ROBERT: The lawyers had to set up paperwork to get a foundation set up, a 501(c)3. We had to get everything going, that type of thing. I think it helped us, because it got us out of bed.

BARBARA: It took me six months to be able to utter a word. I couldn't talk at all.

ROBERT: We did grief counseling.

BARBARA: A doctor from Mount Sinai had volunteered to go down to Ground Zero, and somehow we got hooked up with her. So our family met with her once a week for two years.

ROBERT: And that helped. When we first started going, I remember telling the doctor, "I just want my family to get as normal as they can." I wanted to get back on track, and that was my job. Hopefully it's done. And sometimes it's horrible, for all of us. It's just, like we said, it doesn't go away. If I see two young girls walking down the street talking, and one looks like Brooke, I'm a basket case.

The foundation was very much a family operation in those first couple of years. So we did everything. Sometimes I don't know how we did it. But it was just the will of the whole family to get together to do this. Well, once we announced it, there were all kinds of e-mails that went out at Bear Stearns. I can't tell you how many employees we had at that time—it could have been twelve thousand. The guys in the Boston office did a whole solicitation of everybody there. Because I dealt with most of the other departments in the other offices out of town selling bonds, they all pretty much knew what we were trying to do.

BARBARA: Friends started sending in donations, and people from all over whom we didn't even know, who had read about it in the paper. I can't say how many donations came in—from Australia, Colorado Springs, North Dakota, France. A teacher in France. So many wonderful people.

ROBERT: The first couple of years we got a lot of money. We're amazed that every year we're doing okay, because in general, the further away you get from the event of 9/11 itself, the less interest there is in this. I think everybody in some way was affected by 9/11, whether they lost somebody or didn't. From our point of view, every year is hard. Usually when you lose somebody, you have a mourning period, and it's over. But whenever an article appears about 9/11, or another anniversary is honored, it's a public matter. It's an abrasion, always rubbing—it doesn't go away.

BARBARA: Of course, nothing could ever truly take the place of Brooke. The ache that's in your heart, it just never goes away. There's always something that reminds you. I couldn't walk into our town for two years. I couldn't go into the local supermarket. I would go two towns away, because I would always remember something—she had her first car accident in that parking lot, or it's a place she liked to hang out with her friends. I couldn't go anywhere near that.

But it helps to know that we are helping other people through her. We have expanded all of our programs, as well. Our literacy programs are in so many more sites now.

ROBERT: The first year we gave out one hundred backpacks. We were running around to Staples, buying the packs, filling them with books, and putting them out there. We had a bunch of friends come and help us pack, and we did that for about seven years, at the end of August, for the new school year. People couldn't wait to help.

BARBARA: We eventually used the gymnasium of a school on the Upper East Side, and would sit there for a few days, assembling the backpacks. It was a lot of work. In the beginning there were three books, then four, and this last year it was five. Up until this year we also gave a little Walkman. We wanted the children to be able to listen to books on tape, because they don't always have time to read them. Now we are using MP3 players, and people can download the books from our Web site. This year we also sent out a few hundred to Haiti.

ROBERT: And a couple of years ago to Louisiana.

BARBARA: Right. For the children after Katrina. But most of them go to the metropolitan area—to homeless shelters or family and children shelters.

ROBERT: They've also opened libraries in some of these shelters and in the schools—like PS 111, where my daughter Erin taught.

BARBARA: This year we are giving out three thousand seven hundred backpacks. Now that's way too many for us, and we have them filled in Chicago. We've found that the need grows each year, and that if you love to do something, you'll do it. We just felt that books and reading are sort of the keys to empowering children for a better life.

ROBERT: What we found was that, for a lot of these children, reading was not being reinforced at home. That's how we started our literacy program, where we involve families. We bring them in and give them dinner, and they play word games and different things with the kids. People can't seem to get enough of it. Most of these programs run eight months or nine months.

BARBARA: And then they have a graduation ceremony.

ROBERT: The best thing was the parents that would come up to you—a woman who is now reading on the bus with her daughter as she's going to work, or when she's dropping the kid off in the morning, or in the Laundromat doing the wash, telling us that this has helped her in her job and with her daughter.

BARBARA: She said, "Now we've become readers. We read in the Laundromat, we read on the subway." At a graduation ceremony another parent actually gave my daughter and son roses and said, "We have bloomed just like these flowers. We are readers now." These are very touching. We get little notes all the time.

I also mentioned to a woman, when I went on a school trip, that the children didn't have any hats or mittens, so now she has an organization called Stand to Knit that makes them. And we put them in the backpacks also. Erin is running it all now. She left teaching.

ROBERT: She's the best and only employee we have.

BARBARA: The only paid employee. After the second year I got shingles and I knew I needed help. She volunteered to run the foundation. She has a friend who gave us an office, computer time, telephone, anything that we need. It's very nice. Very generous.

BARBARA: We also have Brooke's Read-a-Thon, which is a two-hour event down at the World Financial Center, where we have officials, the fire commissioner, children's authors, people from the mayor's office, EMTs, and firemen who read to the children.

ROBERT: Twenty-five readers and about a hundred and fifty kids, I'd say. We also do a five-K run in the Oyster Bay area. And our friends come out and help us every year.

BARBARA: And that's grown. One hundred and fifty people this year.

ROBERT: We have a fun run for the little kids and then a five-K race for the adults.

ROBERT: You know, when you go back to that day, I remember being in the office, and Brooke called. And some guy picked up the phone and said, "It sounds like your daughter." I picked it up and there was no sound. And then, next thing I saw on the screen was the tower going down. And you just can't believe that your child's there. I think of the days that we spent going around the city and not admitting to ourselves the worst. I'm just amazed we were able to get through it. You know, you're not supposed to have to give the eulogy for your child. That's not supposed to happen.

Regarding 9/11: The only thing I think about is that somewhere one hand wasn't telling the other what the hell was going on, and it should have been preventable. Those guys should have been caught or stopped. But, you know, these things have happened, and I'm sure maybe there will be more stories about what this group knew and didn't tell that group. Because that's the way the world goes around.

BARBARA: I attend a support group that my daughter Erin suggested. One of the facilitators lives in Chappaqua, near President Clinton, and he wanted to come down and talk to us, but the group voted for him not to come, because as a whole it felt that he didn't do enough, that he could have prevented it. So in the back of my mind, the question is always there: What if he had done more? With the embassy or the *Achille Lauro* or—I don't know. Maybe this wouldn't have happened if he'd taken a stronger stand. But to blame the rest, al Qaeda, it's like a blur to me. You can't even put a face to it. I don't know about blame for this whole thing, because I don't think I've given it that much thought. I just go forward and do what we can do to change. And for me, change comes from education. That's what I hope.

ROBERT: I am not a hater, but who knows what else will come? Someone else will be unhappy with the world because of the way it is. They want a bigger share for themselves. It's been going on for centuries. I guess we are all trying to take our hate and make it positive.

BARBARA: I don't think it's hate. We just want to make something positive of this situation. I can't say that I've ever hated anyone. Bob was in Vietnam, and he wrote a book that was published after he was home, letters he had written to his sister in an elementary school class. He wrote to them that he was in Vietnam to make the world safe for them. That's how he perceived it. It's ironic what happened with us.

ROBERT: Since 9/11, I think I've gotten a little more spiritual. Our kids and my wife have not. They find no solace in organized religion. They feel that organized religion or God or whatever you want to call it has left them. Because if there was a God, Brooke would be here.

BARBARA: Brooke and all the other people that were there.

ROBERT: Our rabbi was new to the temple at the time this happened, and he did a yeoman's job. He didn't even know us, but he was very comforting in the beginning, and still is to this day. I wouldn't say he's extremely religious, but he is extremely learned, and a mensch.

BARBARA: You know, I never thought I would be able to laugh again, because the ache you always feel is there, but you learn to cope, and I think that we are trying to do more than just cope. We want to show our grandchildren that it is a good world, it is a positive world.

ROBERT: Now that they're seven and five they're starting to ask a lot of questions about 9/11.

BARBARA: And their aunt Brooke.

ROBERT: The aunt that they never met. They always talk about her as if she's in the room, which is a little hard sometimes. I hope that as they get older they'll be helping out to raise money for the foundation, with lemonade sales and whatever. I really want them to know what happened, and maybe my analysis of it will help them down the road.

BARBARA: We want people to remember Brooke and everyone else who lost their lives that day. I have been looking at the designs of the 9/11 memorial. You know, I have a few questions about it. I don't like how the names are being placed. I don't know if I like it placed underneath, as it's going to be. But this is what we have, and hopefully it will come out as beautiful as they are telling us it will.

ROBERT: The first time you go down to that open pit, it's heartbreaking, like getting hit in the chest. A stabbing in the heart. And you walk around, and you say, *This is where she is.* We got a couple of fragments back [and] actually had a burial.

BARBARA: And then we had to open the casket again. And that was the worst. She's at the cemetery, but she's not really there.

ROBERT: We put up a headstone because it gives us a place to go. It's very hard.

BARBARA: Brooke's birthday was August 28. So the month of August, leading up to September 11, I feel washed out. It's a terrible time. Sometimes I really don't know why she went to Wall Street. When she graduated she went for book publishing, but she was bored with that. And then she went on the Columbia Web site and saw this opening that she applied for at Cantor Fitzgerald.

She never even had a finance course.

ROBERT: She went, interviewed, and was one of two out of a hundred who got hired. It was never in her makeup to be a trader or to do that type of thing. And I don't know why she took that job. I keep thinking, *Did she go there because I was there? Because my son was there?* Why would she do that?

BARBARA: It was so tragic for so many Cantor Fitzgerald families.

ROBERT: I think Howard [Lutnick, the CEO of Cantor Fitzgerald, a firm that lost 657 employees in addition to Brooke Jackman] did a superb job. He was in a tough position. His brother on the agency desk died. I must have seen the guy eight to ten times over the next two years. He would fly to New York to see all the families whose loved ones worked there, and was always sending little notes and stuff about people to us. In the beginning Howard got very bad publicity, and in the end I think he did an enormous job. I think he did the best he could, and he didn't know what was going to happen to that firm. But he made a promise to everyone, and he stuck to it. Families who lost their sole support got health benefits for five or six years. They took care of their people, more so than any other firm I ever heard of. And now the firm is doing very well. I would never take anything away from the guy.

BARBARA: I just keep wanting to do more. So where do we see the future? Hopefully we will grow. We did three thousand seven hundred back-packs this year, and we will get to ten thousand. Hopefully we'll open more libraries, more literacy programs, more read-a-thons. We just want to grow.

ERIN: A lot of families created named efforts and said they would do them for five years or ten years. We always had a forever outlook. To grow it as big as we possibly could.

BARBARA: I remember that Erin told me about the Susan Komen Foundation, which was started by her sister. And look how it's grown. We said that someday we're going to get ours to grow like that.

ERIN: We can evolve it as the world evolves. We have a library at a domestic abuse center. Children and mothers who are victims of abuse are cared for, and there's a whole system of support for them. While they are there, there's the Brooke Jackman library. And we also started one of our family literacy programs there for the mothers and their children. They come back to utilize it. When they first get there, after they've left their homes in the middle of the night and taken almost no possessions—one mother was with her two traumatized sons in the library, and our backpacks had just arrived, and they were the first two to get them last year. They were just amazed. They saw books, the backpack, the MP3 players, and they were, like, "How did they know? How did they know I need this?" We get to experience many stories like this, and they all inspire us to reach more and more children with Brooke's love of books.

Cameron and Ann MacRae

Cameron MacRae is of counsel to a major New York law firm. His wife, Ann, besides being a wife and a mother, is a natural volunteer and, together with her husband and others, created a foundation that improves the lives of young people, the Cat MacRae Memorial Fund. Their daughter Catherine—Cat—was working as a financial analyst with Fred Alger Management, and on 9/11 she was in her office on the ninety-third floor of the North Tower.

ANN: Both of my daughters grew up right here on the Upper East Side of New York. We lived on Eighty-first Street until Cat was nine, and then moved here, to Seventy-second Street. Her sister Annie was five at the time. They went to the Brearley School on Eighty-fourth Street. And they did have a wonderful New York City life.

Cat was a really great child and always excelled at everything, even in the first grade. All the students who didn't know how to read went downstairs to reading lessons, and all of those who knew how to read stayed upstairs. Of course Cat didn't know how to read, but Brearley made her feel like she was a genius and kept her upstairs the whole time. She thrived there. Both girls loved Brearley, and it was a lovely childhood, with weekends in Southampton. Cameron and I both went to boarding school, and neither one of us liked it, and so we did not send them away to high school. After Brearley Cat went to Princeton, where she really grew. Those were the happiest four years of her life. Because she died at twenty-three we don't have too much to compare to, but she was the happiest at Princeton, where she graduated with honors in economics.

CAMERON: Magna cum laude. She was a very beautiful young lady, and so is Annie. They were both very dynamic and captivating growing up. I speak of Cat as if she's still around, not because I'm delusional, but because she is somewhat very much with us. She loved Princeton, and one of the things that was extraordinarily fun for her was sophomore year. There was a little house next to the dorm called 99 Alexandra, where she'd been assigned to live with nine other girls. That was just a wonderful time for Cat, and she ended up joining the Ivy Club.

ANN: Where there's a portrait of her now.

CAMERON: Yes. If you go into Ivy now, which is probably the most traditional of all the clubs, in the foyer there's a gallery of extraordinary Ivy Club members. The portraits are all men, but they did put a beautiful oil painting of Cat with us. She looks so beautiful.

ANN: Cat met a chap named Andrew Caspersen there. They fell in love and were clearly going to be married. He fell for Cat's interesting combination of being attractive, very nice, and funny—very funny. Great sense of humor. One of the things I remember the most about Cat is, if she'd heard something funny, and if she was eating, she would almost choke. She would just collapse in laughter. She was great on a level plane, and then on the unusual, too. For instance, she was very good in both English and mathematics. She had a perfect little life, and she worked very hard to get everything she achieved. She was naturally smart and naturally athletic and naturally nice, but she was also a hard worker. And that's one of the things that broke our hearts—that she had worked so hard to get to Princeton. She always wanted to go there and had gone to Cameron's reunions because Cameron had gone to Princeton. Since she was six, she had said, "I'm going to go to Princeton," and in 1996 she got an early admission, which was quite a feat. While there she excelled at mathematics and got a math prize.

CAMERON: I sometimes wonder, though, *What if she had not gone directly from college to Goldman Sachs?* I actually had urged her not to immediately go to Goldman, because even though it is the best investment bank, it's certainly not the nicest place to work.

She did leave Goldman, and the final straw was that the previous year she got an assignment the Thursday before Labor Day weekend with a "request" that it be on her boss's desk the following workday. She knew there was no urgency whatsoever for this report, and she'd planned a weekend with Andrew, as they hadn't had much time off during that summer. She eventually allowed herself to be lured away by David Alger, who ran Fred Alger, a fairly prominent money management firm, and she was very happy there, working as an analyst. They manage mutual funds and things like that, strictly in the high-tech area. Unfortunately, David selected the ninety-third floor of the WTC as their office site.

ANN: Well, we all thought it was safe.

CAMERON: It made me a little queasy because when I was a member of the Council of the Banking Commission in 1970–1972, I was in one of the World Trade Center buildings, on the thirty-second floor. I always knew that it was quite a job to get up to the top. You had to go up to the sky lobby, and then change over, and it made me nervous that Cat would be up that high. In retrospect, thinking of the first bombing in 1993, it's now very clear to me that these people kept going after the same target. Which is a worrisome thing in New York City. Cat got a little nervous herself after she began working on the ninety-third floor, so high up.

ANN: She did worry about terrorism. I remember her saying, "I just don't like that building"—and she was aware of the '93 bombing. We are very protective parents. And it's funny, a number of the mothers of victims of the attack whom I've met have all said that safety was a top priority in bringing up their kids. It just did not occur to us. It's absurd that we didn't realize that the World Trade Center would be a target. The '93 bombing should have been enough warning. And Richard Clarke was telling everybody. [Clarke, a counterterrorism adviser, warned the George W. Bush administration about al Qaeda before 9/11.]

CAMERON: What we honestly didn't know, living in New York, was how iconic our city and those buildings were. To the rest of the world the World Trade Center was the center of commerce and power. If we thought our city had a target, we would have thought it would be the Empire State Building.

The thing that really appalled me—and I hold Bush and Cheney extremely responsible for this—was that terrorism was not a priority for Bush. Whatever the pros and cons of the Clinton administration, it was very clear that after the millennium they were very focused on terrorism. Clinton or Gore would attend meetings every day to discuss this kind of threat. When Bush and Cheney came in they rejected everything that Clinton had done. Terrorism was a very low priority. It wasn't in the top ten, probably around number twenty-five. They just dropped the ball.

ANN: The morning of 9/11, I was on the phone to my best friend and Cameron came in and said a plane had hit the World Trade Center. And I said, "Cameron, be quiet, I'm on the phone." And then . . . We didn't know. Cameron said it hit Tower 1, and we didn't know which tower Cat was in. I remember picking up the phone book and looking up Fred Alger.

CAMERON: We tried to call Cat.

ANN: We never heard from her.

CAMERON: And at that point I was watching CNBC. The thought was that maybe it was a private plane.

We have trouble talking about that day because . . .

ANN: I can talk about it. We had called Cat, but there was no answer— I think the call just didn't go through. We went into total shock. Of course we did. Our best friends came over. And a lot of Cat's friends, Princeton girls, came over. I remember going to the dining room window, and fighter jets went over all those little town houses down on the street, and I said, "Oh my God," because when it happens to you, you're not fully aware that it's an international incident. Fighter jets—you can't take it all in. But we knew the government was involved. There were a lot of young people here in our home, and every time the phone rang we thought, *It might be Cat.* I won't use the profanity, but I said, If I don't hear from her by four o'clock . . . I'm not sure I said it would mean she was dead, but it would be bad. And then at four I said, "Oh, it's four o'clock." And then the kids went to work and started calling hospitals.

You know, when you grow up in an apartment building, all the doormen, the superintendent, the tenants, everybody together, it's a village. Everybody knew Cat and was there to help within four hours.

CAMERON: One of the doormen, with whom we were close, and who ultimately enlisted in the marines, had an old jalopy, so he, Dennis the superintendent, and I tried to get down to the World Trade Center site. We couldn't get past Fourteenth Street. We stopped, and I walked around in that area trying to get my cell phone working. I was hopeful, as I thought they all would have gathered in David Alger's office, and he would have led them out.

For the next few days I went to the hospitals—St. Vincent's, Bellevue, even Lenox Hill—but didn't find out anything. We had a little hope when we saw a list of survivors that had had something close to Cat's name on it. And I had some hope that everyone would have gotten down into the subbasements.

ANN: And you called people about that too, to find out how they were constructed.

CAMERON: I don't even like to go back there mentally. It's just so awful, and it was beyond belief. I watched the collapse on TV.

ANN: We both did. With our daughter inside.

CAMERON: It's a horrible thing.

ANN: A friend of ours went to pick up Annie the next day from Amherst and brought her home. Chuck Scarborough [a local TV news anchor], who's a friend of ours from Southampton, put up a picture of Cat on the TV news with our telephone number. We were all in our bedroom watching it, and the phone rang, and someone said, "I know where your daughter is." It was some crank, but for a minute you believed him. You were desperate to believe him.

We had a candlelight vigil in Central Park. Everyone came down to Seventy-second Street and lit candles. There was a picture of Cat on the door of our apartment building. People came up to me and said, I'm so sorry, and I remember saying, We don't know.

CAMERON: Needless to say, neither the city administration under [Mayor Rudy] Giuliani nor the national administration did anything to reach out, or try to coordinate, or to say, Here's a master list. I think they were reasonably confused. It's hard to tell how aggressive their efforts were.

It's understandable that people made errors, but then to use the tragedy as a platform for a political career, which Giuliani tried to do, and then to watch people who, particularly in the case of Bush and Cheney, who were in part responsible—and believe me, I'm an independent—use it successfully in a platform for a political career is absolutely nauseating. It still is.

There was a terrible waste of our resources, and our prestige, and so many lives lost when Bush and Cheney elected to go into Iraq, with no connection to September 11. Anyone with half a brain knew that at the time, and it is clear now. And it's hurt our security. I think that over the last nine years the Iraq war and the failure to clean up Afghanistan have hurt our country.

ANN: This is a big part of our grieving too. Because you have got to get mad.

CAMERON: You can quote me: Cheney can roast in hell. And since Bush followed his ideas and advice, they both can. Our security is internationally weaker because of all this. Domestically it's not very pleasant, to say the least, because of how many of the recommendations of the 9/11 Commission that have not been incorporated—for instance, cargo security. Having a "national security czar" has turned out to be counterproductive. On the positive side, it is quite remarkable that a number of these plots in recent years have been foiled. The New York City Police and Fire departments are as alert as any city's defenses can be. I am impressed that we were able to intercept the Times Square bomber, but, unfortunately, terrorism just keeps going on. Now Germany is on alert for a possible Mumbai-like attack. The problem is that we didn't corral the thing.

The Obama administration has been reasonably successful in providing security, and some of the things the Bush administration did at the end were working. I also think that mistakes are being made by the Obama administration, such as the idea of having civilian trials for terrorists, which is just way-out liberal thinking gone crazy by people who have never been in a courtroom. Why they should be tried in New York City is beyond me, and Attorney General [Eric] Holder has been extremely ill advised in pushing for those kinds of things. Certainly it's beyond me, when you have a quasi-military attack on our facilities abroad, whether it's the USS *Cole* or one of our embassies, [that they] will not admit that we are essentially fighting an ongoing war.

ANN: I know exactly where I was when I realized Cat was truly gone. It was the Friday after September 11. We often go to church, and there were a lot of services that week. But that Friday we went to the Church of the Heavenly Rest, where Cat had actually been confirmed. The church was packed [with people] praying for those lost on September 11. I remember sitting in that pew thinking, and it just came to me: *She's dead.* It was as if she had whispered in my ear. I just knew it; it was a revelation.

Her memorial service was October 6, and we spent a lot of time from September 11 until then planning it. Your focus goes to that. It's concrete. We did a program and decided who was going to talk and what the music would be and how to get everybody there. We had a thousand people at the service in Southampton. They normally close the Episcopal church after the summer season, but they kept the church open for that.

The first five years after losing Cat were pure hell. I'm a docent at the Met [the Metropolitan Museum of Art], where tours start in the middle of October. I give tours to children, and I never missed one. After two weeks Annie went back to Amherst, and it being a small college, they embraced her.

CAMERON: Andrew graduated the year he met Cat, and then he went to Harvard Law School. He was in his second year there when September 11 occurred, and because he wanted to be close to us, he transferred to

NYU and took over Cat's apartment. Harvard and NYU have a program, and he still has a Harvard degree.

ANN: He got married in May of this year to a girl who knew Cat, whom we love.

We stay close to Andrew.

We all picked up our lives, which were just shattered. The first year you are in such shock, just putting one foot in front of the other. I don't know what I felt, but I knew it was so deep. It wasn't like, *Oh, I'm so sad that she's dead.* It was just an awareness, a rather amorphous thing. But I knew it. We were a really close family. Cat called me three or four times a day. She was the first child, so I knew practically every detail of her life.

CAMERON: Another interesting thing about Cat is that she was a force. Not many people are a force. She had a tremendous effect on anyone who knew her but without being a talkative person or a center-of-attention person. That's why we stayed so close to all of her friends, because they wanted to stay close to us, and through us to Cat. That was her force.

ANN: She was energetic and so full of love and beauty. She wasn't just charismatic—she was human too—far from perfect. We wanted to memorialize her life. And we all—myself, Cameron, Annie, and Andrew—had the wonderful idea to create a special fund. And that has helped. I never understood what things like that meant to people, but it has helped me, and Cameron too.

At Thanksgiving of 2001 we wrote a letter proposing the fund, which Andrew and Cameron hand-delivered to nearly everyone on the list who was from New York. The response was extraordinary.

CAMERON: We put money in, and we also used a large part of our proceeds from the Victim Compensation Fund [the federal government's fund for survivors and families of survivors administered by Kenneth Feinberg]. Our fund has created a benefit. All four of us are the trustees. It's much easier to raise money than it is to give it out sensibly. Annie had personal views that it should be focused around the five boroughs of New York City. I actually wanted to do things like Seeds for Peace [a nonprofit organization that trains young people in war-torn regions in leadership and conflict-resolution skills].

ANN: Andrew got a list of schools, and so he and I started going around, meeting with people, and finding things that we liked. It was also really therapeutic for our grief. Now here we are, ten years later, and we've really figured out what works.

In the very beginning I went to Children's Storefront up in Harlem, where we gave funding for a math program, and the headmistress said, Will you come and talk about Cat? Now I don't like to talk in public, but I can talk about Cat until I'm blue in the face and I don't get nervous. And I told them about her. The headmistress had warned me that they would probably get a little iffy after twenty minutes, but it was first through eighth grade [children], and you could have heard a pin drop. And they asked, When she did her homework, was it messy? Did she like sports? Did she keep her room neat? They wanted to know about her. In another program we ran downtown, they told the children about Cat before I got there, and one of the little children said, "Can I tell you something? I know something that will be good for you. If you take a picture of Cat and you light a candle next to it, that will make you feel much better." And this was a little seven-year-old.

CAMERON: There are a number of schools we help fund that are not public schools or parochial schools or charter schools, but somewhere in between. They're privately funded schools that are starting to spring up, and they're extraordinary, offering some unique programs. And we want to help them. The bottom line is, our efforts are helping.

ANN: It's helping us, and helping the world. We have two Cat MacRae libraries: one at Brooklyn Jesuit Prep and one at the George Jackson Academy [for academically capable boys from lower income and underserved families].

CAMERON: Brooklyn Jesuit Prep had been a parochial school next to a great big high school, next to a big church. As the neighborhood changed the Catholic presence moved away, and then a Jesuit priest came and built up within the building a wonderful school, which is better than the one I went to. The library, which we just installed there, is magnificent.

ANN: We've sent four children to parochial high schools so far. We have a reading program, a writing program, cultural enrichment programs. They are really successful. And our friends who gave to Cat's fund are now finding out about the programs that we are running, and they are getting more involved too. One of Cat's teachers at Brearley, Mrs. Smith, writes to everyone who went to the school who loved Cat, and there are still so many of them that we continue to build.

ANN: Two September 11s ago, a friend of Annie's who teaches in the public schools, Katie, said that she was talking to the kids in her second-grade class about what had happened that day. A little girl raised her hand and said, "I know somebody who was killed on September 11." Katie said, "How do you know someone who was killed? You weren't even born yet." The girl answered, "Her name is Cat MacRae. Her name is in all the books that I read." They were from our enrichment program for kids, GO Project, which runs [programs in the] Little Red School House and Grace Church. And we started the Cat MacRae Expository Writing Program, so they all have pencils with little CAT MACRAEs on them and in their little books, and they take the Cat MacRae oath in the summer.

CAMERON: They pack the schools on Saturdays with the children from public schools south of Fourteenth Street. The classes are overseen by a certified teacher and a number of assistants who are studying to be teachers, and they break down the kids into little groups, one tutor for every two children.

Reading is obviously one of its biggest goals, but the program is quite remarkable, because not only is it offered every Saturday of the school year, but because they have concluded that these kids get to a certain level during the school year and then they drop off a bit in the summer, the program also takes them five days a week throughout the summer.

ANN: And then there is the work we do at the Harlem Academy, which Vinny Dotoli built up, grade by grade, each year adding another. It's in the bottom of an office building.

CAMERON: And they attract very bright kids. They insist that the parents pay a little something, but obviously the school is charitable. They are now up to seven grades. And it's wonderful, because the good prep schools are watching and in another year will be beating their doors down to try to attract their students.

ANN: What we do when we're assessing a school is, I'm the guinea pig. I go and see if I like the school and the people I would work with. I meet the headmaster and his development team. If I like it, I bring Cameron. And we ask, "What do you want?" So the second year at Harlem Academy we asked that, and Cameron added, "Cat was so good in math, and we already have all these reading and writing programs and libraries. We need a math program." Vinny said, "I'd love to start the Singapore Math Program. It is a very effective way of teaching mathematics." We had a party here the other night for Harlem Academy, parents and friends, people who supported the Cat Fund. I wanted them to see where the money has gone. It was a bit of an emotional event but a good job. We had little fifth graders there, and they were doing all of the math problems. Presenting their math problems to everybody. It was lovely. And it's part of Cat's legacy.

We're also involved with something called SSP, Student Sponsor Partnership, and they send kids to Catholic high school.

CAMERON: Which is very interesting. Brother Stanley runs it within the workings of the Catholic school system. The program takes kids out of public schools and sends them to the good parochial schools, like this wonderful one on Seventy-sixth Street, St. Jean. However, we were also supporting the program of parochial elementary schools, and there was one eighth-grade girl in them who was dropping between the cracks. I watched her participate in class, and when I asked the headmistress where she was going to high school, I discovered that she couldn't afford to go anywhere. The SSP wouldn't pay for kids from one parochial school to go to another, but that's been changed now, and we want to support their programs.

One of the tragic things about education here in New York is that the parochial schools are four times better than the public schools, and they are run on an efficient budget. But because of the dynamics of life these days there's not enough money to have all these parochial schools continue.

ANN: I think I'm more personally involved in the actual work of the fund. I go to Harlem Academy, and they say, Hi, Annie. I teach them art history, and I bring them to the Met too. Maybe it's just the mother in me who wants to mother. I love being involved in the Cat Fund and getting to know the kids. It's more of an emotional commitment for me. And I need it. It helps me tremendously. But you know, there are always sad times. Always.

CAMERON: It helps me in a little bit of a different way, and not as much as it helps Ann. What it does for me is that in some way Cat, although she only lived twenty-three years, has put quite a mark on a little piece of the world. This fund has done a lot of good, and there will be a number of kids who will benefit from this and who will not be failures. But that's not how I solve every period of downtime. The downtime is the reality. These horrible people.

ANN: I think Cat was murdered, but I also think it was a phenomenon.

Oh, I assign blame. I went to those 9/11 Commission hearings. I really did feel that it could have been prevented. It was shocking that our government knew as much as it did and didn't do anything about it. Shocking.

CAMERON: We all approach this differently. I was very interested in knowing, and really wanted to make sure, that Cat was in a good place. I wanted to understand this from both a religious and a scientific standpoint, so I started studying quite extensively advanced physics, string theory, and unification theory, where you get into the question of other dimensions. I was also studying comparative religion—I wanted to come out on the comparative religion side, as my training had always been to look to the internal. All these traditions—Christianity, Judaism, Buddhism, Confucianism—are very similar, which is the thesis of a number of leading textbooks. But as I got into it I realized that there really are some major differences between the Muslim religion and the other great religions of the world. The differences are that most other religions are very peaceful. In fact, Hinduism and Christianity are probably the two closest; they do not have a militaristic bent, nor should any religion. Whatever you might think of the Western religions and their riches, they do have central authority. There is no centralized dogmatic authority in the Muslim religion, which means that any Muslim can say that he has studied a little bit and run a mosque, or be an imam and proclaim fatwas. Admittedly, the more enlightened Muslims are only going to listen to true scholars. Unfortunately, it's the militant side that is extremely dangerous. People who have no respect for human life, people who blow themselves up, who blow their brothers and sisters up— that is a tremendous foe to have. Twenty or thirty years ago the international concern was a state attacking a state. But now you have failed states like Yemen, Afghanistan, Somalia, and Libya that are creating festering pools for murder.

There's an academic side of Islam that is truly a scholarly and peaceful religion, but there's an extremist side too, and we have unfortunately now gone overboard with being politically correct in pointing this out. For example, this mosque by Ground Zero is an example of something that is in very poor taste. Yes, we're all for freedom of religion, but do you think it's really in good taste or appropriate to build a mosque higher than any other religious building downtown? This is a real estate development story, but it happens to be right next to the World Trade Center.

ANN: I remember someone saying, Does there have to be another September 11 before anybody takes this all seriously? People still think September 11 was just another emergency. America doesn't really get it yet.

Our family gets bigger, which really has helped a lot. Annie just married a wonderful man. So much in the beginning was the three of us. We'd go into restaurants, and wherever we went they'd say, "Are you a party of four?" And we'd say three. And the three of us were brave and had done a good job, but having Annie be married added a new dimension to our family. When he married Annie, Win had never met Cat, but his brother was in Cat's class at Princeton and knew her. Win now talks about Cat as if he knew her too. She just comes along with us.

I noticed in the beginning that my friends didn't quite know what to do, because it's every mother's worst fear, or every parent's worst fear, to lose a child. But all of Cat's friends had lost their good friend, so they would come to me and say, Mrs. MacRae, what are we going to do? So we all became a family together and stayed really close. We go to all of her friends' weddings. When they have babies, they send us pictures. One of them sends Annie a birthday present and a Christmas present every year, because Cat's not sending those presents any longer. We all talk about Cat all the time. We haven't let her go. A lot of grieving is often kept inside, but we reach out, and say, God, we miss her. God, she should be at this wedding, on this trip, at this dinner. And it helps.

CAMERON: It's a journey, and it's not over.

Rudy Abad

Rudy Abad was in the process of retiring from Merrill Lynch, where he was first an analyst, then a broker and options specialist for nearly twenty-five years. When his wife, Marie Rose, died in the South Tower, Rudy returned to his native Philippine Islands, where he was determined to build a memorial to her that would be as meaningful and as consequential as the life taken from her.

I am one of five children and was born in 1945, right in the middle of a brother and three sisters. We were a modest and unassuming family. My parents determined to give us sound educations, and all five of us went to one of the better schools in Manila. I cannot say that I had a really happy family, as my parents were very involved in their work. But so were other parents. Our relationship was not as good as what I might have seen in the families of friends of mine. But it was okay.

My father was a businessman, basically in advertising, and my mom was by his side the whole time. When we were kids it was already a multimillion-dollar business, and so we were very comfortable. We had our own car, a very decent home. We were not in the very, very rich category, but we were certainly not lacking for anything.

I went to a school called Ateneo, probably the most prestigious in Manila, which was something like going to Harvard. But after my first year of college I came to the States to continue school at Berkeley, right at the time of Mario Savio and the Free Speech Movement. Being a student from a foreign country, I stayed out of it, as I didn't know what was going on, and I really was not interested. I took a degree in business and have a master's degree in finance.

It was a difficult time. I had never been alone and was used to having a crowd around me, with me as the leader, and here I was in a foreign country, where I really just stayed on the sidelines. From a very early age I had leadership qualities, and in any undertaking I was the one who was doing the talking, the planning. At Berkeley I definitely knew that I was not in my environment, and that I had a lot to learn. As a foreigner with English as a second language, I was behind the eight ball. But I knew where I stood and I accepted that.

I had come to the States planning to go back home to either help my dad or actually work with him in his business. Part of my education, though, was also having to go to work, for I did not want to add to the cost my dad had in putting four other children through school. This was also a little bit of a learning process for me, because in my younger days I never worked, except to do schoolwork. I had two jobs that became fairly important to my life. One was as a waiter on weekends at the golf and country club. The second was at Berkeley after I posted a notice on a bulletin board [saying] that I was looking for a job. One day I got a call from a placement officer offering work cleaning the school, which was very much against my ego—a person of my background cleaning school floors? Those two jobs broke me down, taking all the time and pride from me. Actually, I got used to them, got to like them, and told myself, *Okay, I'm going to be the best waiter and best cleaner around.* But it was an awakening, being brought down to earth like that.

When I got a job with Merrill Lynch, the stock brokerage house, I started at the very, very bottom. I was two years away from graduating college, and they had an opening for a board marker. During those days, when they had those ticker-tape things, we used a board to mark down when they [the stocks] changed prices, and that was my job. At the time, I was going to school at night, taking fifteen credits and working five hours a day. But again, I was probably the best board marker that office ever had. Very shortly after I graduated I was fortunate to be hired there full time. I started to work in San Francisco and moved there. And Merrill Lynch was really the starting point in my life—a real job, with an office. I learned how to mingle with people. I could now think about goals. I was allowed to do eighteen months of training. So I learned a lot.

I started really liking the environment and what I was doing in the United States. It was far different from where I had come from, but it made me want to develop the ability to make money, to buy things with my own money, and not have to depend on anybody. That felt good. I was always eager to work. Anything that had to be done, I volunteered for. I had bosses who recognized my wanting to do things and to further my ability. Eventually that paid off, because when they needed to appoint a supervisor, I was recommended. That was the opening that I had been looking for. I then eventually became the lead assistant operations manager. My operations manager was one of the brightest people I knew, and I always picked his brain. We were close enough to have gone to basketball games, but there was always that line that I never crossed: He was my boss. But I knew that someday I wanted his job or one like it.

Eventually I was transferred to New York and enrolled in what they called operations management school, which prepared me to be an operations manager somewhere in the Merrill Lynch system. I completed that and I was assigned to Newport Beach, California, where I did well. I did not have authority over the brokers, but I made sure they were compliant with everything that they needed to be compliant with.

On June 30, 1970, just before that assignment, when I was still in New York training, I met Marie Labeglia. Marie was from Queens and had been accepted into a program for high school graduates with Merrill Lynch. I was in my office one day and saw four girls go by. I asked who they were, and one of the guys said, Oh, those are the new June grads. Merrill Lynch's June Grads Program had been established to hire new graduates at the firm. The guy who spoke looked at one of them and said, "She looks like a cutie-pie doll."

But I said, "I like the scrawny one." Marie was eighteen, I was twenty-four, and I fell in love with her the first moment I saw her—a scrawny little thing, plain, just my type of girl.

Marie later went on to Queens College and graduated as one of the outstanding students in the United States, summa cum laude. She was also a Phi Beta Kappa, and I still wear her Phi Beta Kappa key, which I had made into a necklace. She was a superintelligent person, and you could talk to her in many subject areas. Very modest and from a very modest family. Her father was a train inspector in New York, her mother, a dressmaker. She and her brothers lived a very simple life.

I didn't start a relationship with Marie at Merrill Lynch because I was one of the managers and that was naturally taboo. But one day she came to me and said, "Can I talk to you?" She felt badly, because she had applied for the job to keep a friend of hers company, but she was accepted and her friend was not. She had thought, what the heck, I'll try it for the summer, but when the summer was over she wanted to go back to school, and she did not know how to tell her managers. She asked me, "What should I do? Should I go back to school?"

I said, "Yes, that's a no-brainer; you go back to school." I told her I would take care of the problem, because she felt like she had misrepresented herself, and I told her not to worry about it. I would let them know.

So we kind of started having a friendship then—hello, that kind of thing—but still nothing serious. The last day of her job I asked her out to dinner; it was no longer a conflict of interest. We went out to dinner in Chinatown. I did not know what to expect at that time, but after that we had our first phone call, and then it was a series of phone calls, one hour each time, two hours, every single day. I don't know what we discussed, but it was just very pleasant to talk to her, and I would save time for her. One thing she made clear to me: We are just friends. She knew that I wanted more, but she made it very clear that that was all it was going to be. Once in a while I would ask her out, and every six weeks we'd go out for lunch or dinner. But every time I came too close, she would remind me, "We are just friends." The conversations every day continued, and I looked forward to them, to the point that I had become satisfied to just be friends with her. That's what I told myself. And that went on for a year. I was not content, but there was nothing I could do.

Marie lived with her parents in Richmond Hill. They were Italian Catholic, went to church every Sunday, a very close family, and she kept me from them for a long, long time—over a year. She did not want to introduce me, and though I didn't ask why, I kind of knew, as did she, that they would object to my being brown skinned and foreign.

Maybe a year later, another girl and I started dating, but my conversations with Marie every day continued. I told this girl about Marie—I'm that kind of a guy—to the point where it began bothering her. So she asked me to break it off with Marie. I went to Marie, who said, "I like you a lot, but really, nothing is going to happen with us."

So I said, "Well, if that's the case then I have to break off with you." So I did, and began concentrating on Doreen, the young woman I was dating.

About a week later Marie called up and said, "I don't know what I'm feeling; I really don't know what this is. The only thing I know is that I feel for you more than just a friend." And I thought, *Oh, my God, now what do I do?*

But it was not a difficult decision to make after that. The opportunity was there, and shortly afterward I broke off with Doreen and started my relationship with Marie. This relationship lasted probably close to a year, and it was happy—dating and all that, and clean, as she wouldn't let me go past second base. But then I was assigned to California, and was basically told to go or I'd be out of a job. So I went, and did a good job there, and Marie and I continued our telephone conversations, two hours a day. We also had over two thousand pieces of correspondence during the one year that I was there. A card, a letter; sometimes I'd be writing three times a day, she'd write me three times a day. And this was [during] her going through her college, getting her Phi Beta Kappa and everything. So all of my time was going to letters, and all of my money was going to long-distance calls.

Then I started missing her a lot and went to my boss and said, I think I've done a good job. He agreed, and then told me that San Diego was opening up. The San Diego office was everybody's dream, and I thought, *Oh, my God, it looks like I'm being offered San Diego*, but I had to ask him to please send me home. They recognized that I had accomplished quite a bit, so I got my wish and was sent back to New York, where I became assistant manager for the biggest office in the system, at 165 Broadway.

When I came back to New York, Marie and I got engaged, and in November 1974 we were married. Though I now had a very big job, I was not satisfied with it, and after a while they told me that it was time for me to be reassigned to my own office and they set me up in Chicago. It was the first time in her life that Marie had ever been separated by real distance from her family, and it was a difficult adjustment for her. I watched her crying for a year. She wouldn't say anything to me, but she was very unhappy and ended up getting a menial job at a grocery store. She couldn't get a better position because she hadn't had any experience yet. I was afraid if I was brought back to New York, they would switch me again to another office, so I took a job and said [to her], This will be my last move, and then they are never going to move me again. So in 1977 we came back to New York, and I went into sales—basically starting a career all over again.

Marie, at the time, began working for William Rogers, who was the secretary of state, but one day applied at a bond house on Wall Street, FB Cooper. Marie was very bright, always smiling, and had the best personality, so she was a very easy hire, and because she was intelligent, did her job very well. But FB Cooper had to close for lack of cash, so they recommended her to Keefe, Bruyette & Woods, an investment banking firm. She was fortunate enough to be hired there as an administrative assistant, making a very nice salary, and from there just moved up the ladder, time after time after time, until eventually she was the highest-ranking female in the company: senior vice president.

Marie was everybody's friend, was always being kind to people. When I attended Christmas parties or gatherings with her, they would make sure we were at the best table—that's how popular she was. She was very down-to-earth, very honest. In all the years I knew Marie I never heard her say anything negative about anybody. If she felt that way she just would keep it to herself.

During those years the standard executive salary was about a hundred thousand dollars. She eventually passed me. She was the senior vice president at Keefe, and I was an options specialist at Merrill Lynch, a certified options principal. I was a broker and not one of those hotshot traders, as I was not looking for drama or glory or anything like that. I just did my job and brought home not as much money as I could. Almost always the Merrill Lynch bosses would tell me that I could double what I was making, but that was not an incentive for me. Marie and I were living a very comfortable life; not having any children, our lives revolved around each other. We had no debt, we had no finances to worry about. We did everything in cash. We put things on credit cards, but when the bills came we paid them. The one thing we allowed ourselves to do was go on vacation, and we went to Hawaii every year. What she loved most was to read books, and would bring a dozen books to Hawaii, finishing them all. Aside from Hawaii, we had our weekends to do whatever we wanted, and we would go shopping in Philadelphia or to the Amish country.

We also went to the Philippines to visit my family, who, while caring for us, planned our entire visit, what we were going to do, at what time, and all of that. Marie was so dear she never said anything: It was my family, and it was fine with her. And her heart was so big. The first time we got to Manila I was in shock, because I had been gone so long. It had been poor when I left, but driving in from the airport, I was struck by the poverty, the needy children. When we had to drive through the really desperate areas, I remember looking at her and seeing her cringe. She would cry, and I would just hold her hand, as I was moved, and tell her, "You know, this is not the country I left."

Marie and I would jog in the morning, because we were both fit. We were staying close to Antipolo and every day we would go to the cathedral and shrine of the Virgin of Antipolo to say a prayer or go to Mass. One day we were approached by a little girl, four years old, who was selling lottery tickets, saying, Please buy, buy, buy. Neither one of us had money, and it broke Marie's heart. We went home and had breakfast and she came to me and said, "Would you go to the bank with me?" She took out five hundred pesos and had them changed to one-peso coins. I didn't ask her why, but the next morning, when we went jogging, she had the five hundred coins. She began looking for the little girl, who soon came, and then another little girl came, and then the mother. Joe, Joe, Joe—they called Marie, and anybody who was white, Joe. We sat there on a wall for about a half hour, everybody touching her hair, because she was a blonde, and she did not stop until all five hundred were gone. I remember her saying at the time, "Someday, I don't know when or how, but I'm going to come back and I'm going to help these kids." That created such an impact on me, and later on in life it came back to me.

I was the biggest person in her life, and she was the biggest person in my life. We tried to outdo each other with surprises when it came to birthdays. Once I took her on an ecological tour, a three-hour trip on a boat. She was so, so pleased. She thought we were then going home, but no, I had a formal dinner all set up at the same place. When my birthday came I would open at least ten presents from her. Christmas, the same way. She just loved loving me, and vice versa. It grew like that for twenty-seven years. People might often claim, "I love you more today than yesterday, / but not as much as tomorrow," but I could honestly say that I loved Marie every single day more than I loved her the day before. I made her know that every single night and every single morning. I would tell her how much I loved her. I would tell here two and three times a day. We would call each other; I was never too busy for her. She was never too busy for me. We went to work together to different jobs, and we went home together on the Long Island Rail Road.

Keefe, Bruyette was originally at 165 Broadway, but eventually it moved to the World Trade Center, occupying the eighty-eighth and eighty-ninth floors. Marie was on the eighty-ninth floor of the South Tower.

The week before 9/11 was significant only in the sense that, because of our wanting to be together and in order to lengthen our weekends, I drove Marie to work on Monday morning, instead of her taking the train alone. At the time, I was working in our Melville office and sometimes I would work at home. In the city on Mondays, we would sit down for about five or ten minutes and have our cups of coffee by the World Trade Center. That gave us more time together after the weekend. And it never failed, never ever failed, that when I got home I would have an e-mail saying, *Thank you so much for driving me.* She appreciated every single thing that I did for her and she made sure that I knew that. She would leave me notes sometimes where I would see them, when she was already gone. Have a nice day, or thank you for this, or thank you for that. She was such a darling.

The next day, on September 11, I drove her to the station, like I always did. It was just before 6:00 A.M. We said, Good-bye, see you later. How could I know that that was the last time I would see her?

I was working at home that day, and I was working out in the basement when she called and said, "Don't worry, I'm okay." I said, "What are you talking about?" She said, "Do you have the TV on?" I said I was watching a movie, and she told me to turn on CNN. I saw the huge hole burning and said, "It looks like a plane went through your building. What's going on?" She said they didn't know—they had heard a very, very large noise, and papers were going in all directions, and that they had no television signal and so had no idea what had happened. She told me they were okay, just wanting me to feel at ease, so I told her I'd talk to her later. After a while she called me again and said that they had started going down but were told to go back, because the building was secure. The fire marshals in the building made that announcement on the PA system: "Your building is secure." But some of them did not go back. The eighty-eighth floor went down, and some on the eighty-ninth actually left but then returned. I told her, "Your building just got hit," not knowing what else to say. She said, "I got to go, I got to go." "Call me back," I said. And she said, "It's getting very hot up here. The fire marshals are moving us out. I'll talk to you as soon as I can."

We talked one last time. They had gone to the top floor; it was locked. They had to come back down, she said. They went to the stairway, as there were no working elevators. It was pitch-black, no lights. At one point while we were talking she said, "This might be my last call to you." And she said,

"Rudy, pray, okay? Pray." And she said, "Good-bye." I said, "Okay. When you get to a phone, give me a call."

It never dawned on me that she might die. Just as it never dawned on me that this could happen in the United States. *She'll get down*, I kept thinking. It never dawned on me that the building could fall. If the building didn't go down, maybe eventually . . . But I just saw the building go down. . . .

Marie was afraid of only one thing: She feared death. I don't know why. And as I was watching that thing fall I could feel the building blocks hitting her body and feel what she was going through. I felt the fear of being afraid to die. There was nothing I could do.

From the time I had last spoken to her to that of the building collapsing, I really believed there was enough time for her to have made it down, and I was just waiting for that phone call. I believed she survived. There were things on television, things being published on the Internet. There was one Web site that said they had a survivor list, and mistakenly her name was on it. That made me think even more that she had made it.

Everybody began to call me, but I told them I had to keep the lines clear. Marie's mother was frantic, absolutely frantic. People started coming to the house, and stayed with me. They just stayed—our friends, her cousins, my friends from Merrill Lynch and wherever else. We just waited. The police had been in touch with us, and I made a police report. I became numb, walking around not really knowing what to do. You were just waiting. I was just waiting for the phone call. Which never came.

For two full days I believed she was still alive. Her name was on that survivor list, and so I kept clinging to that. Maybe she made it out with no identification, leaving her purse. Maybe she had amnesia, in a hospital someplace, not knowing who she was. I had a life full of maybes. Maybe I was trying to find excuses and reasons why she had not called yet. But after two full days, after not hearing anything about survivors being taken out, and nothing from any hospital, after no phone call, I said, Okay, no more wishful thinking after that. The Red Cross told me there was help available. But I was not thinking of needing help. I mean, really, what kind of help could they give me? Except to return Marie.

After seeing the building come down that shock was very vivid, and stayed with me. And then the television kept showing it coming down again and again. A few days later they stopped showing it.

I now call it naiveté, for I did not even think that the second plane's hitting Marie's building was an attack. It just did not dawn on me. The first one got hit, a plane crashed into it, okay. But when I saw the second plane hit, it still didn't dawn on me that we were under siege. Who? How could they do this to us? And then the building itself. How did a 110-story building just come down? Burn, yes. But an implosion?

Keefe, Bruyette, and Woods lost sixty-seven people that day, including my Marie. Because of attending social events I was very close with the group that she worked with, and there was one service after another for those who died. Anyone that I knew, I attended. I purposely scheduled hers toward the end, October 13. By then I had already gone to twelve or thirteen services, so at each one of them it was, Yeah, I lost my wife also. It seemed that the others who had lost a spouse or a child did not attend the services. I saw the bigwigs, who were attending as many as they could. But they did not lose somebody. I did. So every time I went to a service I would die, and I died all of those deaths.

By the time Marie's came I had nothing left. I was so emotionally drained from all of the crying, and listening, and seeing suffering families, and knowing that these friends had been in my house and now they were gone. It was very, very difficult for me to go through with Marie's service. But I felt obligated to do it, so I did a service for her without her remains.

Three years later, as I was getting used to her being gone, there was a knock at the door. Two policewomen had come to tell me that they had found her body—not her body, but they had identified some of her body, 79 pounds of her body. The detective had her dress, which I identified. She was 118 pounds. Just 79 pounds of her came back to us. It was almost three years to the day that they figured out the DNA. They found her body a month after the incident but could not identify it. They froze it, and during the next three years the DNA technology got better, to the point where they were able to make an identification.

I had the remains cremated and the ashes divided into four vials. I spread two of them out in Hawaii, because of her love for that place. I kept two vials, which I don't know what to do with. Out of respect for my Orphelia, my wonderful new wife, I did not want another memorial here besides the village I had built. Not that Orphelia would object, but I just don't know what to do.

I did nothing for the first year after 9/11. I was told by professionals,

Don't do anything for a year; don't make any major decisions. So I stayed in the house alone. That was very, very difficult. I would see her where she always was. But she was not where I would see her. We lived in that house for twenty-plus years, and in that Long Island neighborhood. I would see her in every place in our memories, be it the grocery store, the drugstore, the train station, the library that she loved so much. Memories were every single place.

Three years passed, and one day I saw a house-for-sale sign on Woodbury Road. I looked up and saw it was my kind of house. It had a 270-foot driveway that went straight up from the street. It was very private, surrounded by rhododendrons and philodendrons, with a patio as big as Texas. I did not see the eight bedrooms, just saw a home that I liked, so I bought it. This was a minor victory for me, trying to find a place to be happy. The house made me happy. But then it haunted me that this beautiful place was not supposed to be just for me—it was supposed to be us two, together. And I could not live there. But I also could not bring myself to sell it. Finally, my agent said, "Your house is going to rot," so I went ahead and sold it. My Filipino friends had started saying to me, You have a very strong, dominant character, and whatever you are looking for, you are not going to find here, alone in this big house. Go home to the Philippines, they said. Go home. Find a quiet girl who will say yes to you, whatever you want.

So I made it known that I was going home, and that I was looking. When I got to the Philippines my friends set me up with this one, and they set me up with that one. But everybody they set me up with was not quite right. There was one really nice-looking lady, but when I went to her house she had this huge picture with what must have been at least 150 people in it: daughters, mothers, cousins, this, that, all the children. I would be marrying into a tribe. And then I noticed that she was interviewing me—How do you feel about this and that?—and she had her checklist. She liked me and I liked her, but it really scared me when I saw that. I'm very American. Don't come to my house unless you call first.

At that point I had pretty much given up, but it just so happened that I went into this place where all the bachelors go on Thursday nights, all schoolmates from Ateneo. I was going one way, and here comes this lady, the same way. We looked at each other, and, wow, what a beautiful smile— what a beautiful girl. I didn't know who she was, no idea. I said, "Are you coming here?" and she said, "Yes." Next thing I know she is on the stage.

She was one of the singers and had a beautiful voice. So I said, "I want to talk to you afterward," but she was kind of ignoring me.

That was the first time I saw Orphelia. I soon invested in the club, and then became the manager too. I made two more attempts to see her. I drove her home, but she wouldn't pay attention to me. I drove her home again, and in the car she began [to talk]: "What do I need men for? To be used and abused? Men are all the same." My driver said, "Are we going to do this again tomorrow?" I said, "No way."

Then one day she texted me, wanting some help. She was working five days a week and needed her day off changed. I made the change, she was very grateful, and that was that. But one day I was talking to one of my partners, who asked, "Did you know that Orphelia was operated on?" I said, "No," and I called her up and told her I wanted to visit. She was very grateful. That weekend she told me she was singing in Tagaytay, so I offered to drive her there. In the Philippines more patience is always needed.

I hadn't realized what an influence Marie had been in my life. I began to see the mistakes that I was making—mistakes I had not been making when Marie was with me, because she had taught me in the particulars of that relationship how to deal with them.

After losing Marie, I wanted to do something meaningful in her memory. Basically, I wanted to help those who needed help. Naturally, being Filipino and having seen how poor it is for many here, I was directing my desires toward home. While I was still living on Long Island I put out word that I was looking for a project in the Philippines and kept being told, Be careful, there's a lot of fraud out here. You're going to get sued. They are going to steal your money. They are going to kidnap you. One day a friend of mine, one of my classmates, mentioned that he was doing volunteer work for Gawad Kalinga, an organization that provides homes to people in the Philippines who have none. I told him that I had been looking for just such a project and asked him to send me material about it. Their goal is to stop only when there is no one else homeless in the Philippines. I sent them enough to buy fifty houses. My friend had told me that if I bought fifty houses—basically enough to build a village—they would name the village after me. I told them to name it after Marie. It was then that it came back to me that Marie had said that someday she was going to come back and help these people.

Gawad Kalinga pays only for the material; everything else is either donated or volunteered, whether the property itself or the services of the architect, engineer, or construction workers. It's all volunteer. Anyone who wants a house helps build all the homes in the community. The poorest of the poorest will get houses this way. Their lives will be changed.

In the beginning this subdivision area was a slum, home to seven hundred or eight hundred families, until a fire destroyed the entire thing. Then Gawad Kalinga came in to try to rebuild, and priority was given to those who had been burned out. Just on the other side of the Marie Rose Abad Village is another subdivision that is all slums—people on the outside looking in, asking, When can I move in there? That's the challenge now: to get those people into respectable housing. Each house is small—a twelve-by-fifteen-foot area to build a bedroom, kitchen, and living room—but effective. Villagers are given a shell, cement, paint, raw walls, and it's up to them to do what they want with them. Some of them have built a second floor, with basket gardens hanging down. People take real pride. It's just good having a roof over your head. It gives them a sense of ownership, and because they get title in twenty years, they have an incentive to keep it clean.

These buildings are a transition for many of them from a cardboard box or a corrugated wood shack to a real house with plumbing.

We now have about three hundred people living in the houses in the Marie Rose Abad Village. When I go there I try to be very low-key, and don't even want to be seen. It is about Marie, not about me. I look at it all and I'm so happy, but also sad, because I can see on the other side of the river a much bigger community waiting in those terrible huts. This had been a very high-crime area, but for the past two years we have not had a single incident. The area used to be a watering hole for drugs, but now there's no longer a single person using them. The house offers a chance to restart something meaningful. Before, all they had was an absence of hope, no life, nothing. Marie has provided shelter and hope for so many of them.

Why was Marie killed? I suppress the rage only because I say to myself, *I cannot win this battle.* My pain is so great that if I start to fight, my pain will continue, and it is a battle that I cannot win. Some people have more anger than I can find. I'm not a coward, but it's just, I don't want to exert all my energy and then say, At least I tried. I do not want to accept defeat, no. But I will support in any way I can other people who are willing to take on the fight against terrorism. How can I win? I get so many e-mails from the Department of Justice about how this hearing is going and how that one has been dismissed. The big 9/11 organization, Tuesday's Children, is continuing the fight, and will go to Washington to be heard. If I was in New York I would go with them, to be a part of them, my friends. But I would be a silent minority, not doing any screaming. That would not bring back Marie; it would only bring me pain. But if you need me to stand up for your issues for you to carry on, I will be there.

If Marie is looking down on us, she would say, I am really, really glad about what you have done in my memory. I know that the people in the village are very grateful. Her picture is on every row of houses in the village, along with the title Marie Rose Abad Village. I wanted her face, not just a name; I wanted people to see that this is the woman whom you thank. I'm not someone who is overly religious, thinking all the time of heaven and earth and hell and whatever. But I do go to church and I naturally always speak to Marie there, telling her that I hope she's okay and happy. I do believe that she is watching over me, as I have had so many problems, and I feel her coming to me, smiling, a guiding hand. I guess I manage to stay okay because she has been watching over me. I believe that part.

I am not all alone. I have my brother, my sister, my mother—a meager family, but it is my family. I have my other family, Orphelia and her daughter, now our daughter, Gianne, and everyone who works in our house, which is eleven people plus six others working in our beach house. I also have a band I am managing. All of these people are now my family. These are the people that I care for, whatever happens, because this is what I have built here, with our village and my church. They all look to me, and if that is my mission, then so be it. I have been fortunate enough in my finances, and the good thing about that is that I know that I am doing positive things—things that, for some people, make life at least a little better.

Sally Regenhard

Sally Regenhard is the mother of two children—a son, Christian, and a daughter, Christina. Her husband, Al, is a retired NYPD detective. Christian was a probationary firefighter just six weeks or so out of the FDNY training school when he responded with his company to the World Trade Center disaster on 9/11. He perished along with four other firefighters from his assigned company that day. Sally describes herself as an activist and an advocate for high-rise building safety and is respected by many in the 9/11 community for the tenacity and spirit that has grown from a mother's love.

I'm usually a little on the hard-nosed side, a kick-butt type of person, especially when it comes to the issues that get placed before us. But when it comes to my son, Christian, that's when I cry. What can I say? I'm currently involved with the controversy down at the Ground Zero area where the building of a mosque is planned, and *60 Minutes* called me about it. They sent a girl for a preinterview, and I didn't know if she knew anything, so I had to go through the whole thing about my son and got so upset that I went off on a crying jag. It's draining. It's emotional. It's very difficult to be a 9/11 parent.

Growing up I was known as Teresa Mary Doughty. I'm the child of Irish immigrants, from Mayo and from Derry. My father was a conductor on the IRT, and early on he moved the family to Mosholu Parkway. We were practically the only Gentiles in this 99 percent Jewish upper-middle-class neighborhood and so didn't exactly fit in. My mother and father had brogues that no one ever understood. I was the only person on the block who went to Catholic school, and my sister and I had to walk ten blocks to get there. I was the first person in my family to go to college, because everyone in my neighborhood went to college. Later on, when I moved to Co-op City, I met activists there—socialists and union leaders. I learned so much from them about challenging the system, and that's why I was able to challenge the system after 9/11.

I was basically a stay-at-home mom for the early years of Christian's life. I went back to work when he was around nine years old. I also have a daughter, who is now a science teacher, and who like Christian is a graduate of Bronx High School of Science. When they were young I was with them, because I think it is very important for a parent. My husband was doing shift work back in those days. Before he became an NYPD detective, he worked in many precincts across the city as a uniformed patrolman. He was in the citywide anticrime unit and the senior citizens' robbery unit. He was undercover. He was in the riots of the 1960s and at Columbia University for the famous anti–Vietnam War protests. There's a famous picture of him and his colleagues at those protests, working the confrontation of a crowd. It was just a part of his thirty-nine years in the NYPD.

After just ten years he passed the sergeant's test and aced it. He was a person who had a lot of talent, especially artistic talents. But in his era of growing up on the Upper West Side, you didn't really become an artist or follow the arts. It was a very blue-collar, macho way of thinking. But he did have a very interesting, multifaceted career, and never took himself too seriously. He became a boss in the detective squad, so he was the sergeant. He had to deal with all these detectives—the good, the bad, and the ugly, but mostly good. And he was known among the detectives as a great boss. Before he retired, he had a remarkable career. I would say he was married to the Police Department. Every time there was a blackout, a snowstorm, riots, he was there. So mainly I was alone with the children while he was out saving the city. But that's all part of the job.

I went to Catholic school, and I hate to admit it, but I didn't get into the Bronx High School of Science, because the science and the math tests were so difficult. In those days the Catholic school system was superb in English, writing, history, and philosophy, but it was really not as demanding in science and, perhaps, in math. I was delighted when my daughter got into the Bronx High School of Science, and I was shocked when Christian got in. They both had one of the finest public educations you could receive in our city. In the early days of Co-op City, where we lived in the Bronx, the school used the open-classroom method of teaching. And so Christian was prepared for the Bronx High School of Science. It is one of the hardest high schools to get into in the whole country.

Christian was always a fantastic thinker, and a very charismatic and beautiful child. He had a Buster Brown haircut, with light blond hair and gorgeous blue eyes. And Christian was blessed with personality. Some children are chronic malcontents. Some are problematic. He was blessed with an easygoing temperament. He was a charming child. Everybody loved him and went crazy over him. I didn't really understand why so many other mothers would just go crazy over Christian. I guess since he was my own, I was too close to him to fully get it. He was just a wonderful child.

As a young boy Christian used to do some drawing, having a knack for the arts like his dad. When we moved to Co-op City in the Bronx, I became friendly with a social worker there. She came to our apartment one day, and after looking at Christian's artwork from nursery school, said, "Sally, I'm seeing that your son is highly intelligent, from the way he made the windows and people in the windows. So when he starts going to grammar school, you have to get him tested." At that time they had started something new in the city school system, a program for exceptionally talented and gifted students. The kids had to take an IQ test to get in, and they had one school for these children in each borough. So, at my friend's suggestion, I seriously considered having Christian take the test.

Now Christian was smart, but he was also a cutup. He was a very funny child, and some teachers didn't like him because he had the ability to make the class laugh. If this happened in a Catholic school back in the day, the worst boy would get hit with the ruler stick. If the teacher asked the students to cite a word with a hard C, for example, kids would say words like "clock" and "cat" and so on. But Christian would always say something unexpected, like "cuckoo." And, of course, the whole class would be in hysterics.

Once I was called to the school, and I went over there with my heart in my hand, I was so scared. I looked at Christian, who looked fine to me. But the teacher was pointing at him, saying, "Look what he did." He had apparently taken a scissors—the little scissors they give to kids at school—and cut his hair into a V-like [style]. The teacher sent me this big official note stating that Christian cut his own hair, with his own assigned scissors, at 12:05 P.M., on such and such a date. I framed that note, and I had that in my home for years and years.

After the hair-cutting incident I went back to the teacher and said, "I've been advised, and I'd like my son to be tested." She goes, "You're just raising your hopes. Your son is an average student and, what's more, he knows he's average." I told her, "You know what, I'd still like him tested." And so he took the exceptionally gifted test while in the second grade. Well, end result: Christian aced the test, a standard IQ test. He scored a 146. The teacher almost collapsed. From there he went on to the gifted student program. My daughter was the studious one, a real brainiac, and although Christian was obviously smart, he was not as studious. He was a more laid-back, casual kid. And when he got into the Bronx High School of Science, I nearly fainted.

Christian did very well at Science for the first three years. But in his fourth year there he spent more time cutting class and hanging out in Harris Field, the park across the street. Now, as a parent, I was typically very easygoing with my children. My husband was the taskmaster, the marine, the cop. I felt from a psychological point of view that children should be able to make their own decisions. But this time I got tough with him and said, "Christian, if you don't graduate from Bronx Science I'm going to kill you." He was shocked I had said that. By hook or by crook, though, he did it.

But soon after came the greatest trauma I had had prior to 9/11, when Christian announced, one week before his nineteenth birthday, that he was joining the United States Marine Corps—for five years. I almost had a nervous breakdown. I spent the weekend in my nightgown and my robe, crying and fighting and going crazy and calling all my relatives trying to find ways to talk him out of it. I didn't succeed—he was determined.

A large part of Christian's determination, I believe, grew from a very traumatic experience he had before joining the marines. He never told me outright, but I think it was a factor in his decision. He and his buddies were down in Manhattan on West Eighty-sixth Street. I don't know exactly how it happened—maybe they were drinking a little beer or something—and Christian accidentally bumped into somebody on the street. This was in the lawless days of New York City, and they went after him with a broken beer bottle, mugged him, and slashed him. They cut him so severely that, thank God, the ambulance attendants said to him, Kid, when you get to the hospital, tell them you want a plastic surgeon. They took him to Lenox Hill Hospital, thank God. I only found out about it after he went to the hospital and received something like twenty-five stitches in his face. They almost ripped off his lower lip, and they almost got his eye. The plastic surgeon reassured me that he had done his best to maintain the integrity of the lower lip. And he really did. Thanks to the plastic surgery, you could hardly see any marks. God blessed Christian that day. Christian was a blessed person up until 9/11.

I believe that it was a result of that horrible incident that Christian joined the Marine Corps. And let me tell you: He never harbored any resentment or hatred, but he had such mastery in everything that he was never going to be a victim again. No matter what happened to him, he would persevere.

In hindsight, even though I was initially opposed, Christian's becoming a marine may have been the best thing that he ever did. He entered the Marine Corps a kid who really didn't know his way so much. He was searching, the way teenagers do, searching and looking and not knowing. He suffered like hell through the training—not that he ever felt sorry for himself—but he gained a competence in so many things. I believe that, often through suffering incredible things, qualities can surface that you didn't know you had. I think Christian's artistic and writing abilities grew tremendously.

Sometimes great suffering can also give you great strength. I know that from my own journey, from the painful and bitter time that I've had. Prior to 9/11 I would not have been able to do the things I've had to do over the past ten years: to confront people; to challenge the system; to go after elected officials. At times I am shocked that I have so much adrenaline, but great suffering propels you.

In the marines Christian became a person whom everyone was drawn to. He had all the qualities of a great friend, and people sought his friendship. He—I'm getting emotional—was a man's man and a lady's man together. Even when he was in grammar school he would get these little notes, and I have a collection of them, that the little girls in his class gave him. They would say, "Christian I love you," with this funny big writing. Or, "I like you." One of these girls wrote, "You can borrow my comb." It was so charming and sweet. Another wrote, "This is the number to my locker." Then the phone calls started when he was in junior high, and they kept coming in high school. I once told him, "If you dare touch these girls, just remember that they have brothers who will come after you." I think he believed me, because throughout his life he had an admiration, respect, and love for women. He was a good guy. Nothing could prove that more than the fact that at his memorial service eight ex-girlfriends showed up. They remained friends with him, and that says a lot. He was a gentleman, and, boy, the world certainly needed people like him.

After the Marine Corps Christian went to San Francisco State University. He lived in the Mission District, which was kind of a dicey area then. It was so cold in this brownstone thing that he lived in that he asked me to send him a quilt. He lived as a bohemian. He went to school. He had no money, but he would never take any from us, even if we offered it to him. That is how independent he was. He did a lot of part-time work in all these crazy jobs. He always bought his clothes from the Goodwill or the Salvation Army. He never wore a name brand or a label. He'd turn the shirt inside out rather than have an icon on it. He was a true bohemian. He studied art and writing. And, whenever he could, he traveled.

Christian loved the culture and language of Latin America, so that is where he did most of his traveling. His first trip was to Mexico and Central America, right after high school. He went with his girlfriend, the first love of his life, and they went on this wonderful expedition, where they would slip some money to the guards and sleep in temples. That was the first time he got Montezuma's revenge, and he was terribly, seriously ill. But it didn't deter him from wanting to go back. So after settling in San Francisco, he made several more trips to Central and South America. He went on an expedition to Patagonia. He was in Guatemala, Honduras, El Salvador, many countries—altogether, including his time in the marines, Christian had been to twenty-two countries around the world. He taught himself Spanish and was a fluent and perfect speaker.

Also on his travels he learned how to make handmade jewelry from the indigenous people of Central America—a silversmith-type of craftsmanship. We found in his room little tools that he would use on a piece of silver or wire to create silver florets, the most amazing silver florets. He made the florets very small and *delicate*, as they say *en español*. He made such beautiful jewelry. I had so many aspirations for him. He could have started his own line of jewelry and called it Christian R, Jewels by Christian R. I have a piece that he made for me, which is detailed with these beautiful, colorful stones. He was a colorful and vibrant person, and so was in love with these colors and the passion of Central and South America. He was not bland. He wasn't a beige person. That's why I wore a red jacket to his memorial. It was because he had *mucho* color. It was also for the Marine Corps. For the Fire Department. But it was really for Christian's heart and his passion. My son wanted to live. My son lived for life. That's why I had the song "Gracias a la Vida," "Thank You for Life," sung in Spanish.

Christian was still living in California when he decided to take the test for the Fire Department. When he got out of the Marine Corps, I remember him once saying, "You know, Mom, hardly anyone likes the cops, but everyone loves the firefighters." Even as the wife of a cop, I have to say that statement's pretty accurate. Of course, I like the cops, but a lot of people out there, especially in the inner city, have a strong dislike for police authority. Maybe it's a little different now, with so much terrorism, and people looking to the police to protect them. And Commissioner Ray Kelly has done such a fantastic job. I'm a critic of the system, but he's the exception.

It all started after a friend, who was also a former marine, once said to me, "Sally, when your son comes out of the Marine Corps, tell him to take all civil service tests." And then, one day, I was reading the *Daily News* and I saw an ad for the Fire Department. I cut it out, and I sent it to Christian in San Francisco and said, "Christian, it wouldn't hurt. Why don't you take the test?" The greatest regret of my life.

Well, the rest is history. He flew back from California to take the test. I bought him a book to study, and I think maybe he only looked at it on the plane. But he was so intelligent and so capable that he aced the test. The physical part, needless to say, wouldn't be a problem either. Christian was a recon sergeant. If you're familiar with the Marine Corps, you know that, first of all, it's not easy to be promoted, and second, recon is the most elite outfit. So he aced the physical exam too. His capability was just unparalleled, and the department wanted him. When he went to the Rock, FDNY's training school on Randall's Island, they saw what he was capable of from day one. And they decided his experience in the Marine Corps made him an efficient platoon leader for his probie—probationary firefighter—group.

Christian told me that he wanted to do the job temporarily, because it was hard to get a job in those days, too, in early 2001. Christian was not a paper pusher; he couldn't be in the rat race. He was a person of integrity, and of action. He felt the Fire Department was something he would do until he could finish his studies in art and writing, either at Pratt Institute or at Cooper Union. But when he started working at the firehouse, he really liked it. Several fire companies wanted him. He was squared away. He was so easygoing, and he was ready to go.

He went to a firehouse in a sort of a depressed area in Red Hook. He never complained. It was grueling, especially the commute from the Bronx. We knew nothing about the Fire Department—the only thing my husband knew was from when he used to coop [a practice, now no longer permitted, in which a police officer could take his lunch or dinner break relaxing in a local firehouse] on patrol—so I asked him, "Christian, what kind of people are firefighters?" He said that there were all kinds of firefighters—lawyers, doctors, college professors—but that there was one thing they all had in common: They were all carpenters. My husband, God bless him, couldn't put a nail in the wall. Nobody in my family was able to fix anything. But Christian was fascinated that they all had these skills, and he learned a lot. But he didn't have a long time to learn.

He graduated from the Fire Academy at Manhattan Community College on July 26, 2001. They graduated in the shadow of Ground Zero—six weeks before 9/11.

When 9/11 came I had no idea where he worked. By that time he had moved out and was living with two other aspiring firefighters in an apartment in Brooklyn. I didn't know anything about Brooklyn. I only knew that my husband got lost there twice, and he was in the car with the kids going crazy, yelling and screaming. Brooklyn was a foreign country to me. But Christian was falling in love with everything Brooklyn. He used to say, "Oh Mom. It's very different. It's all little neighborhoods." Whatever he did, wherever he went, he put himself into it 100 percent.

Before 9/11, the last conversation I ever had with my son was about an old, outdated Mac, which was probably already years old when he got it. I said, "Christian, I'm going to buy you a new computer." And he would never take anything from us. "But there's one condition, Christian. . . . I want you to follow your bliss." I wanted all the members of the family to follow their bliss and to live up to their talents and abilities. He was stunned, because I had never really spoken to him about that. "I want you to do that—follow your bliss."

Christian assured me, "Mom, that's how I'm going to make my money." That was about a week before the attacks.

On September 11, 2001, it was primary day. I was a community activist in Co-op City, and there was a mayoral race going on. A couple of months prior, I had become interested in the possible candidacy of an unknown person who was coming on the scene. I was a volunteer, getting people together. I was going to give out the literature, and I was assigning people to be at the different polling places. This hopeful candidate was a guy who people said didn't have a chance, a little-known candidate named Michael Bloomberg.

In the morning I was getting ready at home. I've always been a news-hound, so I was watching the news on my little TV in the kitchen when I saw a breaking news bulletin: Apparently a plane had hit the World Trade Center. I then saw the damage on TV. I kept watching, and as more things emerged I got this apprehension, because I knew that Red Hook was not far over that cursed Brooklyn Bridge. I'm sorry to offend anyone who lives there, but I can't go to Brooklyn. I can't go there. I know it's irrational, but I feel as if Brooklyn allowed my son to be murdered, because he was work-ing there.

Suddenly I got this foreboding. I never really thought that he would have been sent in there—after all, he was a probie who had just graduated from fire school six weeks before. Then people started calling me. My cousin said, "Oh, Sally, Christian, he would never go in there." I spoke to so-and-so: He would never be sent in there. That's not for probies. That's for seasoned firefighters. Don't worry about it.

Christian had had the room with the best view in our apartment. From his window you could see, as clear as day, the skyline of Manhattan, includ-ing the World Trade Center. You could see it from the thirtieth floor, and we all often looked out the window and looked at the sky. It was a fabulous and fascinating view.

So when I heard the news I kept running from this little TV in the kitchen to Christian's room, and I saw the black smoke, and then came back. Oh, my God, I saw that the building [had] collapsed. First I saw there were two buildings, and then there was only one building there. And the smoke. Then I ran back and was watching the TV when the second build-ing came down. I ran back to the window in Christian's room, and there were no buildings. The buildings were gone. These were buildings that I had looked at for thirty years. We had lived in Co-op City for thirty years.

At that time I couldn't comprehend that my son . . . I thought that he would not have been called there. I could never in my wildest dreams even imagine that something like this could have happened to him. But as the day grew longer and longer, I had this foreboding. I had no information. I knew nothing about the Fire Department. I didn't know a single firefighter. In hindsight I realized that we had a second cousin on my father's side of the family, but we were not in touch with him. I didn't know anything. And everyone was gone that day. I don't remember where my husband was, but he wasn't around, and my daughter wasn't around.

And the day went on, and the day went on, and the day went on. Then, I don't know how, but I got the number of Christian's firehouse. I didn't know where Red Hook, Brooklyn, was. And I started calling until the day had turned to night. I thought, *Christian is macho and self-contained, so the last thing that he ever would do is call his mother.* He might have been young, just twenty-eight, but he was a total man, and a marine, and you don't call your mother. And that's why I didn't know a lot about his job, because he wasn't a momma's boy. I thought to myself, *This is Christian, he's not calling us, he's engaged, he's involved.* But then I went from being a little annoyed . . . and fell into a fear that began growing.

I called the firehouse over and over, and whenever I got through I got every kind of story. They said, Well, they were assigned to different places, and they were reassigned, and they didn't know. This is this, this is that. They kept on telling me stories, and I started getting more and more anxious. By the time it was night they had brought in these retired firefighters, and I got an older guy, and I said, "You have to tell me, where is my son?" And finally, you could tell, in desperation, you could tell he was jaded, he was burned out, and he said to me the words I will never forget, the words I would never want anyone to ever hear. He said to me: "He is unaccounted for."

And I heard those words and I was stunned. I didn't know what to say. I thought to myself, *This is something they say in a war, you know. "He is unaccounted for."* My mind started racing. *What does it mean? And what is happening?* And then I asked, "Well, what should I do?"

He said, "Go to bed, and call us in the morning."

And in my state of shock I actually tried to do that. I don't know what time it was by then. And I actually tried to do that. I'll never forget it. Of course I didn't sleep. I prayed all night. Then this doom and this dark cloud began engulfing me. I was so religious at that point, and I prayed and prayed, to all the saints: prayers from twelve years of Catholic school, all those prayers that I knew from my years with the healing ministry in the Catholic Church, the rosary and the Memorare.

When Christian was in the Marine Corps I used to worry about him. I had everybody praying for him. I had rabbis praying. I had nuns—I used to send money to these nuns, adopt a nun, you know, to pray for him.

In the early morning a feeling came over me that I wanted to be with Christian. I never could believe that anything happened to him, but something inside of me was drawing me to him, like I wouldn't have cared if I died, if I could just be near to him.

But there was no knock at the door. There was no Fire Department chaplain in uniform with the "We regret to inform you." No one ever said to me, "Your son is dead," because they don't know what happened to him. They don't know what happened to his whole company, all five men. In all my efforts so far, I have not been successful in finding out one single thing about what happened to my son. When was he assigned to the Trade Center? What time did he get there? What building was he directed to? What was he supposed to accomplish? Why was he sent into a building that most of the people had already evacuated, that had no water, no communication with radios? And the city of New York had no plans for terrorism, no plans for a disaster. To this day the advocacy work that I have engaged in has been to try to make sure that no other mother will ever hear those dreaded words "He is unaccounted for." And that the system will not be allowed to get away with murder.

The worst part of 9/11 was losing such a precious gem of a human being for society—not just my loss, but what he could have done for this world. After his death I learned many things about Christian's life, great things that I had not known before. Christian was very self-contained. He was really a follower of all religions, but especially Buddhism, in which one of the principles is to keep your gems hidden. So he never told me about the heroic things he did. He never told me anything about the Marine Corps— he didn't want me to worry or suffer. After 9/11, though, there was a gathering of people from all over the country who knew him and loved him—from the marines, from college, and others he had met here and there. His girlfriend told me that they experienced a typhoon in Belize so severe that she was actually drowning. Christian saved her life. I never knew that before. One of the firefighters told me a story about when Chris-

tian went to a fire in the Red Hook projects. There had been a report of a
fire or smoke, and there were lots of Spanish immigrants living there, and
one woman wouldn't open the door. What do you do when someone doesn't
understand English? The lieutenant and the firefighters started talking
loudly, and there was so much yelling that they couldn't make any headway.
But all of a sudden Christian stepped forward and started speaking to her
in the most wonderful Spanish. The whole fire company almost collapsed
in surprise. They didn't know he spoke Spanish. They didn't know he had
been a marine. They didn't know he was a rock climber and a mountain
climber, because he never disclosed it. But he was just so good at being a
firefighter, a straightaway guy, that they were shocked when they found out.

The second worst thing about 9/11 is that in the whole system there was
not one iota of accountability or responsibility on any level, from the city
of New York to the Fire Department to the Police Department, for the lack
of an integrated command.

When I stood in Christian's room on the thirtieth floor in Co-op City,
when I actually witnessed the towers collapsing, instinctively I couldn't
accept it. I didn't know that Christian was in there, but still I could not accept it. The tallest, largest buildings in the world, designed to hold the
largest amount of people, that they would go down like pillars of salt. . . . I
couldn't accept that, ever. I couldn't accept that 343 firefighters, and nearly
3,000 people, were killed. In my mind, I started to absorb information like
an activist.

Then I saw an article by John Jay College professors Glenn Corbett
and Charles Jennings calling for a wider investigation of the systems and
policies used by our government on 9/11. At that time Mr. Frank Gribbon,
the public communications person for the Fire Department, was saying in
the *Daily News* that we didn't need any further investigation. I had to deal
with a mentality that said "We don't need to look further into anything.
We can handle it." Some of us rejected that and started calling for a wider
investigation. We led families to Washington, D.C., to the House Finance
Committee hearing, to insist upon a federal investigation into what happened. It was then that the problem of the firefighters' radios started to
emerge. There was the fact that the same-style radios had failed the firefighters in 1993. They were not able to communicate in the first attack on
the World Trade Center. They were flawed. They were Motorola radios, and
somehow the Fire Department had no power, because there was a higher

level of the city of New York that had contracts with the company that provided the radios. Between 1993 and 2001 there was little to nothing done to improve them. There was an attempt to bring in another type of radio, but apparently they were too advanced or too different. They were put out on the streets to the firefighters, and there were problems with them, so they were immediately shelved, and the old radios were brought back. When 2001 came along, the Fire Department was still equipped with radios that did not work properly in certain big New York City buildings. I never would have recommended that my son join the Fire Department if I had known that the entire Fire Department had radios that did not work predictably. I also didn't know that my son wouldn't even have a radio, and that, I think, it was one person in the whole unit who would have a radio, maybe two people and an officer. I didn't know that until years after 9/11. Little by little I found out more and more.

On 9/11, I was an innocent person. When I got up there on the altar of Saint Patrick's Cathedral on October 26, 2001, and made my speech about my son and about what happened to him, I was looking into a sea of blue who knew the truth. But they were either afraid for me to know or there was this terrible guilt that firefighters had. I know it's the guilt of the survivor, and I know that some of my son's friends in the Fire Department have become racked with guilt. Their lives have been destroyed, and I would never want that. They should not have guilt. The system that controls the Fire Department should have guilt.

I didn't know the truth then, but thank God I found wonderful mentors like Glenn Corbett and Charles Jenning. People like Vincent Dunn, the iconic deputy chief who is an expert on building collapse. People like Al Fuentes, battalion chief, and many other wonderful people. Little by little I found out about the conditions under which the heroic firefighters were sent into those towers. I had to be very careful in the beginning because the Fire Department was not used to a probie's mother speaking out about failures in a system that caused 343 brothers to be massacred. There was a lot of push back, and for me to stick up and question what had happened, it was like I was a heretic.

Little by little I found out about a bizarre contract with Motorola that grew suddenly from a small amount to a huge amount of money. It was a history characterized by such impropriety and, I would say, by a wanton disregard for the human life in the Fire Department. There was not only that, but no coordination of emergency planning and no real incident command. Little by little I found out about one atrocity after another, and I was aghast. My son was murdered by al Qaeda, yes, but also, in my opinion, by a system that he had sworn to uphold, a system of saving lives and protecting property, where he was not given any tools whereby either he could survive or he could really save people in this catastrophic type of scenario. If my son was killed in a fire in a project or in a building, or if he fell off a ladder, I think I could have accepted it more. But he was sent somewhere he never should have been sent. The whole Fire Department should never have been sent in there, for there was no preplanning by the highest level of government in the city of New York to establish a unified command system like they have in California for huge forest fires. It's a military-based plan, and it's what we have now, but look at the price we had to pay. My son died for nothing, because there were woefully few people who could have been saved. He didn't have the radio equipment; he didn't have any water.

And what kind of power manipulation gave the Port Authority of New York and New Jersey the right to build in this city outside of city building laws? The Port Authority is exempt and immune from all New York City building and fire codes, and so they construct buildings above the law. The city of New York knew that. If Chief John O'Hagan [also New York City fire commissioner, 1973–78] had been listened to, things would have been different. When the Twin Towers were going to be built, Chief O'Hagan expressed great concern for so many of these issues. Retired deputy fire chief Vincent Dunn, the collapse expert, told me that when you have an acre of fire ground, it's impossible to defend it with classic methods of water. So these buildings, these towers, were built exempt and immune from the compartmentalization of each floor required by the New York City building and fire codes.

Now, some people were engaged in waving the flag: Wasn't it great? Even some of the families. One of the 9/11 mothers, not of the Fire Department, scolded me: "Why are you going to court trying to get those 9/11 tapes and transmissions?" I had a whole group of parents of firefighters, and we did everything we had to do to expose the failures so that the system could be improved. We spent three years in lower courts with the attorney Norman Siegel, and then got to the New York State Court of Appeals. It was one of the best days of my life. In 2005 we got part of the tapes and transmissions revealed. Now, after years have gone by, firefighters and everyone have realized that I'm working for their good. I'm proud of the things that I pushed for and forced open.

When I heard Rudy Giuliani at the New School, at the last meeting of the 9/11 Commission in May of 2005, he had the audacity to continue the big lie when he said that those firefighters could have left the building but stood their ground after they heard the order to evacuate. Thank God I brought my sign saying LIES AND TRUTH. That's when everyone went crazy, that's when I shouted out, "No, No!" and the whole place erupted. My wonderful colleague Rosaleen Tallon, whose brother, Sean Patrick Tallon, had been in the Ladder 10/Engine 10 firehouse, brought her mother there. And in her wonderful Irish brogue from Cork, she yelled out, "What about the radios and Motorola? We want to hear about Motorola!" And then everyone went crazy. That stopped Giuliani. But it's not about stopping individuals; it's about stopping the big lie and the cover-up. The radios failed. It was the blackest day for the city of New York and for the Fire Department.

You have to change the system when you see it has failed. Because if you don't speak up about the sins of the past, as you know the famous saying goes, you're doomed to repeat them. That's what activism is about. That's what happens.

I'm very sorry to say that despite our best efforts and the best efforts of everyone, the new World Trade Center—all the buildings plus the dangerous and despicable underground museum—is exempt and immune from all New York City building and fire codes. To me you have another death trap waiting for the New York City Fire Department. So I devoted my life to my son's legacy and to the grand legacy of all the 343 firefighters.

I never really voiced that desire, but Professor Glenn Corbett sensed it and suggested we create a Christian Regenhard Center at John Jay College. John Jay lost a large number of firefighters who studied there, the largest number from any academic institution, on 9/11. Apparently Glenn had been discussing his idea with the college officials, and when I heard that . . . well, see, I was afraid to be happy. Number one, because I'm Irish, and number two, because 9/11 parents have lost all of their hope. And so have the siblings. But I was praying for something, and I was so happy to hear that Glenn was creating the Christian Regenhard Center for Emergency Response Studies.

I had been approached to lend my son's stellar name to one or two other things, which I declined, because Christian was a person of such integrity, and he was such a minimalist. I don't even know if he would have agreed to have his name put on anything, for he was so modest. But you know, I was so happy. A center like this could not exist without the full support of everyone at John Jay College, from President Jeremy Travis on down. And John Jay has a national reputation for such excellence in law enforcement, fire science, and homeland security. That's why I agreed to it: I wanted any legacy for Christian to be a legacy of excellence. My son was an intellectual but he was also a firefighter. He loved it for his short time. He loved people and he loved helping people. And this is the right legacy for our dedicated public servants in Fire, Police, EMS, and all the other auxiliary emergency responders. They need that legacy going forward. It's as if we are a wheel, and we will support the spokes, the responders, in all those protection agencies.

I've spent the last six years out of the decade going to Washington, attending these hearings, listening to testimony, meeting with the FBI and DHS [Department of Homeland Security] people. These experts have certainly told us that it's not a matter of *if* there will be another terrorist attack but *when* the terrorists will strike again. Anyone paying attention in New York City knows there have been fourteen confirmed terrorist plots that have been intercepted. The next time—and, I'm sorry, there will be a next time—these terrorists succeed, I want things to go differently from the way they did on 9/11. I want people to be safe. I want the emergency responders to be safe. I couldn't save my son, but going forward I'm hoping that through the Christian Regenhard Center for Emergency Response Studies we will be able to save other mothers' sons, as well as the public.

Dan Nigro

Ray Kelly

Dr. David Prezant

Jay Jonas

Ada Rosario
Dolch

Wendy Wakeford

Peter King

Brendan, Lee, and Jonathan Ielpi

Lee Ielpi

Jim, Patricia, and Moira Smith

John and Dan D'Allara

Zack and Andre Fletcher

Tim, Ken, and Tom Haskell

Jay Winuk

Glenn Winuk

Akiko Takahashi

Keiichiro Takahashi

Barbara Habib

Ray Habib

Brooke Jackman

Robert and Barbara Jackman

Rudy and Marie Abad

Catherine MacRae

Sally and Christian
Regenhard

9/11 Tribute Organizations Mentioned in
A Decade of Hope

Tribute WTC Visitor Center
120 Liberty Street
New York, NY 10006

Tel: (866) 737-1184 or (212) 393-9160 ext. 138

http://www.tributewtc.org/
E-mail: visitorservices@tributewtc.org

Group reservations and information:
(212) 393-9160 ext. 132
E-mail: groupservices@tributewtc.org

Stephen Siller Tunnel to Towers Foundation
2361 Hylan Blvd.
Staten Island, NY 10306

Tel: (718) 987-1931

http://www.tunneltotowersrun.org/

The Brooke Jackman Foundation
c/o Marquis Jet
230 Park Avenue, Suite 840
New York, NY 10169

Tel: (212) 692-2696

http://www.brookejackmanfoundation.org/
E-mail: info@BrookeJackmanFoundation.org

FDNY Fire Family Transport Foundation
PO Box 340949
Brooklyn, NY 11234

http://www.firefamilytransport.org/

The Christian Regenhard Center for Emergency Response Studies (RaCERS)
John Jay College Foundation, Regenhard Center
899 Tenth Avenue
New York, NY 10019

Tel: (646) 557-4430

http://christianregenhardcenter.org/

Research support through donations is greatly appreciated. Donations are tax deductible. The John Jay College Foundation is a registered 501(c)(3) organization. Please make your check payable to: John Jay College Foundation, Regenhard Center.

The Cat MacRae Memorial Fund
125 East 72nd Street
New York, NY 10021

Hope for the Warriors
PMB 48
1335 Suite E, Western Blvd.
Jacksonville, NC 28546

Tel: (910) 938-1817 or (877) 246-7349

http://www.hopeforthewarriors.org/

Information on the Haskell Brothers Annual Golf Outing can also be found at Hope for the Warriors.

The New York Firefighters Burn Center Foundation
21 Asch Loop
Bronx, NY 10475

Tel: (718) 379-1900

http://www.nyffburncenter.com/
E-mail: info@nyffburncenter.com

Billy Burke

Michael Burke

Talat Hamdani

Salman Hamdani

Pete and Toni Ann Carroll

John T.
Vigiano, Jr.

Joseph V. Vigiano

Jan and John
Vigiano

Debra and Chic Burlingame

George and Glenda Siller

Stephen Siller